WHEN WORK DISAPPEARS

WILLIAM JULIUS WILSON

WHEN WORK DISAPPEARS

William Julius Wilson was a member of the faculty at the
University of Chicago for twenty-four years and is currently
the Malcolm Wiener Professor of Social Policy at Harvard
University. He is past president of the American Sociological
Association and has been elected to the National Academy of
Sciences, the American Academy of Arts and Sciences, and
the American Philosophical Society. His previous books
include *Power, Racism, and Privilege*; *The Declining Significance
of Race*; and *The Truly Disadvantaged*. He lives with his wife in
Cambridge, Massachusetts.

Also by WILLIAM JULIUS WILSON

Power, Racism, and Privilege

The Declining Significance of Race

The Truly Disadvantaged

Through Different Eyes (co-editor)

The Ghetto Underclass (editor)

Scociology and the Public Agenda (editor)

Poverty, Inequality and the Future of Social Policy (co-editor)

WHEN WORK DISAPPEARS

WHEN WORK DISAPPEARS

The World of the New Urban Poor

WILLIAM JULIUS WILSON

VINTAGE BOOKS
A Division of Random House, Inc.
New York

FIRST VINTAGE BOOKS EDITION, AUGUST 1997

The Library of Congress has cataloged the Knopf edition as follows:

Wilson, William J., [date]
When work disappears : the world of the new urban poor /
William Julius Wilson.—first ed.
p. cm.
Includes bibliographical references.
ISBN 0-394-57935-6
1. Urban poor—United States.
2. Afro-Americans—Employment.
3. Inner cities—United States.
1. Title
HV4045.W553 1996
362.'0973'091732—dc20   96–11803
CIP

Vintage ISBN: 0-679-72417-6

Random House Web address: http://www.randomhouse.com/

Printed in the United States of America
20 19

To Beverly

CONTENTS

ACKNOWLEDGMENTS

In the preparation of this book I am deeply indebted to a large number of individuals and institutions. I owe a very special debt to Jennifer Hochschild, Alice O'Connor, Sheldon Danziger, Tracey Meares, James Quane, and Robert Sampson, who read the entire first draft of the manuscript and provided detailed comments, including a number of challenging questions, that led to significant revision of parts of the book. Helpful comments were also provided by Brenda Smith, who carefully read Chapter 4. To my editor at Knopf, Victoria Wilson, I am grateful for first making me aware that I needed to go back to the drawing board on some of my policy recommendations and for helping me to improve the flow of the manuscript. To Susan Allen I owe a great deal for her skillful editing of the manuscript to improve its readability for a general audience. Finally, I am indebted to Jackie Harris, my secretary at the Center for the Study of Urban Inequality, who proofread the entire manuscript with considerable care; and to Ellen J. Hickok-Wall, who provided helpful editorial suggestions concerning the revision and reorganization of the final draft.

The research assistants who worked with me in preparing the complex data sets for analysis deserve special recognition. I particularly would like to single out Sophia Pedder, who worked on the ethnographic data and open-ended interviews from the Urban Poverty and Family Life Study (UPFLS); Rowena Abrahams, who worked on the same materials in addition to the UPFLS employers' survey; and Sandra Smith, who worked on the employers' survey. These three individuals displayed great imagination and dedication in analyzing, organizing, and integrating the detailed data sets. Also, I would like to thank Loïc J. D. Wacquant for his help in the analysis of the UPFLS survey; Amit Sevak, Jean Twenge, and Simon Weffer for their work on the ethnographic materials, open-ended interviews, and employers' survey of the UPFLS; Kelly Chong for her assistance in the compilation of the bibliography; and Jeffrey Morenoff for his work on the map of Chicago Community Areas. This book also benefited from the help I received from Bruce Rankin, Research Coordinator for the Center for the Study of Urban Inequality at the University of Chicago. Rankin worked with me in analyzing the data from all three of the studies I directed and on which this book is largely based—the UPFLS, the Woodlawn and Oakland neighborhood study, and the study of the effects of high-risk neighborhoods on adolescent social development.

The data collection for these three studies involved the work of a number of faculty and students at the University of Chicago. The UPFLS included a large team of researchers. The project was administered by Robert Aponte. Raymond Smith and Richard Taub, two faculty members at the University of Chicago, supervised the research of the ethnographic team, which included Nan Astone, Daniel Breslau, Major Coleman, Karen Freel, Antonia Gutierrez-Marquez, Sharon Hicks-Bartlett, Marilyn Krogh, Robert Laseter, Guadalupe Rodriguez-Gomez, Martha Van Haitsma, and Daniel Wolk. Raymond Smith also supervised the work of a team of research assistants who conducted the open-ended surveys of inner-city residents. This group included Major Coleman, Ming Chin, Joleen Kirschenman, Matthew Lawson, Patricia Porter, Michael Reynolds, Martha Van Haitsma, and Loïc J. D. Wacquant. Mark Testa and Marta Tienda, members of the University of Chicago faculty, supervised the data gathering for the large closed-ended survey of the UPFLS. Other faculty members who worked on this survey were Donna Franklin, Delores Norton, and Michael Sosin. I would also like to thank the staff of the National Opinion Research Center (NORC) at the University of Chicago who worked on the large survey, including Sameer Abraham, Virginia Bartot, Barbara Campbell, Martin Frankel, Mary O'Brien, and David Pepper. NORC conducted the face-to-face interviews using the closed-ended questionnaire.

The employers' survey of the UPFLS benefited from the leadership of Joleen Kirschenman and Kathryn Neckerman, who worked with me, Loïc J. D. Wacquant, Daniel Breslau, and Lori Sparzo on the construction of the questionnaire and who conducted the actual interviews along with Breslau, Wacquant, Sparzo, and Judy Mintz.

The Oakland and Woodlawn neighborhood study was supervised by David Campbell and Lena Lundgren-Gaveras. This study also benefited from the work of James Quane and Bruce Rankin, and the tireless effort of research assistant Mignon Moore. Alicia Bassuk and John Davis also served as research assistants on this project. The focus group discussions of residents from Oakland and Woodlawn were ably led by Robert Laseter, and the data from the survey of these two neighborhoods were collected by the Metro Chicago Information Center, a private nonprofit research organization, directed by Garth Taylor.

The study of the effects of neighborhoods on adolescent social outcomes in high-risk areas involved the work and supervision of Michael Sosin and Robert Sampson, two faculty members at the University of Chicago, and the project coordinator for this research, Joleen Kirschenman. Marilyn Krogh and Bruce Rankin were the data analysts for this project, and Sudhir Venketesh and David Reingold worked on the project as research assistants. William McCready and his staff from the University of Northern Illinois Survey Research Center conducted the face-to-face interviews for this study.

The following institutions provided the financial support for these three research projects. The UPFLS was supported by the Ford Foundation, the Rockefeller Foundation, the Carnegie Corporation, the Joyce Foundation, the Spencer Foundation, the William T. Grant Foundation, the Lloyd A. Fry Foundation, the Woods Charitable Fund, the Chicago Community Trust, the Institute for Research on Poverty, and the Department of Health and Human Services. The Woodlawn and Oakland neighborhood study was made possible by generous grants to the Center for the Study of Urban Inequality from the John D. and Catherine T. MacArthur Foundation, the Ford Foundation, the Rockefeller Foundation, and Household International. These same funds, along with a grant from the MacArthur Research Program on Successful Adolescents in High Risk Areas, also supported the study of the effects of neighborhoods on adolescent social outcomes in high-risk areas.

I would also like to thank the French-American Foundation for awarding me a fellowship to spend the 1989–90 academic year in Paris, France, at the Ecole des Hautes Etudes en Sciences Sociales.

During that year I visited a number of European countries and observed and studied their problems of race, poverty, and joblessness. The knowledge gained is reflected in Chapters 6 and 8, where I draw comparisons between Europe and the United States.

Finally, to my wife, I have dedicated this book.

W.J.W.

For the first time in the twentieth century most adults in many inner-city ghetto neighborhoods are not working in a typical week. The disappearance of work has adversely affected not only individuals, families, and neighborhoods, but the social life of the city at large as well. Inner-city joblessness is a severe problem that is often overlooked or obscured when the focus is placed mainly on poverty and its consequences. Despite increases in the concentration of poverty since 1970, inner cities have always featured high levels of poverty, but the current levels of joblessness in some neighborhoods are unprecedented.

The consequences of high neighborhood joblessness are more devastating than those of high neighborhood poverty. A neighborhood in which people are poor but employed is different from a neighborhood in which people are poor and jobless. Many of today's problems in the inner-city ghetto neighborhoods—crime, family dissolution, welfare, low levels of social organization, and so on—are fundamentally a consequence of the disappearance of work.

What causes the disappearance of work? The public debate around this question is not productive because it seeks to assign blame rather than recognizing and dealing with the complex and changing realities that have led to economic distress for many Americans. Explanations and proposed solutions to the problems are often ideologically driven.

Thus, those who endorse liberal ideology have tended to emphasize social structural factors, including race. By social structure I mean the ordering of social positions (or statuses) and networks of social relationships that are based on the arrangement of mutually dependent institutions (economy, polity, family, education) of society. Race, which reflects both an individual's position (in the sense of social status defined by skin color) and network of relationships in society, is a social structural variable. Many liberal explanations of social inequality cite race to the exclusion of other structural variables.

Those who endorse conservative ideology tend to stress the importance of values, attitudes, habits, and styles in explaining the different experiences, behavior, and outcomes of groups. According to this view, group differences are reflected in the culture. To act according to one's culture is to follow one's inclinations as they have been developed by learning or influence from other members of the community to which one belongs or with which one identifies.

This book attempts to demonstrate that social structural factors are important for understanding joblessness and other experiences of the inner-city poor, but that there is much these factors do not explain. Although race is clearly an important variable in the social outcomes of inner-city blacks, much ambiguity remains about the meaning and significance of race in certain situations. Cultural factors do play a role, but any adequate explanation of inner-city joblessness and poverty should take other variables into account. Social psychological variables—a set of factors generally absent from the current debate—must be integrated with social structural and cultural variables. We need a broader vision that includes *all* of the major variables and, even more important, reveals their relative significance and their interaction in determining the experiences and life chances of inner-city residents. Such a vision guides my interpretation and integration of the research reported in the following chapters.

I highlight problems in order to inform the public and social policy debates. A good deal of what we call attention to as social scientists is related to the ultimate objective of our research. Social researchers who wish to inform and influence public policy are more likely to focus on a community's problems than on its strengths. Their purpose is to stimulate thought so that policymakers, concerned citizens, journalists, and others will have a basis for understanding such problems and the need to address them. Given the reemergence of the discussion concerning the importance of genetic endowment, it is urgent that social scientists once again emphasize, for public policy purposes, the powerful and complex role of the social environment in shaping the life experiences of inner-city ghetto residents.

Since the publication of *The Bell Curve* in late 1994, a genetic argument has resurfaced in public discussions about the plight of inner-city residents. This controversial book by Richard Herrnstein and Charles Murray argues that regardless of social, economic, or ethnic background, low intelligence is the root cause of many of our social problems. Herrnstein and Murray attempt to demonstrate that "cognitive ability," as measured by intelligence tests, powerfully predicts not only earnings but a range of other outcomes from parental competence to criminal behavior. *The Bell Curve* questions the extent to which the environment influences group social outcomes and whether intervention programs can compensate for the handicaps of genetic endowment.

Herrnstein and Murray argue, for example, that early intervention programs for children of the "underclass" hold little promise. Why? Because the substantial gains in standardized test scores recorded during the preschool programs quickly erode after the children leave. They point out that within a few years the test scores of the children who attended Head Start programs do not differ significantly from the scores of those who did not. "Cognitive benefits that can often be picked up in the first grade of school are usually gone by the third grade," they state. "By the sixth grade, they have vanished entirely in aggregate statistics." This is what is called "fade-out"—"the gradual convergence in test scores of the children who participated in the program with comparable children who had not." The authors maintain that for the foreseeable future outside intervention programs such as Head Start will not be effective because they do not address the problems associated with low cognitive ability.

Anyone familiar with the harsh environment of the inner-city ghetto should not be surprised by the research findings on the Head Start fade-out. It would be extraordinary if the gains from Head Start programs were sustained in some of these environments. The children of the inner-city ghetto have to contend with public schools plagued by unimaginative curricula, overcrowded classrooms, inadequate plant and facilities, and only a small proportion of teachers who have confidence in their students and expect them to learn. Inner-city ghetto children also grow up in neighborhoods with devastating rates of joblessness, which trigger a whole series of other problems that are not conducive to healthy child development or intellectual growth. Included among these are broken families, antisocial behavior, social networks that do not extend beyond the confines of the ghetto environment, and a lack of informal social control over the behavior and activities of children and adults in the neighborhood.

If enrichment programs like Head Start were extended throughout elementary, middle, and even high school, it is very likely that initial gains would be sustained. In the absence of such programs, however, it is unwarranted and intellectually irresponsible to attribute either the academic failure of these children or their lack of success in postschool employment mainly to their "cognitive ability." Moreover, most geneticists agree that there is currently no definite line separating genetic influences from environmental influences.

Indeed, the test used by Herrnstein and Murray as an indicator of innate intellectual ability, the Armed Forces Qualifications Test (AFQT), is largely an achievement test, not a test of genetic endowment. It reflects the cumulative weight of poverty and racial experiences. Recent research reveals that additional years of schooling and work experience result in significant changes in AFQT scores. Herrnstein and Murray claim that they controlled for environmental experiences using an indicator of family background (parental education, occupational status, family income) measured at the time the youth took the AFQT test (between ages 15 and 23). However, as the economist James Heckman points out, this measure does not capture the 15 to 23 years of cumulative environmental influences, including the long-term effects of living in certain neighborhoods, the cultural milieu, the quality of schooling, the nurturing of parents, the resources they are able to spend or pass on to their children, and so on.

If the importance of the ghetto environment is deemphasized in studies such as *The Bell Curve*, it is also downplayed by those scholars who purport to "defend" inner-city residents and correct what they believe to be distortions in the descriptions of their behaviors and experiences. The earlier proponents of this approach were African-American scholars who reacted angrily in the 1970s to the unflattering depictions of ghetto blacks in *The Negro Family: The Case for National Action*, Daniel Patrick Moynihan's controversial 1965 report on the black family.

These scholars were highly critical of the Moynihan report's emphasis on social pathologies within ghetto neighborhoods not simply because of its potential for embarrassment but also because it conflicted with their claim that blacks were developing a community power base that could become a major force in American society. This power base, they argued, reflected the strength and vitality of the black community. These African-American scholars emphasized the positive aspects of the black experience. In fact, those elements of ghetto behavior described as pathological in the late-1960s studies of the inner city were seen as functional in this new interpretation because, it was argued, inner-city blacks, and especially the black family, were resilient, able to survive and even flourish in a racist environment. These revisionist arguments shifted the focus from the consequences of racial isolation and economic class subordination to inner-city black achievement. In short, as in *The Bell Curve*, but of course for entirely different reasons, the devastating effects of the inner-city environment were either ignored, played down, or denied.

The most prominent and recent "sympathetic" portrayal of inner-city residents which shifts the focus away from the ghetto environment was presented by the sociologist Mitchell Duneier. In a book entitled *Slim's Table*, Duneier reports on his extensive interviews with a small group of working-class men, including one named "Slim," from an inner-city neighborhood on the South Side of Chicago. These men frequent a cafeteria in the nearby affluent neighborhood of Hyde Park, where the interviews were conducted. Duneier argues that sociologists and journalists ignore people like Slim who continue to live in the ghetto. In reaction to the arguments I presented in *The Truly Disadvantaged*, Duneier points out that even in the most troubled neighborhoods one will find hardworking and family-oriented people who are committed to the values of mainstream society.

The arguments in *The Truly Disadvantaged* do not contradict this view. I pointed out that both middle-class and working-class blacks—who have historically reinforced the traditional patterns of work, family, and education in the inner city—have departed many ghetto neighborhoods in significant numbers. I argue that there is a paucity of such families not only because of the exodus (outmigration) of higher-income families but also because of declining employment opportunities associated with the economic restructuring that currently afflicts Americans in all racial and ethnic groups. In other words, the ranks of the stable and employed families in many inner-city neighborhoods have been severely reduced, not totally eliminated.

In this volume the devastating effects of the inner-city ghetto environment are discussed and documented. The residents who live in these environments plainly see this process themselves and many of them discuss the situation in clearer and more graphic terms than the social scientists who are researching these neighborhoods.

Like the older men who eat regularly in the Hyde Park cafeteria, whom Duneier claims are representative of ghetto blacks, the people interviewed in their actual homes and neighborhoods by our researchers spoke with dignity and in their remarks expressed values of work, family, and education. But they also focused on issues not highlighted in the benign portraits in *Slim's Table*—the problems of racial segregation, class subordination, and social isolation that not only make their efforts to survive very difficult but have destroyed so many of their relatives, friends, and neighbors.

In emphasizing the powerful role of the environment in shaping the lives of inner-city residents, we should not ignore or deny the existence of unflattering behaviors that emerge from blocked opportunities. Indeed, as spelled out in Chapter 3, some of these behaviors, which often impede the social mobility of inner-city residents, represent cultural responses to constraints and limited opportunities that have evolved over time. The tendency of some liberals to deny the very existence of culturally destructive behavior and attitudes in the inner city is once again to diminish the importance of the environment in determining the outcomes and life chances of individuals. The environment embodies both structural and cultural constraints and opportunities. In order to fully appreciate and explain the divergent social outcomes of human groups, we must take into account the exposure to different cultural influences.

It is also necessary to account for the exposure to different structural influences. For example, it is important to understand and communicate the overwhelming obstacles that many ghetto residents have to overcome just to live up to mainstream expectations involving work, the family, and the law. Such expectations are taken for granted in middle-class society. Americans in more affluent areas have jobs that offer fringe benefits; they are accustomed to health insurance that covers paid sick leave and medical care. They do not live in neighborhoods where attempts at normal child-rearing are constantly undermined by social forces that interfere with healthy child development. And their families' prospects for survival do not require at least some participation in the informal economy (that is, an economy in which income is unreported and therefore not taxable).

It is just as indefensible to treat inner-city residents as superheroes who are able to overcome racist oppression as it is to view them as helpless victims. We should, however, appreciate the range of choices, including choices representing cultural influences, that are available to inner-city residents who live under constraints that most people in the larger society do not experience.

I argue that the disappearance of work and the consequences of that disappearance for both social and cultural life are the central problems in the inner-city ghetto. To acknowledge that the ghetto still includes working people and that nearly all ghetto residents, whether employed or not, support the norms of the work ethic (see Chapter 6) should not lead one to overlook the fact that a majority of adults in many inner-city neighborhoods are jobless at any given point in time.

This book also emphasizes that the disappearance of work and the growth of related problems in the ghetto have aggravated an already tense racial situation in urban areas. Our nation's response to racial discord in the central city and to the growing racial divide between the city and the suburbs has been disappointing. In discussing these problems we have a tendency to engage in the kind of rhetoric that exacerbates, rather than alleviates, urban and metropolitan racial tensions. Ever since the 1992 Los Angeles riot, the media have focused heavily on the factors that divide rather than those that unite racial groups. Emphasis on racial division peaked in 1995 following the jury's verdict in the O. J. Simpson murder trial. Before the verdict was announced, opinion polls revealed that whites overwhelmingly thought Mr. Simpson was guilty, while a substantial majority of blacks felt he was innocent. The media clips showing public reaction to the verdict dramatized the racial division—blacks appeared elated and jubilant; whites appeared stunned, angry, and somber. Blacks believed that O. J. Simpson had been framed by a racist police conspiracy; whites were convinced that he was guilty of the murder of two people and was being allowed to walk free. The racial divide, as depicted in the media, seemed as wide as ever.

The implications of these developments for the future of race relations and for programs perceived to benefit blacks remain to be seen. As one observer, on the eve of the Simpson verdict, put it: "When O. J. gets off, the whites will riot the way we whites do: leave the cities, go to Idaho or Oregon or Arizona, vote for Gingrich . . . and punish the blacks by closing the day-care programs and cutting off their Medicaid."

The extent of the racial divisions in this country should not be minimized. The different reactions to the Simpson trial and the verdict reflect in part the fundamentally dissimilar racial experiences of blacks and whites in America—the former burdened by racial injustice, the latter largely free of the effects of bigotry and hatred. Nonetheless, the emphasis on racial differences has obscured the fact that African-Americans, whites, and other ethnic groups share many common concerns, are beset by many common problems, and have many common values, aspirations, and hopes.

If inner-city blacks are experiencing the greatest problems of joblessness, it is a more extreme form of economic marginality that has affected most Americans since 1980. As I shall argue in Chapters 7 and 8, solutions to the broader problems of economic marginality in this country, including those that stem from changes in the global economy, can go a long way toward addressing the problems of inner-city joblessness, especially if the application of resources includes wise targeting to the groups most in need of help. Discussions that emphasize common solutions to commonly shared problems promote a sense of unity, regardless of the different degrees of severity to which these problems afflict certain groups. Such messages bring races together, not apart, and are especially important during periods of racial tension. In comparison with the rhetoric highlighting racial divisions, however, messages promoting interracial unity have been infrequent and are generally ignored in the media.

It is important to recognize that racial antagonisms, or the manifestation of racial tensions, are products of economic, political, and social situations. In a 1992 op-ed article in *The New York Times*, I used this argument to point out why it is important for political leaders to channel the frustrations of average citizens in positive or constructive directions during periods of economic duress. I discussed the 1992 political campaign of President Bill Clinton, who not only explicitly acknowledged the growing racial tension in America and the need for political leadership to unite and not divide the races, but who had actually developed a public rhetoric that reflected these concerns. This campaign rhetoric warned Americans against the distraction of pitting race against race; it urged citizens to associate their declining real incomes, increasing job insecurity, and growing pessimism with the complex but real sources of these problems. I pointed out that the use of this positive public rhetoric during a period of intense racial tension enabled Clinton to bring together antagonistic racial groups to form an effective political coalition in the primary elections—even in Louisiana where a majority of white voters supported the former Klansman David Duke in the 1991 gubernatorial election. Unfortunately, the media, preoccupied with allegations surrounding Mr. Clinton's personal life, failed to record the significance of this event.

Because the problems of ghetto joblessness are so severe and because they are associated with social problems that make many of our central cities increasingly unattractive places in which to reside and work, a vision of interracial unity that acknowledges distinctively racial problems but nonetheless emphasizes common solutions to common problems is more important now than ever. Such a vision should be developed, shared, and promoted by all leaders in this country, but especially by political leaders.

I have in mind a vision that promotes values of racial and intergroup harmony and unity and rejects the commonly held view that race is so divisive that whites, blacks, Latinos, and other ethnic groups cannot work together in a common cause. This vision recognizes that if a political message is tailored to a white audience, racial minorities draw back, just as whites draw back when a message is tailored to minority audiences. The foundation of this vision emphasizes issues and programs that concern the families of all racial and ethnic groups so that individuals in these groups will come to see their mutual interests and join in a multiracial coalition to move America forward; it promotes the idea that Americans have common interests and concerns that cross racial and class boundaries—such as unemployment and job security, declining real wages, escalating medical and housing costs, the scarcity of quality child care programs, the sharp decline in the quality of public education, and the toll of crime and drug trafficking in all neighborhoods. This vision encourages Americans to see that the application of programs to combat these problems would benefit everyone, not just the truly disadvantaged; to recognize that the division between the suburbs and the central city is partly a racial one and that it is vitally important to emphasize city-suburban cooperation, not separation; and, finally, to endorse the idea that all groups, including those in the throes of ghetto joblessness, should be able to achieve full membership in society because the problems of economic and social marginality spring from the inequities in society at large and not from group deficiencies. I believe that this vision, supported by a public rhetoric of interracial unity, is essential to address the problems discussed in this book.

Most of the following chapters rely heavily on data collected during the course of three research projects conducted at the Center for the Study of Urban Inequality at the University of Chicago. Appendix B describes each of these studies in some detail, but I would like to point out here that the most important of these projects is the Urban Poverty and Family Life Study (UPFLS). Conducted in 1987 and 1988, this project includes a random survey of nearly 2,500 poor and nonpoor African-American, Latino, and white residents in Chicago's poor inner-city neighborhoods. These are neighborhoods with poverty rates of at least 20 percent. As part of this broad project, the UPFLS includes data from the Social Opportunity Survey, a subsample of 175 UPFLS participants who answered open-ended questions concerning their perceptions of the opportunity structure and life chances; a 1988 survey of 179 employers—in most cases the information came from the highest-ranking official at each firm sampled—selected to reflect the distribution of employment across industry and firm size in the Chicago metropolitan areas; and comprehensive ethnographic research, including participant-observation research and life-history interviews, conducted during the period of 1986 to 1988 by ten research assistants in a representative sample of inner-city neighborhoods.

The first of the two remaining projects includes a 1993 survey of a representative sample of 500 respondents from two high-joblessness neighborhoods on the South Side of Chicago and six focus group discussions involving the residents and former residents of these neighborhoods. The third study is a 1989–90 survey of a representative sample of black mothers and up to two of their adolescent children (ages 11 to 16) in working- and middle-class neighborhoods and high-poverty neighborhoods. The respondents from the households in the high-poverty neighborhoods included 383 mothers and 614 youths. Those from the households in the working- and middle-class neighborhoods were represented by 163 mothers and 273 youths. I have integrated the data from these three studies with census-type information and relevant findings from the research of other scholars.

PART I

THE NEW URBAN POVERTY

CHAPTER I

From Institutional to Jobless Ghettos

An elderly woman who has lived in one inner-city neighborhood on the South Side of Chicago for more than forty years reflected:

> I've been here since March 21, 1953. When I moved in, the neighborhood was intact. It was intact with homes, beautiful homes, mini mansions, with stores, laundromats, with cleaners, with Chinese [cleaners]. We had drugstores. We had hotels. We had doctors over on Thirty-ninth Street. We had doctors' offices in the neighborhood. We had the middle class and upper middle class. It has gone from affluent to where it is today. And I would like to see it come back, that we can have some of things we had. Since I came in young, and I'm a senior citizen now, I would like to see some of the things come back so I can enjoy them like we did when we first came in.

An employed 35-year-old married woman from a South Side neighborhood shared some of her philosophy.

> I feels that . . . that everyone who wants to work and wanta have a job should be able to walk out and get it and not take six months to do it. . . . I think, society should make a greater effort in caring for the sick, the seniors, and the peoples that's just down and out on their luck and just don't have, for whatever means. Another thing, one of my main top concerns, I feel that it's just [slow and coldly outraged], it's awful the way, throughout the city, on your South

and West Side, you see all these vacant lots, all these abandoned buildings, and peoples are living in the streets. Or living four and five and ten peoples in an apartment that was allocated for one or two peoples—you find eight or ten peoples because they have no place to go and no housing available. And throughout the city, you have those abandoned buildings, and vacant buildings, and just, just areas, blocks and blocks of vacant lots, where they could be building affordable, moderate-income houses.

A young truck driver expressed his view regarding the need for improvement in his neighborhood. "It'd be nice to see police walking around here once in a while. We need role models for the kids." A senior typist added: "Need funding to get businesses in the area. A big grocery store would generate more jobs and enable people to shop more safely and without fear."

A 91-year-old woman spoke of safety concerns: "It's not safe anymore because the streets aren't. When all the black businesses and shows closed down, the economy went to the dogs. The stores, the businesses, the shows, everywhere was lighted, the stores and businesses have disappeared."

The negative social forces triggered a decision by a concerned mother to send her son away.

I have a 13-year-old. I sent him away when he was nine because the gangs was at him so tough, because he wouldn't join—he's a basketball player. That's all he ever cared about. They took his gym shoes off his feet. They took his clothes. Made him walk home from school. Jumped on him every day. Took his jacket off his back in subzero weather. You know, and we only live two blocks from the school. . . . A boy pulled a gun to his head and told him, "If you don't join, next week you won't be here." I had to send him out of town. His father stayed out of town. He came here last week for a week. He said, "Mom, I want to come home so bad," I said no!

The social deterioration of ghetto neighborhoods is the central concern expressed in the testimony of these residents. As a representative from the media put it, the ghetto has gone "from bad to worse." Few observers of the urban scene in the late 1960s anticipated the extensive breakdown of social institutions and the sharp rise in rates of social dislocation that have since swept the ghettos and spread to other neighborhoods that were once stable. For example, in the neighborhood of Woodlawn, located on the South Side of Chicago, there were over eight hundred commercial and industrial establishments in 1950. Today, it is estimated that only about a hundred are left, many of them represented by "tiny catering places, barber shops, and thrift stores with no more than one or two employees." As Loïc Wacquant, a member of the Urban Poverty and Family Life Study research team, put it:

> The once-lively streets—residents remember a time, not so long ago, when crowds were so dense at rush hour that one had to elbow one's way to the train station—now have the appearance of an empty, bombed-out war zone. The commercial strip has been reduced to a long tunnel of charred stores, vacant lots littered with broken glass and garbage, and dilapidated buildings left to rot in the shadow of the elevated train line. At the corner of Sixty-third Street and Cottage Grove Avenue, the handful of remaining establishments that struggle to survive are huddled behind wrought-iron bars. . . . The only enterprises that seem to be thriving are liquor stores and currency exchanges, these "banks of the poor" where one can cash checks, pay bills and buy money orders for a fee.

A resident of Woodlawn who had left the neighborhood as a child described how she felt upon her return about the changes that had occurred: "I was just really appalled. When I walked down Sixty-third Street when I was younger, everything that you wanted was there. But now, coming back as an adult with my child, those resources are just gone, completely. . . . And . . . housing, everybody has moved, there are vacant lots everywhere." Another resident describes a similar experience when he returned to the neighborhood after living elsewhere for several years. "[There were all kinds] of stores up and down Sixty-third Street, and it was, you know, just a fun place. Then when I came back in the seventies, it was like . . . barren. It was totally different from what I remembered."

In 1950, almost two-thirds of Woodlawn's population was white; by 1960 the white population had declined to just 10 percent. Despite the sudden white exodus, the number of residents in the neighborhood increased slightly during this period. After 1960, however, a sizable exodus of black residents followed, including a significant number of working- and middle-class families. The population of the neighborhood declined from over 80,000 in 1960 to 53,814 in 1970; it further slipped to 36,323 in 1980 and finally to 24,473 in 1990. The loss of residents was accompanied by a substantial reduction in the economic, social, and political resources that make a community vibrant. Woodlawn is only one of a growing number of poor black neighborhoods in Chicago plagued by depopulation and social and economic deterioration.

When the black respondents in our large UPFLS survey were asked to rate their neighborhood as a place to live, only a third said that their area was a good or very good place to live and only 18 percent of those in the ghetto poverty census tracts felt that their neighborhood was a desirable place to live. (The Bureau of the Census defines a census tract as "a relatively homogeneous area with respect to population characteristics, economic status, and living conditions with an average population of 4,000." Poverty tracts are those in which at least 20 percent of the residents are poor, and ghetto poverty tracts are those in which at least 40 percent are poor.)

A 31-year-old employed laborer and janitor from a Near West Side public housing project described his neighborhood in these emphatic terms:

> See, this is a violent neighborhood. You always hear somebody gettin' shot, just about every day or something like every night. Because you know, like I said, I see people are crowded up together, especially in the high rises. I would say it drags you down, because, you know, when people get crazy and everything, it'll drag you down. They gonna robbin' you, you know, tryin' to beat you. They don't wanta work, you know, they'd rather for you to work and then wait for you, you know, to get your paycheck so they can rob you or something.

A 39-year-old divorced schoolteacher and mother of four talked about a boy who recently had been shot in her South Side neighborhood:

I think he was just gettin', buyin' somethin' or whatever—at the restaurant or somethin' and some kid walked up to him on the street and shot him five times. I—I don't know was it gang related or if kids—you know, just a matter of bein' in the wrong place at the wrong time, you know. Those are the kinds of things that you have to be careful about when you live in an environment like this.

Concern about violent crime was also expressed by a married mother of four children who works as a factory packer. She pointed out that the criminal elements in her South Side neighborhood often

knock old ladies down and take their pension checks. Like on the El [elevated train] station there. Especially when they get their Social Security checks, they be out there, waiting for them, grab their purses and everything. Lot of that happening around here. They borrow and they pawn, breaking in and all. They broke in on me when I first moved in here so I put bars in. They got my stereo. But I haven't any trouble since I put my bars up.

Violence was also a cause for worry for a 32-year-old unemployed and unmarried black father of one child from a ghetto poverty census tract on the Near West Side:

No, I don't like this neighborhood. A lot of friends, they got killed and whatnot, you know, I saw a lot of killing in this neighborhood. It's messed up. My mother is going on sixty-six, she ain't got a chance of a young man running up on her and saying: "Hey, give me your money." She ain't got a chance. The dudes, they do a lot of ripping off around here, they do a lot of stealing, put it that way. They rip off people. Then they got the drug traffic running through in these buildings. It's all messed up, man.

Many of the respondents described the negative effects of their neighborhood on their own personal outlook. An unmarried, employed clerical worker from a ghetto poverty census tract on the West Side stated:

There is a more positive outlook if you come from an upwardly mobile neighborhood than you would here. In this type of neighborhood, all you hear is negative [things] and that can kind of bring you down when you're trying to make it. So your neighborhood definitely has something to do with it.

This view was shared by a 17-year-old college student and part-time worker from an impoverished West Side neighborhood.

I'd say about 40 percent in my neighborhood . . . I'd say 40 percent are alcoholics. . . . And . . . only 5 percent of the alcoholics have homes. Then you got the other 35 percent who are in the street. . . . They probably live somewhere, but they in street, on the corner every day, same old thing, because they don't have no chance in life. They live based on today. [They say,] "Oh, we gonna get high today." "Oh, whoopee!" "What you gonna do to-morrow, man?" "I don't know, man, I don't know." You can ask any of 'em: "What you gonna do tomorrow?" "I don't know, man. I know when [it gets] here." And I can really understand, you know, being in that state. If you around totally negative people, people who are not doing anything, that's the way you gonna be regardless.

The state of the inner-city public schools was another major concern expressed by our respondents. The complaints ranged from overcrowded conditions to unqualified and uncaring teachers. Sharply voicing her views on these subjects, a 25-year-old married mother of two children from a South Side census tract that just recently became poor stated: "My daughter ain't going to school here, she was going to a nursery school where I paid and of course they took the time and spent it with her, 'cause they was getting the money. But the public schools, no! They are overcrowded and the teachers don't care."

A 29-year-old South Side welfare mother of four children pointed out that in her "neighborhood [the kids] can't learn much if they don't have the proper equipment, the proper books and things, because I know that this school, they don't have proper books that the children need to study from. That's what holds them back a lot."

However, a 35-year-old married black mother of two children, who works as a management aide for the city of Chicago, focused mainly on student behavior.

> The junior high schools [are] too infested with overcrowdedness, gang activities, high pregnancy rates. I feel they're so infested with this type of situations, that, uh, it's just a deterral to childrens to want to seek higher education.

Finally, a 40-year-old welfare mother of four children who lives in a ghetto poverty tract on the West Side described how the conditions in her neighborhood could be improved:

> Even this neighborhood, if they would fix it up, and keep it up, keep the drugs out, it would be much better. Take the drugs out. Give, uh, let the peoples have more jobs, you know, working. They're sitting out on the corner, they're doin' nothin'. So I think if a person was workin' . . . I don't think there, maybe it would be as bad as, you know, stickin' up people and killin' people. 'Cause I think they kill, stick up people 'cause they don't have, so they figure they can go take it from someone else.

The respondents were also asked whether their neighborhoods had changed as a place to live over the years. Seventy-one percent of the African-American respondents felt that their neighborhoods had either stayed the same or had gotten worse.

An unemployed black man from a West Side housing project felt that the only thing that had changed in his neighborhood was that it was "going down instead of going back up." He further stated, "It ain't like it used to be. They laid off a lot of people. There used to be a time when you got a broken window, you call up housing and they send someone over to fix it, but it ain't like that no more."

Respondents frequently made statements about the increase in drug trafficking and drug consumption when discussing how their neighborhood had changed. "Well, OK, I realize there was drugs when I was growing up but they weren't as open as they are now," stated a divorced telephone dispatcher and mother of five children from a neighborhood that recently changed from a nonpoverty to a poverty area. "It's nothing to see a 10-year-old kid strung out or a 10-

year-old kid selling drugs. I mean, when they were doing it back then they were sneaking around doing it. It's like an open thing now."

The 17-year-old black college student from the West Side that I quoted above describes how drugs created a problem for his neighborhood:

When I first moved over here this neighborhood was quite OK. After six o'clock you wouldn't see anybody on the street in this neighborhood, you know, even if it was summertime. People might be in the park, but if you walk down the street you may see somebody sitting on they porch, and they wasn't no lot of loud noise, and—and didn't many cars pass by. But, when drugs start flowing in, people start having drugs fights and you couldn't sleep because here were cars coming up and down the street all night long. And, you know, that's bad 'cause that makes your community look bad.

Finally, a 41-year-old nurse's aide, married but separated from her husband, and the mother of two, described how the situation in her neighborhood, a ghetto poverty tract on the West Side, has changed for the children:

Before, you know, the young peoples they had this Youth Corps and all this you know, but they done cut out this all. They don't have anything for the young peoples now. All they do when they get out of school in summertime is rap up and down the street, and get into trouble 'cause they don't have anything to do. And I felt like the Youth Corps, when I was in school, I was in Youth Corps and it really helped out a lot. It taught me a lot, taught me—I learned to hold on a job when I am working it 'cause they train you. But now they don't have anything for the young kids, really you know.

The black respondents' negative feelings about their neighborhood are also reflected in their stated preference to live elsewhere. When asked if they would prefer to live in their neighborhood, another neighborhood in Chicago, in the suburbs, or somewhere else, only 35 percent of the respondents from the poverty census tracts overall stated that they would prefer to live in their own neighborhood; as few as 23 percent of the respondents in the ghetto poverty tracts indicated a preference for their own neighborhood.

Describing why she chose to live in a neighborhood that she dislikes, a 27-year-old West Side welfare mother of three stated that "it's the only place I could afford to live at the time when I moved in." She further remarked: "At the time when I moved I had two children and I've been here eleven years. No, I don't like it. At the present time I can't afford to move out."

This sentiment was echoed by a 24-year-old welfare mother of four children from the same neighborhood: "The reason I moved over here is because of the rent: it's very low, and I don't have to worry about gas bills and light bills. No, I just don't like it living over here, it's too many people, living around, living on top of each other. It's much too overcrowded."

Finally, a welfare mother of three children who also lives in this neighborhood stated: "Taxis don't want to come over here to get you and bring you back either. You know, friends from other places don't want really to come here. And you yourself, you wouldn't want to invite intelligent people here: there's markings and there's writing on the wall, nasty—whatever."

The feelings of many of the respondents in our study were summed up by a 33-year-old married mother of three from a very poor West Side neighborhood:

> If you live in an area in your neighborhood where you have people that don't work, don't have no means of support, you know, don't have no jobs, who're gonna break into your house to steal what you have, to sell to get them some money, then you can't live in a neighborhood and try to concentrate on tryin' to get ahead, then you get to work and you have to worry if somebody's breakin' into your house or not. So, you know, it's best to try to move in a decent area, to live in a community with people that works.

In 1959, less than one-third of the poverty population in the United States lived in metropolitan central cities. By 1991, the central cities included close to half of the nation's poor. Many of the most rapid increases in concentrated poverty have occurred in African-American neighborhoods. For example, in the ten community areas that represent the historic core of Chicago's Black Belt (see Figure 1.1), eight had rates of poverty in 1990 that exceeded 45 percent, including three with rates higher than 50 percent and three that surpassed 60 percent. Twenty-five years earlier, in 1970, only two of these neighborhoods had poverty rates above 40 percent.

In recent years, social scientists have paid particular attention to the increases in urban neighborhood poverty. "Defining an urban neighborhood for analytical purposes is no easy task." The community areas of Chicago referred to in Figure 1.1 include a number of adjacent census tracts. The seventy-seven community areas within the city of Chicago represent statistical units derived by urban sociologists at the University of Chicago for the 1930 census in their effort to analyze varying conditions within the city. These delineations were originally drawn up on the basis of settlement and history of the area, local identification and trade patterns, local institutions, and natural and artificial barriers. There have been major shifts in population and land use since then. But these units remain useful in tracing changes over time, and they continue to capture much of the contemporary reality of Chicago neighborhoods.

Other cities, however, do not have such convenient classifications of neighborhoods, which means that comparison across cities cannot be drawn using community areas. The measurable unit considered most appropriate to represent urban neighborhoods is the census tract. In attempts to examine this problem of ghetto poverty across the nation empirically, social scientists have tended to define ghetto neighborhoods as those located in the *ghetto poverty* census tracts. As indicated earlier, ghetto poverty census tracts are those in which at least 40 percent of the residents are poor. For example, Paul Jargowsky and Mary Jo Bane state: "Visits to various cities confirmed that the 40 percent criterion came very close to identifying areas that looked like ghettos in terms of their housing conditions. Moreover, the areas selected by the 40 percent criterion corresponded closely with the neighborhoods that city officials and local Census Bureau officials considered ghettos." The ghetto poor in Jargowsky and Bane's study are therefore designated as those among the poor who live in these ghetto poverty areas. Three-quarters of all the ghetto poor in metropolitan areas reside in one hundred of the nation's largest central cities; however, it is important to remember that the ghetto areas in these central cities also include a good many families and individuals who are not poor.

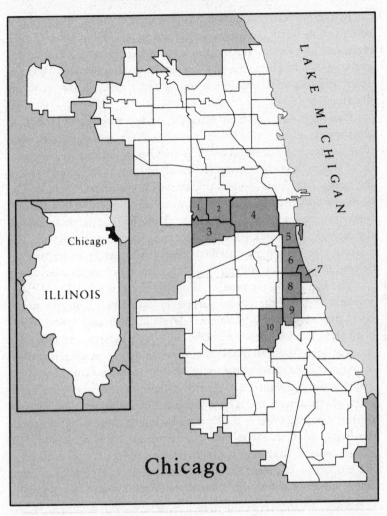

FIGURE I.I

COMMUNITY AREAS IN CHICAGO'S BLACK BELT

1. WEST GARFIELD PARK
2. EAST GARFIELD PARK
3. NORTH LAWNDALE
4. NEAR WEST SIDE
5. NEAR SOUTH SIDE
6. DOUGLAS
7. OAKLAND
8. GRAND BOULEVARD
9. WASHINGTON PARK
10. ENGLEWOOD

In the nation's one hundred largest central cities, nearly one in seven census tracts is at least 40 percent poor. The number of such tracts has more than doubled since 1970. Indeed, it is alarming that 579 tracts fell to ghetto poverty level in these cities between 1970 and 1980, and 624 additional tracts joined these ranks in the following decade.

Paul Jargowsky's research reveals that a vast majority of people (almost seven out of eight) living in metropolitan-area ghettos in 1990 were minority group members. The number of African-Americans in these ghettos grew by more than one-third from 1980 to 1990, reaching nearly 6 million. Most of this growth involved poor people. The proportion of metropolitan blacks who live in ghetto areas climbed from more than a third (37 percent) to almost half (45 percent). Indeed, the metropolitan black poor are becoming increasingly isolated. The poverty rate among metropolitan blacks who reside in ghettos increased while the rate among those who live in nonghettos decreased.

The increase in the *number* of ghetto blacks is related to the *geographical spread* of the ghetto. Jargowsky and Bane found that in the cities they studied (Philadelphia, Cleveland, Milwaukee, and Memphis) areas that had become ghettos by 1980 had been mixed-income tracts in 1970—but tracts have that were contiguous to areas identified as ghettos. The exodus of the nonpoor from mixed-income areas was a major factor in the spread of ghettos in these cities in the 1970s. Since 1980, ghetto census tracts have increased in a substantial majority of the metropolitan areas in the country, including those with fewer people living in them. Nine new ghetto census tracts were added in Philadelphia, even though it experienced one of the largest declines in the proportion of people living in ghetto tracts. In a number of other cities, including Baltimore, Boston, and Washington, D.C., a smaller percentage of poor blacks live in a larger number of ghetto census tracts. Chicago had a 61.5 percent increase in the number of ghetto census tracts from 1980 to 1990, even though the number of poor residing in those areas increased only slightly.

Jargowsky reflects on the significance of the substantial spread of ghetto areas:

> The geographic size of a city's ghetto has a large effect on the perception of the magnitude of the problem associated with ghetto poverty. How big an area of the city do you consider off

limits? How far out of your way will you drive not to go through a dangerous area? Indeed, the lower density exacerbated the problem. More abandoned buildings mean more places for crack dens and criminal enterprises. Police trying to protect a given number of citizens have to be stretched over a wider number of square miles, making it less likely that criminals will be caught. Lower density also makes it harder for a sense of community to develop, or for people to feel that they can find safety in numbers. From the point of view of local political officials, the increase in the size of the ghetto is a disaster. Many of those leaving the ghetto settle in non-ghetto areas outside the political jurisdiction of the central city. Thus, geographic size of the ghetto is expanding, cutting a wider swath through the hearts of our metropolitan areas.

In sum, the 1970s and 1980s witnessed a sharp growth in the number of census tracts classified as ghetto poverty areas, an increased concentration of the poor in these areas, and sharply divergent patterns of poverty concentration between racial minorities and whites. One of the legacies of historic racial and class subjugation in America is a unique and growing concentration of minority residents in the most impoverished areas of the nation's metropolises.

Some have argued that this concentration of poverty is not new but mirrors conditions prevalent in the 1930s. According to Douglas Massey and Nancy Denton, during the Depression poverty was just as concentrated in the ghettos of the 1930s as in those of the 1970s. The black communities of the 1930s and those of the 1970s shared a common experience: a high degree of racial segregation from the larger society. Massey and Denton argue that "concentrated poverty is created by a pernicious interaction between a group's overall rate of poverty and its degree of segregation in society. When a highly segregated group experiences a high or rising rate of poverty, geographically concentrated poverty is the inevitable result." However convincing the logic of that argument, it does not explain the following: In the ten neighborhoods that make up Chicago's Black Belt, the poverty rate increased almost 20 percent between 1970 and 1990 (from 32.5 to 50.4 percent) despite the fact that the overall black poverty rate for the city of Chicago increased only 7.5 percent during this same period (from 25.1 to 32.6 percent).

Concentrated poverty may be the inevitable result when a highly segregated group experiences an increase in its overall rate of poverty. But segregation does not explain why the concentration of poverty in *certain* neighborhoods of this segregated group should increase to nearly three times the group's *overall* rate of poverty increase. There is no doubt that the disproportionate concentration of poverty among African-Americans is one of the legacies of historic racial segregation. It is also true that segregation often compounds black vulnerability in the face of other changes in the society, including, as we shall soon see, economic changes. Nonetheless, to focus mainly on segregation to account for the growth of concentrated poverty is to overlook some of the dynamic aspects of the social and demographic changes occurring in cities like Chicago. Given the existence of segregation, we must consider the way in which other changes in society have interacted with segregation to produce the dramatic social transformation of inner-city neighborhoods, especially since 1970.

For example, the communities that make up the Black Belt in Chicago have been overwhelmingly black for the last four decades, yet they lost almost half their residents between 1970 and 1990. This rapid depopulation has had profound consequences for the social and economic deterioration of segregated Black Belt neighborhoods, including increases in concentrated poverty and joblessness. If comparisons are made strictly between the Depression years of the 1930s and the 1980s, rates of ghetto poverty and joblessness in these neighborhoods will indeed be similar. But such a comparison obscures significant changes that have occurred in these neighborhoods across the fifty-year span between those two points.

In *The Truly Disadvantaged*, I focused mainly on changes in ghetto neighborhoods that began around 1970. Many of the gains made in inner-city neighborhoods following the Depression were wiped out after 1970. To maintain that concentrated black poverty in the 1970s or in the 1980s is equivalent in severity and pervasiveness to that which occurred during the Depression does not explain its dramatic rise since 1970; nor does it address a far more fundamental problem that is at the heart of the extraordinary increases in and spread of concentrated poverty—namely, the rapid growth of joblessness, which accelerated through these two decades. The problems reported by the residents of poor Chicago neighborhoods are not a consequence of poverty alone. Something far more devastating has happened that can only be attributed to the emergence of concentrated and persistent joblessness and its crippling effects on neighborhoods, families, and individuals. The city of Chicago epitomizes these changes.

Since the early twentieth century, Chicago has been a laboratory for the scientific investigation of the social, economic, and historical forces that create and perpetuate economically depressed and isolated urban communities. The most distinctive phase of this research, referred to as the Chicago School of urban sociology, was completed before 1950 and was conducted by social scientists at the University of Chicago. Immediately following World War I, the Chicago School produced several classic studies, many of which were conducted under the guidance of Robert E. Park and Ernest W. Burgess over the next three decades. These studies often combined statistical and observational analyses in making distinctive empirical and theoretical contributions to our understanding of urban processes, social problems and urban growth, and, commencing in the late 1930s, the nature of race and class subjugation in urban areas.

The Chicago social scientists recognized and legitimized the neighborhood—including the ghetto neighborhood—as a subject for scientific analysis. Chicago, a community of neighborhoods, was considered a laboratory from which generalizations about broader urban conditions could be made.

The perspectives on urban processes that guided the Chicago School's approach to the study of race and class have undergone subtle changes through the years. In the 1920s, Park and Burgess argued that the immigrant slums, and the social problems that characterized them, were temporary conditions on the pathway toward inevitable progress. They further maintained that blacks represented the latest group of migrants involved in the "interaction cycle" that "led from conflict to accommodation to assimilation."

The view that blacks fit the pattern of immigrant assimilation appeared in subsequent studies by E. Franklin Frazier in the 1930s. But Frazier, an African-American sociologist trained at the University of Chicago, also recognized and emphasized a problem ignored in the earlier work of Park and Burgess—the important link between the black family structure and the industrial economy. Frazier believed that the availability of employment opportunities in the industrial sector would largely determine the upward mobility of African-Americans and their eventual assimilation into American life.

In 1945, a fundamental revision in the Chicago framework came with the publication of St. Clair Drake and Horace Cayton's classic study, _Black Metropolis._ Drake and Cayton first examined black progress in employment, housing, and social integration using census, survey, and archival data. Their analysis clearly revealed the existence of a color line that effectively blocked black occupational, residential, and social mobility. They demonstrated that any assumption about urban blacks duplicating the immigrant experience had to confront the issue of race. Moreover, as the historian Alice O'Connor puts it, "Drake and Cayton recognized that the racial configuration of Chicago was not the expression of an organic process of city growth, but the product of human behavior, institutional practices and political decisions."

Black Metropolis also deviated from the earlier Chicago School studies in its inclusion of an ethnographic study. Using W. Lloyd Warner's anthropological techniques, Drake and Cayton studied patterns of daily life in three of Chicago's South Side community areas (Washington Park, Grand Boulevard, and Douglas). They labeled these three areas "Bronzeville," a term that was used by the local residents themselves to describe their community. Combining data based on the Chicago School–style research and anthropological methods, _Black Metropolis_ presented a much less encouraging view of the prospects for black progress.

In the revised and enlarged edition of _Black Metropolis_ published in 1962, Drake and Cayton examined the changes that had occurred in Bronzeville since the publication of the first edition with a sense of optimism. They felt that America in the 1960s was "experiencing a period of prosperity" and that African-Americans were "living in the era of integration." Of course, they had no way of anticipating the rapid social and economic deterioration of communities like Bronzeville that would begin in the next decade.

The most fundamental difference between today's inner-city neighborhoods and those studied by Drake and Cayton is the much higher levels of joblessness. Indeed, there is a new poverty in our nation's metropolises that has consequences for a range of issues relating to the quality of life in urban areas, including race relations.

By "the new urban poverty," I mean poor, segregated neighborhoods in which a substantial majority of individual adults are either unemployed or have dropped out of the labor force altogether. For example, in 1990 only one in three adults ages 16 and over in the twelve Chicago community areas with ghetto poverty rates held a job in a typical week of the year. Each of these community areas, located on the South and West Sides of the city, is overwhelmingly black. We can add to these twelve high-jobless areas three additional predominantly black community areas, with rates approaching ghetto poverty, in which only 42 percent of the adult population were working in a typical week in 1990. Thus, in these fifteen black community areas—comprising a total population of 425,125—only 37 percent of all the adults were gainfully employed in a typical week in 1990. By contrast, 54 percent of the adults in the seventeen other predominantly black community areas in Chicago—a total population of 545,408—worked in a typical week in 1990. This was close to the citywide employment figure of 57 percent for all adults. Finally, except for one Asian community area with an employment rate of 46 percent, and one Latino community area with an employment rate of 49 percent, a majority of the adults held a job in a typical week in each of the remaining forty-five community areas of Chicago.

But Chicago is by no means the only city that features new poverty neighborhoods. In the ghetto census tracts of the nation's one hundred largest central cities, there were only 65.5 employed persons for every hundred adults who did not hold a job in a typical week in 1990. In contrast, the nonpoverty areas contained 182.3 employed persons for every hundred of those not working. In other words, the ratio of employed to jobless persons was three times greater in census tracts not marked by poverty.

Looking at Drake and Cayton's Bronzeville, I can illustrate the magnitude of the changes that have occurred in many inner-city ghetto neighborhoods in recent years. A majority of adults held jobs in the three Bronzeville areas in 1950, but by 1990 only four in ten in Douglas worked in a typical week, one in three in Washington Park, and one in four in Grand Boulevard. In 1950, 69 percent of all males 14 and over who lived in the Bronzeville neighborhoods worked in a typical week, and in 1960, 64 percent of this group were so employed.

However, by 1990 only 37 percent of all males 16 and over held jobs in a typical week in these three neighborhoods.

Upon the publication of the first edition of *Black Metropolis* in 1945, there was much greater class integration within the black community. As Drake and Cayton pointed out, Bronzeville residents had limited success in "sorting themselves out into broad community areas designated as 'lower class' and 'middle class.' . . . Instead of middle-class *areas*, Bronzeville tends to have middle-class *buildings* in all areas, or a few middle-class blocks here and there." Though they may have lived on different streets, blacks of all classes in inner-city areas such as Bronzeville lived in the same community and shopped at the same stores. Their children went to the same schools and played in the same parks. Although there was some class antagonism, their neighborhoods were more stable than the inner-city neighborhoods of today; in short, they featured higher levels of what social scientists call "social organization."

When I speak of social organization I am referring to the extent to which the residents of a neighborhood are able to maintain effective social control and realize their common goals. There are three major dimensions of neighborhood social organization: (1) the prevalence, strength, and interdependence of social networks; (2) the extent of collective supervision that the residents exercise and the degree of personal responsibility they assume in addressing neighborhood problems; and (3) the rate of resident participation in voluntary and formal organizations. Formal institutions (e.g., churches and political party organizations), voluntary associations (e.g., block clubs and parent-teacher organizations), and informal networks (e.g., neighborhood friends and acquaintances, coworkers, marital and parental ties) all reflect social organization.

Neighborhood social organization depends on the extent of local friendship ties, the degree of social cohesion, the level of resident participation in formal and informal voluntary associations, the density and stability of formal organizations, and the nature of informal social controls. Neighborhoods in which adults are able to interact in terms of obligations, expectations, and relationships are in a better position to supervise and control the activities and behavior of children. In neighborhoods with high levels of social organization, adults are empowered to act to improve the quality of neighborhood life—for example, by breaking up congregations of youths on street corners and by supervising the leisure activities of youngsters.

Neighborhoods plagued by high levels of joblessness are more likely to experience low levels of social organization: the two go hand in hand. High rates of joblessness trigger other neighborhood problems that undermine social organization, ranging from crime, gang violence, and drug trafficking to family breakups and problems in the organization of family life.

Consider, for example, the problems of drug trafficking and violent crime. As many studies have revealed, the decline in legitimate employment opportunities among inner-city residents has increased incentives to sell drugs. The distribution of crack in a neighborhood attracts individuals involved in violence and lawlessness. Between 1985 and 1992, there was a sharp increase in the murder rate among men under the age of 24; for men 18 years old and younger, murder rates doubled. Black males in particular have been involved in this upsurge in violence. For example, whereas the homicide rate for white males between 14 and 17 increased from 8 per 100,000 in 1984 to 14 in 1991, the rate for black males tripled during that time (from 32 per 100,000 to 112). This sharp rise in violent crime among younger males has accompanied the widespread outbreak of addiction to crack-cocaine. The association is especially strong in inner-city ghetto neighborhoods plagued by joblessness and weak social organization.

Violent persons in the crack-cocaine marketplace have a powerful impact on the social organization of a neighborhood. Neighborhoods plagued by high levels of joblessness, insufficient economic opportunities, and high residential mobility are unable to control the volatile drug market and the violent crimes related to it. As informal controls weaken, the social processes that regulate behavior change.

As a result, the behavior and norms in the drug market are more likely to influence the action of others in the neighborhood, even those who are not involved in drug activity. Drug dealers cause the use and spread of guns in the neighborhood to escalate, which in turn raises the likelihood that others, particularly the youngsters, will come to view the possession of weapons as necessary or desirable for self-protection, settling disputes, and gaining respect from peers and other individuals.

Moreover, as Alfred Blumstein pointed out, the drug industry actively recruits teenagers in the neighborhood "partly because they will work more cheaply than adults, partly because they may be less vulnerable to the punishments imposed by the adult criminal justice system, partly because they tend to be daring and willing to take risks that more mature adults would eschew." Inner-city black youths with limited prospects for stable or attractive employment are easily lured into drug trafficking and therefore increasingly find themselves involved in the violent behavior that accompanies it.

A more direct relationship between joblessness and violent crime is revealed in recent research by Delbert Elliott of the University of Colorado, a study based on National Longitudinal Youth Survey data collected from 1976 to 1989, covering ages 11 to 30. As Elliott points out, the transition from adolescence to adulthood usually results in a sharp drop in most crimes as individuals take on new adult roles and responsibilities. "Participation in serious violent offending behavior (aggravated assault, forcible rape, and robbery) increases [for all males] from ages 11 and 12 to ages 15 and 16, then declines dramatically with advancing age." Although black and white males reveal similar age curves, "the negative slope of the age curve for blacks after age 20 is substantially less than that of whites."

The black-white differential in the proportion of males involved in serious violent crime, although almost even at age 11, increases to 3:2 over the remaining years of adolescence, and reaches a differential of nearly 4:1 during the late twenties. However, when Elliott compared only *employed* black and white males, he found no significant differences in violent behavior patterns among the two groups by age 21. Employed black males, like white males, experienced a precipitous decline in serious violent behavior following their adolescent period. Accordingly, a major reason for the racial gap in violent behavior after adolescence is joblessness; a large proportion of jobless black males do not assume adult roles and responsibilities, and their serious violent behavior is therefore more likely to extend into adulthood. The new poverty neighborhoods feature a high concentration of jobless males and, as a result, suffer rates of violent criminal behavior that exceed those in other urban neighborhoods.

The problems of joblessness and neighborhood social organization, including crime and drug trafficking, are prominently reflected in the concerns expressed by the respondents interviewed in the Urban Poverty and Family Life Study. They are also reflected in the responses to a 1993 survey (see Appendix B) conducted on a random sample of adult residents in Woodlawn and Oakland, two of the new poverty neighborhoods on the South Side of Chicago. In 1990, 37 percent of Woodlawn's 27,473 adults were employed and only 23 percent of Oakland's 4,935 adults were working. When asked how much of a problem unemployment was in their neighborhood, 73 percent of the residents in Woodlawn and 76 percent in Oakland identified it as a *major* problem. The responses to the survey also revealed the residents' concerns about a series of related problems, such as crime and drug abuse, that are symptomatic of severe problems of social organization. Indeed, crime was identified as a major problem by 66 percent of the residents in each neighborhood. Drug abuse was cited as a major problem by as many as 86 percent of the adult residents in Oakland and 79 percent of those in Woodlawn.

Although high-jobless neighborhoods also feature concentrated poverty, high rates of neighborhood poverty are less likely to trigger problems of social organization if the residents are working. This was the case in previous years when the working poor stood out in areas like Bronzeville. Today, the nonworking poor predominate in the highly segregated and impoverished neighborhoods.

The rise of new poverty neighborhoods represents a movement away from what the historian Allan Spear has called an institutional ghetto—whose structure and activities parallel those of the larger society, as portrayed in Drake and Cayton's description of Bronzeville—toward a jobless ghetto, which features a severe lack of basic opportunities and resources, and inadequate social controls.

What can account for the growing proportion of jobless adults and the corresponding increase in problems of social organization in inner-city communities such as Bronzeville? An easy answer is racial segregation. However, a race-specific argument is not sufficient to explain recent changes in neighborhoods like Bronzeville. After all, Bronzeville was *just as segregated by skin color in 1950* as it is today, yet the level of employment was much higher then.

Nonetheless, racial segregation does matter. If large segments of the African-American population had not been historically segregated in inner-city ghettos, we would not be talking about the new urban poverty. The segregated ghetto is not the result of voluntary or positive decisions on the part of the residents who live there. As Massey and Denton have carefully documented, the segregated ghetto is the product of systematic racial practices such as restrictive covenants, redlining by banks and insurance companies, zoning, panic peddling by real estate agents, and the creation of massive public housing projects in low-income areas.

Segregated ghettos are less conducive to employment and employment preparation than are other areas of the city. Segregation in ghettos exacerbates employment problems because it leads to weak informal employment networks and contributes to the social isolation of individuals and families, thereby reducing their chances of acquiring the human capital skills, including adequate educational training, that facilitate mobility in a society. Since no other group in society experiences the degree of segregation, isolation, and poverty concentration as do African-Americans, they are far more likely to be disadvantaged when they have to compete with other groups in society, including other despised groups, for resources and privileges.

To understand the new urban poverty, one has to account for the ways in which segregation interacts with other changes in society to produce the recent escalating rates of joblessness and problems of social organization in inner-city ghetto neighborhoods.

CHAPTER 2

Societal Changes and Vulnerable Neighborhoods

The disappearance of work in many inner-city neighborhoods is partly related to the nationwide decline in the fortunes of low-skilled workers. Although the growing wage inequality has hurt both low-skilled men and women, the problem of declining employment has been concentrated among low-skilled men. In 1987–89, a low-skilled male worker was jobless eight and a half weeks longer than he would have been in 1967–69. Moreover, the proportion of men who "permanently" dropped out of the labor force was more than twice as high in the late 1980s than it had been in the late 1960s. A precipitous drop in real wages—that is, wages adjusted for inflation—has accompanied the increases in joblessness among low-income workers. If you arrange all wages into five groups according to wage percentile (from highest to lowest), you see that men in the bottom fifth of this income distribution experienced more than a 30 percent drop in real wages between 1970 and 1989.

Even the low-skilled workers who are consistently employed face problems of economic advancement. Job ladders—opportunities for promotion within firms—have eroded, and many less-skilled workers stagnate in dead-end, low-paying positions. This suggests that the chances of improving one's earnings by changing jobs have declined: if jobs inside a firm have become less available to the experienced workers in that firm, they are probably even more difficult for outsiders to obtain.

But there is a paradox here. Despite the increasing economic marginality of low-wage workers, unemployment dipped below 6 percent in 1994 and early 1995, many workers are holding more than one job, and overtime work has reached a record high. Yet while tens of millions of new jobs have been created in the past two decades, men who are well below retirement age are working less than they did two decades ago—and a growing percentage are neither working nor looking for work. The proportion of male workers in the prime of their life (between the ages of 22 and 58) who worked in a given decade full-time, year-round, in at least eight out of ten years declined from 79 percent during the 1970s to 71 percent in the 1980s. While the American economy saw a rapid expansion in high technology and services, especially advanced services, growth in blue-collar factory, transportation, and construction jobs, traditionally held by men, has not kept pace with the rise in the working-age population. These men are working less as a result.

The growth of a nonworking class of prime-age males along with a larger number of those who are often unemployed, who work part-time, or who work in temporary jobs is concentrated among the poorly educated, the school dropouts, and minorities. In the 1970s, two-thirds of prime-age male workers with less than a high school education worked full-time, year-round, in eight out of ten years. During the 1980s, only half did so. Prime-age black men experienced a similar sharp decline. Seven out of ten of all black men worked full-time, year-round, in eight out of ten years in the 1970s, but only half did so in the 1980s. The figures for those who reside in the inner city are obviously even lower.

One study estimates that since 1967 the number of prime-age men who are not in school, not working, and not looking for work for even a single week in a given year has more than doubled for both whites and nonwhites (respectively, from 3.3 to 7.7 percent and 5.8 percent to 13.2 percent). Data from this study also revealed that one-quarter of all male high school dropouts had no official employment at all in 1992. And of those with high school diplomas, one out of ten did not hold a job in 1993, up sharply from 1967 when only one out of fifty reported that he had had no job throughout the year. Among prime-age nonwhite males, the share of those who had no jobs at all in a given year increased from 3 percent to 17 percent during the last quarter century.

These changes are related to the decline of the mass production system in the United States. The traditional American economy featured rapid growth in productivity and living standards. The mass production system benefited from large quantities of cheap natural resources, economies of scale, and processes that generated higher uses of productivity through shifts in market forces from agriculture to manufacturing and that caused improvements in one industry (for example, reduced steel costs) to lead to advancements in others (for example, higher sales and greater economies of scale in the automobile industry). In this system plenty of blue-collar jobs were available to workers with little formal education. Today, most of the new jobs for workers with limited education and experience are in the service sector, which hires relatively more women. One study found that the U.S. created 27 clerical, sales, and service jobs per thousand of working-age population in the 1980s. During the same period, the country lost 16 production, transportation, and laborer jobs per thousand of working-age population. In another study the social scientists Robert Lerman and Martin Rein revealed that from 1989 to 1993, the period covering the economic downturn, social service industries (health, education, and welfare) added almost 3 million jobs, while 1.4 million jobs were lost in all other industries. The expanding job market in social services offset the recession-linked job loss in other industries.

The movement of lower-educated men into the growth sectors of the economy has been slow. For example, "the fraction of men who have moved into so-called pink-collar jobs like practical nursing or clerical work remains negligible." The large concentration of women in the expanding social service sector partly accounts for the striking gender differences in job growth. Unlike lower-educated men, lower-educated women are working more, not less, than in previous years. The employment patterns among lower-educated women, like those with higher education and training, reflect the dramatic expansion of social service industries. Between 1989 and 1993, jobs held by women increased by 1.3 million, while those held by men barely rose at all (by roughly 100,000).

Although the wages of low-skilled women (those with less than twelve years of education) rose slightly in the 1970s, they flattened out in the 1980s, and continued to remain below those of low-skilled men. The wage gap between low-skilled men and women shrank not because of gains made by female workers but mainly because of the decline in real wages for men. The unemployment rates among low-skilled women are slightly lower than those among their male counterparts. However, over the past decade their rates of participation in the labor force have stagnated and have fallen further behind the labor-force-participation rates among more highly educated women, which continue to rise. The unemployment rates among both low-skilled men and women are five times that among their college-educated counterparts.

Among the factors that have contributed to the growing gap in employment and wages between low-skilled and college-educated workers is the increased internationalization of the U.S. economy. As the economists Richard B. Freeman and Lawrence F. Katz point out:

> In the 1980s, trade imbalances implicitly acted to augment the nation's supply of less educated workers, particularly those with less than a high school education. Many production and routine clerical tasks could be more easily transferred abroad than in the past. The increased supply of less educated workers arising from trade deficits accounted for as much as 15 percent of the increase in college–high school wage differential from the 1970s to the mid-1980s. In contrast, a balanced expansion of international trade, in which growth in exports matches the growth of imports, appears to have fairly neutral effects on relative labor demand. Indeed, balanced growth of trade leads to an upgrading in jobs for workers without college degrees, since export-sector jobs tend to pay higher wages for "comparable" workers than do import-competing jobs.

The lowering of unionization rates, which accompanied the decline in the mass production system, has also contributed to shrinking wages and nonwage compensation for less skilled workers. As the economist Rebecca Blank has pointed out, "unionized workers typically receive not only higher wages, but also more non-wage benefits. As the availability of union jobs has declined for unskilled workers, non-wage benefits have also declined."

Finally, the wage and employment gap between skilled and unskilled workers is growing partly because education and training are considered more important than ever in the new global economy. At the same time that changes in technology are producing new jobs, they are making many others obsolete. The workplace has been revolutionized by technological changes that range from the development of robotics to information highways. While educated workers are benefiting from the pace of technological change, involving the increased use of computer-based technologies and microcomputers, more routine workers face the growing threat of job displacement in certain industries. For example, highly skilled designers, engineers, and operators are needed for the jobs associated with the creation of a new set of computer-operated machine tools; but these same exciting new opportunities eliminate jobs for those trained only for manual, assembly-line work. Also, in certain businesses, advances in word processing have increased the demand for those who not only know how to type but can operate specialized software as well; at the same time, these advances reduce the need for routine typists and secretaries. In the new global economy, highly educated and thoroughly trained men and women are in demand. This may be seen most dramatically in the sharp differences in employment experiences among men. Unlike men with lower education, college-educated men are working more, not less.

The shift in demand has been especially devastating for those low-skilled workers whose incorporation into the mainstream economy has been marginal or recent. Even before the economic restructuring of the nation's economy, low-skilled African-Americans were at the end of the employment queue. Their economic situation has been further weakened because they tend to reside in communities that not only have higher jobless rates and lower employment growth but lack access to areas of higher employment and employment growth as well. Moreover, as we shall see in Chapter 5, they are far more likely than other ethnic and racial groups to face negative employer attitudes.

Of the changes in the economy that have adversely affected low-skilled African-American workers, perhaps the most significant have been those in the manufacturing sector. One study revealed that in the 1970s "up to half of the huge employment declines for less-educated blacks might be explained by industrial shifts away from manufacturing toward other sectors." Another study reported that since the 1960s "deindustrialization" and the "erosion in job opportunities especially in the Midwest and Northeast . . . bear responsibility for the growth of the ranks of the 'truly disadvantaged.'" The manufacturing losses in some northern cities have been staggering. In the twenty-year period from 1967 to 1987, Philadelphia lost 64 percent of its manufacturing jobs; Chicago lost 60 percent; New York City, 58 percent; Detroit, 51 percent. In absolute numbers, these percentages represent the loss of 160,000 jobs in Philadelphia, 326,000 in Chicago, 520,000—over half a million—in New York, and 108,000 in Detroit.

Another study examined the effects of economic restructuring in the 1980s by highlighting the changes in both the variety and the quality of blue-collar employment in general. Jobs were grouped into a small number of relatively homogeneous clusters on the basis of job quality (which was measured in terms of earnings, benefits, union protection, and involuntary part-time employment). The authors found that both the relative earnings and employment rates among unskilled black workers were lower for two reasons: traditional jobs that provide a living wage (high-wage blue-collar cluster, of which roughly 50 percent were manufacturing jobs) declined, as did the quality of secondary jobs on which they increasingly had to rely, leading to lower relative earnings for the remaining workers in the labor market. As employment prospects worsened, rising proportions of low-skilled black workers dropped out of the legitimate labor market.

Data from the Chicago Urban Poverty and Family Life Survey show that efforts by out-of-school inner-city black men to obtain blue-collar jobs in the industries in which their fathers had been employed have been hampered by industrial restructuring. "The most common occupation reported by respondents at ages 19 to 28 changed from operative and assembler jobs among the oldest cohorts to service jobs (waiters and janitors) among the youngest cohort." Fifty-seven percent of Chicago's employed inner-city black fathers (aged 15 and over and without undergraduate degrees) who were born between 1950 and 1955 worked in manufacturing and construction industries in 1974. By 1987, industrial employment in this group had fallen to 31 percent. Of those born between 1956 and 1960, 52 percent worked in these industries as late as 1978. But again, by 1987 industrial employment in this group fell to 28 percent. No other male ethnic group in the inner city experienced such an overall precipitous drop in manufacturing employment (see Appendix C). These employment changes have accompanied the loss of traditional manufacturing and other blue-collar jobs in Chicago. As a result, young black males have turned increasingly to the low-wage service sector and unskilled laboring jobs for employment, or have gone jobless. The strongly held U.S. cultural and economic belief that the son will do at least as well as the father in the labor market does not apply to many young inner-city males.

If industrial restructuring has hurt inner-city black workers in Chicago, it has had serious consequences for African-Americans across the nation. "As late as the 1968–70 period," states John Kasarda, "more than 70 percent of all blacks working in metropolitan areas held blue-collar jobs at the same time that more than 50 percent of all metropolitan workers held white-collar jobs. Moreover, of the large numbers of urban blacks classified as blue-collar workers during the late 1960s, more than half were employed in goods-producing industries."

The number of employed black males ages 20 to 29 working in manufacturing industries fell dramatically between 1973 and 1987 (from three of every eight to one in five). Meanwhile, the share of employed young black men in the retail trade and service jobs rose sharply during that period (from 17 to almost 27 percent and from 10 to nearly 21 percent, respectively). And this shift in opportunities was not without economic consequences: in 1987, the average annual earnings of 20-to-29-year-old males who held jobs in the retail trade and service sectors were 25 to 30 percent less than those of males employed in manufacturing sectors. This dramatic loss in earnings potential affects every male employed in the service sector regardless of color.

The structural shifts in the distribution of industrial job opportunities are not the only reason for the increasing joblessness and declining earnings among young black male workers. There have also been important changes in the patterns of occupational staffing within firms and industries, including those in manufacturing. These changes have primarily benefited those with more formal education. Substantial numbers of new professional, technical, and managerial positions have been created. However, such jobs require at least some years of postsecondary education. Young high school dropouts and even high school graduates "have faced a dwindling supply of career jobs offering the real earnings opportunities available to them in the 1960s and early 1970s."

In certain urban areas the prospects for employment among workers with little education have fallen sharply. John Kasarda examined employment changes in selected urban centers and found that major northern cities had consistent employment losses in industries with low mean levels of employee education and employment gains in industries in which the workers had higher levels of education. For example, during the 1980s New York City lost 135,000 jobs in industries in which the workers averaged less than twelve years of education, and gained almost 300,000 jobs in industries in which workers had thirteen or more years of education. Philadelphia lost 55,000 jobs in the low-education industries and gained 40,000 jobs for workers with high school plus at least some college. Baltimore and Boston also experienced substantial losses in industries employing low-education workers and major gains in industries employing more educated workers.

Kasarda's study also documents the growing importance of education in nine "economically transforming" northern cities and in Los Angeles. The jobs traditionally held by high school dropouts declined in all nine northern cities between 1980 and 1990, while those held by college graduates increased. "Los Angeles, which experienced a 50 percent increase in city [urban] jobs held by college graduates, also experienced a 15 percent growth in jobs held by those who have not completed high school. The latter no doubt reflects the large immigration of Hispanic workers and other minorities" who have little education.

To some degree, these changes reflect overall improvements in educational attainment within the urban labor force. However, they "were not nearly as great as the concurrent upward shifts in the education of city jobholders." Moreover, much of the increase in the "college-educated" jobs in each city reflected the educational status of suburban commuters, while much of the decrease in the "less than high school" category reflected the job losses of city residents, few of whom could aspire to a four-year postsecondary degree.

As pointed out earlier, most of the new jobs for workers with limited training and education are in the service sector and are disproportionately held by women. This is even more true for those who work in social services, which include the industries of health, education, and welfare. As we have seen, within central cities the number of jobs for less educated workers has declined precipitously. However, many workers stayed afloat thanks to jobs in the expanding social service sector, especially black women with less than a high school degree. Robert Lerman and Martin Rein report that among all women workers, the proportion employed in social services climbed between 1979 and 1993 (from 28 to 33 percent). The health and education industries absorbed nearly all of this increase. Of the 54 million female workers in 1993, almost one-third were employed in social service industries.

Social services tend to feature a more highly educated workforce. Only 20 percent of all female workers with less than a high school degree were employed in social services in 1993. (The figure for comparable males is even less. Only 4 percent of employed less educated men held social service jobs in 1993.) Nonetheless, the proportion of less educated female workers in social services is up notably from 1989.

Indeed, despite the relatively higher educational level of social service workers, the research of Lerman and Rein reveals that 37 percent of employed less educated black women in central cities worked in social services in 1993, largely in jobs in hospitals, elementary schools, nursing care, and child care. In central cities in the largest metropolitan areas, the fraction of low-educated African-American female workers in social services sharply increased from 30.5 percent in 1979 to 40.5 percent in 1993. Given the overall decline of jobs for less educated central city workers, the opportunity for employment in the social service industries prevented many inner-city workers from joining the growing ranks of the jobless. Less educated black female workers depend heavily on social service employment. Even a small number of less educated black males were able to find jobs in social services. Although only 4 percent of less educated employed males worked in social services in 1993, 12 percent of less educated employed black men in the central cities of large metropolitan areas held social service jobs. Without the growth of social service employment, the rates of inner-city joblessness would have risen beyond their already unprecedented high levels.

The demand in the labor market has shifted toward higher-educated workers in various industries and occupations. The changing occupational and industrial mix is associated with increases in the rates of joblessness (unemployment and "dropping out" of, or nonparticipation in, the labor force) and decreases in the relative wages of disadvantaged urban workers.

The factors contributing to the relative decline in the economic status of disadvantaged workers are not solely due to those on the demand side, such as economic restructuring. The growing wage differential in the 1980s is also a function of two supply-side factors—the decline in the relative supply of college graduates and the influx of poor immigrants. "In the 1970s the relative supply of college graduates grew rapidly, the result of the baby boomers who enrolled in college in the late 1960s and early 1970s in response to the high rewards for college degrees and the fear of being drafted for the Vietnam War," state Freeman and Katz. "The growth in supply overwhelmed the increase in demand for more educated workers, and the returns to college diminished." In the 1980s, the returns for college increased because of declining growth in the relative supply of college graduates.

Also in the 1980s, a large number of immigrants with little formal education arrived in the United States from developing countries, and affected the wages of poorly educated native workers, especially those who had dropped out of high school. According to one estimate, nearly one-third of the decline in earnings for male high school dropouts compared with other workers in the 1980s may be linked to immigration. However, although the increase in immigration contributed to the growing inequality, it is only one of several factors depressing the wages of low-skilled workers. As Sheldon Danziger and Peter Gottschalk point out in this connection, "Immigrants are heavily concentrated in a few states, such as California and Florida . . . inequality did rise in these states, but it rose in most areas, even those with very few immigrants."

Joblessness and declining wages are also related to the recent growth in ghetto poverty. The most dramatic increases in ghetto poverty occurred between 1970 and 1980, and they were mostly confined to the large industrial metropolises of the Northeast and Midwest, regions that experienced massive industrial restructuring and loss of blue-collar jobs during that decade. But the rise in ghetto poverty was not the only problem. Industrial restructuring had devastating effects on the social organization of many inner-city neighborhoods in these regions. The fate of the West Side black community of North Lawndale vividly exemplifies the cumulative process of economic and social dislocation that has swept through Chicago's inner city.

After more than a quarter century of continuous deterioration, North Lawndale resembles a war zone. Since 1960, nearly half of its housing stock has disappeared; the remaining units are mostly run-down or dilapidated. Two large factories anchored the economy of this West Side neighborhood in its good days—the Hawthorne plant of Western Electric, which employed over 43,000 workers; and an International Harvester plant with 14,000 workers. The world headquarters for Sears, Roebuck and Company was located there, providing another 10,000 jobs. The neighborhood also had a Copenhagen snuff plant, a Sunbeam factory, and a Zenith factory, a Dell Farm food market, an Alden's catalog store, and a U.S. Post Office bulk station. But conditions rapidly changed. Harvester closed its doors in the late 1960s. Sears moved most of its offices to the Loop in downtown Chicago in 1973; a catalog distribution center with a workforce of 3,000 initially remained in the neighborhood but was relocated outside of the state of Illinois in 1987. The Hawthorne plant gradually phased out its operations and finally shut down in 1984.

The departure of the big plants triggered the demise or exodus of the smaller stores, the banks, and other businesses that relied on the wages paid by the large employers. "To make matters worse, scores of stores were forced out of business or pushed out of the neighborhoods by insurance companies in the wake of the 1968 riots that swept through Chicago's West Side after the assassination of Dr. Martin Luther King, Jr. Others were simply burned or abandoned. It has been estimated that the community lost 75 percent of its business establishments from 1960 to 1970 alone." In 1986, North Lawndale, with a population of over 66,000, had only one bank and one supermarket; but it was also home to forty-eight state lottery agents, fifty currency exchanges, and ninety-nine licensed liquor stores and bars.

The impact of industrial restructuring on inner-city employment is clearly apparent to urban blacks. The UPFLS survey posed the following question: "Over the past five or ten years, how many friends of yours have lost their jobs because the place where they worked shut down—would you say none, a few, some, or most?" Only 26 percent of the black residents in our sample reported that none of their friends had lost jobs because their workplace shut down. Indeed, both black men and black women were more likely to report that their friends had lost jobs because of plant closings than were the Mexicans and the other ethnic groups in our study. Moreover, nearly half of the employed black fathers and mothers in the UPFLS survey stated that they considered themselves to be at high risk of losing their jobs because of plant shutdowns. Significantly fewer Hispanic and white parents felt this way.

Some of the inner-city neighborhoods have experienced more visible job losses than others. But residents of the inner city are keenly aware of the rapid depletion of job opportunities. A 33-year-old unmarried black male of North Lawndale who is employed as a clerical worker stated: "Because of the way the economy is structured, we're losing more jobs. Chicago is losing jobs by the thousands. There just aren't any starting companies here and it's harder to find a job compared to what it was years ago."

A similar view was expressed by a 41-year-old black female, also from North Lawndale, who works as a nurse's aide:

> Chicago is really full of peoples. Everybody can't get a good job. They don't have enough good jobs to provide for everybody. I don't think they have enough jobs period. . . . And all the factories and the places, they closed up and moved out of the city and stuff like that, you know. I guess it's one of the reasons they haven't got too many jobs now, 'cause a lot of the jobs now, factories and business, they're done moved out. So that way it's less jobs for lot of peoples.

Respondents from other neighborhoods also reported on the impact of industrial restructuring. According to a 33-year-old South Side janitor:

> The machines are putting a lot of people out of jobs. I worked for *Time* magazine for seven years on a videograph printer and they come along with the Abedic printer, it cost them half a million dollars: they did what we did in half the time, eliminated two shifts.

"Jobs were plentiful in the past," stated a 29-year-old unemployed black male who lives in one of the poorest neighborhoods on the South Side.

> You could walk out of the house and get a job. Maybe not what you want but you could get a job. Now, you can't find anything. A lot of people in this neighborhood, they want to work but they can't get work. A few, but a very few, they just don't want to work. The majority they want to work but they can't find work.

Finally, a 41-year-old hospital worker from another impoverished South Side neighborhood associated declining employment opportunities with decreasing skill levels:

Well, most of the jobs have moved out of Chicago. Factory jobs have moved out. There are no jobs here. Not like it was 20, 30 years ago. And people aren't skilled enough for the jobs that are here. You don't have enough skilled and educated people to fill them.

The increasing suburbanization of employment has accompanied industrial restructuring and has further exacerbated the problems of inner-city joblessness and restricted access to jobs. "Metropolitan areas captured nearly 90 percent of the nation's employment growth; much of this growth occurred in booming 'edge cities' at the metropolitan periphery. By 1990, many of these 'edge cities' had more office space and retail sales than the metropolitan downtowns." Over the last two decades, 60 percent of the new jobs created in the Chicago metropolitan area have been located in the northwest suburbs of Cook and Du Page counties. African-Americans constitute less than 2 percent of the population in these areas.

In *The Truly Disadvantaged*, I maintained that one result of these changes for many urban blacks has been a growing mismatch between the suburban location of employment and minorities' residence in the inner city. Although studies based on data collected before 1970 showed no consistent or convincing effects on black employment as a consequence of this spatial mismatch, the employment of inner-city blacks relative to suburban blacks has clearly deteriorated since then. Recent research, conducted mainly by urban and labor economists, strongly shows that the decentralization of employment is continuing and that employment in manufacturing, most of which is already suburbanized, has decreased in central cities, particularly in the Northeast and Midwest. As Farrell Bloch, an economic and statistical consultant, points out, "Not only has the number of manufacturing jobs been decreasing, but new plants now tend to locate in the suburbs to take advantage of cheap land, access to highways, and low crime rates; in addition, businesses shun urban locations to avoid buying land from several different owners, paying high demolition costs for old buildings, and arranging parking for employees and customers."

Blacks living in central cities have less access to employment, as measured by the ratio of jobs to people and the average travel time to and from work, than do central-city whites. Moreover, unlike most other groups of workers across the urban/suburban divide, less educated central-city blacks receive lower wages than suburban blacks who have similar levels of education. And the decline in earnings of central-city blacks is related to the decentralization of employment—that is, the movement of jobs from the cities to the suburbs—in metropolitan areas.

But are the differences in employment between city and suburban blacks mainly the result of changes in the location of jobs? It is possible that in recent years the migration of blacks to the suburbs has become much more selective than in earlier years, so much so that the changes attributed to job location are actually caused by this selective migration. The pattern of black migration to the suburbs in the 1970s was similar to that of whites during the 1950s and 1960s in the sense that it was concentrated among the better-educated and younger city residents. However, in the 1970s this was even more true for blacks, creating a situation in which the education and income gaps between city and suburban blacks seemed to expand at the same time that the differences between city and suburban whites seemed to contract. Accordingly, if one were to take into account differences in education, family background, and so on, how much of the employment gap between city and suburbs would remain?

This question was addressed in a study of the Gautreaux program in Chicago. The Gautreaux program was created under a 1976 court order resulting from a judicial finding of widespread discrimination in the public housing projects of Chicago. The program has relocated more than 4,000 residents from public housing into subsidized housing in neighborhoods throughout the Greater Chicago area. The design of the program permitted the researchers, James E. Rosenbaum and Susan J. Popkin, to contrast systematically the employment experiences of a group of low-income blacks who had been assigned private apartments in the suburbs with the experiences of a control group with similar characteristics and histories who had been assigned private apartments in the city. Their findings support the spatial mismatch hypothesis. After taking into account the personal characteristics of the respondents (including family background, family circumstances, levels of human capital, motivation, length of time since the respondent first enrolled in the Gautreaux program), Rosenbaum and Popkin found that those who moved to apartments in the suburbs were significantly more likely to have a job after the move than those placed in the city. When asked what makes it easier to obtain employment in the

DIRECTION OF CAUSATION

suburbs, nearly all the surburban respondents mentioned the high availability of jobs.

The African-Americans surveyed in the UPFLS clearly recognized a spatial mismatch of jobs. Both black men and black women saw greater job prospects outside the city. For example, only one-third of black fathers from areas with poverty rates of at least 30 percent reported that their best opportunities for employment were to be found in the city. Nearly two-thirds of whites and Puerto Ricans and over half of Mexicans living in similar neighborhoods felt this way. Getting to suburban jobs is especially problematic for the jobless individuals in the UPFLS because only 28 percent have access to an automobile. This rate falls even further to 18 percent for those living in the ghetto areas.

Among two-car middle-class and affluent families, commuting is accepted as a fact of life; but it occurs in a context of safe school environments for children, more available and accessible day care, and higher incomes to support mobile, away-from-home lifestyles. In a multitiered job market that requires substantial resources for participation, most inner-city minorities must rely on public transportation systems that rarely provide easy and quick access to suburban locations. A 32-year-old unemployed South Side welfare mother described the problem this way:

> There's not enough jobs. I thinks Chicago's the only city that does not have a lot of opportunities opening in it. There's not enough factories, there's not enough work. Most all the good jobs are in the suburbs. Sometimes it's hard for the people in the city to get to the suburbs, because everybody don't own a car. Everybody don't drive.

After commenting on the lack of jobs in his area, a 29-year-old unemployed South Side black male continued:

> You gotta go out in the suburbs, but I can't get out there. The bus go out there but you don't want to catch the bus out there, going two hours each ways. If you have to be at work at eight that mean you have to leave for work at six, that mean you have to get up at five to be at work at eight. Then when wintertime come you be in trouble.

Another unemployed South Side black male had this to say: "Most of the time . . . the places be too far and you need transportation and I don't have none right now. If I had some I'd probably be able to get one [a job]. If I had a car and went way into the suburbs, 'cause there ain't none in the city." This perception was echoed by an 18-year-old unemployed West Side black male:

> They are most likely hiring in the suburbs. Recently, I think about two years ago, I had a job but they say that I need some transportation and they say that the bus out in the suburbs run at a certain time. So I had to pass that job up because I did not have no transport.

An unemployed unmarried welfare mother of two from the West Side likewise stated:

> Well, I'm goin' to tell you: most jobs, more jobs are in the suburbs. It's where the good jobs and stuff is but you gotta have transportation to get there and it's hard to be gettin' out there in the suburbs. Some people don't know where the suburbs is, some people get lost out there. It is really hard, but some make a way.

One employed factory worker from the West Side who works a night shift described the situation this way:

> From what I, I see, you know, it's hard to find a good job in the inner city 'cause so many people moving, you know, west to the suburbs and out of state. . . . Some people turn jobs down because they don't have no way of getting out there. . . . I just see some people just going to work—and they seem like they the type who just used to—they coming all the way from the city and go on all the way to the suburbs and, you know, you can see 'em all bundled and—catching one bus and the next bus. They just used to doing that.

But the problem is not simply one of transportation and the length of commuting time. There is also the problem of the travel expense and of whether the long trek to the suburbs is actually worth it in terms of the income earned—after all, owning a car creates expenses far beyond the purchase price, including insurance, which is much more costly for city dwellers than it is for suburban motorists. "If you work in the suburbs you gotta have a car," stated an unmarried welfare mother of three children who lives on Chicago's West Side, "then you gotta buy gas. You spending more getting to the suburbs to work, than you is getting paid, so you still ain't getting nowhere."

Indeed, one unemployed 36-year-old black man from the West Side of Chicago actually quit his suburban job because of the transportation problem. "It was more expensive going to work in Naperville, transportation and all, and it wasn't worth it. . . . I was spending more money getting to work than I earned working."

If transportation poses a problem for those who have to commute to work from the inner city to the suburbs, it can also hinder poor ghetto residents' ability to travel to the suburbs just to seek employment. For example, one unemployed man who lives on the South Side had just gone to O'Hare Airport looking for work with no luck. His complaint: "The money I spent yesterday, I coulda kept that in my pocket—I coulda kept that. 'Cause you know I musta spent about $7 or somethin'. I coulda kept that."

Finally, in addition to enduring the search-and-travel costs, inner-city black workers often confront racial harassment when they enter suburban communities. A 38-year-old South Side divorced mother of two children who works as a hotel cashier described the problems experienced by her son and his coworker in one of Chicago's suburbs:

My son, who works in Carol Stream, an all-white community, they've been stopped by a policeman two or three times asking them why they're in the community. And they're trying to go to work. They want everyone to stay in their own place. That's what society wants. And they followed them all the way to work to make sure. 'Cause it's an all-white neighborhood. But there're no jobs in the black neighborhoods. They got to go way out there to get a job.

These informal observations on the difficulties and cost of travel to suburban employment are consistent with the results of a recent study by the labor economists Harry J. Holzer, Keith R. Ihlandfeldt, and David L. Sjoquist. In addition to finding that the lack of automobile ownership among inner-city blacks contributed significantly to their lower wages and lower rate of employment, these authors also reported that African-Americans "spend more time traveling to work than whites," that "the time cost per mile traveled is . . . significantly higher for blacks," and that the resulting gains are relatively small. Overall, their results suggest that the amount of time and money spent in commuting, when compared with the actual income that accrues to inner-city blacks in low-skill jobs in the suburbs, acts to discourage poor people from seeking employment far from their own neighborhoods. Holzer and his colleagues concluded that it was quite rational for blacks to reject these search-and-travel choices when assessing their position in the job market.

Changes in the industrial and occupational mix, including the removal of jobs from urban centers to suburban corridors, represent external factors that have helped to elevate joblessness among inner-city blacks. But important social and demographic changes within the inner city are also associated with the escalating rates of neighborhood joblessness, and we shall consider these next.

The increase in the proportion of jobless adults in the inner city is also related to changes in the class, racial, and age composition of such neighborhoods—changes that have led to greater concentrations of poverty. Concentrated poverty is positively associated with joblessness. That is, when the former appears, the latter is found as well. As stated previously, poor people today are far more likely to be unemployed or out of the labor force than in previous years. In *The Truly Disadvantaged*, I argue that in addition to the effects of joblessness, inner-city neighborhoods have experienced a growing concentration of poverty for several other reasons, including (1) the outmigration of nonpoor black families; (2) the exodus of nonpoor white and other nonblack families; and (3) the rise in the number of residents who have become poor while living in these areas. Additional research on the growth of concentrated poverty suggests another factor: the movement of poor people into a neighborhood (inmigration). And one more factor should be added to this mix: changes in the age structure of the community.

I believe that the extent to which any one factor is significant in explaining the decrease in the proportion of nonpoor individuals and families depends on the poverty level and racial or ethnic makeup of the neighborhood at a given time. For example, as pointed out in *The Truly Disadvantaged*, the community areas of Chicago that experienced the most substantial white outmigration between 1970 and 1980 had moderate rates of family poverty (between 20 and 29 percent) in 1980. Today, four of these communities are predominantly black. Only one, Greater Grand Crossing, is a new poverty area. Unlike the other three black community areas with poverty rates in the 20 percent range in 1980, Greater Grand Crossing remained virtually all black from 1970 to 1990. A clear majority (61 percent) of the adults in Greater Grand Crossing held jobs in 1970. Accordingly, the transformation of this neighborhood into a new poverty area (it had an adult employment rate of only 44 percent in a typical week in 1990) cannot be linked to the exodus of white residents.

Considering the strong association between poverty and joblessness, the sharp rise in the proportion of adults who are not working in Greater Grand Crossing is related to two factors: the outmigration of nonpoor families and, perhaps even more significant, the increase in the number of poor families, probably due to inmigration. From 1970 to 1990, despite a 29 percent reduction in the population (from 54,414 to 38,644), the number of individuals existing at or below the poverty level in Greater Grand Crossing increased by more than half (from 7,058 to 11,073).

Between 1950 and 1960, Greater Grand Crossing underwent a drastic change from being 94 percent white to being 86 percent black. Because few whites lived in the neighborhood by 1960 and because African-Americans are at greater risk of joblessness, the chances of Greater Grand Crossing becoming a new poverty area increased. In other words, even though a white exodus did not directly cause Greater Grand Crossing's deterioration between 1970 and 1990, the emptying of the white population out of the neighborhood from 1950 to 1960 increased the area's vulnerability to changes in the economy after 1970.

Of Chicago's fourteen other new poverty areas, five—including the three Bronzeville neighborhoods of Douglas, Grand Boulevard, and Washington Park—have remained overwhelmingly black since 1950. Therefore, the economic and demographic changes within the African-American community resulted in the transformation of these neighborhoods into new poverty areas.

One of the important demographic shifts that had an impact on the upturn in the jobless rate has been the change in the age structure of inner-city ghetto neighborhoods. Let us again examine the three Bronzeville neighborhoods of Douglas, Grand Boulevard, and Washington Park. As shown in Table 2.1, the proportion of those in the age categories (20–64) that roughly approximate the prime-age workforce has declined in all three neighborhoods since 1950, whereas the proportion in the age category 65 and over has increased. Of the adults age 20 and over, the proportion in the prime-age categories declined by 17 percent in Grand Boulevard, 16 percent in Douglas, and 12 percent in Washington Park between 1950 and 1990. The smaller the percentage of prime-age adults in a population, the lower the proportion of residents who are likely to be employed. The proportion of residents in the age category 5–19 increased sharply in each neighborhood from 1950 to 1990, suggesting that the growth in the proportion of teenagers also contributed to the rise in the jobless rate. However, if we consider the fact that male employment in these neighborhoods declined by a phenomenal 46 percent between 1950 and 1990, these demographic changes obviously can account for only a fraction, albeit a significant fraction, of the high proportion of the area's jobless adults.

The rise in the proportion of jobless adults in the Bronzeville neighborhoods has been accompanied by an incredible depopulation—a decline of 66 percent in the three neighborhoods combined—that magnifies the problems of the new poverty neighborhoods. As the population drops and the proportion of nonworking adults rises, basic neighborhood institutions are more difficult to maintain: stores, banks, credit institutions, restaurants, dry cleaners, gas stations, medical doctors, and so on lose regular and potential patrons. Churches experience dwindling numbers of parishioners and shrinking resources; recreational facilities, block clubs, community groups, and other informal organizations also suffer. As these organizations decline, the means of formal and informal social control in the neighborhood become weaker. Levels of crime and street violence increase as a result, leading to further deterioration of the neighborhood.

The more rapid the neighborhood deterioration, the greater the institutional disinvestment. In the 1960s and 1970s, neighborhoods plagued by heavy abandonment were frequently "redlined" (identified as areas that should not receive or be recommended for mortgage loans or insurance); this paralyzed the housing market, lowered prop-

TABLE 2.1

DEMOGRAPHIC CHANGES IN DOUGLAS, GRAND BOULEVARD, AND WASHINGTON PARK, 1950–1990

DOUGLAS

	1990	1980	1970	1960	1950
Total Population	30,652	35,700	41,276	52,325	78,745
% female	58.3	57.6	55.1	52.2	52.3
% male	41.7	42.4	44.9	47.8	47.7
% age 0–4	10.5	9.0	10.2	15.1	11.0
% age 5–19	24.5	26.2	33.3	29.9	21.7
% age 20–44	34.8	36.4	32.0	33.0	43.3
% age 45–64	15.6	16.5	16.8	15.9	18.7
% age 65+	14.7	11.9	7.7	6.1	5.3

GRAND BOULEVARD

	1990	1980	1970	1960	1950
Total Population	35,897	58,741	80,150	80,036	114,557
% female	55.9	54.4	53.8	52.3	52.7
% male	44.1	45.6	46.2	47.7	47.3
% age 0–4	11.4	9.5	9.4	11.7	8.3
% age 5–19	30.0	31.5	36.4	21.3	16.8
% age 20–44	30.3	27.9	24.8	32.6	45.3
% age 45–64	14.0	17.5	18.4	25.0	24.0
% age 65+	14.3	13.6	11.0	9.4	5.6

WASHINGTON PARK

	1990	1980	1970	1960	1950
Total Population	19,425	31,935	46,024	43,690	56,865
% female	54.5	54.7	53.0	52.0	52.5
% male	45.5	45.3	47.0	48.0	46.8
% age 0–4	11.8	9.9	9.0	9.7	7.2
% age 5–19	28.8	30.8	31.8	18.1	15.7
% age 20–44	33.7	28.5	28.5	34.9	47.0
% age 45–64	14.9	18.8	20.3	27.6	24.5
% age 65+	10.8	12.0	10.4	9.4	5.6

Source: 1990 Census of Population and Housing, File STF3A; and Local Community Fact Book—Chicago Metropolitan Area.

erty values, and further encouraged landlord abandonment. The enactment of federal and state community reinvestment legislation in the 1970s curbed the practice of open redlining. Nonetheless, "prudent lenders will exercise increased caution in advancing mortgages, particularly in neighborhoods marked by strong indication of owner disinvestment and early abandonment."

As the neighborhood disintegrates, those who are able to leave depart in increasing numbers; among these are many working- and middle-class families. The lower population density in turn creates additional problems. Abandoned buildings increase and often serve as havens for crack use and other illegal enterprises that give criminals footholds in the community. Precipitous declines in density also make it even more difficult to sustain or develop a sense of community. The feeling of safety in numbers is completely lacking in such neighborhoods.

Although changes in the economy (industrial restructuring and reorganization) and changes in the class, racial, and demographic composition of inner-city ghetto neighborhoods are important factors in the shift from institutional to jobless ghettos since 1970, we ought not to lose sight of the fact that this process actually began immediately following World War II.

The federal government contributed to the early decay of inner-city neighborhoods by withholding mortgage capital and by making it difficult for urban areas to retain or attract families able to purchase their own homes. Spurred on by massive mortgage foreclosures during the Great Depression, the federal government in the 1940s began underwriting mortgages in an effort to enable citizens to become homeowners. But the mortgage program was selectively administered by the Federal Housing Administration (FHA), and urban neighborhoods considered poor risks were redlined—an action that excluded virtually all the black neighborhoods and many neighborhoods with a considerable number of European immigrants. It was not until the 1960s that the FHA discontinued its racial restrictions on mortgages.

By manipulating market incentives, the federal government drew middle-class whites to the suburbs and, in effect, trapped blacks in the inner cities. Beginning in the 1950s, the suburbanization of the middle class was also facilitated by a federal transportation and highway policy, including the building of freeway networks through the hearts of many cities, mortgages for veterans, mortgage-interest tax exemptions, and the quick, cheap production of massive amounts of tract housing.

In the nineteenth and early twentieth centuries, with the offer of municipal services as an inducement, cities tended to annex their suburbs. But the relations between cities and suburbs in the United States began to change following a century-long influx of poor migrants who required expensive services and paid relatively little in taxes. Annexation largely ended in the mid-twentieth century as suburbs began to resist incorporation successfully. Suburban communities also drew tighter boundaries through the manipulation of zoning laws and discriminatory land-use controls and site-selection practices, making it difficult for inner-city racial minorities to penetrate.

As separate political jurisdictions, suburbs exercised a great deal of autonomy in their use of zoning, land-use policies, covenants, and deed restrictions. In the face of mounting pressures calling for integration in the 1960s, "suburbs chose to diversify by race rather than class. They retained zoning and other restrictions that allowed only affluent blacks (and in some instances Jews) to enter, thereby intensifying the concentration and isolation of the urban poor."

Other government policies also contributed to the growth of jobless ghettos, both directly and indirectly. Many black communities were uprooted by urban renewal and forced migration. The construction of freeway and highway networks through the hearts of many cities in the 1950s produced the most dramatic changes, as many viable low-income communities were destroyed. These networks not only encouraged relocation from the cities to the suburbs, "they also created barriers between the sections of the cities, walling off poor and minority neighborhoods from central business districts. Like urban renewal, highway and expressway construction also displaced many poor people from their homes."

Federal housing policy also contributed to the gradual shift to jobless ghettos. Indeed, the lack of federal action to fight extensive segregation against African-Americans in urban housing markets and acquiescence to the opposition of organized neighborhood groups to the construction of public housing in their communities have resulted in massive segregated housing projects. The federal public housing program evolved in two policy stages that represented two distinct styles. The Wagner Housing Act of 1937 initiated the first stage. Concerned that the construction of public housing might depress private rent levels, groups such as the U.S. Building and Loan League and the National Association of Real Estate Boards successfully lobbied Congress to require, by law, that for each new unit of public housing one "unsafe or unsanitary" unit of public housing be destroyed. As Mark Condon points out, "This policy increased employment in the urban construction market while insulating private rent levels by barring the expansion of the housing stock available to low-income families."

The early years of the public housing program produced positive results. Initially, the program mainly served intact families temporarily displaced by the Depression or in need of housing after the end of World War II. For many of these families, public housing was the first step on the road toward economic recovery. Their stay in the projects was relatively brief. The economic mobility of these families "contributed to the sociological stability of the first public housing communities, and explains the program's initial success."

The passage of the Housing Act of 1949 marked the beginning of the second policy stage. It instituted and funded the urban renewal program designed to eradicate urban slums. "Public housing was now meant to collect the ghetto residents left homeless by the urban renewal bulldozers." A new, lower-income ceiling for public housing residency was established by the federal Public Housing Authority, and families with incomes above that ceiling were evicted, thereby restricting access to public housing to the most economically disadvantaged segments of the population.

This change in federal housing policy coincided with the mass migration of African-Americans from the rural South to the cities of the Northeast and Midwest. Since smaller suburban communities refused to permit the construction of public housing, the units were overwhelmingly concentrated in the overcrowded and deteriorating inner-city ghettos—the poorest and least socially organized sections of the city and the metropolitan area. "This growing population of politically weak urban poor was unable to counteract the desires of vocal middle- and working-class whites for segregated housing," housing that would keep blacks out of white neighborhoods. In short, public housing represents a federally funded institution that has isolated families by race and class for decades, and has therefore contributed to the growing concentration of jobless families in the inner-city ghettos in recent years.

Also, since 1980, a fundamental shift in the federal government's support for basic urban programs has aggravated the problems of joblessness and social organization in the new poverty neighborhoods. The Reagan and Bush administrations—proponents of the New Federalism—sharply cut spending on direct aid to cities, including general revenue sharing, urban mass transit, public service jobs and job training, compensatory education, social service block grants, local public works, economic development assistance, and urban development action grants. In 1980, the federal contribution to city budgets was 18 percent; by 1990 it had dropped to 6.4 percent. In addition, the economic recession which began in the Northeast in 1989 and lasted until the early 1990s sharply reduced those revenues that the cities themselves generated, thereby creating budget deficits that resulted in further cutbacks in basic services and programs along with increases in local taxes.

For many cities, especially the older cities of the East and Midwest, the combination of the New Federalism and the recession led to the worst fiscal and service crisis since the Depression. Cities have become increasingly underserviced, and many have been on the brink of bankruptcy. They have therefore not been in a position to combat effectively three unhealthy social conditions that have emerged or become prominent since 1980: (1) the prevalence of crack-cocaine addiction and the violent crime associated with it; (2) the AIDS epidemic and its escalating public health costs; and (3) the sharp rise in the homeless population not only for individuals but for whole families as well.

Although drug addiction and its attendant violence, AIDS and its toll on public health resources, and homelessness are found in many American communities, their impact on the ghetto is profound. These communities, whose residents have been pushed to the margins of society, have few resources with which to combat these social ills that arose in the 1980s. Fiscally strapped cities have watched helplessly as these problems—exacerbated by the new poverty, the decline of social organization in the jobless neighborhoods, and the reduction of social services—have made the city at large seem a dangerous and threatening place in which to live. Accordingly, working- and middle-class urban residents continue to relocate in the suburbs. Thus, while joblessness and related social problems are on the rise in inner-city neighborhoods, especially in those that represent the new poverty areas, the larger city has fewer and fewer resources with which to combat them.

Finally, policymakers indirectly contributed to the emergence of jobless ghettos by making decisions that have decreased the attractiveness of low-paying jobs and accelerated the relative decline in wages for low-income workers. In particular, in the absence of an effective labor-market policy, they have tolerated industry practices that undermine worker security, such as the reduction in benefits and the rise of involuntary part-time employment, and they have "allowed the minimum wage to erode to its second-lowest level in purchasing power in 40 years." After adjusting for inflation, "the minimum wage is 26 percent below its average level in the 1970s." Moreover, they virtually eliminated AFDC benefits for families in which a mother is employed at least half-time. In the early 1970s, a working mother with two children whose wages equaled 75 percent of the amount designated as the poverty line could receive AFDC benefits as a wage supplement in forty-nine states; in 1995 only those in three states could. As discussed in Chapter 8, even with the expansion of the earned income tax credit (a wage subsidy for the working poor) such policies make it difficult for poor workers to support their families and protect their children. The erosion of wages and benefits force many low-income workers in the inner city to move or remain on welfare.

CHAPTER 3

Ghetto-Related Behavior and the Structure of Opportunity

Seven out of eight people residing in ghettos in metropolitan areas in 1990 were minority group members, most of them African-Americans. But the figure also includes a considerable number of Hispanics. This is not a monolithic socioeconomic group, however; the term embraces all the Spanish-speaking cultures of the New World, which vary broadly. For example, there are significant differences in the socioeconomic status of Mexicans and Puerto Ricans. The latter are largely concentrated in New York City and more closely resemble African-Americans than Mexicans in terms of poverty concentration.

If comparisons are drawn only between the two largest minority groups in the United States—African-Americans and Mexicans—some significant neighborhood differences become clear. In the Urban Poverty and Family Life Study, 85 percent of the inner-city Mexican random sample were first-generation immigrants. Nonetheless, their neighborhoods were on average less poor than those of Chicago's inner-city African-American population. In 1980, 21 percent of blacks but only 7.9 percent of all Mexican immigrants lived in tracts with poverty rates of 30 to 39 percent. And one-fifth of blacks—but only 2 percent of the Mexican immigrant population—resided in ghetto poverty census tracts. Thus, whereas inner-city African-Americans are overrepresented in areas of high to extremely high poverty concentration, inner-city Mexican immigrants are more likely to live in areas of moderate poverty. More important, the Mexican immigrant neighborhoods in the inner city feature lower levels of joblessness and higher levels of social organization than comparable African-American neighborhoods. As Martha Van Haitsma, a member of the UPFLS ethnographic research team, puts it, "Mexican immigrants living in Chicago poverty areas may well be residents of crowded and dilapidated buildings, but they are surrounded by small local businesses, many of them owned and operated by persons of Mexican origin, and by Mexican-targeted social service agencies. Poverty-tract blacks are more isolated from jobs and from employed neighbors than are Mexican immigrants."

As we shall soon see, the residents of these jobless black poverty areas face certain social constraints on the choices they can make in their daily lives. These constraints, combined with restricted opportunities in the larger society, lead to ghetto-related behavior and attitudes—that is, behavior and attitudes that are found more frequently in ghetto neighborhoods than in neighborhoods that feature even modest levels of poverty and local employment. Ghetto-related behavior and attitudes often reinforce the economic marginality of the residents of jobless ghettos.

I choose the term "ghetto-related" as opposed to "ghetto-specific" so as to make the following point: Although many of the behaviors to be described and analyzed below are rooted in circumstances that are unique to inner-city ghettos (for example, extremely high rates of concentrated joblessness and poverty), they are fairly widespread in the larger society. In other words, these behaviors are not unique to ghettos, as the term "ghetto-specific" would imply; rather they occur with greater frequency in the ghetto.

Neighborhoods that offer few legitimate employment opportunities, inadequate job information networks, and poor schools lead to the disappearance of work. That is, where jobs are scarce, where people rarely, if ever, have the opportunity to help their friends and neighbors find jobs, and where there is a disruptive or degraded school life purporting to prepare youngsters for eventual participation in the workforce, many people eventually lose their feeling of connectedness to work in the formal economy; they no longer expect work to be a regular, and regulating, force in their lives. In the case of young people, they may grow up in an environment that lacks the idea of work as a central experience of adult life—they have little or no labor-force attachment. These circumstances also increase the likelihood that the residents will rely on illegitimate sources of income, thereby further weakening their attachment to the legitimate labor market.

On the other hand, many inner-city ghetto residents who maintain a connection with the formal labor market—that is, who continue to be employed mostly in low-wage jobs—are, in effect, working against all odds. They somehow manage to work steadily despite the lack of work-support networks (car pools, informal job information networks), institutions (good schools and training programs), and systems (child care and transportation) that most of the employed population in this country rely on. Moreover, the travel costs, child care costs, and other employment-related expenses consume a significant portion of their already meager incomes. In other words, in order to fully appreciate the problems of employment experienced by inner-city ghetto workers, one has to understand that there is both a unique reality of work (see Chapter 2) and a culture of work (see sections below).

Accordingly, as we examine the adaptations and responses of ghetto residents to persistent joblessness in this chapter, it should be emphasized that the disappearance of work in many inner-city neighborhoods is the function of a number of factors beyond their control. Too often, as reflected in the current public policy debates on welfare reform, the discussion of behavior and social responsibility fails to mention the structural underpinnings of poverty and welfare. The focus is mainly on the shortcomings of individuals and families and not on the structural and social changes in the society at large that have made life so miserable for many inner-city ghetto residents or that have produced certain unique responses and behavior patterns over time. Later I discuss these responses and patterns of behavior, not in isolation but in relation to the constraints and opportunities that shape and provide the context for this action.

A few points highlighted in Chapters 1 and 2 should be reiterated here in order to set up the discussion to follow in this chapter. The reader should keep in mind the point that the current jobless situation evolved from a set of circumstances that must be understood and repeatedly underscored in order to appreciate the particular adaptations to chronic subordination in the ghetto. The inner-city ghetto was not always plagued by low levels of employment and related problems. In the 1950s, employment rates were high. People were poor, but they were still working. Ghetto neighborhoods were as highly segregated as they are now, but people were working.

The disappearance of work in many inner-city neighborhoods is in part related to the nationwide decline in the fortunes of low-skilled workers. Fundamental structural changes in the new global economy, including changes in the distribution of jobs and in the level of education required to obtain employment, resulted in the simultaneous occurrence of increasing joblessness and declining real wages for low-skilled workers. The decline of the mass production system, the decreasing availability of lower-skilled blue-collar jobs, and the growing importance of training and education in the higher-growth industries adversely affected the employment rates and earnings of low-skilled black workers, many of whom are concentrated in inner-city ghettos. The growing suburbanization of jobs has aggravated the employment woes of poor inner-city workers. Most ghetto residents cannot afford an automobile and therefore have to rely on public transit systems that make the connection between inner-city neighborhoods and suburban job locations difficult and time-consuming.

The reader should also be reminded that changes in the class, racial, and demographic composition of inner-city neighborhoods contributed to the high percentage of jobless adults who continue to live there. The proportion of nonpoor families and prime-age working adults has decreased. Today, joblessness is more strongly associated with poverty than in previous years. In the face of increasing and prolonged joblessness, the declining proportion of nonpoor families and the overall depopulation make it more difficult to sustain basic neighborhood institutions or to achieve adequate levels of social organization. The declining presence of working- and middle-class blacks also deprives ghetto neighborhoods of key resources, including structural resources (such as residents with income to sustain neighborhood services) and cultural resources (such as conventional role models for neighborhood children). The economic marginality of the ghetto poor is cruelly reinforced, therefore, by conditions in the neighborhoods in which they live.

Finally, it is important to keep the following point in focus. In addition to changes in the economy and in the class, racial, and demographic composition of inner-city ghetto neighborhoods, certain government programs and policies contributed, over the last fifty years, to the evolution of jobless ghettos. Prominent among these are the early actions of the FHA in withholding mortgage capital from inner-city neighborhoods, the manipulation of market incentives that trapped blacks in the inner cities and lured middle-class whites to the suburbs, the construction of massive federal housing projects in inner-city neighborhoods, and, since 1980, the New Federalism, which, through its insistence on localized responses to social problems, resulted in drastic cuts in spending on basic urban programs. Just when the problems of social dislocation in jobless neighborhoods have escalated, the city has fewer resources with which to address them.

Given the current policy debates that tend to assign blame and attribute failure to personal shortcomings (see Chapter 6), these are the points that the reader should keep in mind as I discuss the responses and adaptations to chronic subordination, including those that have evolved into cultural patterns. The social action—including behavior, habits, skills, styles, orientations, attitudes—discussed in this chapter and in the next chapter ought not to be analyzed as if it were unrelated to the broader structure of opportunities and constraints that have evolved over time. This is not to argue that individuals and groups lack the freedom to make their own choices, engage in certain conduct, and develop certain styles and orientations, but it is to say that these decisions and actions occur within a context of constraints and opportunities that are drastically different from those present in middle-class society.

Many inner-city ghetto residents clearly see the social and cultural effects of living in high-jobless and impoverished neighborhoods. A 17-year-old black male who works part-time, attends college, and resides in a ghetto poverty neighborhood on the West Side stated:

> Well, basically, I feel that if you are raised in a neighborhood and all you see is negative things, then you are going to be negative because you don't see anything positive. . . . Guys and black males see drug dealers on the corner and they see fancy cars and flashy money and they figure: "Hey, if I get into drugs I can be like him."

Interviewed several weeks later, he went on:

> And I think about how, you know, the kids around there, all they see, OK, they see these drug addicts, and then what else do they

see? Oh, they see thugs, you know, they see the gangbangers. So, who do they, who do they really look, model themselves after? Who is their role model? They have none but the thugs. So that's what they wind up being, you know. . . . They [the children in the neighborhood] deal with the only male role model that they can find and most of the time that be pimps, dope dealers, so what do they do? They model themselves after them. Not intentionally trying to but if, you know, that's the only male you're around and that's the only one you come in close contact with, you tend to want to be like that person. And that's why you have so many young drug dealers.

A 25-year-old West Side father of two who works two jobs to make ends meet presented a similar point of view about some inner-city black males:

They try to find easier routes, uh, and had been conditioned over a period of time to just be lazy, so to speak. Uh, motivation nonexistent, you know, and the society that they're affiliated with really don't advocate hard work and struggle to meet your goals such as education and stuff like that. And they see what's around 'em and they follow that same pattern, you know. The society says: "Well, you can sell dope. You can do this. You can do that." A lot of 'em even got to the point where they can accept a few years in jail, uh, as a result of what they might do. . . . They don't see nobody getting up early in the morning, going to work or going to school all the time. The guys they—they be with don't do that . . . 'cause that's the crowd that you choose—well, that's been presented to you by your neighborhood.

Describing how children from troubled neighborhoods get into drugs and alcohol, an unemployed black male who lives in a poor sub-urb south of Chicago stated:

They're in an environment where if you don't get high you're square. You know what I'm saying? If you don't get high some kind of way or another . . . and then, you know, kids are gonna emulate what they come up under. . . . I've watched a couple of generations—I've been here since '61. I watched kids, I saw their fathers ruined, and I seen 'em grow up and do the very same thing.... The children, they don't have any means of recreation whatsoever out here, other than their backyards, the streets, nothing.... The only way it can be intervened if the child has something outside the house to go to, because it is—just go by the environment of the house, he's destined to be an alcoholic or a drug addict.

Some of the respondents relate the problems facing children to the limited opportunity structure in high-jobless neighborhoods. "There's less opportunities over here: it's no jobs. The kids aren't in school, you know, they're not getting any education, there's a lot of drugs on the streets. So, you know, wrong environment, bad associations," reported a 40-year-old mother of six who lives in a ghetto poverty tract on the South Side.

So you have to be in some kind of environment where the kids are more, you know, ready to go to school to get an education instead of, you know, droppin' out to sell drugs because they see their friends, on the corner, makin' money: they got a pocket fulla money, you know. They got kids walkin' around here that's ten years old selling drugs.

According to a 37-year-old unemployed black male from the South Side, the situation is different for males than it is for females. He stated:

Some kids just seem like they don't want to learn, but others, they stick to it. Especially the females, they stick to it. The males either become—they see the street life. They see guys out here making big bucks with fancy cars, jewelry and stuff, and they try to emulate them. That's our problem, you know. The males, they're pretty impressionable. That's why they drop out.... They see their peers out here, they didn't go to school, they makin' it. But they makin' it the wrong way.

In recent years, the process of inner-city neighborhood deterioration has been clearly related to the growth of the inner-city drug industry. The decline of legitimate employment opportunities among inner-city residents increases the incentive to sell drugs. When asked the best way to get ahead in Chicago, a 29-year-old unmarried, employed cook and dishwasher from a poor black neighborhood in which only one in four adults was employed in 1990 stated: "I hate to say it, but it, it look to me dealin' drugs, 'cause these guys make money out there. This is wrong, but, you know, uh—they make a lot of money, fast."

A 35-year-old unemployed male from a nearby neighborhood with a comparable jobless rate emphatically justified his involvement in drug trafficking:

And what am I doing now? I'm a cocaine dealer—'cause I can't get a decent-ass job. So, what other choices do I have? I have to feed my family . . . do I work? I work. See, don't . . . bring me that bullshit. I been working since I was fifteen years old. I had to work to take care of my mother and father and my sisters. See, so can't, can't nobody bring me that bullshit about I ain't looking for no job.

When the people in his poor neighborhood on the South Side run out of money, a 33-year-old janitor stated, they "get depressed, drink, snort, break in other people's houses. Borrow, get on aid, whore—that means prostitute."

A 28-year-old welfare mother from one of the large public housing projects in Chicago also explained what people in her neighborhood resort to when they are out of money.

Shit, turn tricks, sell drugs, anything—and everything. Mind you, everyone is not a stick-up man, you know, but any and everything. Me myself I have sold marijuana, I'm not a drug pusher, but I'm just tryin' to make ends—I'm tryin' to keep bread on the table—I have two babies.

The lack of success in finding full-time employment led a 25-year-old unmarried father of one child from a high-jobless neighborhood on the West Side to sell drugs to augment his income from part-time work.

Four years I been out here trying to find a steady job. Going back and forth all these temporary jobs and this 'n' that. Then you know you gotta give money at home, you know you gotta buy your clothes which cost especially for a big person. Then you're talking about my daughter, then you talking about food in the house too, you know, things like that. . . . Well, lately like I said I have been trying to make extra money and everything. I have been selling drugs lately on the side after I get off work and, ah, it has been going all right. . . . Like I was saying you can make more money dealing drugs than your job, anybody. Not just me but anybody, for the simple fact that if you have a nice clientele and some nice drugs, some nice 'caine or whatever you are selling then the money is going to come, the people are going to come. . . . I can take you to a place where cars come through there like this all day—like traffic—and it got so trafficky that people got to seeing it and they got to calling the police and the police got to staking out the place, raiding the place and all this kind of stuff.

The presence of high levels of drug activity in a neighborhood is indicative of problems of social organization. High rates of joblessness trigger other problems in the neighborhood that adversely affect social organization, including drug trafficking, crime, and gang violence.

The current drug problem began to emerge in the early 1980s when crack—a highly addictive, relatively cheap, and smokable form of cocaine—was widely marketed by dealers on the streets of many American cities, especially in urban ghettos. Addiction to crack reached epidemic proportions in the mid-1980s. Not surprisingly, the rate of drug offense arrests likewise increased, "which, especially for nonwhites (primarily African-Americans), started to move upward in the early 1980s, but accelerated appreciably after 1985." By 1990, the distribution and consumption of crack-cocaine had become widespread in the ghetto neighborhoods of Chicago. In 1994, consumption leveled off "as heroin made a comeback."

In our 1993 survey of two high-jobless neighborhoods on Chicago's South Side (see Appendix B) respondents revealed that the increase in drug trafficking heightened feelings that their neighborhoods had become more dangerous. As a consequence, many residents retreated to the safety of their homes. "More people are dying and being killed," reported one respondent. "There are many drugs sold here every day. It's unsafe and you can't even go out of your house because of being afraid of being shot." Another stated, "I stay home a lot. Streets are dangerous. Killings are terrible. Drugs make people crazy." Similar sentiments were voiced by other residents who felt trapped. One put it this way: "It's scary to see these people. I'm afraid to go outside. I know people who go to work and leave the music on all day and night."

The journalist Isabel Wilkerson points out that "crack has been like a bullet wound to the communities that were already suffering. Even if the bullet can safely be extracted, it has left these neighborhoods deeply scarred." Perhaps the most visible problem associated with the crack-cocaine epidemic may be summed up by Wilkerson's observation of the proliferation of "guns that crack dealers started to carry, the way accountants carry calculators." These weapons filtered down into the hands of adolescents and remain in circulation. "When the epidemic subsided," states the criminologist Jeffrey Fagan, "the guns stayed behind."

When crack landed in a neighborhood, its effect was devastating. Wilkerson described these effects:

The drug's fleeting highs and long, desolate lows created a frenetic field of customers who again and again had to come back for more. In all the chaos, small-time dealers could set up shop practically anywhere, and did. Teenagers who might have otherwise stuck to hustling and shoplifting suddenly had a shot at the big time. As kingpins and upstarts competed for prime locations, disputes were settled with violence. With more guns on the streets, homicides skyrocketed.

No matter the city, homicide charts tell the same story. Whatever year crack took hold, in New York, Washington, Los Angeles, Chicago, the homicide rates soared. The rate has leveled off in these cities, but the toll is still much higher than before crack arrived, because the guns remained, even as crack declined. And the survivors have found that crack has turned the social order of their neighborhood upside down. Armed teen-agers control the streets, residents say. They decide who can stroll on the sidewalk or who can enter an apartment building, while the adults are afraid of the children or depend on them for drugs.

Teenagers with guns, especially rapid-fire assault weapons, increase the danger in these neighborhoods. Adolescents are generally less likely to exercise restraint than mature adults are. Armed with deadly weapons, youngsters are tempted to solve temporary problems in a very permanent fashion. The sharp growth in the number of teenage male homicide victims is directly related to the sudden rise in the number of young male killers. In 1984, there were slightly more than 80 homicide deaths per 100,000 black males ages 15 to 19; by 1992 that figure had ballooned to more than 180 homicide deaths per 100,000.

It is important to emphasize that the norms and actions within the drug industry in ghetto neighborhoods can also affect the behavior of those who have no direct involvement. For example, the widespread possession of guns among drug dealers, and therefore the increased availability of weapons in the neighborhood, prompts others to arm themselves. Some acquire weapons for self-protection, others for settling disputes that have nothing to do with drugs, and still others for the simple purpose of gaining respect from peers and acquaintances in the neighborhood. A National Institute of Justice survey of 758 male students in ten inner-city public high schools in California, Illinois, New Jersey, and Louisiana revealed that "22 percent of the students possess guns," 12 percent carry them all or most of the time, and "another 23 percent carry guns now and then." Within this survey the students revealed that the primary reason for their most recent gun acquisition was self-protection.

As possession of firearms and drug use increase, the residents of troubled neighborhoods become more fearful of leaving the safety of their homes. Such fears decrease their involvement in voluntary associations and informal social control networks essential to maintain the social organization of the neighborhood. One resident who moved from a dangerous housing project to a safer area nearby described the difference in neighborhood informal interaction.

> Well, mostly, you know . . . I know a lot of peoples communicate . . . together . . . try to keep the neighborhood together . . . so far since I lived here . . . and . . . I don't see too many peoples, you know, just hanging out and gettin' high on the street anymore like . . . like when I was livin' in the project. I used to see it all the time, but around here I don't see it too much.

Neighborhoods that feature higher levels of social organization— that is, neighborhoods that integrate the adults by means of an extensive set of obligations, expectations, and social networks—are in a better position to control and supervise the activities and behavior of children. Youngsters know they will be held accountable for their individual and group action; at the same time, they know they can rely on neighborhood adults for support and guidance. In terms of levels of social organization, black working- and middle-class neighborhoods in Chicago stand in sharp contrast to the new poverty neighborhoods. Data from the 1989–90 survey (see Appendix B) reveal that in addition to much lower levels of perceived unemployment than in the poor neighborhoods, black working- and middle-class neighborhoods also have much higher levels of perceived social control and cohesion, organizational services, and social support.

The connectedness and stability of social networks in strong neighborhoods transcend the household because the neighborhood adults have the potential to observe, report on, and discuss the behavior of the children in different circumstances. These networks reinforce the discipline the child receives in the home, because other adults in the neighborhood assume responsibility for maintaining a standard of public or social behavior even on the part of children who are not their own. As Frank Furstenberg put it, "Ordinary parents are likely to have more success when they reside in communities where the burden of raising children is seen as a collective responsibility and where strong institutions sustain the efforts of parents."

The norms and supervision imposed on children are most effective when they reflect what James S. Coleman has called "intergenerational closure"—that is, the overlapping of youth and adult social networks in a neighborhood. Intergenerational closure is exhibited in those neighborhoods where most parents know not only their children's friends but the parents of those friends as well. As a general rule, adolescents seem to benefit directly from the exchange of resources produced by their parents' social integration with others in the neighborhood.

Nonetheless, social integration may not be beneficial to adolescents who live in neighborhoods characterized by high levels of individual and family involvement in aberrant behavior. "Although we tend to think of social integration as a desirable endpoint," state Laurence Steinberg and his colleagues, "its desirability depends on the nature of the people that integration brings one into contact with. There are many communities in contemporary America in which it may be

more adaptive for parents to be socially isolated than socially integrated. Indeed, some of Frank Furstenberg's recent work on family life
in the inner city of Philadelphia suggest that social isolation is often
deliberately practiced as an adaptive strategy by many parents living in
dangerous neighborhoods."

A similar finding emerged from ethnographic research in a
densely populated housing project in Denver. Concerns on the part of
some parents about safety in this housing project affected their degree
of involvement or interaction with their neighbors. Such parents were
skeptical of other parents and youths in the housing project and therefore resisted casual contact with their neighbors, established few
friendships, and did not get involved with neighborhood problems.
They also expressed negative views of their more socially engaged
neighbors and their nonconventional behavior (drinking and "hanging
out"). Analogous views were voiced by some parents in the Urban
Poverty and Family Life Study. As a 42-year-old married father of one
child and an employed part-time salesman from a ghetto poverty area
on the South Side put it: "It makes no difference what's in that street,
you don't have to socialize with the people around here, that's your
personal preference."

On the basis of research conducted by the University of Chicago's
Center for the Study of Urban Inequality on successful adolescent development in high-risk areas (see Appendix B), it appears that what
many impoverished and dangerous neighborhoods have in common is
a relatively high degree of social integration (high levels of local
neighboring while being relatively isolated from contacts in the
broader mainstream society) and low levels of informal social control
(feelings that they have little control over their immediate environment, including the environment's negative influences on their children). In such areas, not only are children at risk because of the lack of
informal social controls, they are also disadvantaged because the social
interaction among neighbors tends to be confined to those whose
skills, styles, orientations, and habits are not as conducive to promoting positive social outcomes (academic success, pro-social behavior,
etc.) as are those in more stable neighborhoods. Although the close interaction among neighbors in such areas may be useful in devising
strategies, disseminating information, and developing styles of behavior that are helpful in a ghetto milieu (teaching children to avoid eye-
to-eye contact with strangers and to develop a tough demeanor in the

public sphere for self-protection), they may be less effective in promoting the welfare of children in the society at large.

Despite being socially integrated, the residents in Chicago's ghetto neighborhoods shared a feeling that they had little informal social control over the children in their environment. A primary reason is the absence of a strong organizational capacity or an institutional resource base that would provide an extra layer of social organization in their neighborhoods. It is easier for parents to control the behavior of the children in their neighborhoods when there exists a strong institutional resource base, when the links between community institutions such as churches, schools, political organizations, businesses, and civic clubs are strong. The higher the density and stability of formal organizations, the less that illicit activities such as drug trafficking, crime, prostitution, and gang formation can take root in the neighborhood. A weak institutional resource base is what distinguishes high-jobless inner-city neighborhoods from stable middle-class and working-class areas. As one resident of a high-jobless neighborhood on the South Side of Chicago put it, "Our children, you know, seems to be more at risk than any other children there is, because there's no library for them to go to. There's not a center they can go to, there's no field house that they can go into. There's nothing. There's nothing at all."

Parents in high-jobless neighborhoods have a much more difficult task of controlling the behavior of their adolescents, of preventing them from getting involved in activities detrimental to pro-social development. Given the lack of organizational capacity and weak institutional base, some parents choose to protect their children by isolating them from activities in the neighborhood, including the avoidance of contact and interaction with neighborhood families. Wherever possible, and often with great difficulty considering the problems of transportation and limited financial resources, they attempt to establish contact and cultivate relations with individuals, families, and institutions outside the neighborhood, such as church groups, schools, and community recreation programs.

When speaking of social isolation, therefore, a distinction should be made between those families who deliberately isolate themselves from other families in dangerous neighborhoods and those who lack contact or sustained interaction with institutions, families, and individuals that represent mainstream society.

As I pointed out earlier, the most impoverished inner-city neighborhoods have experienced a decrease in the proportion of working- and middle-class families, thereby increasing the social isolation of the remaining residents in these neighborhoods from the more advantaged members of society. Data from the UPFLS reveal that the non-working poor in the inner city experience greater social isolation in this sense of the term than do the working poor.

Nonworking poor black men and women "were consistently less likely to participate in local institutions and have mainstream friends [that is, friends who are working, have some college education, and are married] than people in other classes" and ethnic groups. However, there are noticeable gender differences in the structure of interpersonal relations among the nonworking poor blacks in the inner-city neighborhoods of Chicago. Jobless black females (mostly mothers on welfare) were significantly more isolated from mainstream individuals and families than jobless black males. Welfare mothers interacted with other welfare mothers. "It is not simply poverty that isolates women, but being non-working further increases isolation. This lends some credence to the imagery of AFDC [Aid for Families with Dependent Children] women being cut off from others." Overall, the personal friendship network of blacks (both male and female) is more insular, and they are less likely to have at least one employed close friend than are the Mexican immigrants.

This form of social isolation operates in the inner-city black neighborhood as a result of the lack of access to resources provided by stable working residents. Such resources include informal job networks. Analysis of the UPFLS ethnographic data reveals that "social contacts were a useful means of gaining informal work to help make ends meet but far less often successful in helping with steady employment; networks existed but largely lacked the capacity to help lift residents into the formal labor market."

Moreover, UPFLS data on job-search behavior reveal that black men and women in the inner city are less likely than Mexican immigrants to report that they received help from a friend or relative in obtaining their current job. Recognizing the importance of the informal job network system, a 35-year-old welfare mother of two children in the UPFLS stated: "A lot of people get good jobs because they know friends, and they work there. If you know somebody that's been working in an established company for a long time, and they tell you to come in and fill an application, you can get a job. It always pay to know somebody." However, the job-search strategies that black inner-city residents most frequently reported using were filling out an application at a place of business and seeking assistance at an employment office. Also, both black men and women more often use the public transit system to get to and from work than do Mexicans, who rely more heavily on carpooling, itself an important network activity.

In short, social isolation deprives inner-city residents not only of conventional role models, whose strong presence once buffered the effects of neighborhood joblessness, but also of the social resources (including social contacts) provided by mainstream social networks that facilitate social and economic advancement in a modern industrial society. This form of social isolation also contributes to the formation and crystallization of ghetto-related cultural traits and behaviors, a subject to which I now turn.

"Culture" may be defined as the sharing of modes of behavior and outlook within a community. The study of culture involves an analysis of how culture is transmitted from generation to generation and the way in which it is sustained through social interaction in the community. To act according to one's culture—either through forms of nonverbal action, including engaging in or refraining from certain conduct, or in the verbal expression of opinions or attitudes concerning norms, values, or beliefs—is to follow one's inclinations as they have been developed by influence or learning from other members of the community that one belongs to or identifies with.

All communities within the broader society share common modes of behavior and outlook. However, the extent to which communities differ with respect to outlook and behavior depends in part on the degree of the group's social isolation from the broader society, the material assets or resources they control, the benefits and privileges they derive from these resources, the cultural experiences they have accumulated as a consequence of historical and existing economic and political arrangements, and the influence they wield because of those arrangements.

For all these reasons one would expect variations in the culture of subgroups within society, even though many elements of their cultural repertoires are similar. The available research suggests that the total culture of the inner-city ghetto includes ghetto-related elements, but it also includes a predominance of mainstream elements. Many media discussions of the "underclass" often overlook or ignore these mainstream elements. Indeed, one gets the distinct impression from these discussions that the values of people in the inner-city ghetto, to quote *Time* magazine, "are often at radical odds with those of the majority— even the majority of the poor." The UPFLS research reveals, however, that the beliefs of inner-city residents bear little resemblance to such descriptions.

Despite the overwhelming poverty, black residents in inner-city ghetto neighborhoods verbally reinforce, rather than undermine, the basic American values pertaining to individual initiative. For example, the large survey of the UPFLS found that nearly all the black respondents felt that plain hard work is either very important or somewhat important for getting ahead. Indeed, fewer than 3 percent of the black respondents from ghetto poverty census tracts denied the importance of plain hard work for getting ahead in society, and 66 percent expressed the view that it is very important.

Nonetheless, given the constraints and limited opportunities facing people in inner-city neighborhoods, it is altogether reasonable to assume that many of those who subscribe to these values will, in the final analysis, find it difficult to live up to them. Circumstances generally taken for granted in middle-class society are often major obstacles that must be overcome in the inner-city ghetto. Take, for example, the case of a 29-year-old black male from a high-jobless neighborhood on the South Side who is employed in a job without the fringe benefits most workers associate with stable employment, such as paid sick leave. His situation is described in the field notes prepared by a member of the UPFLS research team.

> Clifford is a 29-year-old black male who quit school in eleventh grade and currently works night-shifts (from 7 p.m. to 5 a.m.) as a "dishwasher and assistant cook" in a western suburb of Chicago. He has lived in the city for 16 years and in his present neighborhood for two years. He resides with his mother, a homemaker of 52, his sister of 23, a younger sister of 18, and a little brother of

12. Clifford has never been married and has no children. While he was raised partly on welfare support, he has never received public aid himself.

Clifford has been working for several years as a dishwasher for different employers. He now cooks, mops, and washes dishes for $4.85 an hour. He has held this job since February of 1985 without taking a single day of vacation. His supervisor has made it crystal clear to him that he is expendable and that if he takes too much (that is, any) vacation, they will not keep him. On the day of the interview, he had had a molar pulled and was in great pain (partly due to the fact that, not having any money and having already borrowed cash to pay for the extraction, he could not buy the prescribed pain-killers); yet he was . . . reluctant to call his boss and ask for an evening off.

When I asked if he expects to find a better job soon, he laughed: "I don't know: this is up to the employers, if they wanta hire me." Should he find one, it would be "somethin' in the restaurant business, hospital, or maybe a hotel or somethin', doing dishes."

He has not taken any steps to get further education or training, mainly because his work schedule and lack of resources make such planning quasi-impossible. Yet he clearly would like to get more so he "can better [himself] in life," he says, as he tucks his shirt under his armpits, strokes his belly, yawns as he lays stretched out on the couch. . . . With his present wage, he cannot save any money ("You can't, uh [chuckles], I be right back to my next day. You can't. Don't make enough").

As a result, he frequently finds himself without any money. "Yeah, like today. I had to get my tooth pulled and I had to go out and rent money." When this happens, he borrows small sums (about $20.00) from friends and associates: "I just try to hang in there, whatever I can do." People in the neighborhood often find themselves out of cash too, and the result is that illegal activities are fairly routine: "Oh, man, some of them steal, some of them, uh . . . It's hard to say, man: they probably do anything they can to get a dollar in their pocket. Robbin', prostitution, drug sale, anythin'. Oh boy!" . . . At this point in the interview, Clifford holds his hand to his cheek and constantly moans in pain. . . . Once the interview was over, I explained I'd pay him with a money order because we don't carry cash with us. "I don't blame you for not bringing any money around here, man. I don't blame you. I have been stuck up before."

There are many individuals in the inner-city ghetto like Clifford, people who struggle against the odds at great individual sacrifice to live up to mainstream norms and ideas of acceptability. For example, a woman in one of the new poverty neighborhoods on the South Side described her husband's financial struggles:

My husband, he's worked in the community. He's 33. He's worked at One Stop since he was 15. And right now, he's one of the highest paid—he's a butcher—he's one of the highest paid butchers in One Stop. For the 15—almost 18—years that he's been there, he's only making nine dollars an hour. And he's begged and fought and scrapped and sued and everything else for the low pay he gets. And he takes so much. Sometimes he come home and he'd sit home and he'd just cry. And he'd say, "If it weren't for my kids and my family, I'd quit." You know, it's bad, 'cuz he won't get into drugs, selling it, you know, he ain't into drug using. He's the kind of man, he want to work hard and feel good about that he came home. He say that it feels bad sometime to see this 15-year-old boy drivin' down the street with a new car. He saying, "I can't even pay my car note. And I worry about them comin' to get my car."

There are many people in the inner-city ghetto (like Clifford and the butcher) who are working hard under extremely difficult circumstances to make a go of it. Some are able to maintain their employment only under considerable strain, while others, because of the very nature of their economic circumstances, are sometimes compelled to act in ghetto-related ways—for example, existing for a period of time without a steady job or pursuing illegitimate means of income. They may strongly agree with mainstream judgments of unacceptable behavior and yet feel utterly constrained by their circumstances, forced sometimes to act in ways that violate mainstream norms. Outsiders may observe their overt behavior and erroneously assume that they regard this illegitimate income as rightful.

Thus, in some cases, ghetto-related behavior may not reflect internalized values at all. People are simply adapting to difficult circumstances. In addition to constraints associated with limited access to organizational channels of privilege and influence, there are also constraints on the choices they can make because they lack access to mainstream sources of information needed to make responsible and helpful decisions. For example, research conducted in a Chicago inner-city high school suggested that many of the seniors had attainable goals and could have made a successful post–high school transition had they received adequate information, guidance, and resources. In addition, every counselor at this high school reported that he or she did not have sufficient informational materials, time, and training needed to provide students with effective career counseling.

In other cases, the decision to act in ghetto-related ways, although not necessarily reflecting internalized values, can nonetheless be said to be cultural. The more often certain behavior such as the pursuit of illegal income is manifested in a community, the greater will be the readiness on the part of some residents of the community to find that behavior "not only convenient but also morally appropriate." They may endorse mainstream norms against this behavior in the abstract but then provide compelling reasons and justifications for this behavior, given the circumstances in their community.

A reasonable hypothesis concerning behavior is that in stable neighborhoods, people who are economically marginal and are struggling to make ends meet are more strongly constrained to act in mainstream ways than are their counterparts in high-jobless neighborhoods that feature problems of social organization and ghetto-related modes of adaptation. The former may be able to exercise a range of illegal or unacceptable solutions to their problems, but the widely held mores of their community, reinforced by economic and social resources that keep the community stable, strongly pressure them to refrain from such activity. However, individuals in the latter neighborhoods may be more likely to pursue such activity because it is more frequently manifested and tolerated in the overt behavior of their neighbors, who are also struggling to survive economically. In this case, ghetto-related culture "may be seen as at least to some extent adaptive, in that situationally suitable modes of action are not only made available as techniques but also tend to be given some measure of apparent legitimacy."

Individuals in the inner-city ghetto can hardly avoid exposure to many kinds of recurrent and open ghetto-related behavior in the daily interactions and contacts with the people of their community. They therefore have the opportunity to familiarize themselves with a range and combination of modes of behavior that include elements of both the mainstream and the ghetto. The degree of exposure to culturally transmitted modes of behavior in any given milieu depends in large measure on the individual's involvement in or choice of social networks, including networks of friends and kin. Through cultural transmission, individuals develop a cultural repertoire that includes discrete elements that are relevant to a variety of respective situations. For example, jobless individuals who receive cultural transmissions that grow out of lack of steady employment may find some of the transmitted elements, such as street-corner panhandling, quite relevant to their situation. This, as Ulf Hannerz points out, is why some elements of culture should be seen as *situationally adaptive*—that is, they provide members of a group with models of behavior that apply to situations specific to that community.

As Hannerz also notes, however, not all aspects of cultural transmission involve rational decisions as to which aspects of a person's cultural repertoire are relevant in a given situation. There is also the phenomenon of accidental or nonconscious cultural transmission—also called transmission by precept—whereby a person's exposure to certain attitudes and actions is so frequent that they become part of his or her own outlook and therefore do not, in many cases, involve selective application to a given situation. The cultural sharing exemplified in role modeling epitomizes this process. "When a mode of behavior is encountered frequently and in many different persons," it is more likely to be transmitted by precept. Ghetto-related practices involving overt emphasis on sexuality, idleness, and public drinking "do not go free of denunciation" in inner-city ghetto neighborhoods. But the failure of forces of social organization allow these practices to occur much more frequently there than in middle-class society, so the transmission of these modes of behavior by precept, as in role modeling, is more easily facilitated. As the sociologist Ann Swidler has noted,

> People may share common aspirations, while remaining profoundly different in the way their culture organizes their overall pattern of behavior. . . . When we move from one cultural community to another, action is not determined by one's values. Rather action and values are organized to take advantage of cultural competencies. . . . Students of culture keep looking for cul-

tural values that will explain what is distinctive about the behavior of groups or societies, and neglect other distinctively *cultural* phenomena which offer greater promise of explaining patterns of action. These factors are better described as culturally shaped skills, habits, and styles than as values or preferences.

Skills, habits, and styles are often shaped by the frequency at which they are found in their own community. As Dr. Deborah Prothrow-Stith so clearly shows in her book, *Deadly Consequences*, youngsters in inner-city ghetto neighborhoods are more likely than other children to see violence as a way of life. They are likely to witness violent acts and to have role models who do not adequately control their own violent impulses or restrain their own anger. Accidental cultural transmission can also be seen in the development and crystallization of outlooks or beliefs that grow out of the common experiences of many different people. Elijah Anderson points out that receiving respect from peers, acquaintances, and strangers has become highly valued among inner-city adolescents, who have increasingly been denied status in mainstream terms. Respect is often granted when one is carrying and willing to use an assault weapon. Accordingly, given the ready availability of firearms, knives, and other weapons, adolescents' experiments with aggressive behavior often have deadly consequences.

In short, regardless of the mode of cultural transmission, ghetto-related behaviors often represent particular cultural adaptations to the systematic blockage of opportunities in the environment of the inner city and the society as a whole. These adaptations are reflected in habits, skills, styles, and attitudes that are shaped over time. This was the message articulated in the pioneering works of such authors as Kenneth B. Clark, Ulf Hannerz, and Lee Rainwater and was based on research conducted in the 1960s. These authors demonstrated that it is possible to recognize the importance of macrostructural constraints (that is, to avoid the extreme notion of a "culture of poverty") and still see "the merits of a more subtle kind of cultural analysis of life in poverty." This point can perhaps be most clearly demonstrated in an analysis of the impact of persistent joblessness.

I believe that there is a difference between, on the one hand, a jobless family whose mobility is hampered by constraints in the economy but nonetheless lives in a neighborhood with a relatively high rate of employment and, on the other hand, a jobless family that lives in a new poverty neighborhood that is affected not only by these same constraints but also by the behavior and outlook of other jobless families in the neighborhood.

As Pierre Bourdieu demonstrated, <u>work</u> is not simply a way to make a living and support one's family. It also constitutes a framework ~,~ B. for daily behavior and patterns of interaction because it <u>imposes disciplines and regularities</u>. Thus, in the absence of regular employment, a person lacks not only a place in which to work and the receipt of regular income but also a coherent organization of the present—that is, a system of concrete expectations and goals. Regular employment provides the anchor for the spatial and temporal aspects of daily life. It determines where you are going to be and when you are going to be there. In the absence of regular employment, life, including family life, becomes less coherent. Persistent unemployment and irregular employment hinder rational planning in daily life, the necessary condition of adaptation to an industrial economy.

One of the earliest studies to examine the effects of persistent unemployment was conducted over fifty years ago by Marie Jahoda, Paul F. Lazarsfeld, and Hans Zeisel in Marienthal, a small industrial community in Austria "at the time of a depression that was much worse than anything the United States went through." During the period of the research, the entire community of Marienthal was unemployed. "One of the main theses of the Marienthal study was that prolonged unemployment leads to a state of apathy in which the victims do not utilize any longer even the few opportunities left to them."

Before this economic depression, when people in the community were working, political organizations were active. People of the town read a lot, "entered eagerly into discussions, and enjoyed organizing a variety of events." The factory was at the center of this lively community. It "was not simply a place of work. It was the center of social life." All of this disappeared when the factory shut down. Describing the situation during their field research in 1930, the authors stated:

> Cut off from their work and deprived of contact with the outside world, the workers of Marienthal have lost the material and moral incentives to make use of their time. Now that they are no longer under any pressure, they undertake nothing new and drift

gradually out of an ordered existence into one that is undisciplined and empty. Looking back over any period of this free time, they are unable to recall anything worth mentioning.

For hours on end, the men stand around in the street alone or in small groups, leaning against the wall of a house or the parapet of the bridge. When a vehicle drives through the village they turn their heads slightly; several of them smoke pipes. They carry on leisurely conversations for which they have unlimited time. Nothing is urgent anymore; they have forgotten how to hurry.

The idleness due to joblessness in Marienthal is not unlike the idleness associated with joblessness in today's inner-city neighborhoods. A 25-year-old employed, unmarried father of one child who works two full-time jobs talked to a UPFLS researcher about his life as an employed worker and his experiences when he was out of work and on drugs.

The guys in my neighborhood, I used to be with them a few years ago when I was drugging. But, once I quit I found if someone was my friend so-called, all we had in common was drugs and once I quit drugs we had nothing to talk about because things that I was trying to do such as being at work on time and not being able to stay out until two o'clock on a weeknight 'cause I had to get up in the morning in order for me to be punctual at the job, that wasn't their concern because they didn't have no job and a job was furthest from their mind.

It should be clear to the reader that when I speak of joblessness or the disappearance of work, I am referring to the declining involvement in or lack of attachment to the formal labor market. It could be argued that "joblessness," in the general sense of the term, does not necessarily mean "nonwork." To be officially unemployed or officially outside the labor market does not mean that one is totally removed from all forms of work activity. Many people who are officially jobless are nonetheless involved in informal kinds of work activity, ranging from unpaid housework to work in the informal or illegal economies that provide income.

Housework is work, baby-sitting is work, even drug dealing is work. However, what distinguishes work in the formal economy from work in the informal and illegal economies is that work in the formal economy is characterized by greater regularity and consistency in schedules and hours. The demands for discipline are greater. It is true that some work activities outside the formal economy also call for discipline and regular schedules. Several studies reveal that the social organization of the drug industry is driven by discipline and a work ethic, however perverse. But as a general rule, work in the informal and illegal economies is far less governed by norms or expectations that place a premium on discipline and regularity. It is also negatively sanctioned by state authorities and therefore discourages open and continuous participation. For all these reasons, when I speak of the disappearance of work, I mean work in the formal economy, work that provides a framework for daily behavior because it readily imposes discipline and regularity.

The problems associated with the absence of work are most severe for a jobless family in a low-employment neighborhood because they are more likely to be shared and therefore reinforced by other families in the neighborhood through the process of accidental or nonconscious cultural transmission. One of these shared problems is a perception of a lack of self-efficacy.

In social cognitive theory, perceived self-efficacy refers to beliefs in one's own ability to take the steps necessary to achieve the goals required in a given situation. Such beliefs affect the level of challenge that an individual feels he or she is able to tackle, the amount of effort expended in a given venture, and the degree of perseverance when encountering difficulties. As Albert Bandura has put it, "Inability to influence events and social conditions that significantly affect one's life can give rise to feelings of futility and despondency as well as to anxiety." Two sources of perceived futility are distinguished in self-efficacy theory: people may (1) seriously doubt their ability to accomplish what is expected or (2) feel confident of their abilities but nonetheless give up trying because they believe that their efforts will ultimately be futile due to an environment that is unresponsive, discriminatory, or punitive. "The type of outcomes people expect depends largely on their judgments of how well they will be able to perform in given situations."

Unstable work and low income, I would hypothesize, will lower one's perceived self-efficacy. A recent study on the adverse effects of economic pressure on mental health and parental behavior, based on data from a sample of both black and white inner-city parents in Philadelphia, provides some support for this view. The study reported that mounting economic pressures, caused by unstable work and low income, created feelings of emotional depression and thereby tended to lower the parents' sense of efficacy in terms of what they believed to be their influence over their children and on their children's environment. Strong marriages effectively minimized such effects on the behavior of parents in both racial groups, whereas marriages marked by conflict and single-parent households compounded them.

I would therefore expect lower levels of perceived self-efficacy in ghetto neighborhoods—which feature underemployment, unemployment, and labor-force dropouts, weak marriages, and single-parent households—than in less impoverished neighborhoods. Considering the importance of cultural learning and influence, I would also expect the level of perceived self-efficacy to be higher among those individuals who experience these same difficulties but live in working- and middle-class neighborhoods than among their counterparts in ghetto neighborhoods.

In the more socially isolated ghetto neighborhoods, networks of kin, friends, and associates are more likely to include a higher proportion of individuals who, because of their experiences with extreme economic marginality, tend to doubt that they can achieve approved societal goals. The self-doubts may exist for either of the two reasons stated earlier: these individuals may have questions concerning their own capabilities or preparedness, or they may perceive that severe restrictions have been imposed on them by a hostile environment.

The longer the joblessness persists, the more likely these self-doubts will take root. I think it is reasonable to assume that the association between joblessness and self-efficacy grows over time and becomes stronger the longer a neighborhood is plagued by low employment. This hypothesis cannot be directly tested, but my assumption is that there are lower levels of self-efficacy in the inner city today than there were in previous years when most of the adults were working and involved in informal job networks.

Since joblessness afflicts a majority of the adult population in the new poverty neighborhoods, I think it is likely that problems of self-efficacy stem more from perceived environmental restrictions than from doubts about individual capability. In contrast, I would hypothesize that problems of perceived self-efficacy among jobless families in neighborhoods with moderate to high employment may suffer more from feelings of low individual capability because a majority of families in the neighborhood have jobs whereas they do not.

Many of the UPFLS respondents expressed the view that growing up in poverty and living in an environment plagued by joblessness and other problems make it difficult to sustain motivation. A 28-year-old unmarried welfare mother of two children who lives in a large housing project put it this way:

> Because, like I said, to get discouraged, if—I don't care how far you are down the road, to get discouraged takes you back halfway. Because then you got to get your self-esteem up again, you know, you got to get the motor goin' again. And that's what I feel is one of the biggest downfalls for people in the neighborhood. They just—give up. . . . I feel like this [the housing project] was meant to be a stepping stone, you can come here, you can save you a little money. I don't save a damn dime. I don't know who brought that one up, who thought that you could save something. You know, on my public aid application, they actually asked me if I had a savings account! I can't—what am I going to save?

Another unmarried welfare mother of three children who is 35 years old and lives in one of the poor neighborhoods on the South Side stated:

> Sometimes you can try and then you say "I'm tired of trying." I have did that. You try so hard it seems as if when you just about to get up, something happen to knock you back down and you just forget it, then. 'Cause I did that many a time.

The open-ended survey of the UPFLS revealed that although a number of respondents have relatively high aspirations and seem to display confidence in their ability to get ahead, many others were despondent and were pessimistic about their ability to succeed. They insisted that despite the opportunities that may be available to many people, they are destined to remain in a state of poverty and live in troubled neighborhoods. The respondents argued that inner-city blacks will not be able to progress because inferior education has placed them at a disadvantage. They blame racism and the rising number of immigrants in the United States as major reasons for their inability to improve their position in life. They are frustrated by the unrewarding process of seeking employment. Some blame their employment difficulties on competition from foreigners; others feel that the problem stems from a scarcity of jobs and that the government does not provide enough jobs for its citizens. They believe that because of the limited number of jobs available, the more qualified workers are taking positions from the less qualified. Others feel that the jobs that are available do not pay enough to adequately support a family and that the only decent jobs available are to be found in the suburbs and not the city. Many of the women feel that they cannot find employment because they have to care for their children. Finally, a few respondents insisted that racial prejudice is the main reason they have difficulty in finding a job and that most of the good jobs are taken by white people.

An individual's feelings of low self-efficacy grow out of experiences involving unstable work and low income and are reinforced or strengthened by the similar feelings and views of others who share the conditions and culture of the neighborhood. This represents the process of accidental cultural transmission, whereby the individual's exposure to certain attitudes and actions is so frequent that they actually become part of his or her own perspective. The end result, to use a term from Bandura's work, is lower collective efficacy in the inner-city ghetto. Research on the *transmission* of such views and feelings would represent a cultural analysis of life in poverty. The psychological self-efficacy theory is used here not in isolation but in relation to the *structural problem* of weak labor-force attachment—that is, the marginal economic position (unstable work, joblessness, and low income) of some people in the labor force because of structural constraints or limited opportunities, including constraints or opportunities in their immediate environment—and the *cultural problem* of the transmission of self and collective beliefs in the neighborhood.

However, I do not want to overemphasize the importance of the cultural transmission of individual and collective beliefs in accounting for decisions made by people with unstable work and low income. It is quite clear from research at the University of Chicago's Center for the Study of Urban Inequality that residents of the inner city constantly reflect on the economic constraints and restricted opportunities they face and often make rational decisions based on the choices available to them, regardless of whether the decisions are influenced by personal feelings of low self-efficacy.

For example, one welfare mother in a new poverty neighborhood on the South Side explained her decision to remain on welfare even though she would like "to go out there and get a job."

> I was workin' and then I had two kids. And I'm struggling. I was making, like, close to seven dollars an hour. . . . I had to pay a babysitter. Then I had to deal with my kids when I got home. And I couldn't even afford medical insurance. . . . I was so scared, when my kids were sick or somethin' . . . because I have been turned away from a hospital because I did not have a medical card. I don't like being on public aid and stuff right now. But . . . what do I do with my kids when my kids get sick?

A 31-year-old welfare mother of three children who is separated from her husband and lives in a poor South Side neighborhood provides another example of the economic constraints that force women to go or remain on welfare:

> Like when I moved I got behind. The telephone and moving expenses. Like one month's [rent for a] security [deposit], the telephone company eat your tail out and all the other little bills I have. I have to take it more slowly to get back on my feet. I never liked public aid. I'm on public aid now. I've been on and off for eleven years with [my daughter], I had to get on with her. I was tryin' to collect some of my unemployment. I was tryin' to get a job where I could get off completely, but you just don't know. 'Cause you may lose your job. I have to do something to keep these kids going through, otherwise if I was by myself, I could do other little things like, you know, 'cause I cannot see myself workin' the streets. I cannot see myself doin' that. I can't see it at all.

Research by Kathryn Edin provides the clearest evidence on the rational decisions made by many disadvantaged women to either remain or go on welfare instead of seeking low-wage employment.

"Once we look at single-parent families' budgets, their reason for non-work becomes crystal clear," Edin states. "[I]t is the gap between what most unskilled or semiskilled single mothers *need* to earn and what they can *expect* to earn in the labor market that is responsible for much of their AFDC receipt."

Edin points out that we often fail to consider that "states set AFDC benefits too low to live on. Because of this basic fact, women must supplement their welfare income with either unreported work or covert contributions from boyfriends, friends or relatives." Moreover, we also often ignore the fact that "low-wage jobs do not pay enough to support a family either and offer little access to better-paying jobs." Indeed, Edin found that "those who leave [welfare] for work are even more likely to be poor in the second year after leaving welfare than they were in the first." Let us briefly examine some of the important findings based on this research to establish firmly the point that many nonwork decisions on the part of welfare mothers reflect the rational and realistic options open to them given the existing constraints and limited opportunities facing them.

Edin and her colleague interviewed a sample of 214 recipients of AFDC and 165 single mothers "who worked at jobs paying what welfare mothers reported having earned in the past" in four cities in the United States. The AFDC mothers had an average monthly income of $307 in cash and $222 in food stamps. Yet, according to their budgets, an average of $876 a month was needed to pay their expenses. Thus, the present benefit level of AFDC was not sufficient to cover their living expenses.

Similar findings were reported in a study by LaDonna Pavetti. She found that many welfare recipients attempted to leave welfare for employment but were unable to stay off welfare because doing so was not economically feasible. They frequently found jobs as bartenders, waitresses, car dispatchers, and baby-sitters that paid about $5 an hour and lacked health benefits. But these mothers felt that in order to make ends meet, including covering health care and child care costs, they needed jobs that paid about $8 or $9 an hour and provided health benefits.

Respondents in the UPFLS also pointed out the difficulty of subsisting on welfare. A 41-year-old mother of two children from a poor West Side neighborhood, married but separated from her husband,

and employed as a nurse's aide, described her financial struggle after her daughter got pregnant and applied for assistance from AFDC:

> My daughter . . . got pregnant when she was 21, OK? She had finished school, and she had gone one year of college. And after she got pregnant she really hadn't worked too many places, you know, 'cause she had the baby, so she found out she couldn't get right to work. She had to wait until the kid is old enough, then she can go back to work. So she went and applied for public aid, you know. And of course they didn't want to give her public aid, 'cause she was stayin' home with me, which I thought they were very wrong: hey, she's 21 years old, and she had a child. . . . I wasn't making enough money really to support her, her and the child. So then the first they did, they give her like . . . $80. What is $80 a month, hey? So I called myself and I asked him, the case-worker or whatever it was, and I said: "Why do you want to give $80 for a child?" And he went on and say, "Well, after all, you're the mother and you be workin' in." I said, "Yeah, but I only bring home somethin' like . . . and if they gonna take it on me, I only bring home somethin' like $600 somethin', a little over somethin' like $600 a month. How can you expect me to take care two kids and the baby, two grown, I mean, you know, adults and the small baby and myself, and pay $300 a month for rent, you know. I mean, hey! Come on!" So he went on, decide, well, OK, I see if I can make arrangements. So I had to give him my social security number, I had to go down there, sign all these papers so they just gave her $250, you know. So with $250 and my income, both our income, it's, what, $800, $850. And $850 for four people, it's no money. Especially you payin' rent, you have to pay your light and gas, food to buy.

Edin points out that in order to keep their families together welfare mothers have to supplement their monthly AFDC checks. Some acquire extra income from piecework—sewing or knitting in the home—and other jobs; others receive money from their boyfriends or from their children's fathers. In theory, welfare mothers are required to report any extra income, which would result in a reduction of their welfare checks by an equivalent amount. Since the extra income is necessary to maintain their households, this rule is usually ignored.

If the welfare mothers are still unable to make ends meet by supplementing their incomes, they frequently move in with relatives or friends. A woman from a poor West Side neighborhood commented on this situation in the UPFLS:

> They ought to build jobs, build houses or buildings where people can live. You got three or four families staying together because they can't find nowhere to stay or they can't afford where this rent is at. So everybody that can, they huddle up together. Then you have to fix it, and give an address somewhere else in order to get your check. They don't understand that the rent is so high that the only thing you can do is live with somebody. "Well, all you all living in the same house together, you all just trying to get all the money you can." They don't realize how things is.

If the option of moving in with relatives or friends is not available and if they are unable to get into subsidized housing, welfare mothers either have to break up their families or must move to a homeless shelter. For many families, a shelter provides their last hope of staying together.

Severe economic problems are not limited to welfare recipients. Working mothers with comparable incomes face, in many cases, even greater difficulty. Why? Simply because many low-wage jobs do not provide health care benefits, and most working mothers have to pay for transportation, spend more for child care, and purchase better clothing. Working mothers also have to spend more for housing because it is more difficult for them to qualify for housing subsidies. With these additional expenses, Edin found that the average low-income working mother would have to spend $317 a month more than her welfare counterpart to maintain the same standard of living. Edin states:

> These figures mean that the average mother who left welfare for full-time work would experience at least a 33 percent gap between what she could expect to earn and what she would need to earn to meet her expenses. Any profit she might gain from her work would be eaten up by the extra costs associated with leaving

welfare for a job, meaning that she would have to continue generating large amounts of outside income. However, since she would be working a full-time job she would have less available time in which to do so.

Edin's research revealed that since the working mothers could not live solely on the income from their full-time, low-wage jobs, they had to generate considerable outside income to make ends meet, including income from overtime hours or second jobs, earned income tax credits, food stamps, Social Security Insurance, and the contributions of relatives and friends.

It is not surprising, therefore, that many welfare-reliant mothers choose not to enter the formal labor market. It would not be in their best economic interest to do so. Given the economic realities, it is also not surprising that many who are working in these low-wage jobs decide to rely on or return to welfare.

"Women calculate not only how their incomes will compare with their welfare benefits, but how much they will lose in housing subsidies as well," states Edin. "For women living in subsidized housing, working means a double tax on earnings. Housing subsidies are determined on the basis of cash income. For welfare mothers, only their cash AFDC payment (and not their food stamp benefit) is used to determine their subsidy. This means that even if a mother takes a job that pays exactly what her combined AFDC and food stamp benefit would have netted her, she will receive less subsidy and thus pay more rent."

In the final analysis, a typical unskilled or semiskilled single mother is likely to make the transition from dependency to self-sufficiency only if her job provides full family health care benefits, she has minimal or no child care costs, and her other living costs are relatively low. Recognizing this problem, the state of Illinois introduced a program in late 1993 called "Work Pays." This program encourages welfare recipients to move toward self-sufficiency by allowing them to take a job and not only keep a fraction of their cash assistance but also remain eligible for food stamps, medical coverage, and child care payments as well. Still, this program is available only to those already on welfare. And although it does enable welfare recipients to accept legitimate employment without severe financial consequences, it does not address the plight of working mothers who are not on welfare. Moreover, neither it nor any other government program will enable mothers to move off welfare as long as jobs in the low-wage sector provide little overall income and do not include health insurance.

Since the idea of remaining permanently on welfare is anathema to an overwhelming majority of the mothers receiving aid, the typical AFDC recipient contemplates the following: leaving welfare for work as soon as her child care and other arrangements, including employment training, enable her to cover basic living expenses with her earnings.

One does not have to draw conclusions about accidental cultural transmission to understand the rational choices of low-skilled single women to opt for welfare given the economic constraints of low-wage employment. As stated previously, because of the very nature of their economic situations, many people in the inner city are often compelled to act in ghetto-related ways—for example, entering a period of time without a steady job or engaging in activities to obtain income that are deemed inappropriate in middle-class society. They may strongly endorse the mainstream judgments of such behavior and yet at the same time feel forced by circumstances to violate the normative expectations of the larger society. Middle-class whites and others who do not share the "Catch-22" conditions of support at the margins of society may find it easy to judge those ghetto residents who receive welfare and resort to illegitimate means of generating income.

It would be a mistake, however, to describe such behavior as purely situational. As I have stated previously, economically marginal people from stable neighborhoods who are struggling to make ends meet feel more moral pressure to act in mainstream ways than do those in high-jobless neighborhoods featuring problems of social organization and ghetto-related attitudes and behaviors. Thus, although many of the welfare mothers in the inner-city ghetto make rational and realistic choices to remain or go on welfare in light of the problems associated with low-wage employment, their decisions are made easier in two ways: the greater frequency with which similar decisions are made by other mothers in the neighborhood and the more tolerant neighborhood attitude toward welfare receipt.

The relatively bleak socioeconomic situation of inner-city black mothers probably accounts for why they have also developed some attitudes that differ from those of the other mothers. In the UPFLS,

African-American mothers in the inner city, regardless of whether they were welfare recipients, expressed far stronger opposition to the statement that the government was spending too much on welfare than did either inner-city white or Hispanic nonwelfare and welfare mothers. But, as Marta Tienda and Haya Stier argue, ethnic differences toward welfare reflect, to some extent, "perceived and actual differences in opportunities rather than different values toward welfare." When asked whether the high receipt of public assistance was because individuals refused to work or because of the shortage of "decent" jobs, 80 percent of the black mothers who had ever received AFDC—compared to two-thirds of the white and Puerto Rican mothers, and only half the Mexican mothers who had ever received AFDC—answered that it was because of the shortage of jobs.

Welfare receipt is not a desirable alternative for many of the black single mothers. As one 27-year-old welfare mother of three children from an impoverished West Side neighborhood put it, "I want to work; I do not work but I *want to work*. I don't want to just be on public aid." A 32-year-old welfare mother of five children from a South Side neighborhood who had been receiving AFDC for more than thirteen years also described her dislike of welfare:

> If I get my GED going, get me off in a training program, get me a job, make me feel a little better about myself. Tired of being on aid, tired of waiting. Can't get nothing, you know. Not being on aid, you need to get a job. My mother and father worked and took care of me, and I can do the same, work and take care of my family. Aid, you know, when you dependent on—once they start sending you this money every month, and you start depending on it, every month, like I say, it make you lazy! I used to like it, but now I'm sort of tired of it.

Although some culturally transmitted behavior is accidental, as noted in the example of role modeling, some of these behaviors can be seen as situationally adaptive since people draw those elements from their cultural repertoire that are considered relevant to their situation. In other words, the decisions on the part of inner-city mothers to prevent their families from sliding deeper into poverty by choosing welfare over low-paying work not only are rational but might be made in many cases regardless of the degree to which welfare is sanctioned in the community; but in the eyes of others in the community, welfare is seen as legitimate and, for some, even morally appropriate. These ghetto-related attitudes are part of the cultural repertoire and are used by the residents to justify and explain the prevalence of welfare receipt in the neighborhood. They have evolved over time and represent perceived and real differences in opportunities.

CHAPTER 4

The Fading Inner-City Family

As the disappearance of work has become a characteristic feature of the inner-city ghetto, so too has the disappearance of the traditional married-couple family. Only one-quarter of the black families whose children live with them in inner-city neighborhoods in Chicago are husband-wife families today, compared with three-quarters of the inner-city Mexican families, more than one-half of the white families, and nearly one-half of the Puerto Rican families (see Figure 4.1). And in census tracts with poverty rates of at least 40 percent, only 16.5 percent of the black families with coresident children are husband-wife families.

Changes in the family structure in the inner-city ghetto, although resulting in a drastic decline in husband-wife families, are part of a process that now affects all racial and ethnic groups in the United States. Nationally, the birth rate among unmarried women has recently soared. However, whites have largely accounted for this increase. Between 1980 and 1992, when the rate of births outside of marriage increased nationally by 54 percent, it rose 94 percent for whites and only 9 percent for blacks. In 1993, 27 percent of all children under the age of 18 were living with a single parent. This figure includes 57 percent of all black children, 32 percent of all Hispanic children, and 21 percent of all white children.

Although the annual increase in the number of infants born outside marriage slowed some in the 1980s, the number of children living with a single parent who *has never married* grew from 243,000 in 1960 to 3.7 million in 1983, and then to 6.3 million in 1993. As of 1993,

FIGURE 4.1

UPFLS PARENTS WITH SPOUSE AND CHILDREN IN HOUSEHOLD IN CENSUS TRACTS WITH 20% OR MORE FAMILIES IN POVERTY

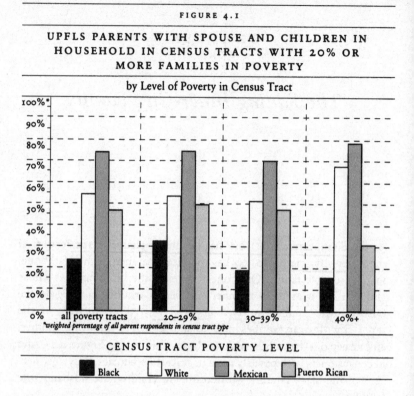

by Level of Poverty in Census Tract

*weighted percentage of all parent respondents in census tract type

CENSUS TRACT POVERTY LEVEL

■ Black   □ White   ▨ Mexican   ▨ Puerto Rican

9 percent of all children under the age of 18 were living with a never-married parent. This includes 31 percent of black children, 13 percent of Hispanic children, and 5 percent of white children.

In the African-American community, rates of marriage are positively correlated with levels of education. Better-educated black women are more likely to marry than black women with less education. These rates are reversed for white women, for whom less education correlates with higher rates of marriage. Also, the more highly educated divorced and separated African-American women are more likely to remarry than those with less education, whereas the level of education is unrelated to the question of whether divorced and separated white women remarry. The positive association between education and marriage among African-Americans is in part due to the extraordinarily low rate of marriage among less educated black Americans, many of whom are concentrated in inner-city neighborhoods.

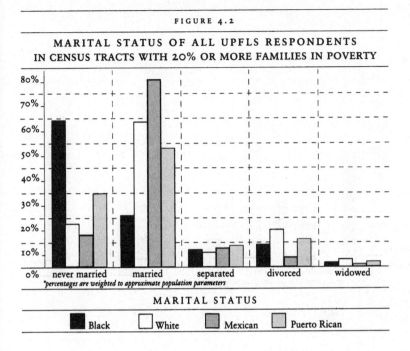

FIGURE 4.2

MARITAL STATUS OF ALL UPFLS RESPONDENTS
IN CENSUS TRACTS WITH 20% OR MORE FAMILIES IN POVERTY

percentages are weighted to approximate population parameters

MARITAL STATUS

■ Black □ White ▨ Mexican ▨ Puerto Rican

In Chicago's inner-city neighborhoods, as shown in Figure 4.2, almost 60 percent of the black adults ages 18 to 44 have never been married. Moreover, Figure 4.3 reveals that only 28 percent of the African-American parents ages 18 to 44 are currently married, compared with 75 percent of the Mexican parents, 61 percent of the white parents, and 45 percent of the Puerto Rican parents from the same age group. And of the black parents living in census tracts with rates of poverty of at least 40 percent, only 15.6 percent are married. Furthermore, 47 percent of black parents in the inner city of Chicago have never been married, compared with 14 percent of the Mexican parents, 18 percent of the white parents, and 30 percent of the Puerto Rican parents. And of the black parents living in neighborhoods with poverty rates of 40 percent or more, more than half (56 percent) have never been married.

After analyzing the Urban Poverty and Family Life Study data, Mark Testa, a member of the UPFLS research team, estimated that only 6 percent of the single inner-city expectant black fathers marry

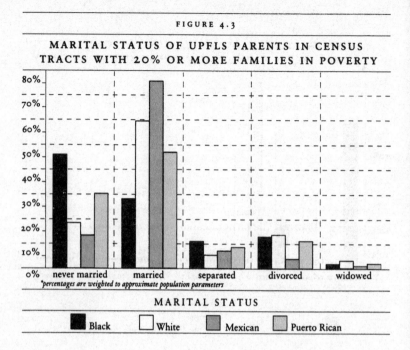

FIGURE 4.3

MARITAL STATUS OF UPFLS PARENTS IN CENSUS
TRACTS WITH 20% OR MORE FAMILIES IN POVERTY

percentages are weighted to approximate population parameters

MARITAL STATUS

■ Black   □ White   ▨ Mexican   ▨ Puerto Rican

during the prenatal period (from conception to birth)—the period popularly dubbed the "shotgun wedding" interval. Testa furthermore found, after taking class background and economic status into account, that inner-city Mexican and non-Hispanic white single fathers are respectively 2.6 and 3 times more likely to marry after the birth of their first child than are their black American counterparts. This shift away from marriage among black fathers in the inner-city neighborhoods of Chicago, although extreme, represents a historic trend across the nation.

"Black men born in the early 1940s were twice as likely as [black] men born in the late 1950s to wed at a given age, and the rate has continued to fall for the post 'baby boom' cohort," reports Testa. "With fewer black men marrying prior to their partner's pregnancy, the proportion of infants conceived in marriage has dropped over time. The result is that in spite of near constant rates of nonmarital fertility [that is, the number of births per thousand unmarried women], the out-of-wedlock birth ratio among African-Americans surged past 50 percent in the 1980s." In Chicago's inner city, single African-American men born during or immediately after World War II were more than twice as likely to marry after the conception of their child, regardless of their economic and educational background, than black men born in the late 1950s who became fathers at a similar age.

The decline of the married-parent family, not only among blacks but among all groups across the nation, has been a controversial topic featured in political debates about "family values." According to one observer,

> Ever since the growth of the one-parent family, there has been a tendency to accept it as virtually normal. Too many social commentators portray the birth of children out of wedlock as part of the "norm." What actually amounts to abandoning children, usually by the father, is becoming increasingly acceptable without penalty to anyone except to the neglected child. Too many social scientists and policymakers play down the advantages of the two-parent family; some even ridicule it as an outmoded middle-class ideal.

One reason for concern about the sharp decline in the marriage rate is that children living in one-parent families in the United States, especially those in families where the parent has never married, suffer from many more disadvantages than those in married-parent families. A study relying on longitudinal data (data collected on a specific group over a substantial period) found that the persistently poor families (defined as having family incomes below the poverty line during at least eight years in a ten-year period) in the United States tended to be headed by women, and that 31 percent of all persistently poor households were headed by nonelderly *black* women. This is a startling figure when you realize that, according to the 1990 census, African-Americans account for just over 12 percent of the entire U.S. population.

As Kathryn Edin has pointed out, "More children are poor today than at any time since before Lyndon Johnson's War on Poverty began three decades ago. Children living in households headed by single mothers are America's poorest demographic group. This fact is not surprising, since single mothers who work seldom earn enough to bring their families out of poverty and most cannot get child support, medical benefits, housing subsidies, or cheap child care."

In 1993, whereas the median income of married-couple families was $43,578, the median income of single-parent families in which the mother was divorced was $17,014. In families where the mother had never been married, the median income was only $9,272. Likewise, whereas only one-tenth of children in husband-wife families were living below the poverty line, over one-third of those living with divorced mothers and two-thirds living with mothers who had never married were classified as poor. Finally, longitudinal studies also reveal that mothers who have never been married receive AFDC for a significantly longer period than do separated or divorced mothers.

In addition to the strong links between single parenthood and poverty and welfare receipt, the available research indicates that children from mother-only households are more likely to be school dropouts, to receive lower earnings in young adulthood, and to be recipients of welfare. Moreover, the daughters who grew up in black single-parent households are more likely to establish single-parent households themselves than are those who were raised in married-couple households. Furthermore, single-parent households tend to exert less control over the behavior of adolescents. Reviewing their research findings, Sanford Dornbusch and his colleagues concluded:

> We do not know whether it is lack of surveillance, lack of appropriate teaching, or lack of social support for the single parent that leads to a reduction in control of adolescents, especially males, in mother-only families. But we do know, and perhaps this has broad implications, that the presence of any other adult in a mother-only household brings control levels closer to those found in two-parent families—nontraditional groupings that can do the job of parenting—and that the raising of adolescents is not a task that can easily be borne by a mother alone.

While nonmarital birth statistics provide some sense of the extent to which mothers are parenting alone, UPFLS data indicate that the decline in ongoing relationships among inner-city parents is substantially less than nonmarital birth statistics suggest. First, a proportion of the parents who have nonmarital births marry following the birth (a postpartum marriage). Of the UPFLS respondents whose first child was born out of wedlock, nearly one-third had married by the time they were interviewed. Second, the decrease in the proportion of married parents over the past thirty years has been partially offset by an increase in the proportion of parents who are unmarried but maintain a relationship, either as cohabiting or visiting partners. Whereas the percentage of parents who were married at the time of their first child's birth declines by 61 percent when parents born in the 1940s are compared to parents born in the 1960s, the percentage of parents who maintain a relationship declines by only 27 percent when the same age groups are compared.

However, despite the extent to which cohabiting- and visiting-partner relationships offset the decline in married-couple families, black mothers in the inner city are far more likely than mothers of other ethnic groups to reside in households where no other adults are present and therefore to face greater challenges in raising children. Whereas 44 percent of the black women living with their children in Chicago's inner city have no other adults in the household, only 6.5 percent of comparable Mexican women are the sole adults in their household. Also, inner-city black women whose children are under 12 years of age are eight times more likely than comparable Mexican women to live in a single-adult household.

Analyzing data from the UPFLS, Martha Van Haitsma found that "network differences translate into childcare differences. Mexican women with young children are significantly more likely than their black counterparts to have regular childcare provided by a friend or relative." The high proportion of two-adult Mexican households with working fathers, particularly among immigrant Mexicans, may be an important factor in the mother's greater access to network child care.

Also, the high percentage of black mothers who live with young children in a single-adult household is associated with problems of labor-force attachment. If a single mother in Chicago's inner city lives in a coresidential household—that is, a household that includes at least one other adult—and receives informal child support, she significantly improves her chances of entering the labor force. Among the inner-city mothers who were not receiving AFDC, those who lived in a coresidential household and received informal child care had a very high (90 percent) probability of labor-force activity. On the other hand, those who maintain sole-adult households and did not receive informal child care had a much reduced (60 percent) probability of working. Of the 12 percent of inner-city women on AFDC who candidly reported that they worked at least part-time—probably in the informal economy—those who lived in a coresidential household and received informal child care were more than five times as likely to work as were those who lived in single households and did not receive informal child care.

There are many factors involved in the precipitous decline in marriage rates and the sharp rise in single-parent families. The explanation most often heard in the public debate associates the increase of out-of-wedlock births and single-parent families with welfare. Indeed, it is widely assumed among the general public and reflected in the many recent proposals for welfare reform that a direct causal connection exists between the level of welfare benefits and the likelihood that a young woman will bear a child outside marriage.

However, the *scientific* evidence offers little support for the claim that AFDC benefits play a significant role in promoting out-of-wedlock births. Research examining the association between the generosity of welfare benefits and out-of-wedlock childbearing and teen pregnancy indicates that benefit levels have no significant effect on the likelihood that African-American girls and women will have children outside marriage; likewise, welfare rates have either no significant effect or only a small effect on the odds that whites will have children outside marriage. There is no evidence to suggest that welfare is a major factor in the rise of childbearing outside marriage.

The rate of out-of-wedlock teen childbearing has nearly doubled since 1975, despite the fact that during the period the real value of AFDC, food stamps, and Medicaid had fallen, after adjusting for inflation. And the smallest increases in the number of out-of-wedlock births have not occurred in states that have had the largest declines in the inflation-adjusted value of AFDC benefits. Indeed, while the real value of cash welfare benefits has plummeted over the past twenty years, not only has out-of-wedlock childbearing increased, but postpartum marriages (marriages following the birth of a couple's child) have decreased as well.

In *The Truly Disadvantaged*, I argued that the sharp increase in black male joblessness since 1970 accounts in large measure for the rise in the rate of single-parent families, and that since jobless rates are highest in the inner-city ghetto, rates of single parenthood are also highest there. Still, recent research on the relationship between employment on the one hand and rates of marriage and single parenthood on the other are mixed. Some studies reveal that a man's employment status is not related to the likelihood of his conceiving a child out of wedlock. For example, one national study based on state-level data (data gathered state by state) reported that there was no relationship between the ratio of single employed men to single women of the same race and the probability that a woman who had never been married will become a mother by age 19.

However, if the focus of research shifts from the birth of a child out of wedlock to the probability of the parents' subsequent entry into marriage, the employment status of the male becomes an important factor. Data from the UPFLS reveal that although the employment status of the man is unrelated to the risk of his becoming an unmarried father, as we shall soon see, for the younger black father it is strongly associated with his entry into marriage after the birth of his child.

A study by Andrew Sum and Neal Fogg based on national-level data revealed a very strong relationship between the annual earnings of young black men and their marital status. They found that whereas more than half of young black men (ages 18 to 29) with annual earnings of over $20,000 were married in 1987, the marriage ratio decreased steadily for those earning less than that—39 percent for those earning between $15,000 and $20,000, 29 percent for those earning between $10,000 and $15,000, 7 percent for those earning between $1,000 and $5,000, and only 3 percent for those with no reported earnings.

Although there is a strong association between rates of marriage and both employment status and earnings at any given point in time, national longitudinal studies suggest that these factors account for a relatively small proportion of the overall *decline* in marriage among African-Americans. Christopher Jencks points out that the decline in the proportion of African-American men who were married and living with their wives was almost as large among those who had worked throughout the previous years as among black men in general. Also, Robert Mare and Christopher Winship found only modest support for the hypothesis linking the sharp rise in poor single-parent families to the declining employment status of young black men. After examining two national data sets, they concluded that changes in the employment of young African-American men account for approximately one-fifth of the decline in their rates of marriage since 1960. A study by Saul Hoffman, Greg Duncan, and Ronald Mincy reported that about one-quarter of the decline in marriage among young African-American women in their mid-20s can be accounted for by the decline in income of young black men. Finally, David Ellwood and David Rodda found no significant change in the relative impact of work and earnings on marriages between the two periods they observed—1967–71 and 1980–86.

These studies, however, are based on national data. How much of the decline in the black marriage rate in the inner city can be accounted for by the increasing joblessness among black males? The UPFLS is not a longitudinal study, but it did collect retrospective (or life-history) marriage and employment data that allow the estimation of trends over time. An analysis of respondents' retrospective data comparing the employment experiences of different age groups (cohorts) reveals that marriage rates have dropped much more sharply among jobless black fathers than among employed black fathers. But this drop applies only to the younger cohorts. Mark Testa and Marilyn Krogh found that while employment had no significant effect on the likelihood that UPFLS single fathers ages 32 to 44 would eventually marry, it increased the likelihood of legitimation by eight times for those single fathers ages 18 to 31.

Testa and Krogh analyzed findings from the UPFLS survey. Although most of the people in the large UPFLS survey live above the officially designated poverty line and although the sample includes a number of middle-class families, these findings should only be generalized to the inner city and not to the urban population as a whole. In other words, the sample is drawn from urban poverty or inner-city neighborhoods. In recent years these neighborhoods have experienced a significant outmigration of working- and middle-class families. "Since the likelihood of out-migration most probably increases with age," state Testa and Krogh, "black men who were employed when they got married may be systematically underrepresented among the older cohorts in [the UPFLS] sample. Consequently, our estimate of the employment effect for the older cohorts . . . could be misleadingly small." If the outmigration of older cohorts results in a much stronger association between joblessness and the decline in marriage rates among the younger cohorts in the inner city, it is a phenomenon unique to the inner city. Still, even though the joblessness among black men is a significant factor in their delayed entry into marriage and in the decreasing rates of marriage after a child has been born, it can account for only a proportion of the decline in marriages in the inner city, including postpartum marriages.

In the inner-city ghetto community, not only have the norms in support of husband-wife families and against out-of-wedlock births become weaker as a result of the general trend in society, they have also gradually disintegrated because of worsening economic conditions in the inner city, including the sharp rise in joblessness and declining real incomes. The weakening of social sanctions has had the most severe impact on the jobless, but it has also affected many who are employed, especially those whose jobs are not very secure or stable and/or those who are experiencing declining real incomes. The decreasing marriage rates among inner-city black parents is a function not simply of increased economic marginality or of changing attitudes toward sex and marriage, but of, as Testa emphasizes, "the interaction between material and cultural constraints." The point that should be emphasized is that "variation in the moral evaluations that different sociocultural groups attach to premarital sex, out-of-wedlock pregnancy, and nonmarital parenthood affects the importance of economic considerations in a person's decision to marry." The weaker the norms against premarital sex, out-of-wedlock pregnancy, and nonmarital parenthood, the more that economic considerations affect decisions to marry.

Some of the differences between inner-city black, white, and Hispanic nonmarital parenthood can be accounted for by the higher levels of joblessness and concentrated poverty in the black community. But even when ethnic-group variations in work activity, poverty concentration, education, and family structure are taken into account, significant differences between inner-city blacks and the other groups, especially the Mexicans, still remain. Accordingly, it is reasonable to consider whether cultural variables should be included among the interrelated factors that account for these differences.

A brief comparison between inner-city blacks and inner-city Mexicans (many of whom are immigrants) in terms of family perspectives provides some evidence for these cultural differences. Richard Taub, another member of the UPFLS research team, points out that marriage and family ties are subjects of "frequent and intense discourse" among Mexican immigrants. Mexicans come to the United States with a clear conception of a traditional family unit that features men as breadwinners. Although extramarital affairs by men are tolerated, "a pregnant, unmarried woman is a source of opprobrium, anguish, or great concern." Pressure is applied by the kin of both parents to enter into marriage.

The family norms and behavior in inner-city black neighborhoods stand in sharp contrast. The husband-wife relationship is only weakly supported. UPFLS ethnographic data reveal that the relationships between inner-city black men and women, whether in a marital or nonmarital situation, are often fractious and antagonistic. Inner-city black women routinely say that they distrust men and feel strongly that black men lack dedication to their families. They argue that black males are hopeless as either husbands or fathers and that more of their time is spent on the streets than at home. As one woman, an unmarried welfare mother of three children from a new poverty neighborhood on the South Side, put it, "And most of the men don't have jobs . . . but if things were equal it really wouldn't matter, would it? I mean OK if you're together and everything, you split, whatever. . . . The way it is, if they can get jobs then they go and get drunk or whatever." When asked if that is why she did not get married, she stated:

> I don't think I want to get married but then . . . see you're supposed to stick to that one and that's a fantasy. You know, stick with one for the rest of your life. I've never met many people like that, have you? . . . If they're married and have kids. Them kids come in and it seems like the men get jealous 'cause you're spending your time on them. OK, they can get up and go anytime. A woman has to stick there all the time 'cause she got them kids behind their backs.

The women in the inner city tend to believe that black men get involved with women mainly to obtain sex or money, and that once these goals are achieved women are usually discarded. For example, one woman from a poor neighborhood on the West Side of Chicago was asked if she still saw the father of her child. She stated: "He left before the baby was born, I was about two weeks pregnant and he said that he didn't want to be bothered and I said 'Fine—you go your way and I go mine.' " Another woman—a 21-year-old part-time employed, unmarried mother of two children who also lives in a poor neighborhood on the West Side—voiced this general complaint about men.

> Some mens can't speak to one woman. Some man might try to force theyself to do that, then again you really can't believe it so a, a female have to be careful, really careful. She have to learn really if this man really care about her, if he gonna do what he really does, what he say he, what he plan on doing, you know. So, you know—'cause they be out to get one thing, nothing but sex from a female.

There is a widespread feeling among women in the inner city that black males have relationships with more than one female at a time. And since some young men leave their girlfriends as soon as they become pregnant, it is not uncommon to find a black male who has fathered at least three children by three separate women. Despite the problematic state of these relationships, sex among inner-city black teenagers is widely practiced. In the ethnographic phase of the research, UPFLS respondents reported that sex is an integral and expected aspect of the male/female relationship. Males especially feel peer pressure to be sexually active. They said that the members of their peer networks brag about their sexual encounters and that they feel obligated to reveal their own sexual exploits. Little consideration is given to the implications or consequences of sexual matters for the longer-term relationship.

Whereas women blame men for the poor gender relations, men maintain that it is the women who are troublesome. The men complain that it is not easy to deal with the women's suspicions about their behavior and intentions. They also feel that women are especially attracted by material resources and that it is therefore difficult to find women who are supportive of partners with a low living standard.

These antagonistic relationships influence the views of both men and women about marriage. The ethnographic data reveal especially weak support for the institution of marriage in the inner-city ghetto among black men. For many of the men, marriage ties a man down and results in a loss of freedom. "Marriage. You can't have it, you can't do the things you wanna do then," stated an unemployed 21-year-old unmarried father of one child from a poor neighborhood on the West Side.

> She [the spouse] might want you in at a certain time and all, all this. You can't hang out when you married, you know. You married to be with her. . . . I like, you know, spending my time, half the time with my friends and then come in when I want to. . . . In my book it [marriage] is something that is bad. Like, like fighting, divorce.

A 27-year-old unmarried, employed father of one child makes a similar point. Marriage "cuts down a lot of things you used to do, like, staying out late, stuff like that, hanging with the fellows all day, like, now you can do what the hell you want to do, now, when you—when you married, got a family, it cuts a lot of that stuff off."

The men in the inner city generally feel that it is much better for all parties to remain in a nonmarital relationship until the relationship dissolves rather than to get married and then have to get a divorce. A 25-year-old unmarried West Side resident, the father of one child, expressed this view:

> Well, most black men feel now, why get married when you got six to seven womens to one guy, really. You know, 'cause there's more women out here mostly than men. 'Cause most dudes around here are killing each other like fools over drugs or all this other stuff. And if you're not that bad looking of a guy, you know, and you know a lot of women like you, why get married when you can play the field the way they want to do, you know?

An 18-year-old senior in high school and father of a five-week-old son described why he was not ready for marriage:

> I don't think that marriage is for me right now but I think that there is a certain age where I think that I would want to get mar-

ried to somebody that I really love. I say that I would be about 25 years old but right now I don't have it on my conscience. I'm always farsighted for the future but not marriage, but like I said at a certain age I will probably decide on doing that.

No, that is not on my conscience right now. Also of people, they tell me don't get married because once you stay with that one woman you probably start having problems. I know a lot of boyfriends and girlfriends, you know they have problems but then when they decide to get married I don't think things will turn out right. I just feel that I have a child by her and I am going to go ahead and support that child but thinking about marriage I ain't got it on my conscience right now.

A 25-year-old part-time worker with a 7-year-old daughter explained why he'd avoided marriage following the child's birth:

For years I have been observing other marriages. They all have been built on the wrong foundation. The husband misuses the family or neglects the family or the wife do the same, ah, they just missing a lot of important elements. I had made a commitment to marry her really out of people pleasing. My mom wanted me to do it; her parents wanted us to do it. Taking their suggestions and opinions about the situation over my own and [I] am a grown man. These decisions is for me to make and I realized that they were going to go to expect it to last for 20, 40 years so I evaluated my feelings and came to the honest conclusion that was not right for me, right. And I made the decision that the baby, that I could be a father without necessarily living there.

Others talk about avoiding or delaying marriage for economic reasons. "It made no sense to just get married because we have a baby like other people . . . do," argued an 18-year-old unmarried father of a two-week-old son. "If I couldn't take care of my family, why get married?"

Thus, marriage is "not in the forefront of the men's minds." The dominant attitude among the young single black fathers in the UPFLS is, "I'll get married in the future when I am no longer having fun and when I get a job or a better job." Marriage limits their ability to date other women or "hang out" with the boys. The ethnographic data

clearly reveal that the birth of a child does not create a sense of obligation to marry, and that most young fathers feel little pressure, from
either their family or their partner's family, to marry. Having children
and getting married are not usually connected.

There is very little research on changing norms and sanctions regarding the family in the inner city, but there does seem to be some indication that the norms have changed. In a study of fathering in the
inner city based on a series of interviews with the same respondents
over several years, Frank Furstenberg notes:

> I have no way of knowing for sure, but I think that families now
> exert less pressure on men to remain involved than they once did.
> I found no instance, for example, of families urging their children
> to marry or even to live together as was common when I was
> studying the parents of my informants in the mid-1960s.

Yet the data from the UPFLS indicate that the young men do "feel
some obligation to contribute something to support their children."
The level of financial support is low and often erratic, however, varying from occasionally buying disposable diapers to regularly contributing several hundred dollars a month. As Frank Furstenberg has
pointed out,

> When ill-timed pregnancies occur in unstable partnerships to
> men who have few material resources for managing unplanned
> parenthood, they challenge, to say the least, the commitment of
> young fathers. Fatherhood occurs to men who often have a per-
> sonal biography that poorly equips them to act on their inten-
> tions, even when their intentions to do for their children are
> strongly felt. And fatherhood [in the inner city] takes place in a
> culture where the gap between good intentions and good perfor-
> mance is large and widely recognized.

Black women in the inner city are more interested in marriage, but
their expectations for matrimony are low and they do not hold the
men they encounter in very high regard. The women feel that even if
they do marry, it is unlikely to be successful. They maintain that husbands are not as dedicated to their wives as in previous generations

and that they would not be able to depend on their husbands even if they did get married.

A young welfare mother of three children from a new poverty neighborhood on the West Side of Chicago made the following point:

Well, to my recollection, twenty years ago I was only seven years [old] but ... twenty years ago, men, if they got a woman pregnant, that if they didn't marry her, they stood by her and took care of the child. And nowadays, when a man makes you pregnant, they're goin' off and leave you and think nothing of it. And also ... also, uh, twenty years ago, I find that there were more people getting married and when they got married they were staying together. I found that with a lot of couples nowadays, that when they get married they're so quick to get a divorce. I've thought about marriage myself many times, uh, but nowadays, it seems to me that when it comes to marriage, it just doesn't mean anything to people. At least the men that I talk to. And also, twenty years ago, I think families were closer [police siren]. I found now families are drifting apart, they're not as loving as they were twenty years ago. I find with a lot of families now, they're quicker to hurt you than to help you.

The view that welfare enables some women to avoid marriage was expressed by a 31-year-old divorcée and welfare mother of four children from a South Side new poverty neighborhood:

I still say I wouldn't get married. You know, like some people say, there's a lot of elderly people that say, "It's best to get a child a father's name, it's best to do that." But I think that by having public aid, and if you do happen to wind up with a lot of kids, until you're able to get on your feet, its better not to get married. Because the actual status between an unmarried woman on welfare and an unmarried man on welfare is a lot different when they have kids or have no kids. If you have kids, you say, "OK, he's going to do it better for me anyway," so we get married, change the names of the kids. And then, "I'm not working, thems not my kids." If you're not married to the person you say, "They're not yours? Hit the door then!" But if you're married to them, you say, "Hit the door, please?" You know, you start nagging and they say,

"I'm not going nowhere." So you say, "Well, I'll put you out." But you can't put them out, can't do nothing. You're stuck with them just like all the other people stuck with their marriage and stuff. I think it's best, once you get a family started, and you're not as educated as well as you wanted to be, it's not good to get married. That's one thing I would never do again is get married. . . . I think it's best not to get married. Unless you're pretty sure that person's going to take care of you.

Finally, a 27-year-old single woman (who is childless, has four years of college, works as a customer service representative, and lives in a new poverty neighborhood on the South Side) talked about changes in the family structure in relation to her own personal situation. She stated that there has been

a definite change in the family structure as far as the mother and father being together. The way things are going now you'll find more single women having kids, but not totally dependent on the guy being there. I know there's a change in friends of mine who have kids, the father isn't there with them. They're not so totally dependent on him anymore. They're out there doing for themselves. . . . You have to make it one way or another, and you can't depend on him to come through or him to be there. And a lot of them are searching for someone to be with, but if [he] comes he does and if he doesn't. Because I always say by the time I'm thirty, if I'm not married, I know I'll still have me a child. But I wouldn't be so hung up on the idea of having somebody be there. I probably wouldn't have a child by anyone I was seeing or anything. I'd probably go through a sperm bank. I think financially I could do it, but I would need help as far as babysitting and stuff.

The ethnographic data reveal that both inner-city black males and females believe that since most marriages will eventually break up and since marriages no longer represent meaningful relationships, it is better to avoid the entanglements of wedlock altogether. For many single mothers in the inner city, nonmarriage makes more sense as a family formation strategy than does marriage. Single mothers who perceive the fathers of their children as unreliable or as having limited financial means will often—rationally—choose single parenthood. From the point of view of day-to-day survival, single parenthood reduces the emotional burden and shields them from the type of exploitation that often accompanies the sharing of both living arrangements and limited resources. Men and women are extremely suspicious of each other, and their concerns range from the degree of financial commitment to fidelity. For all these reasons, they often state they do not want to get married until they are sure it is going to work out.

Changing patterns of family formation are not limited to the inner-city black community. As revealed earlier in this chapter, they are part of a current societal trend. The commitment to traditional husband-wife families and the stigma associated with out-of-wedlock births, separation, and divorce have waned significantly in the United States. "The labor market conditions which sustained the 'male breadwinner' family have all but vanished." This has gradually led to the creation of a new set of orientations that places less value on marriage and rejects the dominance of men as a standard for a successful husband-wife family.

The major argument advanced in this section is that inner-city black single parents, unlike their Mexican-immigrant counterparts, feel little pressure to commit to a marriage. They emphasize the loss of freedom, the lack of dedication to one's partner, and the importance of having secure jobs and financial security before seriously considering matrimony. They have little reason to contemplate seriously the consequences of single parenthood because their prospects for social and economic mobility are severely limited whether they are married or not. These responses represent a linkage between new structural realities, changing norms, and evolving cultural patterns. The new structural realities may be seen in the diminishing employment opportunities for low-skilled workers. The decline of the mass production system and the rise of new jobs in the highly technological global economy requiring training and education have severely weakened the labor-force attachment among inner-city workers.

As employment prospects recede, the foundation for stable relationships becomes weaker over time. More permanent relationships such as marriage give way to temporary liaisons that result in broken relationships, out-of-wedlock pregnancies and births, and, to a lesser extent, separation and divorce. The changing norms concerning marriage in the larger society reinforce the movement toward temporary liaisons in the inner city, and therefore economic considerations in marital decisions take on even greater weight. The evolving cultural patterns may be seen in the sharing of negative outlooks toward marriage and toward the relationships between males and females in the inner city, outlooks that are developed in and influenced by an environment plagued by persistent joblessness. This combination of factors has increased out-of-wedlock births, weakened the family structure, expanded the welfare rolls, and, as a result, caused poor inner-city blacks to be even more disconnected from the job market and discouraged about their role in the labor force.

The intensity of the commitment to the marital bond among Mexican immigrants will very likely decline the longer they remain in the United States and are exposed to U.S. norms, patterns of behavior, and changing opportunity structures for men and women. Nonetheless, cultural arrangements reflect structural realities. In comparison with African-Americans in the inner city, Mexican immigrants have a stronger attachment to the labor force, as well as stronger households, networks, and neighborhoods. Therefore, as long as these differences exist, attitudes toward the family and family formation among inner-city blacks and Mexican immigrants will contrast noticeably.

The complex interaction between social constraints and cultural attitudes and behavior over time has not only weakened the inner-city black family structure, it has also reduced the family's effectiveness in socializing children and preparing them for future participation in society. Weak families do not prepare youngsters for the labor market. And this is even more true in neighborhoods where family management (that is, the steps taken by parents to supervise and control the behavior of their children) is undermined rather than reinforced by neighborhood influences.

For example, a youngster who grows up in a family with a steady breadwinner and in a neighborhood in which most of the adults are employed will tend to develop some of the disciplined habits associated with stable or steady employment—habits that are reflected in the behavior of his or her parents and of other neighborhood adults. These might include attachment to a routine, a recognition of the hierarchy found in most work situations, a sense of personal efficacy attained through the routine management of financial affairs, endorsement of a system of personal and material rewards associated with dependability and responsibility, and so on. Accordingly, when this youngster enters the labor market, he or she will have a distinct advantage over the youngsters who grow up in households without a steady breadwinner and in neighborhoods that are not organized around work—in other words, in a milieu in which one is more exposed to the less disciplined habits associated with casual or infrequent work.

With the sharp recent rise of solo-parent families, black children who live in inner-city households are less likely to be socialized in a work environment for two main reasons. Their mothers, saddled with child care responsibilities, can prevent a slide deeper into poverty by accepting welfare over low-wage employment, especially if such employment is not covered by health insurance. Their fathers, removed from family responsibilities and obligations, are more likely to respond to restricted employment opportunities by becoming idle, which further weakens their influence in the household and reduces their contact with the family.

In communities where the young people have little reason to believe that they have a promising future—including the prospects of stable employment and stable marriages—the absence of strong normative pressure to resolve out-of-wedlock pregnancies through marriage has resulted in an explosion of single-parent families. In such communities, adolescents and young adults are more likely to engage in behavior that jeopardizes their chances for social and economic mobility. For example, the teenagers most likely to bear a child are those with the least to lose. "Young people who are raised with a sense of opportunity and are able realistically to picture a better life are often successful in avoiding the draw of the street culture," notes Elijah Anderson. "For girls, the belief that they can become successful in the wider community prevails over the lure of becoming somebody by having a prize baby at age fifteen." But far too few girls in the inner-city ghetto can realize such dreams. For them, having a baby proves that they are attractive to "desirable (good-looking) men. Such recognition from peers, along with the status of grown woman, which accrues to her upon becoming a mother, is often the most she hopes for."

A 30-year-old welfare mother of two children from an impoverished South Side neighborhood of Chicago put it this way: "A lot of them is having babies 'cause they ain't got nothing better to do. Now I have one 13 and one 8 years old. I had mine when I was 16 years old. I had mine 'cause I was curious. I wanted to see what it was like."

Thirty years ago, Kenneth B. Clark pinpointed this problem in distinguishing the way that poor black ghetto residents and those of the black middle class approach the issue of sex. Clark pointed out that the attitude toward sex among black middle-class families is vastly different from that among the ghetto poor. For the middle-class African-American girl, like her middle-class white counterpart, sex is tied to aspirations and status. "She wants to make a good marriage . . . and the motivation to avoid illegitimate pregnancy is great." On the other hand, the young people in the inner-city ghetto, involved in tentative and sporadic relationships, pursue acceptance, love, and affection more desperately than young people in other neighborhoods. For many, person-to-person relationships compensate for society's rejection. The boy and girl in the inner-city ghetto are "forced to be quite elemental in their demands, and sex becomes more important for them than even they realize," stated Clark. "They act in a cavalier fashion about their affairs, trying to seem casual and cool, but it is clear nonetheless that they are dominated by the complexity of their needs."

Neither the girl nor the boy in the ghetto has any illusions. Realistic about the nature of her situation, the girl does not expect to hold on to the boy. "Sex is important to her but it is not, as in middle-class society, a symbol of status, to be used to rise into a better family class or a higher income bracket." Rather, sex is used to gain personal affirmation. "She is desired and that is almost enough." If the relationship results in an out-of-wedlock birth, the child's acceptance is unambiguous. An illegitimate child in the ghetto is not stigmatized. There is no ultimate disgrace, no demand for abortion, no pressure to give up the child to an adoption agency that one found in the sixties in more advantaged neighborhoods. The stigma of illegitimacy in the middle class derives from personal and family aspirations. The girl from a poor inner-city ghetto family, however, only sacrifices a few of her already limited options by having a child out of wedlock. As Clark put it, "She is not going to make a 'better marriage' or improve her economic and social status either way. On the contrary, a child is a symbol of the fact that she is a woman, and she may gain from having something of her own." Likewise, the boy who fathers a child out of wedlock has little to lose because his prospects for social and economic mobility are bleak or nonexistent. Reflecting on the prevalence of births outside marriage in the ghetto, Clark stated:

> Illegitimacy in the ghetto cannot be understood or dealt with in terms of punitive hostility, as in the suggestion that unwed mothers be denied welfare if illegitimacy is repeated. Such approaches obscure, with empty and at times hypocritical moralizing, the desperate yearning of the young for acceptance and identity, the need to be meaningful to someone else even for a moment without implication of a pledge of undying fealty and foreverness. If, when the girl becomes pregnant, the boy deserts or refuses to marry her, it is often because neither can sustain an intimate relationship; both seem incapable of the tenderness that continues beyond immediate gratification. Both may have a realistic, if unconscious, acceptance of the fact that nothing else is possible; to expect—to ask—for more would be to open oneself to the inevitable rejections, hurts, and frustrations.

Kenneth Clark's thirty-year-old, insightful analysis of the relationship between sex and social status is perhaps even more apt today. What is apparent is that many of the problems connected with male-female relationships in the ghetto have deepened in the new poverty neighborhoods. Concepts that are now being discussed to explain ghetto experiences, such as "social isolation," certainly apply to the earlier descriptions of inner-city life, including male-female sexual relationships, detailed in Clark's *Dark Ghetto*. What has changed is that ghetto neighborhoods in large central cities like New York and Chicago have much higher rates of joblessness because of shifts in the broader economy. Also, the impact of joblessness on the neighborhood is much greater because there is a smaller proportion of nonpoor families to absorb or cushion the economic shock. Since 1970, the combination of economic change and the departure of many working- and middle-class families has sharply increased joblessness and problems of social organization in the inner-city ghetto, problems that exacerbate the already tenuous relations between the sexes that Clark so aptly describes.

What remains to be addressed is the question of how the interpretation of these environmental influences by mainstream society affects hiring decisions, decisions that can reinforce or strengthen the economic marginality of inner-city blacks, including their high rate of joblessness.

CHAPTER 5

The Meaning and Significance of Race: Employers and Inner-City Workers

Blacks reside in neighborhoods and are engaged in social networks and households that are less conducive to employment than those of other ethnic and racial groups in the inner city. In the eyes of employers in metropolitan Chicago, these differences render inner-city blacks less desirable as workers, and therefore many are reluctant to hire them. The degree to which this perception is based on racial bias or represents an objective assessment of worker qualifications is not easy to determine. Although empirical studies on race and employer attitudes are limited, the available research does suggest that African-Americans, more than any other major racial or ethnic group, face negative employer perceptions about their qualifications and their work ethic.

The Urban Poverty and Family Life Study's survey of a representative sample of Chicago-area employers (see Appendix B) indicates that many consider inner-city workers—especially young black males—to be uneducated, unstable, uncooperative, and dishonest. Furthermore, racial stereotyping is greater among employers with lower proportions of blacks in their workforce—especially blue-collar employers, who tend to stress the importance of qualities, such as work attitudes, that are difficult to measure in a job interview.

The survey featured face-to-face interviews with employers representing 179 firms in the city of Chicago and in surrounding Cook County that provided entry-level jobs. The sample is representative of the distribution of employment by industry and firm size in the county. The survey included a number of open-ended questions concerning employer perceptions of inner-city workers that yielded views concerning job skills, basic skills, work ethic, dependability, attitudes, and interpersonal skills. Of the 170 employers who provided comments on one or more of these traits, 126 (or 74 percent) expressed views of innercity blacks that were coded as "negative"—that is, they expressed views (whether in terms of environmental or neighborhood influences, family influences, or personal characteristics) asserting that inner-city black workers—especially black males—bring to the workplace traits, including level of training and education, that negatively affect their job performance.

The chairman of a car transport company, when asked if there were differences in the work ethic of whites, blacks, and Hispanics, responded with great certainty:

> Definitely! I don't think, I know: I've seen it over a period of 30 years. I have it right in here. Basically, the Oriental is much more aggressive and intelligent and studious than the Hispanic. The Hispanics, except Cubans of course, they have the work ethnic [sic]. The Hispanics are mañana, mañana, mañana—tomorrow, tomorrow, tomorrow.
>
> Interviewer: You mentioned the case of native-born blacks.
> Respondent: They're the laziest of the bunch.
> Interviewer: That would relate to your earlier remarks about dependability. What is the reason for that?
> Respondent: The parents are that way so, what the hell, they didn't have a role model to copy, that's part of it.

The personnel manager of a suburban bakery stated: "We have some problems with blacks. . . . I find that the blacks aren't as hard workers as the Hispanics and—or the Italian or whatever. Their ethic is much different where they have more of the pride. The black kind of has a, you-owe-me kind of an attitude." According to another employer, the general manager of an inner-city hotel,

> I hate to admit it, yes. I see far more blacks thinking the employer has the obligation to give him a check for doing nothing. There are some whites that think that way, but, far more blacks. Not so

much the Hispanics. It even aggravates my black housekeeping supervisor. Why they think they're going to come in here and get a check for sitting around God only knows.

Interviewer: Do you think the whites' work ethic has changed?

Respondent: Yeah. In the last ten years, you know. I'd say some of the black attitude is rubbing off on them, that's what I'd say.

A manufacturer introduced a class distinction with this blunt assertion about the work ethic among blacks: "The black work ethic. There's no work ethic. At least at the unskilled. I'm sure with the skilled . . . as you go up, it's a lot different." A more nuanced discussion of the work ethic among blacks in terms of economic class status was provided by the director of an inner-city human resources firm:

The question is, Is there a difference in the work ethic? . . . I see a tremendous amount of difference in the work ethics of the individuals who come out of different income groups . . . and that's where the difference is and if a black individual we're talking about comes out of an income group of, uh . . . you know, middle class, successful situation, I think the work ethic is probably exactly what it is for a white person coming out of the same kind of background. The reality, of course, is that there are many, many, many more black persons that come out of the other kind of milieu, but I don't know whether I'm begging the question or not. I really don't think it's a racial thing.

If some employers view the work ethic of inner-city poor blacks as problematic, many also express concerns about their honesty, cultural attitudes, and dependability—traits that are frequently associated with the neighborhoods in which they live. A suburban retail drugstore manager expressed his reluctance to hire someone from a poor inner-city neighborhood. "You'd be afraid they're going to steal from you," he stated. "They grow up that way [laughs]. They grow up dishonest and I guess you'd feel like, geez, how are they going to be honest here?" Concerns about theft prompted a suburban employer at an electrical services firm to offer this unique explanation of why he would not hire inner-city ghetto residents.

If you're in a white neighborhood . . . and you have a manufacturing firm and a ghetto person comes there to apply, it doesn't make
any difference what color his skin is . . . if you know that's where
he's from you know several things. One is that if you give him a
job there, he's going to be unbelievably pressured to give information to his peer group in the ghetto . . . about the security system, the comings and goings of what's of value there that we
could rip off. He's not a crook. He wants no part of it. But he lives
in an area where he may be physically or in danger of his life if he
doesn't provide the information to the people that live around
him. As a manager, I know that. And I'm not going to hire him
because of that. I'm not discriminating against him because he's
black, I'm discriminating against him because he has a problem
that he's going to bring to me. Now the fact that he is black and it
happens that the people around him are black is only coinciden-
tal. In Warsaw they were Jews. They had the same problem.

The president of an inner-city manufacturing firm expressed a different concern about employing residents from certain inner-city
neighborhoods.

If somebody gave me their address, uh, Cabrini Green, I might
unavoidably have some concerns.
    Interviewer: What would your concerns be?
    Respondent: That the poor guy probably would be frequently
unable to get to work and that . . . I probably would watch him
more carefully even if it wasn't fair, than I would with somebody
else. I know what I should do, though, is recognize that here's a
guy that is trying to get out of his situation and probably will
work harder than somebody else who's already out of there and
he might be the best one around here. But I, I think I would have
to struggle accepting that premise at the beginning.

Questions about the employment woes of blacks sometimes involved assumptions about cultural and family influences in the inner
city. One employer asserted that "part of the culture that is dented in
their minds [is] that the best thing to do is just go on to welfare and
have the state support them"; another argued that blacks in the poorer
neighborhoods are "culturally not prepared to work"; and a vice pres-

ident of an inner-city health service firm related the high jobless rate in the inner city to the disproportionate number of families that have weak employment histories:

> I think it depends on previous generations . . . as to whether a family member has . . . worked, what kind of jobs they've held, how successfully they've held jobs and the like. I think that's where the difference is. . . . I think statistics will show that in your black and Hispanic areas there . . . are greater numbers who have not worked and therefore the work ethic of future generations is less.

An industrial relations manager of a Chicago water-heater firm had similar concerns.

> I would think it's because . . . because of the values or the lack of values that those children grow up not having. . . . Not understanding why you come to work every day or why you have to work at all. They're in the mode . . . where they see more people not working . . . it's a way of life. It's not part of a framework. You know, I grew up . . . my father—he went to work every day. He could be half dead, you know, you don't realize those values that are instilled on you. Those children didn't have that benefit and they grew up screwed up because of that. . . . And that's a problem for us as employers, because we're . . . we're not a social agency.

The most common belief among the employers was that the social dislocations in the inner city are mainly a function of the environment in which blacks live. As one employer, a retail caterer, put it, "You and I can grow up going to school, coming home, looking forward to coming home or looking forward to going to a movie. In the inner-city neighborhood, they don't look forward to going to school because the streets are unsafe, the schools are unsafe. They don't look forward to coming home because home for them is on the street basically. And it becomes a way of life." A plant manager at an inner-city firm added:

> The neighborhood itself that they live in is a real tough place to work and there's a lot of outside pressure that causes these people not to come to work and I believe a lot of employers look at past

history and it seems like nowadays you can't really get a true background from an employee.

Concerns about certain aspects of the inner-city milieu often resulted in specific statements about why the workers from that environment would not be hired. The following statements were made by an employer at an inner-city advertising agency:

I necessarily can't tell from looking at an address whether someone's from Cabrini Green or not, but if I could tell, I don't think I'd want to hire them. Because it reflects on your credibility. If you came in here with this survey, and you were from one of those neighborhoods, I don't know if I'd want to answer your questions. I'd wonder about your credibility.

Some employers pointed out that certain areas of the inner city were to be avoided. For example, one stated:

Before I took this job there was an area of Chicago on the West Side that we'd hired, you know, some groups of employees from . . . and our black management people, who do know the areas, they'd say, "No, stay away from that area. That's a bad area. Anybody who comes from that area . . ." And then it came out, too, that sooner or later we did terminate everybody from that certain area for stealing or, you know . . . things worse than attendance, drinking . . . and uh . . . so there probably was some merit to what they were saying.

In addition to qualms about the work ethic, character, family influences, cultural predispositions, and the neighborhood milieu of inner-city residents, the employers frequently mentioned concerns about applicants' language skills and educational training. A blue-collar employer made the following observation:

My guess is that the problem is related to the level of education. I think, even for your minimal jobs, for some of those jobs you know you have to have a little bit of math backgrounds, for example, in some of our machine operations. If you're handicapped by not having some of the basic skills you need, if you're hired and you can't make it on the job because you don't even have the basic skills, that's part of the problem.

An employer from a computer software firm in Chicago expressed the view "that in many businesses the ability to meet the public is paramount and you do not talk street talk to the buying public. Almost all your black welfare people talk street talk. And who's going to sit them down and change their speech patterns?" A Chicago real estate broker made a similar point:

> A lot of times I will interview applicants who are black, who are sort of lower class. . . . They'll come to me and I cannot hire them because their language skills are so poor. Their speaking voice for one thing is poor . . . they have no verbal facility with the language . . . and these . . . you know, they just don't know how to speak and they'll say "salesmens" instead of "salesmen" and that's a problem. . . . They don't know punctuation, they don't know how to use correct grammar, and they cannot spell. And I can't hire them. And I feel bad about that and I think they're being very disadvantaged by the Chicago Public School system.

Another respondent defended his method of screening out most job applicants on the telephone on the basis of their use of "grammar and English."

> I have every right to say that that's a requirement for this job. I don't care if you're pink, black, green, yellow or orange, I demand someone who speaks well. You want to tell me that I'm a bigot, fine, call me a bigot. I know blacks, you don't even know they're black. So do you.

Finally, an inner-city banker claimed that many blacks in the ghetto "simply cannot read. When you're talking our type of business, that disqualifies them immediately; we don't have a job here that doesn't require that somebody have minimum reading and writing skills."

Although many of the employers' negative comments reflected general criticisms of inner-city blacks, when specific reference was made to gender, black males bore the brunt of their criticisms. Indeed, as we shall soon see, employers expressed a clear preference for black females over black males. A significant number of the employers stated that previous experiences had soured their opinion of inner-city black male workers. As seen in Table 5.1, a substantial percentage of the employers in each occupational category feel that a lack of basic skills and a lack of work ethic are the two main reasons why inner-city black males have difficulty finding and retaining employment.

The following explanation for the inner-city black male's employment woes was offered by an employer at a two-year suburban college.

> If they get the job, in the first couple of weeks or so, everything seems to be fine, or maybe even the first 90 days but somehow when they get past that, you see a definite, a marked difference.... They tend to laziness or there's something there. I've seen this pattern over and over again, you know. I think people are willing to give them a chance and then they get the chance and then it's like they really don't want to work.

The vice president of a Chicago offset-printing firm stated:

> Well, I worked with them in the military, and the first chance they get, they'll slack off, they don't want to do the job, they feel

---

TABLE 5.1

OBSERVATIONS AS TO WHY INNER-CITY BLACK MALES CANNOT FIND OR RETAIN JOBS EASILY

Rationale	Frequency (%) of Responses by Employers' Profession				
	Customer Service	Clerical	Craft	Blue-Collar	All Employers
Lack of job skills	9.0	7.1	12.5	17.6	11.7
Lack of basic skills	44.5	37.5	37.5	36.8	38.5
Lack of work ethic	25.0	48.0	25.0	52.9	36.9
Lack of dependability	13.6	14.3	12.5	22.0	16.8
Bad attitude	15.9	16.1	25.0	19.1	17.3
Lack of interpersonal skills	18.2	10.7	0	3.0	8.9
Racial discrimination	15.9	14.3	0	13.2	13.4
Unweighted N	44	56	8	68	179

Source: Data from the 1988 employers' survey conducted as a part of the Urban Poverty and Family Life Study, Chicago.

like they don't have to, they're a minority. They want to take the credit and shift the blame. It's like this guy who runs the elevator [a young black man operated the elevator in the buildings], he's like that. They procrastinate. Some of them try. The ones that have higher education are better than that, but a lot of them don't get an education.

A suburban employer drew upon previous experience to offer the following reasons why inner-city black men cannot find jobs:

It's not every case but the experiences that I've had is the fact that they're not willing to set themselves straight, put 100% effort into their job and try to develop and build within a company. The experiences that I've run into with it is that they develop bad habits, I guess is the best way to put it. Not showing up to work on time. Not showing up to work. Somewhere down the road they didn't develop good work habits.

Employers at inner-city firms tended to be the most critical of inner-city black male workers. One stated: "I just personally, I've had problems with them in the past. . . . They seem to have a lot of associated problems going on at the same time, personal problems, marital problems, that made it difficult for them to get to work every day on time. . . . It's mostly a problem of just getting to work." An inner-city manufacturer at a tool, die, and metal-stamping plant cited past interviews of job seekers when discussing the reasons for his unfavorable opinion of black male workers:

Ah, let's see, I just went through spot welder and I interviewed over 30 of them, the majority of them were black, pretty bad. Yes, I would say that the majority of them have an unstable history. And you can tell attitude just by talking to a person, you know. It's subjective, but it's me talking with 30 years experience, but yeah, I can stake my claim, my reputation, and I can do it. I can interview, and somebody comes in with cut-off shorts on and looking for a job, I just send them away.

A hotel employer in Chicago indicated that he had had some good success with black male workers but that one of the reasons so many of them do not find employment is that their applications reveal high job turnover. He pointed out that when asked why they had left their previous job,

> they'll, on the application itself, just say something like "didn't get along with supervisor" and then the next job, reason for leaving, "didn't get along with supervisor," next job reason for leaving, "didn't like it," and they'll have gone through three or four jobs in a matter of six or eight months and then they don't understand why they don't get hired here.

A suburban employer added: "They don't know how to dress when they come to an interview. They bring fourteen other people with them."

Tardiness and absenteeism was a concern expressed by several employers. "We've hired black guys before and they don't show up and they call in sick," stated the general manager of an inner-city restaurant. The chairman of a car transport service voiced a similar complaint. When asked why inner-city black men cannot find jobs, he stated:

> Number 1 . . . they're not dependable. They have never been taught that when you have a job you have to be there at a certain time and you're to stay there until the time is finished. They may not show up on time. They just disappear for an hour or two at a time. They'll call you up and say, "Ahhh, I'm not coming in today" and they don't even call you up.
> *Interviewer*: So they're undependable, that's one.
> *Respondent*: And the second thing is theft.

Another employer expressed his misgivings about inner-city black males in the course of relating his experiences with one of his previous workers. Agreeing that discrimination probably plays a role among most employers in the hiring of blacks, he went on to explain why:

> I think one of the reasons in all honesty is because we've had bad experience in that sector . . . and believe me I've tried. And as I say, if I find . . . whether he's black or white, if he's good and you know we'll hire him. We are not shutting out any black specifically. But I will say that our experience factor has been bad. We've

had more bad black employees over the years than we had good. . . . We hire a young black [as a stockman] and he just absolutely hated anybody telling him anything. I mean if you criticized him or if you gave him an order or an instruction he absolutely resented it. And after a while he started fighting with the other employees. . . . One of the women says, look, I need a case of this or this or this and he doesn't do it, doesn't get it for them and they are waiting to fill an order and he ignores them and then when they complained he would get mad and start swearing at them. You know so it's things like this that you know you can't, can't tolerate it. And he was one of the few that we have let go. And believe me I can count on one hand over the years how many employees we've actually fired. We don't do it indiscriminately. . . .

Interviewer: So do you think because of experiences like that, do you think that you are a little bit more leery when a black man comes in here than a white man?

Respondent: Yes, in all honesty I probably am, but . . . as I say, I hired this other one, he was a gem.

Other employers expressed reservations about inner-city black men in terms of work-related skills. They "just don't have the language skills," stated a suburban employer. The president of an inner-city advertising agency highlighted the problem of spelling.

I needed a temporary a couple months ago, and they sent me a black man. And I dictated a letter to him, he took shorthand, which was good. Something like "Dear Mr. So and So, I am writing to ask about how your business is doing." And then he typed the letter, and a good while later, now not because he was black, I don't know why it took so long. But I read the letter, and it's "I am writing to *ax* about your business." Now you hear about them speaking a different language and all that, and they say *ax* for ask. Well, I don't care about that, but I didn't say *ax*, I said ask.

Several of the employers of blue-collar workers drew a connection between the problems of inner-city black male joblessness and the failure of some applicants to pass drug-screening tests. For example, the manager of a suburban glass-container firm pointed out:

We've got the unfortunate situation of, through our drug screening, disqualifying roughly 30 percent of those people that get
through the screening process and get to the physical exam.
We're losing about 30 percent of them through the drug screening process. I think it's a shame, I think it's a sin, it's a disgrace to
our society, and as far as I'm concerned it's one of the number one
things that we've got to attack.

The president of an inner-city trucking firm likewise stated: "You're
going to find a lot of them coming through that comes in there—
we've found—we drug test them as part of the physical—and there's a
lot of them on drugs. We used to—we were a customs bonded carrier
and we used to polygraph them all and we would find that a lot of
them are thieves."

Many employers often develop negative opinions of black male
workers in the absence of previous firsthand experience. A manufacturer explained that nobody wanted to hire the inner-city black male
because of the stereotype that

they don't want to work, they don't want to do anything. I think
that's a big part of it. I don't think anybody wants to admit it but I
think that's primarily it. . . . They're ignorant, they don't work,
they don't want to work . . . they got a real bad rap, and uh . . . nobody, I don't think anybody will come out and admit it, but I
think that's the first thing they consider in a black applicant.

The UPFLS employer survey clearly suggests that although black
women also suffer as a consequence of the negative attitudes held by
employers, nonetheless, in an overwhelming majority of cases in
which inner-city black males and females are compared, the employers
preferred black women. When asked how the situation of inner-city
black males compares with that of black females, almost one-half of
the employers stated that there is a gender difference in inner-city
workers' success in finding and retaining employment. Only 14 percent indicated that there was no difference between the employment
experiences of inner-city black males and those of black females. A
large proportion (43 percent) had no opinion, however, mainly because they had not had any direct employment-related experiences
with blacks in general or with black men or black women in particular.

TABLE 5.2

EMPLOYERS' OBSERVATIONS ABOUT GENDER
DIFFERENCES IN INNER-CITY BLACKS' ABILITIES TO FIND
AND RETAIN A JOB

Frequency (%) of Responses by Employers' Profession

Observations on Blacks' Chances for Employment	Customer Service	Clerical	Craft	Blue-Collar	All Employers
Positive toward women	61.1	93.1	100	71.4	77.9
Negative toward women*	5.6	3.4	0	28.6	13.0
Unweighted *N*	18	29	2	28	77

* Employers with negative feelings about black women's chances for employment expressed concerns about child care and other family responsibilities.

Source: Data from the 1988 employers' survey conducted as a part of the Urban Poverty and Family Life Study, Chicago.

As revealed in Table 5.2, of those respondents who felt that the employment situation of inner-city black men and that of black women differ, almost 78 percent felt that black women have a better chance of finding and retaining employment because they are either more responsible and determined or have better attitudes and a better work ethic.

"I think that probably they [inner-city black females] are much more responsible in what we've found," stated the general manager of a suburban luggage retail store. "So many single-family homes right now you'll find that they're working two jobs trying to support a family. You see it all the time. In many, many cases they're the ones that are supporting their four kids and the husband's whereabouts are unknown."

The associate vice president of a health services firm in the inner city commented: "I think probably because employers' experience . . . historically, has been better with black females or minority females than with minority males in terms of the basics—attendance, productivity, work ethic and all that, there is less hesitancy to hire black women." The vice president of an interstate trucking firm offered the following opinion: "No, I think they're a little steadier in that many of them have families that they're concerned with and the job is very important to them." According to the vice president of an inner-city general hospital services firm, the image of black women differs from that of black men. He remarked:

I think there's a different perception of—generally about black women. I think the perception—whether it's right or wrong—may be that they very likely are the heads of households, very likely the ones that are assuming the responsibility for the care of children, very possibly ones that appear to be a little bit more stable in the work environment in terms of their reliability and that type of thing.

Inner-city black women "have a need to work," stated a Chicago employer, "and I think that need translates in many cases into a very responsible employee. Certainly the education can still be a problem, but the stigma of crime, of gangs, of lack of responsibility, I certainly think they don't suffer the same problems that a black male would have in terms of getting a job."

The manager of a computer technology business located in the inner city stated:

Well, I think black women have so much responsibility at home and so many—you know, the single working mother that white women are experiencing now, the black woman has always experienced that. And she's out taking care of other people's children and nobody's home taking care of hers or, you know, she is providing for, oftentimes, several families, not just her own but her children's families, a multiple-family situation. So, because of personal problems she may have poor attendance or may not be able to concentrate on a job all the time and that—which I think a lot of is becoming a problem for white women too, but, I think it's been more prevalent for black women in the past. White women are starting to learn what those kinds of problems are.

A small number of the respondents remarked that black males were less successful than black females because they were more threatening to employers. According to one respondent who hires clerical workers:

Black men present a particularly menacing demeanor to white men. I think they are frightened by them. I think they do not speak the same language. I don't think they use the same codes, I think the whole communication process is a very threatening one.

2

And to the black male, whose need to assert himself is so crucial, because he feels so totally battered in his environment, his sense of manhood is very turned off or intimidated or feels the need to rail against any efforts on the part of the white male establishment to in any way emasculate him further. And I think, there's a tremendous communications block that they come to because both are in some ways frightened and intimidated by the other. Therefore I think many times, when companies hire black males, they hire the most complacent, the least aggressive, the most eunuchish type they can get because they don't want to have some crazy, who's going to become some kind of warmonger, running around the company and spatting. They hire the ones that are most acceptable, and sometimes they're not necessarily the brightest or the most capable.

The executive director of an inner-city charity had similar views:

People are afraid of black men. If it is a choice of a black man or a woman to do the job I think that an employer would take a black woman. But, if I were going to hire for a job I would take a black woman over a black man because of this situation and then also I would be less afraid of a black woman. I would say, well, maybe he's got a criminal record, but, he's—or I would just be a little bit more apprehensive.

Of the few respondents (12.9 percent) who felt that inner-city black women had greater difficulty than black men in finding and retaining employment, most felt it was because women were burdened with family and child care responsibilities. As one employer put it:

I think it's a little different. Um . . . I think in most cases . . . or at least in the cases we've had to deal with . . . or in the cases we've had any problems with . . . even when we've had successes with. The biggest problem is the children . . . the child care problem. I mean the inner-city women not only have all the other things they have to deal with and all these changes and all these new rules and everything else trying to learn all that crap, they also have to worry about where are their kids and who's taking care of them and is Grandma going to be there or a sister or a mom or whoever it happens to be taking care of the kid. And I think that just adds to that burden and makes it more difficult. And I think in some cases it must look real frustrating to them ... that no matter how they're trying to get ahead there's everything else is against them. I mean, everything is working against them to make it easier for them to stay home than it is to come here.

Finally, a categorically negative view of inner-city women was expressed by a suburban employer.

You have the circumstance where you have inner-city women who are, in effect, paid to have more children that they can't support. Doesn't make any difference whether they have a husband or not. They will have more children because the welfare check will be bigger. They will abandon them ... the bad ones will abandon them. ... They have no intention of looking for a job. They will make all the moves they need to make to make it look like they are, but their intention is to have enough children to support themselves. ... Men can't decide, "Well, I'm going to have more children and support myself that way." Can't do that, but the woman can. That's an option for her. It tends to make her less aggressive in looking for a job than the men.

It is difficult to determine whether these views represent a recent shift in employers' attitudes or whether they represent a long-held pattern of negative views toward the residents of inner-city neighborhoods. The employers' strongly disapproving views of inner-city black male workers are interesting to consider in this connection. The success that black men had in obtaining manufacturing and other blue-collar jobs in previous years suggests that these views may have emerged only recently. If you examine the UPFLS survey data on the employment patterns of employed inner-city black fathers born between 1941 and 1955 (the 1941–55 birth cohort), you find that their participation in manufacturing was higher than that of employed inner-city Latino fathers and only slightly below that of employed inner-city white fathers by 1978. For the 1956–69 birth cohort, the proportion of employed black fathers in these industries was equal to that of employed inner-city Mexican fathers and only slightly behind that of employed inner-city white and Puerto Rican fathers by

1978. However, by 1987 the proportion of employed black fathers in manufacturing industries was significantly below the proportion of employed inner-city white and Latino fathers (see Appendix C).

Regardless of whether there has been a shift in attitudes among employers, race is obviously a factor in many of their current decisions; however, the issues are complex and cannot be reduced to the simple notion of employer racism. Let me pursue this point by first focusing on the way in which employers themselves perceive the issues of prejudice and discrimination and, second, examining black employers' perceptions of inner-city workers.

If discrimination is a significant factor in the employment woes of inner-city blacks, it is not recognized as such by a substantial majority of the employers in this survey. When asked the reason for the high levels of unemployment in Chicago's inner-city neighborhoods, only 4 percent of the 179 employers mentioned discrimination. Indeed, employers tend to dismiss the charge of discrimination, even though some of their statements indicate that it does exist.

When asked about the problem of discrimination in connection with the employment experiences of inner-city blacks, the director of personnel at a Chicago department store said, "I have a different view on it because I think it's used as an excuse many times. I've found that to be true in the experience here that it is a real convenient excuse for a minority to use and it's frustrating to me as an employer."

Several other employers complained about charges of racial discrimination from black employees. "If we hire a black male and for some reason he doesn't work out, or is let go during the ninety-day probationary period or shortly after," stated an employer at an inner-city discount department store, "they file a discrimination charge. Whether there's any validity to it or not. It just seems to be an automatic thing." The president of a marketing and promotion firm in the inner city pointed out that once the minority female employees are hired, " if they didn't perform, then you had a problem of great enormity, it was, you can't fire them. There's difficulty in terminating those services because now you have racial discrimination or what have you."

An inner-city employer echoed these feelings:

One thing that some of our management fears in hiring them is problems if they do have to terminate them. I probably shouldn't say that, but that is a real fear of the management because they are a protected class.

    Interviewer: So a lawsuit on the basis of discrimination?

    Respondent: Yes.

The views of the director of personnel at a Chicago hospital perhaps best capture the sentiments of many employers: "People are much more aware . . . of their rights and their—a lot of them abuse it too. A lot of frivolous claims. There's a lot of unjustified filing of charges. . . . It's a big problem."

    In addition to the belief that many formal claims of racial discrimination in the workplace are not justified, there was also the feeling among the respondents that if an employer avoids hiring inner-city workers, it has more to do with concerns about performance and safety than with prejudice against a person because of skin color. As an inner-city employer put it:

I do not believe that it is the result of blatant racism. I do not believe that. I think that it is the result of the experience on the part of the employer communities.

    Interviewer: You said you didn't think it was blatant racism? . . .

    Respondent: You're asking me how much of a problem is racial discrimination?

    Interviewer: How much or what kind of a role it plays, if it does play a role at all.

    Respondent: Yes, it does play a role. Yes, it does. . . . I think a related question is . . . how much of [it] . . . is the fear on the part of the majority community of the violence and the criminal activities that generally are black people acting upon black people. . . . I think the reality of that, then, is that not many white individuals understand that and therefore there is fear of security and safety. Particularly when we're talking about a population of young black males. Now, how much of it is fear and concern for your safety or your welfare, uh . . . and how much of it is real racial discrimination. . . . I'm not sure how you break those out. I certainly think that a black kid . . . a black man in a city is discriminated against. . . . I would like to believe that the issue is . . . is more one of fear than it is one of skin color.

But a few employers candidly admitted that racial prejudice is a factor in the hiring process in the Greater Chicago area. An inner-city manufacturer emphatically expressed this sentiment:

> Well, I don't know about their ability to hang onto the job, or retain it, but their ability to find them is probably rooted in the fact that there's, now I'm going to go back twenty years now, I think that today there's more bias and prejudice against the black man than there was twenty years ago. I think twenty years ago, fifteen years ago, ten years ago, white male employers like myself were willing to give anybody and everybody the opportunity, not because it was the law, but because it was the right thing to do, and today I see more prejudice and more racial bias in employers than I've ever seen before. Not here, and our employees can prove that, but when we hear other employers talk, they'll go after primarily the Hispanic and Oriental first, those two, and ... I'll qualify that even further, the Mexican Hispanic, and any Oriental, and after that, that's pretty much it, that's pretty much where they like to draw the line, right there.

Finally, the director of a packing and assembly firm located in the inner city expressed a view that some economists would describe as a subtle form of *statistical discrimination*—that is, making judgments about an applicant's productivity, which are often too difficult or too expensive to measure, on the basis of his or her race, ethnic background, or class. "My experience has been that the competency is not present with blacks. But I'm wondering whether it's not also that you don't test in your hiring process and therefore simply worked off your perception built over time, having hired someone who later proved to be incompetent."

Conclusions about the role of prejudice and discrimination in the labor market are usually based on analyses of the interaction between white employers and minority employees. Many readers will interpret the negative comments of the employers as indicative of the larger problem of racism and racial discrimination in American society. It is therefore instructive to consider, for separate analysis, the perceptions of the African-American employers who were interviewed in our survey. Their responses suggest that it would be a mistake to characterize the overall comments of the employers in our survey as racist, even though some clearly contain racist sentiments. Indeed, it is significant to note that of the fifteen African-American employers in our survey, twelve expressed views about inner-city black workers, in response to our open-ended questions, that were coded as negative. Only two of the black employers offered comments that could be described as positive, and one expressed views that were coded as neutral. Thus, whereas 74 percent of all the white employers who responded to the open-ended questions expressed negative views of the job-related traits of inner-city blacks, 80 percent of the black employers did so as well.

The black president and CEO of an inner-city wholesale firm described what he saw as the effects of living in a highly concentrated poverty area:

> So, you put . . . a bunch of poor people together, [rushed and emphatic] I don't give a damn whether they're white, green or grizzly, you got a bad deal. You're going to create crime and everything else that's under the sun, dope. Anytime you put all like people together—and particularly if they're on a low level—you destroy them. They not, how you going to expect . . . one's going to stand up like a flower? He don't see no reason to stand up. When he gets up in the morning he sees people laying around doing nothing. He goes to bed at night, the same damn thing. All they think of, do I get to eat and sleep?
> *Interviewer:* So, you understand this wariness of some employers?
> *Respondent:* Sure.

The black president of a business college offered a sophisticated account of the intersection of class and race:

> I think there are differences in the work ethic of people, depending on where you find them valuewise and economically and socially. You can find middle-class blacks who would parallel white American values straight up and down the line, almost you'd find a value set that's interchangeable. What's happening, you're finding fewer of those people, because of the abyss of unemployment and misery in the black community is so widespread that you're

getting people now in this lower end and that creates such bizarre kinds of behavior that it breeds a different set of values, so you get these subcultural effects that just spews out all these bizarre range of things that happen. And as long as people are going to have to live like that, then yes, we're going to have a clear distinction between [the] work ethic of that group of people and the work ethic of this other group of people who aren't dealing with those same kinds of survival phenomenon. . . . It's really an economic value rather than a racial one.

When asked why black men cannot find jobs, the black personnel manager of a retail food and drug store stated: "I think that's really the culture. I think that a lot of the black males look at some of the jobs that they feel are beneath their dignity to work and rather than accept any job, they'd rather stay out of employment rolls." A black employer in a Chicago insurance company argued that

there is a perception that most of your kids are black and they don't have the proper skills . . . they don't know how to write. They don't know how to speak. They don't act in a business fashion or dress in a business manner . . . in a way that the business community would like. And they just don't feel that they're getting a quality employee. . . .

Interviewer: Do you think—is that all a false perception or is something there or—?

Respondent: I think there's some truth to it.

In answer to the same question, another black employer gave this negative response:

Attitude. Poor attitude. I'm very vocal on that. They lazy, a lot of them. You know, when you trapped, you realize you're trapped, but if you don't try to do something about it yourself, then you'll always be trapped. If you get into a welfare mode then you becomes a slave. And if that's what you want to be, so be it as an individual but I don't want to be a slave. I'm going to work. It's an attitude problem, that's all I can tell you and I've known, I been around them. I know what's happening.

Finally, the black personnel manager of a security services firm dismissed the problem of job discrimination: "It's a myth to me and it's something that has been another part where our society constantly has pushed it in the minds of a lot of people and they lean on this as a crutch. And when you lean on this as a crutch well, then how will you ever pick up yourself or apply yourself to anything? So, no. Discrimination can be thrown out the window."

Although the criticisms of employers were directed at both inner-city black males and females, the harshest and most frequent criticisms were aimed at the black male. Employer comments about inner-city black males revealed a wide range of complaints, including assertions that they procrastinate, are lazy, belligerent, and dangerous, have high rates of tardiness and absenteeism, carry employment histories with many job turnovers, and frequently fail to pass drug screening tests.

Many of their comments clearly suggest a direct link between their assessment of the quality of the black inner-city workforce and their hiring strategies. There are many ways in which employers can deny inner-city workers employment or access to employment if they are reluctant or do not want to hire them. Direct, overt discrimination in refusing to consider any black applicants at all or in not seriously reviewing their applications for employment is the most obvious, but only a handful of employers admitted to such practices. Others consider black job applicants but frequently screen them out because their applications are not considered strong, or they do not make a good impression during the interview process, or they fail to pass an employment or skills tests.

The job interview provides job applicants with an opportunity to challenge employer stereotypes. However, as Kathryn Neckerman and Joleen Kirschenman, two of the six researchers who conducted the interviews for the UPFLS employer survey, pointed out:

> Inner-city black job seekers with limited work experience and little familiarity with the white, middle-class world are also likely to have difficulty in the typical job interview. A spotty work record will have to be justified; misunderstanding and suspicion may undermine rapport and hamper communication. However qualified

they are for the job, inner-city black applicants are more likely to fail subjective "tests" of productivity during the interview.

Skills tests are less biased than the subjective assessments used in the typical interview. The data reveal that city employers—that is, those with firms within the city of Chicago—who apply skills tests have a higher average proportion of black workers in entry-level jobs than do those who do not use these tests, even when one takes into consideration the size of the firm, the occupation, and the percentage of blacks in the neighborhood.

However, many Chicago employers engage in recruitment practices that automatically eliminate or significantly reduce the number of inner-city applicants who could apply for entry-level jobs in their firms. Selective recruitment—that is, limiting the search for job candidates in various ways—is widely practiced by the Chicago employers in this survey. Although some of the employers justified this strategy in terms of practicality and efficiency, noting that they save time and money by relying on the referrals of employees instead of screening large numbers of applicants from newspaper ads, most indicated that it yields a higher-quality applicant.

Although the formal criteria of applicant quality were based on neither race nor class, the recruitment strategies designed to attract high-quality applicants were. Inner-city populations were often overlooked if employers limited their recruitment efforts to certain neighborhoods or institutions and placed ads only or mainly in ethnic or neighborhood newspapers. Indeed, the recruitment practices of the employers reflect their perceptions of the quality of the inner-city workers.

An effective way to screen the applicant pool is to avoid placing ads in the Chicago newspapers. Over 40 percent of the employers from firms within the city of Chicago did not advertise their entry-level job openings in the newspaper. And for many of those who did place ads in the local newspapers, it was often only after the informal employee referral network produced an insufficient number of applicants. Furthermore, roughly two-thirds of the city employers who placed ads in newspapers did so in ethnic, neighborhood, or suburban newspapers instead of or in addition to the metropolitan newspapers.

Advertising job vacancies in neighborhood or ethnic newspapers ("local" newspapers) facilitated the targeting of particular groups, mainly Hispanics or white (including "ethnics") populations of recent East European immigrants. A partner with a downtown law firm indicated that his firm puts "ads in the Northwest side of the city" because the "work ethic is better" among the residents there. He stated: "It's a Polish [neighborhood], you know, it's a strong work ethic neighborhood. That's not, I'm not trying to be . . . prejudiced or anything else. It's reality I have to deal with." A few of the white-collar employers, however, placed ads in the *Defender*, a black newspaper, out of a commitment to hire blacks or to satisfy affirmative action guidelines. City employers who placed ads only in local or neighborhood papers, not likely to circulate among inner-city residents, averaged 16 percent black in their entry-level jobs, compared to an average of 32 percent black for those who placed ads in the metropolitan papers.

Determining the location or quality of the schools was another way in which employers conducted screening. A number of employers mentioned that education in the Chicago public schools, which are overwhelmingly black, has become a negative signal, and therefore many applicants from this system are passed over for those from Catholic or suburban schools. As an employer from an inner-city wholesale business put it, "Why the hell would I want to hire someone . . . from a Chicago public high school? Because I don't think they've got it. Is that a prejudice? It's not a prejudice on race, but it's a prejudice on what you think their educational background is."

An employer at a blue-collar firm offered these comments about the educational system:

> We're finding that what comes out of the school is really not what we want. The educational system doesn't prepare them for this type of work.
> *Interviewer:* How do you think it does prepare them?
> *Respondent:* I'm not sure if it does very good at all. We only find criticisms because they're unable to do certain things that we would assume they would learn, particularly in the field of math, which is important in our business, to be able to count, read a ruler, read, actually do reading at all.

The employers who volunteered information on the schools they recruited from usually mentioned Catholic schools or those from Chicago's largely white Northwest Side communities. Although employees recruited from the Catholic schools were more likely to be white, black students from Catholic schools were also viewed more favorably than those from the public schools. For example, an employer at a suburban department store pointed out that although minority students fail the skills test more frequently than white students, "the minorities that go to parochial school test as well as the whites. They come here dressed as well, and this is a totally different act. Now this is a difference that I can spot, is between your parochial school and your public school."

If employers do not like to recruit from the overwhelmingly black Chicago public schools, they also disdain recruiting from welfare programs and state employment service programs. The UPFLS employer survey revealed that only 16 percent of the employers from city firms recruited from welfare agencies, and only one-third from state employment agencies. These programs mainly serve blacks from the inner city, and employers felt that they sent applicants who were unqualified or inappropriate. As one employer put it:

> Any time I've taken any recommendation from state agencies, city agencies, or welfare agencies I really get people who are not prepared to come to work on time, not prepared to see that a new job is carried through, that it's completed. I mean there just doesn't seem to be a work ethic involved in these people.

Of the city employers, those from the inner-city neighborhoods relied most heavily on selective recruiting. They were less likely to place ads in local newspapers or recruit from schools, and they relied very heavily on the informal job networks. One inner-city hospital decided against the use of newspaper ads and recruited workers from community jobs programs and through informal employee networks. As a representative from the hospital put it, "If you are just a cold applicant, chances of you getting in are almost nil."

One inner-city retailer, who complained about young workers being disrespectful and inclined to steal and who recruited some of her employees from a youth mentoring program, put it this way: "I think I'm getting the best of what I've got to select from. . . . I know the guy at the gas station, the guy who runs the Burger King, and all of us say the same thing."

In light of what this employers' survey tells us, the selective recruitment practiced by many city employers results in the systematic exclusion of numerous inner-city blacks from jobs in Chicago. And given the negative view that employers have of inner-city workers, it is reasonable to conclude that although these practices are characterized by employers as necessary to recruit a higher-quality worker, they in fact are <u>deliberately designed to exclude inner-city blacks</u> from the employment applicant pool.

How should we interpret the negative attitudes and actions of employers? To what extent do they represent an aversion to blacks per se and to what degree do they reflect judgments based on the job-related skills and training of inner-city blacks in a changing labor market? As pointed out earlier, the statements made by the African-American employers concerning the qualifications of inner-city black workers do not differ significantly from those of the white employers. This raises a question about the meaning and significance of race in certain situations—in other words, how race intersects with other factors. A key hypothesis is that given the recent shifts in the economy, employers are looking for workers with a broad range of abilities: "hard" skills (literacy, numeracy, basic mechanical ability, and other testable attributes) and "soft" skills (personalities suitable to the work environment, good grooming, group-oriented work behaviors, etc.). While hard skills are the product of education and training—benefits that are apparently in short supply in inner-city schools—soft skills are strongly tied to culture, and are therefore shaped by the harsh environment of the inner-city ghetto. If employers are indeed reacting to the difference in skills between white and black applicants, it becomes increasingly difficult to discern the motives of employers: are they rejecting inner-city black applicants out of overt racial discrimination or on the basis of qualifications? In this connection, one study conducted in Los Angeles found that even after education, income, family background, and place of residence were taken into account, <u>dark-skinned black men were 52 percent less likely to be working than light-skinned black men</u>. Although this finding strongly suggests that racial discrimination plays a significant role in the jobless rate of black men, the study did not pursue the extent to which employers associate darkness of skin color with the social and cultural environment of the inner-city ghetto.

Nonetheless, many of the selective recruitment practices do represent what economists call statistical discrimination: employers make assumptions about the inner-city black workers *in general* and reach decisions based on those assumptions before they have had a chance to review systematically the qualifications of an individual applicant. The net effect is that many black inner-city applicants are never given the chance to prove their qualifications on an individual level because they are systematically screened out by the selective recruitment process. Statistical discrimination, although representing elements of class bias against poor workers in the inner city, is clearly a matter of race. The selective recruitment patterns effectively screen out far more black workers from the inner city than Hispanic or white workers from the same types of backgrounds. But race is also a factor, even in those decisions to deny employment to inner-city black workers on the basis of objective and thorough evaluations of their qualifications. The hard and soft skills among inner-city blacks that do not match the current needs of the labor market are products of racially segregated communities, communities that have historically featured widespread social constraints and restricted opportunities.

Many inner-city residents have a strong sense of the negative attitudes which employers tend to have toward them. A 33-year-old employed janitor from a poor South Side neighborhood had this observation: "I went to a coupla jobs where a couple of the receptionists told me in confidence: 'You know what they do with these applications from blacks as soon as the day is over?' Say 'we rip them and throw 'em in the garbage.' " In addition to concerns about being rejected because of race, the fears that some inner-city residents have of being denied employment simply because of their inner-city address or neighborhood are not unfounded. A welfare mother who lives in a large public housing project put it this way:

> Honestly, I believe they look at the address and the—your attitudes, your address, your surround—you know, your environment has a lot to do with your employment status. The people with the best addresses have the best chances, I feel so, I feel so.

Another welfare mother of two children from a South Side neighborhood expressed a similar view:

I think that a lot of peoples don't get jobs over here because they lives—they live in the projects. They think that just 'cause people living in the projects they no good. Yes, yes. I think so! I think so! I think a lot of people might judge a person because you out—because they got a project address. You know, when you put it on an application, they might not even hire you because you live over here.

A 34-year-old single and unemployed black man put it this way: "If you're from a nice neighborhood I believe it's easier for you to get a job and stuff. I have been on jobs and such and gotten looks from folks and such, 'I wonder if he is the type who do those things that happen in that neighborhood.' "

Although the employers' perceptions of inner-city workers make it difficult for low-income blacks to find or retain employment, it is interesting to note that there is one area where the views of employers and those of many inner-city residents converge—namely, in their attitudes toward inner-city black males. Inner-city residents are aware of the problems of male joblessness in their neighborhoods. For example, more than half the black UPFLS survey respondents from neighborhoods with poverty rates of at least 40 percent felt that very few or none of the men in their neighborhood were working steadily. More than one-third of the respondents from neighborhoods with poverty rates of at least 30 percent expressed that view as well. Forty percent of the black respondents in all neighborhoods in the UPFLS felt that the number of men with jobs has steadily decreased over the past ten years. However, responses to the open-ended questions in our Social Opportunity Survey and data from our ethnographic field interviews reveal a consistent pattern of negative views among the respondents concerning inner-city black males, especially young black males.

Some provided explanations in which they acknowledged the constraints that black men face. An employed 25-year-old unmarried father of one child from North Lawndale stated:

I know a lot of guys that's my age, that don't work and I know some that works temporary, but wanna work, they just can't get the jobs. You know, they got a high school diploma and that . . .

but the thing is, these jobs always say: Not enough experience. How can you get some experience if you never had a chance to get any experience?

Others, however, expressed views that echoed those of the employers. For example, a 30-year-old married father of three children who lives in North Lawndale and works the night shift in a factory stated:

I say about 65 percent—of black males, I say, don't wanna work, and when I say don't wanna work I say don't wanna work hard— they want a real easy job, making big bucks—see? And, and when you start talking about hard labor and earning your money with sweat or just once in a while you gotta put out a little bit—you know, that extra effort, I don't, I don't think the guys really wanna do that. And sometimes it comes from, really, not having a, a steady job or, really, not being out in the work field and just been sittin' back, being comfortable all the time and hanging out.

A 35-year-old welfare mother of eight children from the Englewood neighborhood on the South Side agreed:

Well, I mean see you got all these dudes around here, they don't even work, they don't even try, they don't wanna work. You know what I mean, I wanna work, but I can't work. Then you got people here that, in this neighborhood, can get up and do somethin', they just don't wanna do nothin'—they really don't.

The deterioration of the socioeconomic status of black men may have led to the negative perceptions of both the employers and the inner-city residents. Are these perceptions merely stereotypical or do they have any basis in fact? Data from the UPFLS survey show that variables measuring differences in social context (neighborhoods, social networks, and households) accounted for substantially more of the gap in the employment rates of black and Mexican men than did variables measuring individual attitudes. Also, data from the survey reveal that jobless black men have a lower "reservation wage" than the jobless men in the other ethnic groups. They were willing to work for less than $6.00 per hour, whereas Mexican and Puerto Rican jobless men expected $6.20 and $7.20, respectively, as a condition for working; white men, on the other hand, expected over $9.00 per hour. This would appear to cast some doubt on the characterization of black inner-city men as wanting "something for nothing," of holding out for high pay.

But surveys are not the best way to get at underlying attitudes and values. Accordingly, to gain a better grasp of the cultural issues, I examined the UPFLS ethnographic research that involved establishing long-term contacts and conducting interviews with residents from several neighborhoods. Richard Taub points out:

> Anybody who studies subgroups within the American population knows that there are cultural patterns which are distinctive to the subgroups and which have consequences for social outcomes. The challenge for those concerned about poverty and cultural variation is to link cultural arrangements to larger structural realities and to understand the interaction between the consequences of one's structural position on the one hand and pattern group behavior on the other. It is important to understand that the process works both ways. Cultures are forged in part on the basis of adaptation to both structural and material environments.

Analysis of the ethnographic data reveals identifiable and consistent patterns of attitudes and beliefs among inner-city ethnic groups. The data, systematically analyzed by Taub, reveal that the black men are more hostile than the Mexican men with respect to the low-paying jobs they hold, less willing to be flexible in taking assignments or tasks not considered part of their job, and less willing to work as hard for the same low wages. These contrasts in the behavior of the two groups of men are sharp because many of the Mexicans interviewed were recent immigrants.

"Immigrants, particularly Third World immigrants," will often "tolerate harsher conditions, lower pay, fewer upward trajectories, and other job related characteristics that deter native workers, and thereby exhibit a better 'work ethic' than others." The ethnographic data from the UPFLS suggest that the Mexican immigrants are harder workers because they "come from areas of intense poverty and that even boring, hard, dead-end jobs look, by contrast, good to them." They also fear being deported if they fail to find employment.

Once again, it should be emphasized that the contrasts between blacks and Mexicans in our ethnographic sample are sharp because most of the latter in our sample were recent immigrants. Our ethnographic research was conducted mainly in black and Latino inner-city neighborhoods, and the ethnographic data that were sufficient to draw systematic comparisons concerning work attitudes were those based on intensive field interviews with Mexican men and African-American men. However, as indicated earlier, the large UPFLS survey revealed that white men in the inner city have a much higher reservation wage than either African-American or Latino inner-city men. Accordingly, there is no reason to assume that their attitude toward dead-end menial jobs is any less negative than that of black men.

Since our sample was largely drawn from poverty areas, it includes a disproportionate number of immigrants, who tend to settle initially in poverty areas. As previous research has consistently shown, migrants who leave a poorer economy for a more developed economy in the hope of improving their standard of living tend to accept, willingly, the kinds of employment that the indigenous workers detest or have come to reject. It is reasonable to hypothesize that the more "Americanized" they become, the less inclined they will be to accept menial low-wage and hazardous jobs.

In contrast to the Mexican men, the inner-city black men complained that they get assigned the heaviest or dirtiest work on the job, are overworked, and are paid less than nonblacks. They strongly feel that they are victims of discrimination. "The Mexican-American men also report that they feel exploited," states Taub, "but somehow that comes with the territory." Taub argues that the inner-city black men have a greater sense of "honor" and often see the work, pay, and treatment from bosses as insulting and degrading. Accordingly, a heightened sensitivity to exploitation fuels their anger and gives rise to a tendency to "just walk off the job."

One has to look at the growing exclusion of black men from higher-paying blue-collar jobs in manufacturing and other industries and their increasing confinement to low-paying service laboring jobs to understand these attitudes and how they developed. Many low-paying jobs have predictably low retention rates. For example, one of the respondents in the UPFLS employer survey reported turnover rates at his firm that exceeded 50 percent. When asked if he had considered doing anything about this problem, the employer acknowledged that the company had made a rational decision to tolerate a high turnover rather than increasing the starting salary and improving working conditions to attract higher-caliber workers: "Our practice has been that we'll keep hiring and, hopefully, one or two of them are going to wind up being good."

As Kathryn Neckerman points out, "This employer, and others like him, can afford such high turnover because the work is simple and can be taught in a couple of days. On average, jobs paying under $5.00 or $6.00 an hour were characterized by high quit rates. In higher-paying jobs, by contrast, the proportion of employees resigning fell to less than 20 percent per year." Yet UPFLS data show that the proportion of inner-city black males in the higher-paying blue-collar positions has declined far more sharply than that of Latinos and whites (see Appendix C). Increasingly displaced from manufacturing industries, inner-city black males are more confined to low-paying service work. Annual turnover rates of 50 to 100 percent are common in low-skill service jobs in Chicago, regardless of the race or ethnicity of the employees.

Thus, the attitudes that many inner-city black males express about their jobs and job prospects reflect their plummeting position in a changing labor market. The more they complain and manifest their dissatisfaction, the less desirable they seem to employers. They therefore experience greater rejection when they seek employment and clash more often with supervisors when they secure employment.

Residence in highly concentrated poverty neighborhoods aggravates the weak labor-force attachment of black males. The absence of effective informal job networks and the frequency of many illegal activities increases nonmainstream behavior such as hustling. As Sharon Hicks-Bartlett, another member of the UPFLS research team, points out, "Hustling is making money by doing whatever is necessary to survive or simply make ends meet. It can be legal or extra-legal work and may transpire in the formal or informal economy. While both men and women hustle, men are more conspicuous in the illegal arena of hustling."

In a review of the research literature on the experiences of black men in the labor market, Philip Moss and Christopher Tilly point out that criminal activity in urban areas has become more attractive because of the disappearance of legitimate jobs. They refer to a recent study in Boston that showed that while "black youth in Boston were evenly split on whether they could make more money in a straight job or on the street, by 1989 a three-to-one majority of young black people expressed the opinion that they could make more on the street."

The restructuring of the economy will continue to compound the negative effects of the prevailing perceptions of inner-city black males. Because of the increasing shift away from manufacturing and toward service industries, employers have a greater need for workers who can effectively serve and relate to the consumer. Inner-city black men are not perceived as having these qualities.

The restructuring of the urban economy could also have long-term consequences for inner-city black women. Neckerman argues that a change in work cultures accompanied the transformation of the economy, resulting in a mismatch between the old and new ways of succeeding in the labor market. In other words, there is a growing difference between the practices of blue-collar and service employers and the practices of white-collar employers. This mismatch is important in assessing the labor-market success of inner-city workers.

Low-skilled individuals from the inner city tend to be the children of blue-collar workers or service workers, and their work experience is thus largely confined to blue-collar or service jobs. What happens "when employees socialized to approach jobs and careers in ways that make sense in a blue-collar or service context enter the white-collar world?" The employer interviews suggest that workers from blue-collar or service settings seek positions that carry high entry-level salaries that provide all the necessary training on the job and that grant privileges and promotion in accordance with both seniority and performance. But in a white-collar setting, inner-city workers face entry-level positions that require more and continuous training and employers who are looking for people who are energetic, intelligent, and possess good language skills. Promotions in this environment seldom depend on seniority. Accordingly, "their advancement may depend on fairly subtle standards of evaluation, and on behavior that is irrelevant or even negatively sanctioned in the blue-collar and service settings." Interviews with inner-city workers revealed that most recognize the changing nature of the labor market and that a greater premium is placed on education and training for success, but many "did indeed espouse blue-collar ways of getting ahead."

In summary, the issue of race in the labor market cannot simply be reduced to the presence of discrimination. Although our data suggest that inner-city blacks, especially African-American males, are experiencing increasing problems in the labor market, the reasons for those problems are seen in a complex web of interrelated factors, including those that are race-neutral.

The loss of traditional manufacturing and other blue-collar jobs in Chicago resulted in increased joblessness among inner-city black males and a concentration in low-wage, high-turnover laborer and service-sector jobs. Embedded in ghetto neighborhoods, social networks, and households that are not conducive to employment, inner-city black males fall further behind their white and Hispanic counterparts, especially when the labor market is slack. Hispanics "continue to funnel into manufacturing because employers prefer Hispanics over blacks and they like to hire by referrals from current employees, which Hispanics can readily furnish, being already embedded in migration networks." Inner-city black men grow bitter and resentful in the face of their employment prospects and often manifest or express these feelings in their harsh, often dehumanizing, low-wage work settings.

Their attitudes and actions, combined with erratic work histories in high-turnover jobs, create the widely shared perception that they are undesirable workers. The perception in turn becomes the basis for employers' negative hiring decisions, which sharply increase when the economy is weak. The rejection of inner-city black male workers gradually grows over the long term not only because employers are turning more to the expanding immigrant and female labor force, but also because the number of jobs that require contact with the public continues to climb.

The position of inner-city black women in the labor market is also problematic. Their high degree of social isolation in impoverished neighborhoods reduces their employment prospects. Although Chicago employers consider them more acceptable as workers than the inner-city black men, their social isolation is likely to strengthen involvement in a work culture that has few supports allowing a move into white-collar employment. Also, impoverished neighborhoods, weak networks, and weak household supports decrease their ability to develop language and other job-related skills necessary in an economy that increasingly rewards employees who can work and communicate effectively with the public.

Despite the attitudes of employers, joblessness in inner-city ghetto neighborhoods would decline if the U.S. economy could sustain high levels of employment over a long period of time. In a slack labor market—a labor market with high unemployment—employers are—and indeed, can afford to be—more selective in recruiting and in granting promotions. They overemphasize job prerequisites and exaggerate the value of experience. In such an economic climate, disadvantaged minorities suffer disproportionately and the level of employer discrimination rises. In a tight labor market, job vacancies are numerous, unemployment is of short duration, and wages are higher. Moreover, in a tight labor market the labor force expands because increased job opportunities not only reduce unemployment but also draw into the labor force those workers who, in periods when the labor market is slack, respond to fading job prospects by dropping out of the labor force altogether. Conversely, in a tight labor market the status of all workers—including disadvantaged minorities—improves because of lower unemployment, higher wages, and better jobs.

The economic recovery during the first half of the 1990s lowered the unemployment rates among blacks in general. For the first time in more than two decades, the unemployment rate for African-Americans dipped below 10 percent in December 1994. Indeed, "the unemployment rate for black adults dropped faster in 1994 than it did for white adults." This was in part due to a brief expansion of manufacturing jobs. By contrast, the economy saw a slight decrease in manufacturing jobs during the economic recovery period in the late 1980s and more than 1.5 million positions were eliminated from January 1989 to September 1993. However, 301,000 manufacturing jobs were created during the next sixteen months, significantly benefiting black workers who are heavily concentrated in manufacturing.

Nonetheless, the unemployment rate represents only the percentage of workers in the labor force—that is, those who are actively looking for work. A more significant measure is the employment-to-population ratio, which corresponds to the percentage of adults 16 and older who are working. For example, whereas the unemployment rate for black youths 16 years old and older was 34.6 percent in December of 1994, compared with a white youth unemployment rate of 14.7 percent, only 23.9 percent of all black youths were actually working, compared with 48.5 percent of white youths. In previous years, labor-market demand stimulated by fiscal or monetary policy not only absorbed the technically unemployed (that is, those jobless workers who are in the official labor force) but also enlarged the employment ranks by drawing back workers who were not in or had dropped out of the labor force. Today, it appears that inner-city residents who are not in the labor force tend to be beyond the reach of monetary or fiscal policy. The problem is that in recent years tight labor markets have been of relatively short duration, frequently followed by a recession which either wiped out previous gains for many workers or did not allow others to fully recover from a previous period of economic stagnation. It would take sustained tight labor markets over many years to draw back those discouraged inner-city workers who have dropped out of the labor market altogether, some for very long periods of time. The disappearance of work in the inner-city ghetto presents a serious challenge to society. The consequences of such joblessness are not restricted to the inner-city ghettos, they affect the quality of life and race relations in the larger city as well.

PART 2

THE SOCIAL POLICY CHALLENGE

CHAPTER 6

The American Belief System
Concerning Poverty and Welfare

Historically, Europe and the United States have contrasted sharply in terms of the nature of urban inequality. No European city has experienced the level of concentrated poverty and racial and ethnic segregation that is typical of American metropolises. Nor does any European city include areas that are as physically isolated, deteriorated, and prone to violence as the inner-city ghettos of urban America. In short, there is no real European equivalent to the plight of the American ghetto. Nonetheless, the situation is changing rapidly. European cities are beginning to experience many of the problems of urban social dislocations—including increasing unemployment, concentrated poverty, and racial and ethnic conflicts—that have traditionally plagued American cities.

European cities differ in the origins of their racial and ethnic problems. The rising ethnic conflicts in eastern Europe which have accompanied the breakdown of the Soviet empire stem from nationalist political struggles in the period of democratization, not from immigration. However, there are significant differences even among the countries of western Europe. Since the late 1960s, northern European economies have received workers from Turkey, the Maghreb countries of northwest Africa, North Africa, the Middle East, and former British, Dutch, and French territories. These influxes of immigrants have widened the cultural experiences of European nations, and differences between immigrants and indigenous populations are disturbing the traditionally homogeneous makeup of communities.

In discussions of urban poverty and racial tensions, the European countries that have most frequently been contrasted with the United States are Britain, France, Holland, and Belgium. All of these countries were once colonial powers, and racial groups from former colonies have been prominently represented among recent immigrants. A number of other countries, including Switzerland, Norway, Sweden, and Germany, have seen an influx of immigrants who have come mainly as laborers from southern Europe and as refugees from countries outside Europe. Finally, the southern part of Europe, which for most of the mid-twentieth century represented "sending countries" (countries whose own citizens often became immigrant workers), is now experiencing a fairly rapid growth of immigration from the Maghreb countries of northwest Africa.

The immigrants in all of these countries are disproportionately represented in areas that feature the highest levels of unemployment. Although they are far from matching the depth and severity of the social dislocations that plague the inner-city ghettos of the United States, many inner-city communities and outer-city public housing estates in countries like France and the Netherlands have been cut off from mainstream labor market institutions and informal job networks, creating the vicious cycle of weak labor force attachment, growing social exclusion, and rising tensions.

Although these European inner-city communities still feature many indigenous residents and are therefore more mixed than the nearly black-only ghettos of the United States, their population is invariably drawn disproportionately from the various first- and second-generation immigrant minorities. Trends in a number of European countries suggest the beginnings of the kind of urban social polarization typical of American metropolises.

More important, however, the economic and industrial restructuring of Europe, which includes the decline of traditional manufacturing areas, has decreased the need for unskilled immigrant labor. Thousands of the immigrants who had been recruited during periods of national labor shortages have now been laid off. A substantial number of the new jobs in the next several decades will require levels of training and education that are beyond the reach of most immigrant minorities. Being the last hired and the first fired, immigrant minorities were unemployed at rates that soared during the late 1970s through the 1980s and reached levels ranging from 25 to 50 percent in the cities with unprecedented high levels of unemployment overall. This is not unlike the situation facing residents of the inner-city ghettos of the United States. The economic origins of the problems are also similar, and they deserve a closer look.

It is important to recognize that much of the sharp rise in inner-city joblessness in the United States and the growth of unemployment in Europe and Canada stems from the swift technological changes in the global economy. First of all, there has been a decline in mass production. The effects of this change are perhaps most clearly seen in the U.S. economy, which has traditionally enjoyed rapid growth in productivity and living standards. As outlined in Chapter 2, the mass production system benefited from large quantities of cheap natural resources, economies of scale, and processes that generated higher uses of productivity through shifts in market forces and that caused improvements in one industry to lead to advancements in others.

The skill requirements of the mass production system were reflected in the system of learning. Public schools in the United States were principally designed to provide low-income native and immigrant students with the basic literacy and numeracy skills required for routine work in mass production factories, service industries, or farms. On the other hand, families with professional, technical, and managerial backgrounds had access to elite learning processes in public and private schools and were able to utilize family connections and experiences to prepare their children for higher-paying occupations. "The school-to-work transition processes were informal and largely family related, but were perpetuated through the formal learning system."

Today's close interaction between technology and international competition has eroded the basic institutions of the mass production system. In the last several decades, almost all of the improvements in productivity have been associated with technology and human capital, thereby drastically reducing the importance of physical capital and natural resources. Moreover, in the traditional mass production system only a few highly educated professional, technical, and managerial workers were needed because most of the work "was routine and could be performed by workers who needed only basic literacy and numeracy." Accordingly, workers with limited education were able to take home wages that were comparatively high by international and historical standards. "This was especially true after the New Deal policies of the 1930s provided social safety nets for those who were not expected to work, collective bargaining to improve workers' share of system's gains, and monetary and fiscal policies to help the mass production system running at relatively low levels of unemployment."

At the same time that changes in technology are producing new jobs, however, they are making many others obsolete. The workplace has been revolutionized by technological changes that range from the development of robotics to the creation of information highways. A widening gap between the skilled and unskilled workers is developing because education and training are more important than ever. Indeed, because of low levels of education, more and more unskilled workers are out of work or poorly paid in both the United States and Europe. While educated workers are benefiting from the pace of technological change, less skilled workers, such as those found in many inner-city neighborhoods, face the growing threat of job displacement. For example, highly skilled designers, engineers, and operators are needed for the jobs created by the development of a new set of computer-operated machine tools, an advance that also *eliminates* jobs for those trained only for manual, assembly-line work. Also, advances in word processing have increased the demand for those who not only know how to type but can operate specialized software as well; the need for routine typists and secretaries is, accordingly, reduced.

The impact of technological change has been heightened by international competition. In order to adjust to changing markets and technology, competitive systems were forced to become more flexible. Companies can compete more effectively in the international market either by improving productivity and quality or by reducing workers' income. The easier approach is this latter low-wage strategy, which the United States has tended to follow. According to Ray Marshall, the former secretary of labor in the Carter administration, "Most other industrialized nations have rejected this strategy because it implies lower and more unequal wages, with serious political, social, and economic implications." To encourage western European and Japanese companies to follow high-wage strategies, several actions have been taken. First, governments have worked to create a national consensus concerning recovery strategies—perhaps the most important step toward effective changes. Companies were then pushed to pursue high-wage strategies in a political and regulatory environment that included adjustment processes to shift resources from low- to high-productivity activities, trade and industrial policies, wage regulations, relatively generous family support systems and unemployment compensation, and universal national health care. But with a recent sharp rise in un-employment there is growing pressure on European nations to adopt the low-wage strategy pursued by the United States.

A few years ago when unemployment rose in all the major indus-trial democracies during the worldwide recession, "the conventional wisdom was that the upturn in the business cycle would solve most of the problem." When the United States entered a period of economic recovery in the early 1990s and the worst of the recession was over in Europe, there remained a scarcity of new high-wage jobs on both sides of the Atlantic, a situation that created fears that the duration of the shortage would be lengthy.

In the highly integrated global marketplace of today, economies can grow, stock markets can rise, corporate profits can soar, and yet many workers may remain unemployed or underemployed. Why? Be-cause "capital and technology are now so mobile that they do not al-ways create good jobs in their own backyard." Corporate cutbacks, made in an effort to streamline operations for the global economy, have added to the jobless woes of many workers. In short, economic growth today does not necessarily produce good jobs.

In comparisons between the United States and other industrial-ized nations, the problem of jobs can be seen in different dimensions. Europe and Canada have continued to increase wages and benefits for their workers, but at the price of high levels of unemployment for the many who are kept afloat with generous unemployment insurance. In 1994, 11 percent of the European workforce, or 18 million people, were unemployed. By contrast, the United States, which moved out of the recession earlier, has created more jobs mainly by getting workers to accept low-paying employment. The result has been a widening gap in the United States between the highest- and lowest-paid workers.

Because of Europe's relatively munificent social safety nets, many eschew the kind of low-paying jobs taken by low-skilled workers in the United States. They rely instead on relatively generous unemploy-ment compensation. "In most of the European Union, an unemployed worker can receive close to $1,000 a month indefinitely. In addition, Europe's highly regulated job markets, where it is very difficult to dis-miss workers, have left employers wary of creating jobs." This has led not only to a steady growth in unemployment and increases in wages and social security contributions but to a less and less competitive Eu-ropean industry as well.

The U.S. economy created 35 million jobs between 1973 and 1991. Europe added just 8 million during the same period despite having about one-third more people. As noted in Chapter 2, most of the new jobs in the United States were in the service sector—including those for workers with limited education and training disproportionately held by women. The growth of employment in the service sector reduced, but did not offset, the overall job declines for less educated workers in the U.S. central cities. Indeed, most of the jobs growth occurred outside central cities.

In the more flexible labor market in the United States, real wages grew each year by less than .5 percent, whereas annual real wage growth in Europe rose three times as fast. "Minimum wage levels tend to be higher in Europe, with cost-of-living increases and four-week annual vacations virtually guaranteed." Total compensation—wages, health benefits, vacations—for the typical U.S. worker in manufacturing has either remained flat or declined since the mid-1970s, while it has increased by 40 percent for a European worker in a comparable job. Average compensation for a manufacturing worker in the United States is $16 an hour; in Germany it is $26. During the 1980s, the wages for low-income U.S. workers who lacked any college education dropped 15 percent when adjusted for inflation, whereas those for comparable workers in Europe increased 15 to 20 percent.

There is mounting pressure on European countries to make some adjustments in order to become more globally competitive. Some European observers have argued that there will have to be a massive reduction in the continent's labor force. Others emphasize that production will have to be transferred to lower-wage parts of the world. Both strategies will lead to even greater unemployment. Still other strategists claim that one way to combat the growing problems of unemployment, including those stemming from industrial cost-cutting of the kind engaged in by American industries, is to develop the service sector, even if the jobs do carry lower wages. In so doing, restrictions on zoning laws and store-opening hours would have to be relaxed. Also, the welfare state would have to be altered by lowering taxes and nonwage contributions that significantly increase total labor costs. This strategy would create more low-wage jobs, but it would also, as in the United States, lead to greater inequality among workers.

A recent report based on interviews with leading government officials, corporate executives, economists, and union leaders in Europe reveals pessimism about the efficacy of future action to address the problem of global competition. These leaders feel that Europe lacks both the time and the political will to change social and political habits enough to enable the private sector to better compete in the global economy and thus create enough new jobs to contain the unemployment. "Most everyone agrees on the desirability of slashing regulatory red tape, taxes, and the nonwage labor costs that support Europe's encrusted social protection programs, but few believe it will happen any time soon."

Despite the increasing strains on the European welfare state and cries to cut back on welfare benefits so as to combat unemployment, there are notable differences between the United States and Europe in the extent to which problems of poverty and inequality are addressed. In contrast to many European nations, the United States has not created comprehensive programs to promote the *social* rights of American citizens. Anti-poverty programs have been narrowly targeted and fragmented.

In comparison with Canada and most western European countries, social citizenship rights in the United States are less developed and less intertwined with rights of political and civil citizenship. Although social citizenship rights increased in the United States after World War II, they have yet to reach the levels enjoyed by the citizens of western Europe. For example, American housing policies to promote home ownership have tended to benefit the working and middle classes, not the poor. "Direct financial housing subsidies for low-income families, common in European welfare states, have been virtually non-existent in the United States." The housing made available to the poor tends to be confined to a limited number of public projects disproportionately concentrated in inner-city neighborhoods far from employment opportunities and informal job information networks as well. Moreover, western European societies have always had a much more comprehensive program of unemployment insurance, and the gap has widened each year since the U.S. program lost ground in the early years of the Reagan administration. Indeed, "in every year from 1984 through 1988 the proportion of the jobless receiving unemployment insurance benefits in an average month registered a record low. While a number of factors were at work here, including lower rates of application by eligible unemployed workers, federal and state cuts in the program played a role."

Finally, in western European countries, where services such as medical care are considered basic collective goods, the poor tend to be covered by the same comprehensive medical programs as the working and middle classes. In the United States, however, a Federal Advisory Commission recently reported that Medicaid, a health program for poor people, pays doctors much less than either Medicare or private health insurers pay for the same services. As a result, many doctors refuse to take Medicaid patients.

Those at the bottom of the class ladder in the United States have always suffered greater economic deprivation and insecurity. The most rapid growth in expenditures for U.S. welfare programs has been in universal entitlements such as Social Security and Medicare—programs whose elderly recipients tend to be members of the working and middle classes.

A number of means-tested or targeted programs for the poor have been created in recent years, but the relief they provide is so minimal that they could not prevent the poor from slipping even deeper into poverty. In 1975, 30 percent of all the poor in the United States had incomes below 50 percent of the amount officially designated as the poverty line; in 1992, 40 percent did so. Among blacks, the increase was even sharper, from 32 percent in 1975 to nearly half (49 percent) in 1992. Moreover, the overall poverty rate actually increased after 1978. These discouraging figures are related to such factors as "general income stagnation, the erosion of wages for lower-skilled jobs in the private sector (average hourly wages were lower in real terms in 1989 than in any year since 1970), the increase in the proportion of families headed by single women, and the large decrease in real benefit levels provided by states under the AFDC program."

Food stamps, Medicaid, and the Supplemental Security Income program (SSI) do provide some relief, but as currently designed, they have virtually no effect on the continuing poverty rates among the nonelderly. In short, targeted programs for the poor in the United States do not even begin to address inequities in the social class system. Instead of helping to integrate the recipients into the broader economic and social life of mainstream society—to "capitalize" them into a different educational or residential stratum, as the GI bill and the postwar federal mortgage programs did for working- and middle-class whites—they tend to stigmatize and separate them.

Recent economic crises in Europe have made it difficult to sustain programs that embody universal and integrative social citizenship rights. With the growth of mass unemployment and the increasing fragmentation of European labor markets, pressures to cut back on welfare state benefits have mounted. And the increase of racial and ethnic diversity has led some to reexamine the postwar commitment to universal programs and social inclusion—a commitment originally based on conceptions of citizenship that assumed a fair degree of cultural homogeneity.

Recent challenges questioning this social welfare commitment often reflect racial bias. The latest economic and social changes in urban Europe have already created situations ripe for the demagogic mobilization of racism and anti-immigrant feelings. As economic conditions have worsened, many in the majority white population have come to view the growth of minorities as part of the problem. Stagnant economies and slack labor markets have placed strains on the welfare state at the very time that the immigrant population, facing mounting problems of joblessness, has become more dependent on public assistance for survival.

When the European economies enjoyed tight labor markets and positive economic growth, the welfare state could be financed easily; welfare services, with strong popular support, were either maintained or increased. Calls to cut back on welfare programs, however, accompanied economic stagnation and were influenced by two developments in the 1980s. One was the growing cost of social service programs and entitlements during periods of high unemployment and limited public revenues. The other was the rise to power of a conservative government in the United Kingdom whose views about the need to reduce welfare were buttressed by the political ascendancy of Reaganism in the United States.

In various parts of Europe, ethnic and racial antagonisms have worsened. Algerians and black Africans have been attacked in several French cities, and to the dismay of French progressives, Jean-Marie Le Pen's anti-immigrant National Front movement has had surprising electoral successes. Rioting occurred in several black neighborhoods in Britain. African immigrants have also been attacked in a number of

Italian cities. And tensions have surfaced in several Dutch cities between Christians and Muslims and between racial minorities and whites. Unfortunately, in view of the growing economic and social dislocations in Europe, both spontaneous and organized expressions of overt racism will likely increase if the economic and social problems I have described are not addressed. In many respects, the "postwar" Europe that we know today may not resemble the Europe we will see at the turn of the century.

As western Europe enters a period of economic uncertainty and experiences growing problems of poverty, poverty concentration, and joblessness among the disadvantaged, individuals concerned about preserving social citizenship rights in democratic states should pay close attention to what has happened in urban America. I say this in part because of the way in which some members of the general public in Europe have responded to the increasing visibility of, and deteriorating economic and social situation of, minority and immigrant populations. Although the conditions for expressions of racial antagonisms have increased, official and scholarly explanations of the widening gap between the haves and have-nots in Europe still tend to focus much more on the changes and inequities in the broader society, not on individual deficiencies and behavior. Therefore, public rhetoric lends much greater support to the ideology of social citizenship rights. Furthermore, welfare programs that benefit wide segments of the population, such as child care, children allowances (an annual benefit per child), housing subsidies, education, medical care, and unemployment insurance have been firmly institutionalized in many western European democracies. Efforts to cut back on these programs in the face of growing joblessness do not just threaten the poor, and thus they have met firm resistance from working- and middle-class citizens.

However, in the United States not only do welfare programs that benefit the poor lack institutional safeguards, but, as we shall soon see, the basic belief system concerning the nature and causes of poverty and welfare frames economic and social outcomes mainly in individual terms. This allows conservative intellectuals and policymakers to overemphasize the negative aspects of persistent joblessness and the receipt of welfare by playing on the key individualistic and moralistic themes of this dominant American belief system. Accordingly, the tragic nature and social causes of such problems are lost on a public that holds truly disadvantaged groups, such as inner-city blacks, largely responsible for their plight.

The public framing of social outcomes has profound implications not only for the approach scholars take in studying sensitive problems like ghetto joblessness and poverty but also for the proposals advanced by members of society to address those problems. Beliefs that associate joblessness and poverty with individual shortcomings do not generate strong support for *social* programs intended to end inequality. No one understood this idea better than the British social scientist T. H. Marshall. If we follow his classic thesis on the development of citizenship, we see that when the fundamental principle linking poverty to the social class and racial structure is recognized or acknowledged in Western society, the emphasis on the rights of citizens will tend to go beyond civil and political rights to include social rights—that is, "the whole range from the right to a modicum of economic welfare and security to the right to share to the full in the social heritage and to live the life of a civilized being according to the standards prevailing in the society."

However, as critics of American approaches to the study of poverty and welfare have shown repeatedly, concerns about the civil and political aspects of citizenship in the United States (unlike in Europe) have overshadowed concerns about the social aspects of citizenship (a right to employment, economic security, education, and health care) because of a strong belief system that deemphasizes the social origins and social significance of poverty and welfare.

After analyzing findings from national survey data collected in 1969 and then again in 1980, James Kluegel and Eliot Smith concluded that "most Americans believe that opportunity for economic advancement is widely available, that economic outcomes are determined by individuals' efforts and talents (or their lack) and that in general economic inequality is fair." Indeed, responses to questions in these two national American surveys revealed that individualistic explanations for poverty (lack of effort or ability, poor morals, poor work skills) were overwhelmingly favored over structural explanations (lack of adequate schooling, low wages, lack of jobs, and so on). The most frequently selected items in the surveys were "lack of thrift or proper money management skills," "lack of effort," "lack of ability or talent," attitudes from one's family background that impede social mobility, "failure of society to provide good schools," and "loose morals and drunkenness." Except for the "failure of society to provide good schools," all of these phrases represent individualistic understandings of the causes of poverty. The Americans in the survey considered structural factors, such as "low wages," "failure of industry to provide jobs," and "racial discrimination," least important of all. The ordering of these factors remained virtually unchanged between 1969 and 1980.

A 1990 survey using these same questions showed a slight increase among those who associate poverty with institutional and structural causes, especially the "failure of industry to provide enough jobs." The proportion of American adults who would not ascribe any importance to this item as a cause of poverty declined from one in three in 1969 to roughly one in five in 1990. Nonetheless, despite the slight increase in the support for structural explanations of the causes of poverty, Americans remain strongly disposed to the idea that individuals are largely responsible for their economic situations. Each of the three times the survey was administered, the most popular individualistic explanation was "lack of effort by the poor themselves." Across the 1969–90 time span, more than nine out of ten American adults felt that lack of effort was either very or somewhat important as a cause of poverty. Fewer than 10 percent felt that it was not important.

Their findings sharply contrast with those based on a similar survey conducted in twelve European countries (the United Kingdom, Ireland, France, Denmark, Belgium, the Netherlands, Spain, Germany, Greece, Luxembourg, Portugal, and Italy) in 1990. Citizens of these countries favored structural explanations over individual explanations for the causes of poverty by a wide margin. Two-thirds of the Europeans associated poverty with either social injustice, misfortune, or changes in the modern world. Only 17 percent felt that poverty was the result of laziness or a lack of willpower. Given the growing economic uncertainty in Europe and the rising ethnic and racial tensions, it is uncertain whether these attitudes will come to approach those of Americans. At the present time, however, both the attitudes of ordinary citizens and the public rhetoric focus much more on changes and inequities in the society at large, rather than on individual behavior and deficiencies, in accounting for poverty.

In 1978, the French social scientist Robert Castel argued that the paradox of poverty in affluent American society has rested on the notion that "the poor are individuals who themselves bear the chief responsibility for their condition. As a result, the politics of welfare centers around the management of individual deficiencies." From the building of almshouses in the late nineteenth century to President Johnson's War on Poverty, Americans have failed to emphasize the social rights of the poor, "rights whose interpretation is independent of the views of the agencies charged with dispensing assistance."

Data from public opinion polls support this argument. They indicate that Americans tend to be far more concerned about the *duties* or social obligations of the poor, particularly the welfare poor, than about their social *rights* as American citizens. As far back as the New Deal, Americans have persistently debated whether recipients of welfare checks should be required to work. Public opinion polls over the years have revealed strong support for a work requirement for those on welfare. For example, a Harris poll taken in 1972 showed that 89 percent of the respondents were "in favor of making people on welfare go to work." A 1977 NBC poll revealed that 93 percent of the respondents felt that able-bodied welfare recipients should be required to work at public jobs.

Survey data also suggest that public sentiment against welfare has increased over the past few years. The percentage of respondents in a national poll who said they agreed with the anti-welfare statement that we are "spending too much money on welfare programs in this country" increased from 61 percent in 1969 to 81 percent in 1980; those who agreed with the anti-welfare statement that "most people getting welfare are not honest about their needs" rose from 71 percent in 1969 to 77 percent in 1980; finally, those who concurred with the pro-welfare view that "most people on welfare who can work try to find jobs so they can support themselves" declined from 47 percent in 1969 to 31 percent in 1980. "In the post-1980 period there was a small but real rise in support for increased welfare spending. Many have interpreted this as a reaction against Reagan-era efforts to cut welfare programs." Still, a substantial majority of Americans opposed increased spending for welfare.

A more recent survey suggests that underlying such overwhelming public sentiment against welfare is the belief that the moral character of individuals, not inequities in the social and economic structure of society, is at the root of the problem. Indeed, this survey uncovered widespread support for the notion that most welfare recipients do not share the majority view about the importance of hard work. A majority of the whites polled in this study disagreed with the pro-welfare statement that "most welfare recipients do need help and could not get along without welfare." There was strong sentiment for the view that welfare reform, in the words of one respondent, should be "to get people motivated and become part of the system." Finally, this study emphasized "that there is today, as there has been for years, general agreement—shared by whites and nonwhites alike—that many people on welfare could be working, that many people on welfare cheat, and that a lot of money spent on behalf of the poor has been wasted."

Reactions to the label "welfare" should not be interpreted as an indication of the public's support for aiding the poor. "The term 'welfare' has become a red flag, apparently signaling waste, fraud, and abuse to many Americans." Also, the notion of welfare conjures up racial feelings. A recent study of attitudes toward poverty among white middle-class Americans revealed that the image of unmarried black women with babies evoked strong negative responses when the race of the person in poverty was considered. Young black women were more likely to be held responsible for their plight and much less worthy of government support than single white welfare mothers.

Nonetheless, Americans clearly want to support those living in poverty. For example, from 1983 to 1991 the General Social Survey, conducted by the National Opinion Research Center, found that whereas a substantial majority of Americans felt that too little was being spent to help the poor, only slightly more than 20 percent in any given year felt that too little was being spent to help those on welfare. Paradoxically, it would seem that helping the poor is good, but helping them through the established channels—that is, through welfare—is not.

The heavy emphasis on the individual traits of the poor and on the duties or social obligations of welfare recipients is not unique to the general public. This "common wisdom" has been uncritically integrated into the work of many poverty researchers. Throughout the 1960s and 1970s, the expanding network of poverty researchers in the United States paid considerable attention to the question of individuals' work attitudes and the association between income maintenance programs and the work ethic of the poor. These poverty researchers, however, consistently ignored the effects of basic economic transformations and cyclical processes on the work experiences and prospects of the poor.

It would be interesting to look at an examination of American approaches to the study of poverty from a European perspective. The Swedish scholar Walter Korpi has pointed out that "efforts to explain poverty and inequality in the United States ... appear primarily to have been sought in terms of the characteristics of the poor." Whereas poverty researchers in the United States have conducted numerous studies on the work motivation of the poor, problems of human capital (in which poverty is discussed as, if not reduced to, a problem of lack of education and occupational skills), and the effects of income maintenance programs on the supply of labor, he argued, they have largely neglected to study the impact of the extremely high levels of unemployment that have plagued impoverished Americans since the end of World War II. Writing in 1980, before the rise of high levels of unemployment in Europe, Korpi pointed out that "in Europe, where unemployment has been considerably lower, the concerns of politicians as well as researchers have been keyed much more strongly to the question of unemployment. It is an intellectual paradox that living in a *society that has been a sea of unemployment* [emphasis added], American poverty researchers have concentrated their research interests on the work motivation of the poor" rather than on the cyclical nature of employment in the United States.

Another irony is that despite this narrow focus, these very same American researchers have consistently uncovered empirical evidence that undermines, rather than supports, common assumptions about how welfare negatively affects individual initiative and motivation. Yet these assumptions persist among policymakers, and "the paradox of continuing high poverty during a period of general prosperity has contributed to the recently emerging consensus that welfare must be reformed." Although it is reasonable to argue that policymakers are not aware of a good deal of the empirical research on the effects of welfare, the General Accounting Office (GAO), an investigative arm of Congress, released a study in early 1987 reporting that there was no conclusive evidence to support the prevailing common beliefs that welfare discourages individuals from working, breaks up two-parent families, or affects the childbearing rates of unmarried women, even young unmarried women.

The GAO reached these conclusions after reviewing the results of more than one hundred empirical studies on the effects of welfare completed since 1975, analyzing the case files of more than 1,200 families receiving public assistance in four states, and interviewing officials from federal, state, and local government agencies. Although these conclusions should come as no surprise to poverty researchers familiar with the empirical literature, they should have generated a stir among members of Congress, many of whom have no doubt been influenced by the highly publicized works of conservative scholars such as George Gilder, Charles Murray, and Lawrence Mead which ascribe, without direct empirical evidence, persistent poverty and other social dislocations to the negative effects of welfare.

But systematic scientific argument is no match for the dominant belief system: the views of members of Congress have apparently not been significantly altered by the GAO report. The growth of social dislocations among the inner-city poor and the continued high rates of joblessness and poverty have led policymakers to conclude that something must be done about the welfare system, which they perceive to be causing the breakdown of the norms of citizenship among recipients. Indeed, a liberal-conservative consensus on welfare reform has recently emerged that features two themes: (1) The receipt of welfare should be predicated on reciprocal responsibilities whereby society is obligated to provide assistance to welfare applicants, who, in turn, are obligated to behave in socially endorsed ways, and (2) Able-bodied adult welfare recipients should be required to prepare themselves for work, to search for employment, and to accept jobs when they are offered. These points of agreement were reflected in the discussions of the Family Support Act passed by the United States Congress in 1988. They have also been the focus of a good deal of the public discussions concerning welfare reform since then.

These two themes are based on the implicit assumption that a sort of mysterious "welfare ethos" exists that encourages public assistance recipients to avoid their obligations as citizens to be educated, to work, to support their families, and to obey the law. In other words—and in keeping with the dominant American belief system—*"it is the moral fabric of individuals, not the social and economic structure of society, that is taken to be the root of the problem."* This belief system is a factor in the drastic decline in state support for the Aid for Families with Dependent Children (AFDC) program.

AFDC is a joint federal and state program that provides cash benefits to eligible poor families with children. The federal government provides 50 to 75 percent of the costs to run the program, but individual states establish the dollar amount for financial assistance and the level of benefits granted. The cash benefit is supposed to enable an eligible family to meet its basic needs—shelter, food, clothing, and household and personal necessities. A family on AFDC also can qualify for food stamps to help cover food costs. As discussed later, the 1995 Congress introduced legislation to convert the AFDC program into a federal block grant with fixed funding.

An average of 9.5 million children in 5 million families (representing a total of 14.3 million children and adults) received AFDC each month during fiscal year 1993. However, the total number of AFDC families during that fiscal year was 7.3 million. Since new families entered the program throughout the year and some families receiving AFDC departed each month, the total number of AFDC recipients in a year exceeded the number who received aid in any one month.

Families receiving AFDC were far worse off in 1995 than those who had received public assistance twenty years earlier. Between 1975 and 1995, after adjusting for inflation, the benefit level had declined in every state, so much so that the average real value of AFDC nationwide had plummeted 37 percent during this period. Increases in food stamp benefits slightly cushioned, but far from offset, the losses in AFDC purchasing power. "Between July 1972 and 1992, the combined value of AFDC and food stamps for a three-person family with no countable income dropped 26% on average, from $874 in July 1972 (measured in 1992 dollars) to $649 in July 1992."

The erosion of AFDC benefits became a landslide after 1991. Only six states (Alabama, Arizona, Hawaii, Montana, New Mexico, and South Dakota) maintained or increased the level of benefits between January 1991 and January 1994. Benefit levels were actually cut in nine states, sometimes more than once, and they did not keep pace with inflation in the remaining states. "At no other time in the past twenty-five years, and perhaps never in the history of the program, have so many states enacted such deep cuts for so many families over such a short time period."

When Congress initiated the legislative process to convert AFDC to block grants, the plight of AFDC families could perhaps best be assessed by relating benefit levels to housing costs. In nearly every state, the full monthly AFDC benefit was not sufficient to cover the costs of "what the U.S. Department of Housing and Urban Development (HUD) considers to be 'decent, safe, and sanitary' housing of a 'modest' nature." The Center on Social Welfare Policy and Law found that in 78 of 95 representative localities across the United States, the fair market rent (FMR) for two-bedroom housing is more than the total monthly benefit for an AFDC family of three. "In cities like Newark, Chicago, Philadelphia, Denver, Atlanta, New Orleans, St. Louis, and Memphis, the AFDC benefit is less than two-thirds of the FMR for two-bedroom housing." Housing subsidies did not offset these deficiencies. In fact, only 23 percent of all AFDC families received some form of housing subsidy or lived in public housing in 1992.

The collapse of support for AFDC recipients is related to fundamental assumptions about the nature of welfare and welfare families, including the beliefs that most welfare families are long-term recipients and that most are black women with many children. But studies that analyze welfare data, including monthly data on who receives how much welfare, challenge these assumptions. Only a minority of the AFDC recipients were African-American in 1995, and the average number of children in welfare families was slightly less than the average number in nonwelfare families. Moreover, the research based on monthly data indicates that the welfare population is very dynamic—that is, subject to frequent change.

People tended to go on and off welfare in short spurts, and about one-third had been on welfare more than once. Half of all welfare recipients exited welfare during the first year, and three-quarters departed within two years. Many of those who quickly exited the welfare rolls during the first year, however, returned. As noted in Chapter 3, there is considerable movement between welfare and work. Many mothers go off welfare and enter low-wage employment, try unsuccessfully to make ends meet, and then return to welfare. Some repeated this pattern again and again. Also, as discussed in Chapter 3, it is not the lack of work ethic that causes these mothers to return to or remain on welfare. Not only do they prefer work to welfare, but permanent welfare receipt is anathema to them.

As unemployment in the general population rises, the probability of exiting welfare diminishes. It is not surprising that those who are least employable in terms of skills and training are least successful in avoiding welfare. The longer a mother remains off welfare, the less likely it is that she will return. An examination of the long-term data on multiple spells of welfare reflects the high turnover. Thirty percent of welfare recipients were on AFDC for less than two years, and 50 percent received welfare for less than four years. These figures include recipients who have gone off and then returned to welfare during these periods. Only 15 percent remained *continuously* on welfare for five years. Long-term welfare mothers tended to be racial minorities, never-married, high school dropouts, and those who lack employment experiences. "The overall picture is that one group uses welfare for relatively short periods of time and never return. A middle group cycles on and off, some for short periods and others for longer periods, but again, not for five continuous years. And a third, but quite small group, stays on for long periods of time."

Some liberals have used these figures to argue that long-term welfare dependency is a myth. However, even though most periods of welfare receipt are relatively short, at any given point in time 65 percent of those on the welfare rolls are long-term users. "This is because the probability of being on welfare at a given time is necessarily higher for longer-term recipients than for those who have shorter welfare spells." The following example, used by the House Ways and Means Committee, illustrates this point.

> Consider a 13-bed hospital in which 12 beds are occupied for an entire year by 12 chronically ill patients, while the other bed is used by 52 patients, each of whom stays exactly 1 week. On any given day, a hospital census would find that about 85 percent of the patients (12/13) were in the midst of long spells of hospitalization. Nevertheless, viewed over the course of a year, short-term use clearly dominates: out of 84 patients using hospital services, about 80 percent (52/64) spent only 1 week in the hospital.

In order to counter some of the stereotypes about welfare receipt that form part of the dominant American belief system, liberals have frequently emphasized that only a minority of the total number of AFDC recipients are African-American. This is true. But it actually plays into the hands of conservatives to ignore the fact that the percentage of AFDC recipients who were African-American (39.2 percent) in 1995 was roughly equal to the percentage who were non-Hispanic white (39.9 percent), despite the fact that blacks make up only 12.4 percent of the nation's population. Instead of masking such statistics, the best way to defeat the stereotypes about welfare is to emphasize the hard realities of the inner-city ghetto and the larger society that give rise to welfare receipt. This would more effectively challenge some of the underlying assumptions that have led to calls for welfare reform, especially those that put forth draconian measures either to cut benefits severely or to end them altogether.

In the mid-1990s, two drastically opposed approaches to the issue of welfare reform came to the fore. One recognizes that although welfare is not the major cause of urban social dislocations, efforts should be made to facilitate the transition from welfare to work for several reasons: Welfare recipients prefer work over welfare and would readily accept jobs that will not result in their slipping deeper into poverty; not working has certain debilitating effects on individuals and on family life over time; and children are worse off if they are widely exposed to an environment where few or no people work. Accordingly, welfare reform should not be undertaken in isolation. It should be tied to efforts to create jobs for the disadvantaged. Welfare reform should also be conjoined with programs to establish universal health insurance so that public aid recipients who want to "go out there and get a job" do not face the dilemma posed by a Chicago welfare mother: "I don't like being on public aid right now. But without a medical card, what do I do when my kids get sick?"

Accordingly, advocates of this approach, which involves the assumption that welfare mothers prefer work over welfare, are likely to support enthusiastically those aspects of social reform that are designed to "make work pay," principally through the expansion of the earned income tax credit, the creation of universal health insurance, the development of child care programs, and the establishment of child support provisions to ensure contributions from absent parents.

All of these subsidies and benefits designed to make low-wage work pay were originally incorporated into the initial proposals discussed by President Clinton and his advisers in 1993. Welfare reform was thus part of a more comprehensive agenda of social reform. It was argued that to ease the transition from welfare to work it is not only necessary to help local government create public-sector jobs when private-sector jobs are lacking and to turn welfare offices into "transitional" centers for training and job placement, it is also important to have in place universal health insurance to make any kind of welfare reform program viable.

President Clinton's welfare reform proposal did, however, include a feature that reflected the liberal-conservative consensus on reciprocal obligations—namely, that welfare receipt should end after two years. In the original Clinton proposal, a welfare recipient would be required to undergo training and job placement during the two-year maintenance period and then accept jobs in the private sector. If private-sector jobs were not available at that time, then a number of public-sector jobs would have to be created. As Joel F. Handler appropriately noted, the conservatives, as well as many others in the nation, "seized on the time-limits and paid only lip service to the other provisions." Work preparation continues to be talked about, but the all-important components of guaranteed jobs and guaranteed child support at the end of the two-year period were rarely mentioned.

Following the Republican landslide in the 1994 congressional elections, discussions of welfare reform reflected even more the individualistic beliefs that many Americans hold concerning poverty and welfare. These discussions represent the second major approach to welfare reform and are embodied in the Personal Responsibility Act (PRA) in the House Republican "Contract with America."

Unlike President Clinton's proposal and other, earlier bills which required or allowed states to provide work slots for welfare recipients who reached a time limit (including legislation presented by Republicans that called for workfare after two years for recipients who have not yet found employment), the PRA called for terminating eligibility for both cash aid *and* work slots. Mothers who accumulated five years of AFDC receipt over their lifetime would be excluded permanently from receiving cash aid or a work slot, regardless of whether they can find work. In addition to the time-limit provisions, the bill would deny cash assistance to poor children whose mothers are under 18 and unmarried, and would eliminate any increases in the AFDC benefits for women who had more than two children while receiving welfare. This version of welfare reform was passed by the House of Representatives in the spring of 1995.

An important feature of the bill is that it replaces the current system of federal funding for AFDC with a block grant "that would provide states with a fixed amount of funding for cash assistance and welfare-to-work programs over the next five years. The funding level would be set at $15.4 billion without an adjustment for inflation." According to the Center on Budget and Policy Priorities, a policy research center in Washington, D.C., the block grant—with its inflexible funding requirements—could create a serious problem for some states.

> If the number of poor families increases, states would be faced with unpalatable choices, such as meeting additional need entirely with state funds, denying the newly poor entry into the program, creating waiting lists, or cutting benefits across-the-board for the remainder of the fiscal year. Among those hardest hit could be working families that usually do not receive cash assistance but lose their jobs in a recession and need temporary help. Substantial numbers of such families apply for aid during economic downturns.

It does not take much imagination to see the devastating consequences for the welfare poor if the "Contract with America" proposals are enacted into law. In 1994, 4.5 million children were living in families that had received AFDC for a cumulative total of five years. Accordingly, millions of poor children would become ineligible for aid if the five-year limit were imposed. Homeless shelters would be inundated with mothers and children, and the already overburdened foster care system would have to find "foster care and institutional replacements for large numbers of children whose parents were forced to give them up because they were destitute."

A Senate version of welfare reform was passed in September 1995. The Senate version is less severe and, unlike the measure in the House, received bipartisan support. It does not deny increases in the AFDC benefits for women who have more than two children while receiving AFDC and cash assistance to poor children whose mothers are under 18 and unmarried. Nonetheless, like the House version, it would abolish AFDC as an entitlement and replace it with block grants, thereby allowing states to spend as much or as little as they wish to help poor families. According to one estimate, whereas the House welfare bill would push 2.1 million children who are not poor now into poverty, the Senate bill would increase the ranks of poor children by 1.2 million. For those families already in poverty, "the Senate welfare bill would deepen poverty for families with children by more than one-quarter while the House welfare bill would deepen poverty by 50 percent." Reacting to such legislation, Senator Daniel Patrick Moynihan stated: " 'Welfare reform' in fact means welfare repeal. The repeal, that is, of Title IV-A of the Social Security Act. Everyone is to blame for this duplicity, everyone is an accomplice."

A compromise version (conference agreement) of the House and Senate bills was passed by Congress and vetoed by President Clinton in January 1996. The conference agreement included reductions in means-tested entitlement programs totaling almost $80 billion over seven years. The Office of Management and Budget (OMB) estimated that these cuts would move an additional 1.5 million children into poverty and increase the depth of child poverty (that is, make those who are already poor even poorer) by one-third. At the time of this writing, congressional leaders are contemplating submitting another welfare reform bill for the President's signature, which is closer to the Senate's version.

I believe that the growing assault on welfare mothers is part of a larger reaction to the mounting problems in our nation's inner cities. When many people think of welfare they think of young, unmarried black mothers having babies. This image persists even though almost as many whites as blacks were AFDC recipients in 1995, and there were also a good many Hispanics on the welfare rolls. Nevertheless, blacks were disproportionately represented. The rise in the number of black AFDC recipients was said to be symptomatic of such larger problems as the decline in family values and the dissolution of the family. The receipt of welfare, it is argued, contributes to or aggravates these problems. Ending welfare by forcing people to assume personal and family responsibilities is said to be one way to reverse the trend of rising inner-city social dislocations, including joblessness.

The public dialogue with respect to these issues has been decidedly one-sided for years, embellishing the basic assumptions of the American belief system concerning poverty and welfare. It affects the way in which both conservatives and some liberals describe and discuss the problems. The conservatives stress the personal shortcomings of individuals and families while virtually ignoring the deleterious aspects of the environment. On the other hand, whereas some liberals focus on important aspects of the environment and provide structural explanations, others react to the dominant themes of the American belief system by emphasizing the strengths and positive experiences of inner-city families alone. They even criticize those liberals who try to relate inner-city social dislocations to aspects of the environment.

These tendencies affect the discussion of public policy issues.

They shift attention away from the devastating effects of the *interaction of structural and cultural constraints* in the inner-city environment.

Two developments took place in the latter half of the 1960s that affected the public discussion of the causes of and remedies for ghetto poverty. They were (1) the controversy over the 1965 Moynihan report on the black family, *The Negro Family: The Case for National Action*, and (2) a strong emphasis in the African-American community on a black perspective in the analysis of matters pertaining to race.

The controversy over the Moynihan report, like so many controversies, raged in large measure because his ideas were misrepresented and distorted, particularly by the popular media. Moynihan emphasized that the socioeconomic system in the United States was ultimately responsible for producing unstable poor black families, and that, in turn, this instability is "the principal source of most of the aberrant, inadequate, or antisocial behavior that did not establish, but now serves to perpetuate, the cycle of poverty and deprivation." The critical commentary that followed the report, however, ignored the first part of Moynihan's argument and left the erroneous impression that he had placed the blame for black social dislocations solely on black family instability. If this created a problem for the reception of the Moynihan report, it was exacerbated by a changing political climate in the black community. To be more specific, some blacks were highly critical of the Moynihan report's emphasis on social pathologies within ghetto neighborhoods, regardless of their origin. This emphasis was decried not only because of its potential for embarrassment but also because it conflicted with the claim that blacks were developing a community power base that could become a major force in American society, a power base that reflected the strength and vitality of the African-American community.

This critical reaction reflected a new definition, description, and explanation of the black condition that accompanied the emergence of the Black Power movement in the late 1960s. This new approach, proclaimed as the "black perspective," revealed an ideological shift from interracialism to racial solidarity. It first gained currency among militant black spokespersons in the late 1960s and became a recurrent theme in the writings of black academics and intellectuals by the early 1970s. Although the "black perspective" represented a variety of views and arguments on issues of race, the trumpeting of racial pride and self-affirmation was common to all the writings and speeches on the subject.

The declining support for interracialism and the rising emphasis on black solidarity in the late 1960s was typical of a pattern that has been repeated throughout the history of dominant-subordinate group relations in multiethnic societies. Perhaps the sociologist Robert K. Merton comes closest to providing a theoretical explanation for this shift: "When a once powerless collectivity acquires a socially validated sense of growing power, its members experience an intensified need for self-affirmation. Under such conditions, collective self-glorification, found in some measure among all groups, becomes a predictable and intensified counterresponse to long-standing belittlement from without."

In this atmosphere of race chauvinism, a series of studies written by scholars proclaiming the black perspective appeared. The arguments set forth in these studies made it clear that a substantial and fundamental shift in both the tone and focus of race-relations scholarship was occurring. Consistent with the emphasis on black glorification and the quest for self-affirmation, arguments maintaining that some aspects of ghetto life were pathological—even the liberal position holding that racial isolation and class subordination force individuals to adapt to the realities of the ghetto community and therefore become seriously impaired in their ability to function in any other community—were categorically rejected in favor of those underscoring black community strengths. Arguments declaring the deterioration of the poor black family were dismissed in favor of those extolling the "virtues" and "strengths" of black families. Behavior described as destructive by some scholars was reinterpreted as creative by black-perspective proponents—creative in that blacks were displaying the ability to survive and even flourish in a ghetto milieu. Ghetto families were described as resilient and were seen as imaginatively adapting to an oppressive racist society.

The argument put forth by the proponents of the black perspective explanation is interesting because destructive behavior in the ghetto is not even acknowledged. This represents a unique response to the dominant American belief system concerning the causes of poverty and welfare. Instead of challenging the validity of the assumptions underlying this belief system, this approach sidesteps the issue altogether by denying that social dislocations in the inner city represent a special problem. Researchers who emphasized those dislocations, even those who rejected "blaming the victim" by focusing on the structural roots of these problems, were denounced. Because of these developments there was little motivation in the early 1970s to develop a research agenda that pursued the structural roots of ghetto social dislocations. The vitriolic attacks and acrimonious debate that characterized this controversy proved too intimidating to scholars, especially liberal scholars. Indeed, in the aftermath of this controversy and in an effort to protect their work from the charge of racism or of "blaming the victim," liberal social scientists tended to avoid describing any behavior that could be construed as unflattering or stigmatizing to racial minorities. Accordingly, for a period of several years, and well after this controversy had subsided, the problems of social dislocation in the inner-city ghetto did not attract serious research attention. Until the mid-1980s, the void was partially filled by journalists and therefore conclusions about the behavior of inner-city residents were reached without the benefit of a systematic structural framework to help explain the dynamics of poverty and joblessness.

After serious research on the ghetto came to an abrupt halt in the early 1970s, several trends that had earlier worried Daniel Patrick Moynihan became much more pronounced. First of all, poverty had become more urban, more concentrated, and more deeply rooted in large cities, particularly the older industrial cities with immense, highly segregated black and Hispanic populations.

Even though little serious research on life in the ghetto was conducted during this period, there was a general perception, as occasionally reported in the media, that things were getting worse. For example, in the aftermath of the famous New York City power shortage that occasioned widespread looting, *Time* magazine ran a cover story in August 1977 that dramatized conditions in the ghettos of Chicago and New York. The article, entitled "The American Underclass: Minority Within a Minority," was a trendsetter not only because it was the first major popular publication to prominently feature the term "underclass" but also because it set the tone for future media reports on the world of the underclass. "Affluent people know little about this world," stated the *Time* report, "except when despair makes it erupt explosively onto Page 1 or the seven o'clock news. Behind its crumbling walls lives a large group of people who are more intractable, more socially alien and more hostile than almost anyone had imagined. They are the unreachables: the American underclass." The *Time* article pointed out that the concept of "underclass," first used in "class-ridden Europe," was "applied to the U.S. by Swedish economist Gunnar Myrdal and other intellectuals in the 1960s" and "has become a rather common description of people who are seen to be stuck more or less permanently at the bottom, removed from the American dream." The article goes on to state:

> Though its members come from all races and live in many places, the underclass is made up mostly of impoverished urban blacks, who still suffer from the heritage of slavery and discrimination. . . . Their bleak environment nurtures values that are often at radical odds with those of the majority—even the majority of the poor. Thus the underclass minority produces a highly disproportionate number of the nation's juvenile delinquents, school dropouts, drug addicts and welfare mothers, and much of the adult crime, family disruption, urban decay, and demand for social expenditures.

However, it was not until the early 1980s, following the publication of a series of popular books written by conservative analysts, that the arguments made in this article were widely covered in the media. In a political atmosphere created during the first term of the Reagan administration, when the dominant ideology of poverty and welfare was strongly reinforced, conservative analysts rushed to explain the apparent paradox of a sharp rise in inner-city social dislocations after years of sweeping antipoverty and antidiscrimination legislation, beginning with the Great Society programs and the civil rights legislation of the Johnson administration.

Building implicitly on the basic premises of the culture-of-poverty thesis, these analysts, thrust to the fore of the policy debate by the political ascendancy of Reaganism, argued that the growth of liberal social policies since the mid-1960s had exacerbated, rather than alleviated, ghetto-related cultural tendencies. Widely read neo-conservative books such as George Gilder's *Wealth and Poverty* (1981), Charles Murray's *Losing Ground* (1984), and Lawrence Mead's *Beyond Entitlement* (1986) presented a range of arguments dealing with the presumed adverse effects of liberal social policies on urban underclass values and behavior. Thus, the Great Society and other liberal programs were portrayed as self-defeating because they ignored the behavioral problems of the underclass, made the very poor less self-reliant, increased their joblessness, and promoted both their births outside marriage and the tendency among families to be headed by women rather than employed, productive husbands and fathers. It did not seem to matter that these arguments were not supported by any rigorous scientific evidence. Liberal intellectuals had retreated from the discussion of social dislocations in inner-city ghettos and therefore had no alternative explanations to advance. This allowed conservative analysts to dominate the public discourse on the subject throughout the first half of the 1980s. Their themes were echoed in a series of reports on America's underclass in the popular media that provided unprecedented journalistic endorsement of the culture-of-poverty arguments now cloaked in the epithet the "underclass."

In a July 1986 *New Republic* article entitled "The Work-Ethic State," Mickey Kaus emphatically stated that "no one who has watched Bill Moyers's 'CBS Reports' on the black family's decline, or read Leon Dash's series on black teenage pregnancy in the *Washington Post*, or Nicholas Lemann's recent *Atlantic* article on 'The Origins of the Underclass,' or Ken Auletta's book on the same subject, can doubt that there is a culture of poverty out there that has taken on a life of its own." However, these journalistic accounts failed to establish a convincing case for a culture-of-poverty thesis that in effect ignores structural factors.

Kaus correctly points out that "Lemann stresses a fairly direct connection between those blacks who worked in the sharecropping system in the South and those who formed the lower class of the ghettos after the great migration to the North." Indeed, Lemann, in an otherwise perceptive article, went so far as to suggest that "every aspect of the underclass culture in the ghetto is directly traceable to roots in the South." Yet systematic research on poverty and urban migration, including three major studies since 1975, consistently shows that southern-born blacks who have migrated to the North have lower unemployment rates, higher labor-force-participation rates, and lower welfare rates than northern blacks.

Kaus refers to the Dash articles when stating that teenage girls in the inner-city ghetto "are often ridiculed by other girls if they remain virgins too long into their teens." Kaus argues that "once AFDC benefits reach a certain threshold that allow poor single mothers to survive, the culture of the underclass can start growing as women have babies for all the various nonwelfare reasons they have them." This statement overlooks the fact that actual black teenage birth rates in 1983—that is, the number of live births per thousand women—were 35 percent lower than in 1970, and 40 percent lower than in 1960. How does the culture-of-poverty argument regarding black teenage childbearing explain this? The real problem, you see, is not the *rate* of teenage childbearing but the *proportion* of teenage births that are out of wedlock which has substantially increased. As discussed in Chapter 4, structural factors have interacted dramatically with cultural responses to chronic subordination to produce the high rates of out-of-wedlock births.

The television documentary "The Crisis on Federal Street," which aired on PBS in 1986, effectively related the dismal job prospects of young ghetto men and women to declining employment opportunities in the industrial sector. This important point, however, was obscured in Bill Moyers's 1985 "CBS Report" on the decline of the black family, wherein the personal inadequacies of characters such as "Timothy," who had fathered several children out of wedlock, were highlighted. And although Ken Auletta's study of the underclass provided more balanced coverage of possible explanations of inner-city social dislocations, his lack of a clear framework relating behavior and culture to the structure of opportunity stands in sharp contrast to the earlier ethnographic studies of Lee Rainwater, Kenneth Clark, Elliot Liebow, and Ulf Hannerz.

Nonetheless, the Kaus article and the works cited in it are still among the more dispassionate journalistic reports on the ghetto poor. Lurid descriptions of a culture of poverty in a series of other accounts have brought back memories of the 1977 *Time* magazine article. For example, in a *Fortune* magazine piece Myron Magnet stated that what defines the American underclass is "not so much their poverty or race as their behavior—their chronic lawlessness, drug use, welfare dependency, and school failure. 'Underclass' describes a state of mind and a way of life. It is at least as much a cultural as an economic condition." Similar views were echoed in a 1986 Chicago *Tribune* article.

> Members of the underclass don't share traditional values of work, money, education, home and perhaps even of life. This is a class of misfits best known to more fortunate Americans as either

victim or perpetrator in crime statistics. Over the last quarter-century in America, this subculture has become self-perpetuating. It devours every effort aimed at solving its problems, resists solutions both simple and complicated, absorbs more than its share of welfare and other benefits and causes social and political turmoil far out of proportion to its members.

In an article published in *Esquire*, Pete Hamill stated,

> The heart of the matter is the continued existence and expansion of what has come to be called the Underclass ... [individuals] who are trapped in cycles of welfare dependency, drugs, alcohol, crime, illiteracy, and disease, living in anarchic and murderous isolation in some of the richest cities on the earth. As a reporter, I've covered their miseries for more than a quarter of a century. ... And in the last decade, I've watched this group of American citizens harden and condense, moving further away from the basic requirements of a human life: work, family, safety, the law.

One has the urge to shout, "Enough is enough!"

It is interesting to note how the media perceptions of "underclass" values and attitudes contrast sharply with the views actually expressed by the residents of the inner-city ghetto. For example, a 28-year-old un-married welfare mother of two children who lives in one of Chicago's large public housing projects described to one of the UPFLS interviewers how the media create the impression that the people who live in her housing project are all bad or are thugs and killers.

> OK, I don't know where you live at, but you read the papers ... they say, "Oh, Cabrini! Oh, they have gang killings ... they have gang killings on the South Side! But the media and ... and I guess the public, you know, they build it up so big. I mean, it's bad everywhere. Did anyone offend you when you came up here? My neighbor stopped you and gave you the message. You're white, you're white and they don't know you here, see, see, but you read the paper and your parents will say "Don't go over there, girl!" I read where they said, you know, well, I read where there they kill

blacks . . . whites, and they do this and they do that, and they, I
mean, we're people, too. But it's . . . that's just the system. It
makes us look like we're all the same, and we're all bad. . . . But
that's not true.

A 28-year-old welfare mother from another South Side housing
project raised a similar point:

'Cause a lot of people when they meet me, they say "You live in a
project?" I say "yeah." "Well, you don't look like the type of person." "How is a person supposed to look?" You know, like I tell
them, the project don't make nobody, you make yourself. Now, if
you want to get out there and carry that project name, be tough
and rowdy and sloppy, disrespectful, well, shoot, that's lowlife.
"You don't look like the type that lives in a project!" "Well, how
am I supposed to look?" Just because I live in a project, that don't
mean I have to come outside looking like a tramp, because I'm
not. But they all, they like, "You too nice to be living in a project."
You know, sometimes I get offended. . . . That just really gets on
my nerves. You know, don't no building make you, you make
yourself. You live in a home, you know. Look at all these people
that's got Hollywood kids, busted for cocaine, o.d.'in' on it, you
know, what's happened to them?

Our research reveals that the beliefs of inner-city residents bear
little resemblance to the blanket media reports asserting that values
have plummeted in impoverished inner-city neighborhoods or that
people in the inner city have an entirely different value system. What
is so striking is that despite the overwhelming joblessness and poverty,
black residents in inner-city ghetto neighborhoods actually verbally
endorse, rather than undermine, the basic American values concerning individual initiative.

For example, in the large UPFLS survey of individuals who reside
in poor neighborhoods in the city of Chicago, nearly all the respondents felt that plain hard work is either very important or somewhat
important for getting ahead (see Table 4 in Appendix C). In a series of
open interviews conducted by members of the UPFLS research team,
the respondents overwhelmingly endorsed the dominant American
belief system concerning poverty. The views of some of the individuals

who live in some of the most destitute neighborhoods of the city were particularly revealing. A substantial majority agreed that America is a land of opportunity where anybody can get ahead, and that individuals get pretty much what they deserve.

The response of a 34-year-old black male, a resident of the South Side of Chicago in a ghetto poverty area in which 29 percent of the population is destitute (that is, with incomes 75 percent below the poverty line), was typical: "Everybody get pretty much what they deserve because if everybody wants to do better they got to go out there and try. If they don't try they won't make it." Another black male who resides in an equally impoverished South Side neighborhood stated that "for some it's a land of opportunity, but you can't just let opportunity come knock on your door, you just got to go ahead and work for it. You got to go out and get it for yourself." A similar view was expressed by a 31-year-old unemployed black female who lives on the West Side of the city in a ghetto poverty area in which nearly half of the population is destitute: "Life is what you make it. . . . If you want something from life you have to go for it. Everybody can go for it, you see, but there's nobody that's gonna give you somethin' for nothin': you gotta work for what you want."

A 33-year-old welfare mother of five who lives in a public housing project located in a census tract in which 61 percent of the population is destitute introduced a little pop psychology into her endorsement of these views: "I think that everybody has a chance to get ahead but it's all where your mind's at: where you were raised, your self-esteem—a lot of that has to do with getting ahead. If you don't have any self-esteem, you can't get ahead. If nobody's taught you that there's opportunities out there—I think everybody's got a fair chance to get ahead if they want to." Finally, a South Side welfare mother of five who resides in a ghetto poverty neighborhood in which almost one-third of the population is destitute related her own personal situation to this typically American explanation of social advancement: "Yes, opportunities are out there, it's up to you if you want to do what it takes. I have not taken advantage of all the things that I should have or could have, for the most part the position I am in is totally up to me."

A divorced mother of five children, with two years of college education, who works as a telephone dispatcher and resides in a poor South Side neighborhood, described her own experience in the course of talking about the need for perseverance.

I think basically, if you get out there and really push yourself the opportunity is there. But if you sit at home waiting for someone to hand you something, you'll never get anything. I remember I was working for a temporary agency for four years and I got all the training that I needed. So one day I went down to the telephone company and put in for a application for a job. And the lady kept telling me to call back every thirty days to update your transfer. . . . I called more than every thirty days, I called every two weeks to show that I was really interested and really wanted the job with the telephone company. Keep my name in there. And I didn't give up.

These comments and the responses to questions on values pertaining to work in the UPFLS survey suggest that people in the inner-city ghetto do internalize the basic American idea that people can get ahead in life if they try. Although their support for this abstract American idea is not always consistent with their perceptions and remarkably detailed description of the social barriers that impede the social progress of inner-city ghetto residents, it is clear that these endorsements and the views of those in the large UPFLS random survey contradict the myth that inner-city residents do not share the values and aspirations of mainstream society.

Nonetheless, the social and cultural constraints that confront people in inner-city neighborhoods will cause many who subscribe to these values to fail. Americans in the larger society often conclude, as reflected in the media reports, that the frequency with which behavior in the inner-city ghetto departs from mainstream normative expectations is the result of a different value system. What is clear from our research is that the residents share values that cut across groups in the United States. Little effort is made in these reports to explore the fact that people experience great difficulty as they try to conform to the basic values of the larger society in the face of restrictions unknown to middle-class whites and blacks alike. We need only be reminded that the absence of a strong institutional resource base in many inner-city ghetto neighborhoods undermines parental efforts to control the behavior of their children and therefore makes it exceedingly difficult to satisfy the family value of promoting pro-social development among the children. The institutional resource base in inner-city ghetto neighborhoods has always been weaker than that in middle-class society. It is even worse today due to the staggering rise of joblessness mainly brought about by fundamental changes in the global economy, changes that have affected the job prospects and income of citizens in both the United States and Europe.

The society's lack of appreciation and understanding of the problems that plague inner-city ghetto residents has implications for the state of urban race relations and the degree of support for race-based social policy.

CHAPTER 7

Racial Antagonisms and Race-Based Social Policy

One of the consequences of the rise of new poverty neighborhoods has been the souring of race relations in the city. The problems associated with high joblessness and declining social organization (for example, individual crime, hustling activities, gang violence) in inner-city ghetto neighborhoods are perceived to spill over into other parts of the city. The result is not only fierce class antagonisms in the higher-income black communities located near these deteriorated neighborhoods but, as we shall see, heightened levels of racial animosity toward blacks, especially among lower-income white ethnic and Latino groups whose communities border or are situated near jobless neighborhoods.

It is important to understand the underlying factors that have exacerbated these tensions and magnified the problem of race in America's consciousness. I shall try to demonstrate this important point by showing how the interaction between political policies and economic and social processes directly and indirectly affect racial antagonisms in urban America.

Recent books such as Andrew Hacker's *Two Nations* (1992) and Derrick Bell's *Faces at the Bottom of the Well* (1992) promote the view that racial antagonisms are so deep-seated, so primordial, that feelings of pessimism about the possibility of Americans' overcoming their racist sentiments and behaviors are justified. Media reports on a series of sensational racial attacks heightened these feelings. New York has been the scene of some of the most dramatic incidents. For example, a white jogger was raped and severely beaten in Central Park by a mob of black and Latino youths. A black teenager named Yusef Hawkins was chased and beaten to death by a mob of white youths from the neighborhood of Bensonhurst. A black man named Michael Griffin was struck and killed by a car on the Belt Parkway in Queens while fleeing a group of bat-wielding whites from Howard Beach. And a black teenager named Tawana Brawley falsely claimed that she had been kidnapped and sexually assaulted by a group of white men.

Around the nation, media reports of drive-by shootings and car-jackings have fueled racial animosities and fear, as the perpetrators are frequently identified as black inner-city males. Moreover, the media coverage of a series of attacks against foreign white tourists in Florida by inner-city blacks increased awareness of the random nature of violence and further poisoned the atmosphere in terms of race relations. Although most murders and other violent crimes involve individuals who are acquainted, the sense that such crimes are being committed without provocation against strangers has heightened anxiety and fear among the general public. When victims are murdered by strangers, young people are more likely to be the perpetrators. "During 1976–1991, only 20 percent of all homicides were between strangers, whereas 34 percent of those committed by male juveniles were between strangers," states Alfred Blumstein. "Thus, the perception of the random nature of the growth in murders is reinforced by this difference in the relationship between offenders and victim."

Finally, the recent rebellion in Los Angeles, the worst race riot in the nation's history, and the events surrounding it did more to dramatize the state of American race relations and the problems in the inner city than all the other incidents combined. In the present atmosphere of heightened racial awareness, however, we forget or overlook the fact that racial antagonisms are the product of situations—economic situations, political situations, and social situations.

To understand the manifestation of racial antagonisms during certain periods is to comprehend, from both an analytic and a policy perspective, the situations that increase or reduce them. A discussion of this idea will enable me to examine the problem of race and the new urban poverty in an intergroup context. It will also set up my discussion of social policy options. Let me begin, therefore, with some thoughts on racial antagonisms and demographic changes.

Since 1960, the proportion of whites inside central cities has decreased steadily, while the proportion of minorities has grown. In 1960, the nation's population was evenly divided between cities, suburbs, and rural areas. By 1990, both urban and rural populations had declined, so that suburbs contained nearly half of the nation's population. Urban residents dipped to 31 percent of the U.S. population by 1990. As cities lost population they became poorer and darker in their racial and ethnic composition. Thus, in the eyes of many in the dominant white population, the minorities symbolize the ugly urban scene left behind. Today, the divide between the suburbs and the city is in many respects a racial divide. For example, whereas minorities (blacks, Hispanics, and Asians) constituted 63 percent of all the residents in the city of Chicago in 1990, 83 percent of all suburban residents in the Chicago metropolitan area were white. Across the nation in 1990, three-quarters of the dominant white population lived in suburban and rural areas, while a majority of blacks and Latinos resided in urban areas.

These demographic changes are related to the declining influence of American cities and provided the foundation for the New Federalism, an important political development that has increased the significance of race in metropolitan areas. Beginning in 1980, the federal government drastically decreased its support for basic urban programs. In addition, the most recent economic recession further reduced the urban revenues generated by the cities themselves, thereby resulting in budget deficits that led to additional cutbacks in basic services and programs and increases in municipal taxes.

The combination of the New Federalism and the recession created a fiscal and service crisis in many cities, especially the older cities of the East and Midwest. Fiscally strapped cities helplessly watched as the problems of poverty and joblessness in the inner city multiplied, as the homeless population grew and vicious waves of crack-cocaine addiction and the violent crimes that accompanied them swept through. These problems combined to reduce the attractiveness of the city as a place to live. Accordingly, many urban residents with the economic means to relocate have left the central city for the suburbs and other areas, worsening even further the city's tax base and reducing its revenue even more.

The growing suburbanization of the population influences the extent to which national politicians will support increased federal aid to large cities and to the poor. Indeed, we can associate the sharp drop in federal support for basic urban programs since 1980 with the declining political influence of cities and the rising influence of electoral coalitions in the suburbs. Suburbs cast 36 percent of the vote in the presidential election of 1968, 48 percent in 1988, and a majority of the vote in the 1992 election.

In each of the three presidential races before the 1992 election, the Democratic presidential candidate captured huge majorities in large cities but the electoral votes went to the Republican opponent who gained an even larger number of votes from the suburban and rural residents of the states where these cities were located.

But although there is a clear racial divide between the central city and the suburbs, racial tensions in metropolitan areas continue to be concentrated in the central city. They affect relations and patterns of interaction among blacks, other minorities, and the urban whites—especially the lower-income whites—who remain.

Like inner-city minorities, lower-income whites have felt the full impact of the urban fiscal crisis in the United States. Moreover, lower-income whites are more constrained by financial exigencies to remain in the central city than are their middle-class counterparts and thereby suffer the strains of crime, higher taxes, reduced services, and inferior public schools. Furthermore, unlike the more affluent whites who choose to remain in the wealthier sections of the central city, poor or working-class whites cannot escape the problems of deteriorating public schools by sending their children to private schools, and this problem has been exacerbated by the sharp decline in the number of parochial schools (Roman Catholic) in U.S. cities.

Many of these people originally bought relatively inexpensive homes near their industrial jobs. Because of the dispersion of industry, the changing racial composition of bordering communities, rising neighborhood crime, and the surplus of central-city housing created by the population shift to the suburbs, housing values in their neighborhoods have failed to keep pace with those in the suburbs. As the industries that employ them move away to the suburbs and even to outlying rural areas, a growing number of lower-income whites in our central cities are caught in a double trap. Their devalued property cannot be sold at a price that will permit them to purchase suburban housing, and they become physically removed from their jobs and new opportunities alike. This situation increases the potential for racial tension as they compete with blacks and the rapidly growing Latino population for access to and control of the remaining decent schools, housing, and neighborhoods.

Thus, the racial struggle for power and privilege in the central city is essentially a battle of the have-nots; it is a struggle exemplified by the black-white friction over attempts to integrate working-class ethnic neighborhoods like Marquette Park on Chicago's South Side; to control local public schools, as dramatically acted out in the racial violence that followed the busing of black children from the Boston ghettos of Roxbury and Dorchester to the working-class neighborhoods of South Boston and Charlestown in the 1970s; to exercise political control of the central city, as exhibited in Chicago, Newark, Cleveland, and New York in recent years, where the mayoral races were engulfed by racial antagonism and fear.

Problems in the new poverty or high-jobless neighborhoods have also created racial antagonism among some of the high-income groups in the city. The high joblessness in ghetto neighborhoods has sapped the vitality of local businesses and other institutions and has led to fewer and shabbier movie theaters, bowling alleys, restaurants, public parks and playgrounds, and other recreational facilities. Therefore, residents of inner-city neighborhoods more often seek leisure activity in other areas of the city, where they come into brief contact with citizens of markedly different racial or class backgrounds. Sharp differences in cultural style and patterns of interaction that reflect the social isolation of both poor and middle-class neighborhoods often lead to clashes.

Some behavior on the part of residents from inner-city ghetto neighborhoods—for example, the tendency to enjoy a movie in a communal spirit by carrying on a running conversation with friends and relatives or reacting in an unrestrained manner to what they see on the screen—is considered at least inappropriate and possibly offensive by other groups, particularly black and white members of the middle class. Expressions of disapproval, either overt or with subtle hostile glances, tend to trigger belligerent responses from the inner-city ghetto residents, who then purposefully intensify the behavior that is the source of irritation. The white and even the black middle-class moviegoers then exercise their option and exit, to use Albert Hirschman's term, by taking their patronage elsewhere, expressing resentment and experiencing intensified feelings of racial or class antagonism as they depart.

The areas surrendered in such a manner become the domain of the inner-city ghetto residents. The more expensive restaurants and other establishments serving the higher-income groups in these areas, having lost their regular patrons, soon close down and are replaced by fast-food chains and other local businesses that cater to or reflect the economic and cultural resources of the new clientele. White and black middle-class citizens, in particular, complain bitterly about how certain conveniently located areas of the central city have changed—and thus become "off-limits"—following the influx of ghetto residents.

Although the focus of much of the racial tension has been on black and white encounters, in many of the urban neighborhoods incidents involve Latinos. The UPFLS ethnographic field research indicates that antagonism toward inner-city blacks is frequently expressed in the Latino neighborhoods that border the new poverty areas. An example of this appears in the following field notes made by a UPFLS research assistant:

I asked how the neighborhood was for safety in general and they said around there it was fine if you stayed in at night. They don't go out at night. They said it was the blacks that are responsible for the crime. It was a black man that took her wallet when they went to buy a sewing machine. She said that they come through the neighborhood and are even moving in to live there more. She said that they are surrounded by black neighborhoods and that it isn't safe. I asked if there weren't also Mexican gangs around that area and they said they didn't know much about that, but that it was really the blacks that caused the problems.

A Latino male in the same community expressed his bitterness toward the jobless blacks from the surrounding neighborhood:

The blacks, well, there are very few . . . who work here in Chicago. The ones who work are very nice and respectable, but the ones who don't work, well, you have to hide yourselves from them. Chicago is maybe one third pure black, like in the south and you know how they are. They are a case that you can't change until the blacks start to behave themselves or get jobs. . . . The blacks have robbed me two times. . . . I have been hit and hit with a bat and they raped a girl. How can one ever hang around with them if they do that kind of thing? . . . They don't try to respect and they don't have the character to change. One is already afraid of them at night. One is bitter and we could never live with or associate with them.

According to several demographic projections, the Latino population, which by 1990 had exceeded 22 million in the United States, will replace African-Americans as the nation's largest minority group between 1997 and 2005. They already outnumber African-Americans in Houston and Los Angeles and are rapidly approaching the number of blacks in Dallas and New York. In cities as different as Houston, Los Angeles, and Philadelphia, "competition between blacks and Hispanic citizens over the drawing of legislative districts and the allotment of seats is intensifying." In areas of changing populations, Latino residents increasingly complain that black officials currently in office cannot represent their concerns and interests. The tensions between blacks and Latinos in Miami, to cite one example, have emerged over competition for jobs and government contracts, the distribution of political power, and claims on public services.

It would be a mistake to view the encounters between the two groups solely in racial terms, however. In Dade County, there is a tendency for the black Cubans, Dominicans, Puerto Ricans, and Panamanians to define themselves by their language and culture and not by the color of their skin. Indeed, largely because of the willingness of Hispanic whites and Hispanic blacks to live together and to mix with Haitians and other Caribbean blacks in neighborhoods relatively free of racial tension, Dade County is experiencing the most rapid desegregation of housing in the nation.

By contrast, native-born, English-speaking African-Americans continue to be the most segregated group in Miami. They are concentrated in neighborhoods characterized by high levels of joblessness and marred by pockets of poverty in the northeast section of Dade County. Although there has been some movement by higher-income groups from these neighborhoods in recent years, the poorer blacks are more likely to be trapped because of the combination of extreme economic marginality and residential segregation.

Perhaps the most intense form of racial tension among minority groups has been between inner-city blacks and Korean entrepreneurs.

Following the 1965 revision of the U.S. immigration law, the flow of Asian immigrants, including Korean immigrants, increased sharply. As the Korean population in the United States grew, so too did the presence of Korean businesses in the inner-city ghetto. Relations between black inner-city residents and Korean store owners have been strained.

Many Korean immigrants, before entering the United States, had completed college and were employed in professional, technical, administrative, and managerial positions. Yet neither their educational nor their occupational experience in Korea is recognized in the American labor market. With their employment opportunities restricted to either low-wage manual and service occupations or self-employed small business, many opted for the latter. For example, it is estimated that 60 percent of all adult Korean immigrants in Los Angeles are self-employed in small businesses.

But "for many Koreans, small business is a bittersweet livelihood, which entails enormous physical, psychological, familial, and social costs for moderate income." Enduring racial tension in jobless inner-city neighborhoods is one of the social costs. Take, as the most dramatic example, the experiences of Korean small-business owners during the 1992 Los Angeles disruption. The most destructive riot in the nation's history, the Los Angeles melee resulted in 58 deaths, 2,383 injuries, and 17,000 arrests. Estimates of property damage ranged from $785 million to $1 billion. Approximately 4,500 businesses were either partially or totally destroyed. About half of the businesses damaged (2,300) were owned or operated by Koreans in South Central Los Angeles and nearby Koreatown.

In angry protest against the verdict that found white policemen not guilty in the beating of Rodney King, black residents of South Central Los Angeles burned and looted local property. They were joined by immigrant Hispanics and undocumented workers who, for the most part, participated in the looting of stores. Korean store owners bore the brunt of the anger and destructive behavior displayed by the local residents for several reasons. During the three days of the riot, Korean businesses were vulnerable because of their location in poor neighborhoods left unprotected by the Los Angeles police force. This same location factor meant that these businesses were easily accessible because they were located in or near the riot sites. They were also highly visible, as Korean entrepreneurs are part of a culturally and racially distinct group and their businesses are disproportionately concentrated in what turned out to be the riot area.

The factors involved in Korean and black conflicts are complex and include, in addition to prejudice, language and cultural barriers that become apparent in over-the-counter disputes. As In-Jin Yoon points out:

> Merchandise sold in Korean stores is cheap and thus not built to last. Korean store owners expect that their customers accept that risk when they purchase the merchandise. In addition, due to small profit margins of their merchandise, Korean store owners either deny entirely a refund or an exchange for used merchandise or allow only a three-day or one-week warranty period. This is the most frequent source of dispute between Korean store owners and black customers. Black customers who are accustomed to a lenient refund and exchange policy in larger department stores expect the same services at smaller Korean stores. When their request for refund or exchange is rejected, they engage in verbal disputes with Korean store owners, which often develop into racial epithets between the two parties.

In Los Angeles and New York, local-based black nationalist organizations, which often perceive the presence of Korean businesses in the inner city as a threat to the black economy, turned these over-the-counter disputes into boycotts of Korean businesses.

But if inner-city blacks have antagonistic views toward Korean store owners, the latter hold extremely negative views toward blacks, views that, even if they do not play a role in the alleged mistreatment of customers, make rapprochement difficult once a dispute begins. In a scientific survey of 198 Korean store owners in Koreatown and South Central Los Angeles, In-Jin Yoon found that 78 percent of the respondents thought blacks lazy, and 76 percent felt that blacks live off welfare. A comparison of the Korean store owners' attitudes toward blacks, whites, Asians, and Hispanics revealed that blacks were perceived to be "the least hard working, the most prone to violence, the least intelligent, and the most welfare dependent." Although Hispanics were also perceived in an unfavorable light, they were ranked higher than blacks on all of these traits. Moreover, in answer to the question "If you would hire an employee between Hispanics and blacks, whom would you hire?" 80 percent of the Korean store owners chose Hispanics over blacks, whereas only 10 percent chose blacks over Hispanics.

The Korean store owners "maintain smoother relations with Hispanics" and report fewer clashes with inner-city Hispanic customers. As Yoon puts it:

> As immigrants, the two groups suffer from similar disadvantages and are not in a position to claim a nativistic sense of superiority over the other. Consequently, the Korean in small business is not perceived as a threat to the Hispanic economy, but a desirable path to success Hispanics want to follow. By contrast, the different nativity status between Koreans and blacks make Korean store owners feel less confident in their relations with native-born blacks, who are more assertive than Hispanics toward Koreans. As long-time residents of the United States, blacks claim that they have [a right to] an economic advancement before immigrants. As a result, Korean immigrant businesses in their neighborhoods are perceived as a threat to the black economy, and as part of the white system that has been oppressing and exploiting blacks. With these attitudes, blacks resent more strongly than Hispanics any signs of disrespect and mistreatment of customers.

These racial tensions are being played out during hard economic times as most Americans struggle with the problem of declining real wages, increasing job displacement, and job insecurity in the highly integrated and highly technological global economy. During hard economic times, it is important that political leaders channel the frustrations of citizens in positive or constructive directions. For the last few years, however, just the opposite has frequently occurred. In a time of heightened economic insecurities, the poisonous racial rhetoric of certain highly visible spokespersons has increased racial tensions and channeled frustrations in ways that severely divide the racial groups. During hard economic times, people become more receptive to simplistic ideological messages that deflect attention away from the real and complex source of their problems. Instead of associating their problems with economic and political changes, these divisive messages encourage them to turn on each other—race against race.

As the sharp increase in joblessness has drained many inner-city communities, many of these messages associate inner-city crime, out-breaks of riots, family breakdown, and welfare receipt with individual shortcomings. Arguments that blame the victim resonate with many Americans because of their very simplicity. They not only reinforce the salient belief that joblessness and poverty reflect individual inade-quacies, they also discourage support for new and stronger programs to combat inner-city social dislocations.

Indeed, as we shall soon see, many white Americans have turned against a strategy that emphasizes programs they perceive as benefiting only racial minorities. In the 1960s, efforts to raise the public's aware-ness and conscience about the plight of African-Americans helped to enact civil rights legislation and, later, affirmative action programs. The "myth of black progress," a phrase frequently invoked by black leaders to reinforce arguments for stronger race-based programs, played into the hands of conservative critics. While the strategy may have increased sympathy among some whites for the plight of black Americans, it also created the erroneous impression that federal anti-discrimination efforts had largely failed, and it overlooked the signifi-cance of the complex racial changes that had been unfolding since the mid-1960s. Perhaps most pernicious of all, it also fed a growing con-cern, aroused by demagogic messages, that the politicians' sensitivity to black complaints had come at the expense of the white majority.

As the turn of the century approaches, the movement for racial equality needs a new political strategy that will appeal to a broader coalition and address the many problems that originate in historical racism and afflict inner-city residents. We must recognize that these problems cannot be solved through race-based remedies alone.

At the beginning of the 1980s, the accomplishments of the civil rights struggle were clear—rising numbers of blacks in professional, techni-cal, managerial, and administrative positions. Progress was also evi-dent in the increasing enrollment of blacks in colleges and universities and the growing number of black homeowners. The expansion of par-ticipation in these areas was proportionately greater for blacks than for whites because such a tiny percentage of blacks had property or higher education before this time. As Jennifer Hochschild has pointed out, "One has not really succeeded in America unless one can pass the chance for success on to one's children." Until the 1960s, even the few members of the old black middle class "had great difficulty in doing so." Empirical research on the occupational attainments and mobility of blacks in the early 1960s could "uncover no evidence of class effects on occupation or income achievements that could rival the effect of race on those outcomes of the stratification process. Race was such a powerful variable that even the more modest of class effects that stratified whites were canceled by the skin color of blacks." In other words, states Hochschild, blacks "experienced a perverse sort of egalitarianism—neither the disadvantages of poverty nor the advantages of wealth made much difference in what they could achieve or pass on to their children. Discrimination swamped everything else."

Research by Michael Hout, however, reveals that between 1962 and 1973, class began to affect career and generational mobility for blacks as it had regularly done for whites. In particular, blacks from the most advantaged backgrounds experienced the greatest upward mobility. "Well-off black men thus could begin for the first time in American history to expect their success to persist and cumulate. Since 1973 these trends have continued, although less dramatically."

On the other hand, among the disadvantaged segments of the black population, especially the ghetto poor, many dire problems—joblessness, concentrated poverty, family breakup, and the receipt of welfare—were getting even worse between 1973 and 1980.

The differential rates of progress in the black community have continued through the 1980s and early 1990s. Family incomes among the poorest of the poor reveal the pattern. From 1977 to 1993, the percentage of blacks with incomes below 50 percent of the amount designated as the poverty line (the measurement of "poverty" was $14,335 for a four-person family and $11,522 for a three-person family in 1993) increased from 9.3 percent of the total black population in 1977 to 16.7 percent in 1993. In 1977, fewer than one of every three poor blacks (29.9 percent) fell below half of the poverty-line amount, but by 1993 the proportion rose to more than half (50.4 percent). Moreover, whereas poor black families fell an average of $5,481 below the poverty line in 1977, they fell an average of $6,818 below in 1993. The average poor black family in 1993 slipped further below the poverty level than in any year since the Census Bureau started collecting such data in 1967 (these figures and those that follow have been adjusted for inflation).

From 1975 to 1992 (see Table 7.1), while the average income of the lowest quintile of black families in the United States declined by 33 percent (from $6,333 to $4,255) and that of the second-lowest quintile by 13 percent (from $13,186 to $11,487), the average income of the highest quintile of black families climbed by 23 percent (from $55,681 to $68,431) and that of the top 5 percent by 35 percent (from $76,713 to $103,827). Although income inequality between whites and blacks is substantial—and the financial gap is even greater between the two races when wealth is considered (total financial assets, not just income)—in 1992 the highest fifth of black families nonetheless secured a record 48.8 percent of the total black family income, compared to the 43.8 percent share of the total white income received by the highest fifth of white families, also a record. So, while income inequality has widened generally in America since 1975, the divide is even more dramatic among black Americans. If we are to fashion remedies for black poverty, we need to understand the origins and dynamics of inequality in the African-American community. Without disavowing the accomplishments of the civil rights movement, black leaders and policymakers now need to give more attention to remedies that will make a concrete difference in the lives of the poor.

· · ·

TABLE 7.1

AVERAGE INCOME OF BLACK FAMILIES BY INCOME GROUP

	1975*	1985*	1992	1975–92
Lowest fifth	$6,333	$5,169	$4,255	–$2,078
Second fifth	13,186	12,653	11,487	–1,699
Middle fifth	21,816	21,877	21,047	–769
Fourth fifth	32,811	35,049	35,029	+2,218
Highest fifth	55,681	64,499	68,431	+12,750
Top 5 percent	76,713	93,427	103,827	+27,114

*adjusted for inflation to 1992 dollars

Source: U.S. Bureau of the Census, "Money Income of Households, Families, and Persons in the United States: 1992," in Current Population Reports, series P-60, no. 184 (Washington, D.C.: Government Printing Office, 1992).

The demands of the civil rights movement reflected a general assumption on the part of black leaders in the 1960s that the government could best protect the rights of individual members of minority groups not by formally bestowing rewards and punishments based on racial group membership but by using antidiscrimination legislation to enhance individual freedom. The movement was particularly concerned about access to education, employment, voting, and public accommodations. From the 1950s to 1970, the emphasis was on freedom of choice; the role of the state was to prevent the formal categorization of people on the basis of race. Anti-bias legislation was designed to eliminate racial discrimination without considering the proportion of minorities in certain positions. The underlying principle was that individual merit should be the sole determining factor in choosing candidates for desired positions. Because civil rights protests against racial discrimination clearly upheld a fundamental American principle, they carried a degree of moral authority that leaders such as Martin Luther King, Jr., were able to repeatedly and effectively emphasize.

It would have been ideal if programs based on the principle of freedom of individual opportunity were sufficient to remedy racial inequality in our society. Long periods of racial oppression can result, however, in a system of inequality that lingers even after racial barriers come down. As we have seen in earlier chapters, the most disadvantaged minority individuals, crippled by the cumulative effects of both race and class subjugation, disproportionately lack the resources to compete effectively in a free and open market.

Eliminating racial barriers creates the greatest opportunities for the better-trained, talented, and educated members of minority groups because these members possess the resources to compete most effectively. Those resources reflect a variety of advantages—family stability, financial means, peer groups, schooling—provided or made possible by their parents.

By the late 1960s, a number of black leaders began to recognize this. In November 1967, Kenneth B. Clark said, "The masses of Negroes are now starkly aware of the fact that recent civil rights victories benefited a very small percentage of middle-class Negroes while [poorer blacks'] predicament remained the same or worsened." Simply eliminating racial barriers was not going to be enough. As the late black economist Vivian Henderson put it, "If all racial prejudice and discrimination and all racism were erased today, all the ills brought by the process of economic class distinction and economic depression of the masses of black people would remain."

Accordingly, black leaders and liberal policymakers began to emphasize the need not only to eliminate active discrimination but also to counteract the effects of past racial oppression. Instead of seeking remedies only for individual complaints of discrimination, as specified in Title VII of the Civil Rights Act of 1964, they sought government-mandated affirmative action programs designed to ensure adequate minority representation in employment, education, and public programs.

However, if the more advantaged members of minority groups benefit disproportionately from policies that embody the principle of equality of individual opportunity, they also profit disproportionately from affirmative action policies based solely on their racial group membership. Minority individuals from the most advantaged families tend to be disproportionately represented among those of their racial group most qualified for preferred status, such as college admissions, higher-paying jobs, and promotions. Thus, policies of affirmative action are likely to enhance opportunities for the more advantaged without adequately remedying the problems of the disadvantaged.

To be sure, affirmative action was not intended solely to benefit the more advantaged minority individuals. As William L. Taylor, the former director of the United States Civil Rights Commission, has stated, "The focus of much of the [affirmative action] effort has been not just on white-collar jobs, but also on law enforcement, construction work, and craft and production in large companies—all areas in which the extension of new opportunities has provided upward mobility for less advantaged minority workers." Taylor also notes that studies show that many minority students entering medical schools during the 1970s were from low-income families.

Affirmative action policies, however, did not really open up broad avenues of upward mobility for the masses of disadvantaged blacks. Like other forms of "creaming," they provided opportunities for those individuals from low socioeconomic backgrounds with the greatest educational and social resources. A careful analysis of data on income, employment, and educational attainment would probably reveal that only a few individuals who reside in the inner-city ghettos have benefited from affirmative action.

Since the early 1970s, as discussed in Chapter 2, urban minorities have been highly vulnerable to structural changes in the economy,

such as the shift from goods-producing to service-producing industries, the increasing polarization of the labor market into low-wage
and high-wage sectors, destabilizing innovations in technology, and
the relocation of manufacturing industries outside the central city.
These shifts have led to sharp increases in joblessness and the related
problems of highly concentrated poverty, welfare dependency, and
family breakup, despite the passage of antidiscrimination legislation to
correct discriminatory patterns through litigation and the creation of
affirmative action programs that mandate "goals and timetables" for
the employment of minorities.

Race-based programs have helped to bring about sharp increases
in the number of blacks entering higher education and gaining professional and managerial positions. Moreover, as long as minorities are
underrepresented in higher-paying and desirable positions in society,
affirmative action programs will be needed. Nonetheless, in response
to cries from conservatives to abolish affirmative action altogether,
some liberals have argued for a shift from an affirmative action based
on race to one based on economic class position or need.

The major distinguishing characteristic of affirmative action based
on need is the recognition that the problems of the disadvantaged—
low income, crime-ridden neighborhoods, broken homes, inadequate
housing, poor education, cultural and linguistic differences—are not
always clearly related to previous racial discrimination. Children who
grow up in homes plagued by these disadvantages are more likely to be
denied an equal chance in life because the development of their aspirations and talents is hindered by their environment, regardless of race.
Minorities would benefit disproportionately from affirmative opportunity programs designed to address these disadvantages because they
suffer disproportionately from the effects of such environments, *but
the problems of disadvantaged whites would be addressed as well*.

An affirmative action based solely on need would result, however,
in the systematic exclusion of many middle-income blacks from desirable positions because the standard or conventional measures of performance are not sensitive to the cumulative effects of race. By this I
mean the long-term intergenerational effects of having one's life
choices limited by race, regardless of class, including the effects of living in segregated neighborhoods—for example, exposure to culturally
shaped habits, skills, and styles of behavior—the quality of de facto

segregated schooling, and the nurturing by parents whose experiences have also been limited by race, and the resources these parents are able to pass on to their children, and so on. For example, if we were to rely solely on the standard criteria for college admission, such as Scholastic Aptitude Test (SAT) scores, even many children from black middle-income families would be denied admission in favor of more privileged whites who are not weighed down by the accumulation of disadvantages that stem from racial restrictions and who tend to score higher on these conventional measures as a result. The extent to which standard aptitude tests—such as the SAT and those used in the promotion of police officers—are measuring merit or real potential to succeed, as opposed to privilege, is difficult to determine. Ideally, we should develop *flexible criteria* of evaluation (or performance measures), as opposed to numerical guidelines or quotas, that would not exclude people with background handicaps, including minority racial background, who have as much potential to succeed as those admitted without those handicaps. While some test scores may correlate well with performance, they do not necessarily measure important attributes that also determine ability to perform, such as perseverance, motivation, interpersonal ability, reliability, and leadership skills.

Accordingly, since race is one of the components of "disadvantaged," the ideal affirmative action program would emphasize flexible criteria of evaluation based on both need and race. The cumulative effects of historical discrimination and racial segregation are reflected in many subtle ways that result in the underrepresentation of blacks in positions of high status and their overrepresentation in positions of low status. Some of these problems can be easily addressed with affirmative action programs that are at least in part based on race; others have to be combated by means of race-neutral strategies. As indicated earlier, less advantaged blacks are extremely vulnerable to changes in our modern industrial society, leading to problems that are difficult to combat by means of race-based strategies alone—either those that embody equality of individual opportunity, such as the Civil Rights Act of 1964, or those that represent affirmative action. Now more than ever, we need broader solutions than those we have employed in the past. I will return to this issue in the last section of this chapter.

Finally, if there were a race-based program that would substantially benefit poor inner-city minorities, it would be one that effectively reduces the levels of racial segregation. Strategies representing either equality of individual opportunity or affirmative action are not designed to address the important problem of racial segregation. As demonstrated in Part 1 of this discussion, living in segregated ghettos creates barriers to employment and adequate employment preparation. Accordingly, the reduction of racial segregation would surely improve the job prospects of African-Americans. However, "a federal policy of rapid desegregation in housing is a political and practical impossibility." As long as there are areas to which whites can retreat, it will be difficult to reduce the overall level of segregation. Blacks move in, whites move out. And this process can be surprisingly rapid, as we have seen in neighborhoods like Greater Grand Crossing in Chicago (see Chapter 2).

Perhaps it would be possible to stem this pattern if restrictions were placed on the freedom of movement of whites or if somehow it became very costly to move. But government restrictions on the freedom of movement in a democratic society would be both unrealistic and undesirable. The curtailment of exclusionary zoning practices and more aggressive enforcement of the Fair Housing Act, however, could trigger a gradual decline in racial segregation. This would clear the path for the construction of more affordable housing for low-income families and might enable many poor families to secure residence in neighborhoods with more employment opportunities. The gains, over a period of decades, could be substantial.

Several small steps have already been taken in this direction. For example, in Chicago, the Gautreaux program was created under a 1976 court order following a finding of widespread discrimination in the public housing projects of Chicago. Since then the program has relocated more than 4,000 residents from public housing into subsidized housing in neighborhoods throughout the Greater Chicago area. Careful research by two scholars who have examined this program reveals that the families who were relocated in housing in the suburbs enjoyed significant gains in employment and education. The success of this program is partly a function of its relatively small size. Since only a few families are relocated to other housing sites each year, they remain relatively invisible and do not present the threat of a mass invasion. In 1994, the federal government created a Gautreaux-type program called "Moving to Opportunity." Only $234 million will be spent on the project over a two-year period to help 6,200 families re-locate from poor neighborhoods to more prosperous ones. "But the experiment is being closely watched among housing experts, who say that it could lead to a significant shift in the way the needy receive sub-sidized housing."

No group has a greater stake in the promotion of social rights (the right to employment, economic security, education, and health) in the United States than the inner-city black poor. Unfortunately, for some time there has been considerable resistance to programs for the truly disadvantaged. In view of the current political climate, any pro-gram designed to significantly improve their life chances, including increased job opportunities, would have to be broadly applicable. That is, it would have to address the concerns of wide segments of the U.S. population, not just those of the residents of inner-city ghettos.

Almost two decades ago, the late African-American economist Vi-vian Henderson argued that "the economic future of blacks in the United States is bound up with that of the rest of the nation. Politics designed in the future to cope with the problems of the poor and vic-timized will also yield benefits to blacks. In contrast, any efforts to treat blacks separately from the rest of the nation are likely to lead to frustration, heightened racial animosities, and a waste of the country's resources and the precious resources of black people."

Henderson's warning seems to be especially appropriate in periods of economic stagnation, when public support for programs targeted to minorities—or associated with real or imagined material sacrifice on the part of whites—tends to wane. The economy was strong when af-firmative action programs were introduced during the Johnson ad-ministration. When the economy turned down in the 1970s, the public's view of affirmative action increasingly soured.

Furthermore, as Joseph A. Califano, Johnson's staff assistant for do-mestic affairs, observed in 1988, such programs were generally accept-able to whites "only as a temporary expedient to speed blacks' entry into the social and economic mainstream." But as years passed, many whites "saw continuing such preferences as an unjust insistence by Democrats that they do penance for an era of slavery and discrimination they had nothing to do with." They also associated the decline in public schools not with broader changes in society, but with "forced integration."

The Democrats also came under fire for their support for programs that increasingly were misrepresented as being intended for poor blacks alone. Virtually separate medical and legal systems developed in many cities. Public services became identified mainly with blacks, private services mainly with whites. In an era of ostensible racial justice, many public programs ironically seemed to constitute a new and costlier form of segregation. White taxpayers saw themselves as being forced, through taxes, to pay for medical and legal services that many of them could not afford to purchase for their own families.

White reaction to race-based problems has several dimensions, however. It is important to understand the nature of these reactions as we think about public policies intended to address the problems of inner-city joblessness and related ills. Over the past fifty years, there has been a steep decline in white support for racial segregation and discrimination. For example, although in 1942 only 42 percent of white Americans supported integrated schooling, by 1993 that figure had skyrocketed to 95 percent. Public opinion polls reveal similar patterns of change during the last five decades in white support for the integration of public accommodations and mass transportation and the principle of integrated residential areas.

Nonetheless, the virtual disappearance of Jim Crow attitudes in support of racial segregation has not resulted in strong backing for *government* programs to aggressively combat discrimination, increase integration, enroll blacks in institutions of higher learning, or enlarge the proportion of blacks in higher-level occupations. Indeed, as evidenced in the public opinion polls, whites overwhelmingly object to government assistance targeted to blacks. Whereas eight of every ten African-Americans believe that the government is not spending enough to assist blacks today, only slightly more than one-third of white Americans feel this way. The idea that the federal government "has a special obligation to help improve the living standard of blacks" because they "have been discriminated against so long" was supported by only one in five whites in 1991 and has never exceeded more than one in four since 1975. And the lack of white support for this idea is unrelated to background factors such as age and education level.

Perhaps the most widely discussed racial policy issue in recent years has been affirmative action. Despite a slight decrease in opposition to affirmative action programs in education and employment between 1986 and 1990, sentiments against these programs remain strong. In 1990, almost seven in ten (69.1 percent) white Americans opposed quotas to admit black students into colleges and universities and more than eight in ten (82.5 percent) objected to the idea of preferential hiring and promotion of blacks.

In the previous chapter, I discussed the dominant American belief system that associates poverty and reliance on welfare with individual shortcomings. Studies of racial attitudes suggest that such beliefs are connected with white opposition to programs targeted to blacks. "People whose attitudes blend antiblack feelings and a belief that blacks violate values such as the work ethic and self-reliance are more likely to oppose affirmative action policies." Indeed, among those most hostile to policies meant to uplift blacks are those whites who associate the disadvantages experienced by African-Americans with individual traits. This is perhaps one of the reasons why there is such overwhelming white opposition to welfare. Analyzing data from the NORC General Social Survey, Lawrence Bobo and Ryan Smith reported a positive relationship between hostile feelings toward blacks and opposition to welfare. But these social scientists quickly pointed out that general values, beliefs, and ideology, not racial attitudes, account for most of whites' views on welfare spending.

Racial attitudes do play a significant role in the degree of support individuals are willing to lend to expressly race-based policies invoked by the government to improve the living standard of blacks. Bobo and Smith found that even after controlling for socioeconomic status and a number of measures on general values, beliefs, and ideology, racial attitudes continued to be a substantial factor in the degree to which white Americans support race-based government policies.

Nonetheless, the strong *overall* association between negative racial attitudes and opposition to race-targeted policies should not lead us to overlook the fact that there are some race-based policies that are supported by wide segments of the white population, regardless of racial attitudes. While opposing "preferential" racial policies such as college admission quotas or job hiring and promotion strategies designed to achieve equal outcomes, recent studies reveal that most white Americans approve of "compensatory" affirmative action policies, such as race-targeted programs of job training, special education, and special recruitment efforts. For example, in the 1990 General Social Survey, 68 percent of all whites favored spending more money on the schools in black neighborhoods, especially for preschool and early education programs. Furthermore, 70 percent favored granting special college scholarships to black children who maintain good grades.

Accordingly, programs that enable blacks to take advantage of opportunities, such as race-targeted early education programs and job training, are less likely to be "perceived as challenging the values of individualism and the work ethic." In other words, compensatory or opportunity-enhancing affirmative action programs are supported because they reinforce the belief that the allocation of jobs and economic rewards should be based on individual effort, training, and talent. As Bobo and James Kluegel put it:

> Opportunity-enhancing programs receive greater support because they are consistent with the norm of helping people help themselves. In addition, opportunity-enhancing programs do not challenge principles of equity. Indeed, requirements that beneficiaries of such programs make the effort to acquire the training and skills needed to improve their economic positions are fully consistent with reward on the basis of individual effort.

Furthermore, unlike "preferential" racial policies, support for opportunity-enhancing programs has a relatively weak connection to antiblack attitudes.

In the promotion of social rights today, it is important to appreciate that the poor and the working classes of all racial groups struggle to make ends meet, and even the middle class has experienced a decline in its living standard. Indeed, Americans across racial and class boundaries worry about unemployment and job security, declining real wages, escalating medical and housing costs, the availability of affordable child care programs, the sharp decline in the quality of public education, and crime and drug trafficking in their neighborhoods.

These concerns are reflected in public opinion surveys. For the last several years, national opinion polls consistently reveal strong public backing for government labor-market strategies, including training efforts, to increase employment opportunities. A 1988 Harris poll indicated that almost three-quarters of its respondents would support a tax increase to pay for child care. A 1989 Harris poll reported that almost nine out of ten Americans would like to see fundamental change in the health care system of the United States. A September 1993 *New York Times*/CBS poll, on the eve of President Clinton's health care address to the nation, revealed that nearly two-thirds of the nation's citizens would be willing to pay higher taxes "so that all Americans have health insurance that they can't lose no matter what." Finally, recent surveys conducted by the National Opinion Research Center at the University of Chicago reveal that a substantial majority of Americans want to see more money spent on improving the nation's educational system, and on halting the rise in crime and drug addiction.

Programs created in response to these concerns—programs that increase employment opportunities and job skills training, improve public education, promote better child and health care, and reduce neighborhood crime and drug abuse—would, despite being race-neutral, disproportionately benefit the most disadvantaged segments of the population, especially poor minorities.

A comprehensive race-neutral initiative to address economic and social inequality should be viewed as an extension of—not a replacement for—opportunity-enhancing programs that include race-based criteria to fight social inequality. I feel that such programs should employ flexible criteria of evaluation in college admission, hiring, job promotion, and so on, and should be based on a broad definition of disadvantage that incorporates notions of both *need and race*. Although recent public opinion polls indicate that most Americans would support race-based programs intended to enhance opportunities, mobilizing and sustaining the political support for such programs will be much more difficult if they are not designed to reach broad segments of the American population.

Nonetheless, there are other programs that can be accurately described as purely race-neutral, such as national heath care, school reform, and job training based on need rather than race, that would strongly and positively impact racial minority populations but would benefit large segments of the dominant white population as well. National opinion poll results suggest the possibility of a new alignment in support of a comprehensive social rights initiative that would include such programs. If such an alignment is attempted, perhaps it ought to feature a new public rhetoric that would do two things: (1) focus on problems that afflict not only the poor but the working and middle classes as well, and (2) emphasize integrative programs that would promote the social and economic improvement of all groups in society, not just the truly disadvantaged segments of the population. After all, the joblessness of the inner-city poor represents the most extreme form of economic marginality, stemming in large measure from changes in the organization of the economy, including the global economy.

CHAPTER 8

A Broader Vision: Social Policy Options in Cross-National Perspective

Changes in the global economy are placing strains on the welfare state in both the United States and Europe and are contributing to growing social dislocations, including racial conflicts. The question that Secretary of Labor Robert Reich raised at a 1994 conference of finance and labor ministers from seven industrial democracies is central and timely: "Are we condemned to choose between more jobs but greater inequality and insecurity, as we have in this country, or better jobs but higher unemployment and a thicker social safety net, as in Europe?" This question implicitly asks whether Europeans and Americans can learn from one another in the creation of programs that simultaneously address the problems of economic growth, joblessness, and wage inequality.

There is a growing recognition that proposed solutions to the problems of jobs and wages in any of the major industrial democracies cannot ignore developments in the highly integrated global marketplace. Indeed, because of concerns about the problem of creating good jobs in the global economy, the finance and labor ministers from the major industrial democracies (Britain, Canada, France, Germany, Italy, Japan, and the United States, or the Group of Seven, commonly called G7) held a jobs conference in Detroit in March 1994. In previous years, only heads of state and finance ministers met "to discuss high diplomacy and the high finance exchange rates and interest rate management." However, that exalted approach was considered insufficient to address the concrete issue of jobs that now confronts all of these nations.

In addition to the more familiar themes, such as the importance of stimulating economic growth and of avoiding protectionist policies to safeguard shrinking job markets, the officials at the conference also agreed "that the only way to create more jobs in the face of rapid technological change was to upgrade education, particularly for those who are least skilled." It was the first time the G7 policymakers had addressed, as a global problem, the widening gap in wages between skilled and unskilled workers and the strong association between low levels of education, joblessness, and poorly paid work.

Although the conference did more to highlight than to solve these problems, the main hope of the ministers was that the discussions could "teach them something about what each of them has done right, and wrong, in confronting the jobs question." As I examine possible policy prescriptions in cross-national perspective, a framework for discussing the appropriateness of long-term solutions to the jobs problem in the United States (solutions that take several years before the desired ends are achieved or realized) and one for discussing more immediate solutions come to mind.

My framework for long-term solutions outlines two types of relationships in an effort to address the issues of generating good jobs and combating the growing wage inequality among workers—namely, the relationship between employment and education and family support systems and, in the metropolitan context, the relationship between the cities and the suburbs. My framework for immediate solutions delineates ways in which to either revise current programs or create new programs to decrease joblessness among disadvantaged adults. Each framework involves the integration of programs that involve both the public sector and the private sector.

I hasten to point out that the following presentation and discussion of policy frameworks is not constrained by an awareness of the current political climate in the United States. The dramatic retreat from using public policy as a means to fight social inequality has effectively discouraged calls for bold new social programs. Indeed, at the time of this writing, the trend is toward slicing or reducing social programs and the spending for such programs. The emphasis is on personal responsibility, not inequities in the larger society, and therefore the assumption is that people should help themselves and not turn to the government for handouts. It is said that the growth of joblessness and welfare receipt mainly reflects a declining commitment to the core values of society and therefore that the incentives for idleness or the factors that lead to a lack of personal and family responsibilities ought to be removed.

These arguments have been advanced with such force and consistency in public discussions since the 1994 congressional elections that even some of the most dedicated liberals feel intimidated and powerless. Accordingly, traditional programs benefiting the poor, such as AFDC, Medicaid, and the earned income tax credit, have either been eliminated or are being threatened with severe reductions.

This retreat from public policy as a way to alleviate problems of social inequality will have profound negative consequences for the future of disadvantaged groups such as the ghetto poor. High levels of joblessness, growing wage inequality, and the related social problems discussed in this book are complex and have their source in fundamental economic, social, and cultural changes. They therefore require bold, comprehensive, and thoughtful solutions, not simplistic and pious statements about the need for greater personal responsibility. Progressives who are concerned about the current social conditions of the have-nots and the future generation of have-nots not only have to fight against the current public policy strategies; they are morally obligated to offer alternative strategies designed to alleviate, not exacerbate, the plight of the poor, the jobless, and other disadvantaged citizens of America.

My aim, therefore, is to galvanize and rally concerned Americans to fight back with the same degree of force and dedication displayed by those who have moved us backward, rather than forward, in combating social inequality. I therefore do not advance proposals that seem acceptable or "realistic" given the current political climate. Rather, I have chosen to talk about what *ought to be done to address the problems of social inequality*, including record levels of joblessness in the inner-city ghetto, that threaten the very fabric of our society.

Some who acknowledge the need to confront the growing social inequality also feel that new social programs should be put on hold until the huge budget deficit has been significantly reduced. In the final analysis, however, we must recognize that spending is directly related to political priorities. Decisions about budget cuts for federal programs now indisputably favor the advantaged segments of the population at the expense of the disadvantaged (see Figure 8.1, page 236).

I believe that steps must be taken to galvanize Americans from all walks of life who are concerned about human suffering and the public policy direction in which we are now moving. I therefore present policy frameworks that call for the integration and mobilization of resources from both the public and the private sectors. We need to generate a public/private partnership to fight social inequality. In the final analysis, I hope to stimulate thought about what ought to be done and how we should do it among those who support positive social reforms and see the need for action now. The following policy frameworks, therefore, are suggestive and provide a basis for further discussion and debate. Let me begin by first focusing on the part of my framework for long-term solutions that involves relationships between employment and education, and family support systems.

The United States can learn from industrial democracies like Japan and Germany. These countries have developed policies designed to increase the number of workers with "higher-order thinking skills," including policies that require young people to meet high performance standards before they can graduate from secondary schools and that hold each school responsible for meeting these national standards. As Ray Marshall points out, "Standards are important because they provide incentives for students, teachers and other school personnel; information to employers and postsecondary institutions; and a means for policymakers and the public to evaluate schools. Indeed, by strengthening linkages, standards have helped fashion systems out of disjointed activities."

Students who meet high standards are not only prepared for work, they are ready for technical training and other kinds of postsecondary education. Currently, there are no national standards for secondary students or schools in the United States. Accordingly, students who are not in college preparatory courses have severely limited options with respect to pursuing work or secondary technical training after high school. A commitment to a system of national performance standards for every public school in the United States would be an important first step in addressing the huge gap in educational performance between the schools in advantaged and disadvantaged neighborhoods.

But because the quality of local public schools in the United States is in large measure related to the resources of local governments, national standards may not be attractive to taxpayers and local officials in some areas. Also, some schools will encounter greater difficulties in meeting a national performance standard because of fewer resources and a greater concentration of students from disadvantaged backgrounds and neighborhoods. The question raised by the Columbia University educator Linda Darling-Hammond is important in this connection: "Can the mere issuance of standards really propel improvements in schooling, or are there other structural issues to contend with—issues such as funding, teachers' knowledge and capacities, access to curriculum resources, and dysfunctional school structures?" She goes on to state:

> If the goal of standard setting is the improvement of education for all children, rather than merely a more efficient means of sorting students and schools into "worthy" and "unworthy" categories, attention must be paid to building the capacity for schools to teach in the manner envisioned by these learning goals. This requires carefully developed policy efforts in the areas of teacher development, school development, and equalization of resources.

Accordingly, if standard-setting is to be a meaningful route to reform, it will have to address the current inequalities in the public school system in the United States. In contrast to the more central and equal supports for schools in European countries, funding for public education in the United States is dramatically uneven, "with wealthy schools commonly spending two to three times as much as poor ones." The result is significant differences in educational experiences. Whereas public school students in advantaged neighborhoods enjoy airy facilities and well-equipped small classes, those in poor neighborhoods are more likely to enter dilapidated schools and attend classes that are large and poorly equipped. Even more important is the differential student access to a high-quality curriculum and well-trained teachers, all of which can be traced to the unequal allocation of funds. As Iris C. Rotberg and James J. Harvey put it:

> More often than not, the "best" teachers, including experienced teachers offered greater choice in school assignment because of their seniority, avoid high-poverty schools. As a result, low-income and minority students have less contact with the best-

qualified and more experienced teachers, the teachers most likely
to master the kinds of instructional strategies considered effective
for all students.

Recent research on the nationwide distribution of science and
mathematics opportunities indicates that low-income, minority, and
inner-city students are in school environments that are not as conducive to learning because of less qualified teachers, fewer material resources, less engaging activities for learning in the classroom, and
considerably less exposure to good training and knowledge in mathematics and science. The problem of finding qualified teachers is particularly acute. Teacher shortages in many central-city and poor rural
schools have resulted in a disproportionate number of underprepared
and inexperienced teachers, many of whom provide instruction in
fields outside their areas of preparation, and a continuous flow of
short-term and long-term substitutes.

A system of national performance standards should include the
kind of support that would enable schools in disadvantaged neighborhoods to meet the standards that are set. State government, with federal support, not only would have to create equity in local school
funding and give birth to programs that would foster teacher development (through scholarships and forgivable loans for teacher education
to attract more high-quality teachers, through increased supports for
teacher training in schools of education, and through reforms in
teacher certification and licensing) but would also have to ensure that
highly qualified teachers are distributed in local school districts in
ways that provide all students with access to excellent instruction. In
some cases this would require greater flexibility in the public school
system, not only to attract and hire qualified teachers, but also to displace those who perform poorly in the classroom and lack a dedication
to teaching. Local education agencies and state education departments
should be helped to identify schools that need support in curriculum
development and assessment, teacher development, educational and
material resources, and so on.

One important area that could be addressed in programs to equal-
ize resources in the public schools is the availability of computer facilities. Since two-thirds of all new jobs will require the use of computers,
all schools should require that students become competent in the use of

computers. According to the U.S. Bureau of the Census, only 35 percent of black youths ages 3 to 17 use a computer at school. Half of their white counterparts have access to in-school computers. It is imperative that the public schools provide each student with a computer workstation in the elementary, secondary, and high schools and develop linkage to the information superhighways, including access to the Internet. Some public schools already have this capacity and will not need to be upgraded, but others, such as many inner-city schools, must be earmarked for more resources.

Targeting education would be part of a national effort to raise the performance standards of all public schools in the United States to a desirable level, including schools in the inner city. Every effort should be made to enlist the support and involvement of the private sector in this national effort. Corporations, local businesses, civic clubs, community centers, churches, and community-based organizations should be encouraged to work with the schools to enhance computer-competency training. Some examples of private-sector involvement in such endeavors should be touted to spur others on. For example, Frank C. Weaver, director of the Office of Commercial Space Transportation at the U.S. Department of Transportation, reported:

Bell Atlantic and Tele-Communications, Inc. announced in 1994 that they would provide free linkage to the information superhighways for 26,000 elementary and secondary schools in areas served by the two companies. Under the plan, known as the Basic Education Connection (BEC), the school would receive free educational cable television programming and free access to certain data and online services, such as access to the Internet.

Another project, the Hughes Galaxy Classroom, is enabling 51,000 elementary school children around the country to access more of the educational resources on television available via satellite. Under the auspices of the Galaxy Classroom Foundation, which provides antenna dishes and related equipment to schools, the project offers a science and English curriculum beamed into classrooms through satellite transmissions. Student feedback and questions are faxed to the producers of the program for inclusion in subsequent shows. Particular attention is paid to inner-city and minority schools. There are 480 schools participating this year, and the goal for next year is 1,500 schools with 150,000 to 200,000 students.

Since the creation of national performance standards would provide a clear means for the public to evaluate the different schools, data on school performances could be widely disseminated. This would enable parents of all backgrounds, including those in disadvantaged neighborhoods, to compare nearby schools and make appropriate decisions about which ones their children should attend. However, families from disadvantaged neighborhoods would be in a much better position to make and act on such decisions if an effective public school choice program were in place. This would involve the availability not only of vouchers for the selection of public schools but also information about school performance that could be interpreted with ease. Although the empirical data on the effectiveness of existing school choice programs on student achievement is scant, new evidence suggests that increased competition among public schools (as reflected by a larger number of school districts in a metropolitan area) improves average student performance and restrains levels of spending.

A step toward the development of national performance standards was taken in the spring of 1994 when Congress passed the Goals 2000: Educate America Act. This act identified a number of goals to be achieved by the year 2000, ranging from student-demonstrated competence in challenging subjects (science, English, mathematics, geography, and history) to the professional development of teachers. The basic assumption underlying the act is that the role of the federal government is to "encourage experimentation within the framework of broad federal guidelines," not to mandate uniform changes in the educational system.

Congress appropriated $125 million for Goals 2000 in 1994 and $700 million for 1995. The act encourages states to apply for grants so that their schools can participate in educational improvements outlined in the legislation. Communities and local schools are encouraged to develop clear and high standards pertaining to instruction, curriculum, technology, professional development, and parental and community involvement. The Goals 2000: Educate America Act is a first step toward the development of national performance standards, but since it is not mandatory and only a small amount of money was appropriated, it is unlikely to produce major and widespread changes in the nation's educational system. Yet educational issues are critical and, as suggested in my discussion of the requirements for an adequate system of national performance standards, will require a much stronger commitment to change.

The learning system in other industrial democracies has also been strengthened by family policies to support children. Among industrialized countries, the United States is alone in having no universal preschool, child-support, or parental leave programs. "The absence of such policies makes many of our families, particularly low-income families, very poor learning systems," states Ray Marshall. "Many of our children therefore start school far behind their more advantaged counterparts, and subsequently receive inadequate learning opportunities at home as well as in school." The family structure has undergone fundamental changes in the last several decades. There has been a sharp increase in single-parent families, and many of them are trapped in persistent poverty. Also, in many "intact" families both the husband and wife must work outside the home to make ends meet. The absence of widely available high-quality preschool and child-support assurance programs places additional stress on these families and hampers their ability to provide a learning environment that prepares children for school and reinforces the learning process.

The French system of child welfare stands in sharp contrast to the American system. In France, children are supported by three interrelated government programs—child care, income support, and medical care. The child care program includes establishments for infant care, high-quality nursery schools (*écoles maternelles*), and paid leave for parents of newborns. The income support program includes child-support enforcement (so that the absent parent continues to contribute financially to his or her child's welfare), children allowances, and welfare payments for low-income single mothers. Finally, medical care is provided through a universal system of national health care financed by social security, a preventive care system for children, and a group of public health nurses who specialize in child welfare.

The *école maternelle* is perhaps the most distinctive institution in the French system. Children who are no longer in diapers may enter the nursery school and attend until they are enrolled in the first grade. Because parents view participation in the *école maternelle* as highly beneficial to their children, even those mothers who are not working send their children.

As the economist Barbara Bergmann points out:

The *école maternelle* serves the integration of all children, minority children included, to full participation in regular school and as future citizens. One of its most important functions, especially for the 4- and 5-year-olds, is getting the children ready for the regular school. Each year a child spends at an *école maternelle* reduces considerably the likelihood that the child will fail the rigorous first grade and have to repeat it. Of children from poorer backgrounds who have not attended an *école maternelle*, more than half fail the first grade. Four years of preschool attendance for such poorer children cuts their first grade failure rate in half. Children from more affluent backgrounds are also materially helped to pass.

The combination of a system of national performance standards in public schools and family policies to reinforce the learning system would greatly facilitate the transition from school to work in the United States. "America has the worst school-to-work transition process of any industrialized nation," states Ray Marshall. "Put simply, we have no systematic processes to assist high school graduates to move smoothly from school into employment." The focus of U.S. secondary schools and counseling programs is to encourage young people to enter college and obtain a degree. But high school graduates who are not college-bound represent nearly one-half of each graduating class. Thus, they "are left to sink or swim—without advice or career counseling and without any job placement assistance."

Unlike employers in Germany and Japan, employers in the United States who have jobs that offer good wages, career potential, and attractive benefits usually do not hire workers immediately out of high school. America's largest and best corporations virtually ignore youthful workers. As Marshall points out, "Only a handful of the Fortune 500 firms hire fresh high school graduates for entry jobs offering career opportunities." The larger firms in America do eventually hire high school graduates, but normally not until they have reached their mid-20s, have accumulated some work experience, and have "matured and settled down." The practices of the larger firms are emulated by other employers. Even the "average starting apprentice in the United States is in his/her late twenties. This delay in hiring for career-track jobs results in many youths spending five or six years floundering in jobs that offer neither learning nor advancement opportunities."

The delay in hiring youths has a number of critical consequences for school-to-work transition in the United States. It gives young people in Germany and Japan a five-to-ten-year head start in obtaining access to crucial occupational skills training; it removes our best corporations and their important learning systems from involvement in the processes of molding young workers; it eliminates a natural communication network for feeding employer information to schools about the changing skills required in the workplace; and, most important, it disconnects achievements in school from rewards in the workplace, thereby undermining the incentive for academic success.

The problem of school-to-work transition confronts young people of all ethnic and racial backgrounds, but it is especially serious for black youths. According to a recent report by the U.S. Bureau of Labor Statistics, only 42 percent of black youths who had not enrolled in college had jobs in October after graduating from high school a few months earlier in June, compared with 69 percent of their white counterparts. The figures for black youngsters in inner-city ghetto neighborhoods are obviously even lower. The inadequate system of school-to-work transition has also contributed significantly to the growing wage gap between those with high school diplomas and those with college training. In the 1950s and 1960s, when school-to-work transition was compatible with the mass production system, the average earnings of college graduates was only about 20 percent higher than those of high school graduates. By 1979, it had increased to 49 percent, and then rapidly grew to 83 percent by 1992.

Thus, the school-to-work transition is a major problem in the United States, and it has reached crisis proportions in the inner-city ghetto. In an initial step meant to address this problem, Congress passed the School-to-Work Opportunities Act (SWOA) in the spring of 1994. Providing the framework for the development of a national school-to-work program, the basic objective of the SWOA "is to build on the high standards encouraged by the Goals 2000 Act." The SWOA assumes that the best way to develop a national system of school-to-work transition is to begin with voluntary demonstrations by state and local areas, including demonstrations whereby businesses work with educators in reforming school systems and integrating work and school. The act encourages federal, state, and local partnerships.

It also, through an emphasis on business and education partnerships in local areas, follows the lead of Germany and Japan in stressing the critical importance of private-sector investment in education.

But once again, only a relatively small amount of money was allocated for this program. Total funding for SWOA for fiscal years 1994 and 1995 is less than $500 million. Also, there is no guarantee that the demonstration grants to states will ultimately lead to a more comprehensive national program of school-to-work transition. But such a program is critically needed not only to address the overall problem of growing wage inequality and economic marginality among high school graduates but also as one important weapon in the fight against acute joblessness in the inner-city ghetto.

If the other industrial democracies offer lessons for a long-term solution to the jobs problem involving relationships between employment, education, and family support systems, they also offer lessons on the importance of another solution from a metropolitan perspective—namely, city-suburban integration and cooperation. None of the other industrialized democracies has allowed its city centers to deteriorate as has the United States. In European countries, suburbanization has not been associated with the abandonment of cities as residential areas. "The central governments continued to treat cities as a national resource to be protected and nurtured." Indeed, the city centers in Europe remain very desirable places to reside because of better public transportation, more effective urban renewal programs, and good public education that is more widely available to disadvantaged students. Moreover, unlike in the United States, cheap public transportation makes suburbanized employment sites more accessible.

It will be difficult to address growing racial tensions in U.S. cities unless we tackle the problems of shrinking revenue and inadequate social services and the gradual disappearance of work in certain neighborhoods. The city has become a less desirable place in which to live, and the economic and social gap between the cities and suburbs is growing. The groups left behind compete, often along racial lines, for declining resources, including the remaining decent schools, housing, and neighborhoods. The rise of the new urban poverty neighborhoods has exacerbated these problems. Their high rates of joblessness and social disorganization have created problems that often spill over into other parts of the city at large. All of these factors aggravate race relations and elevate racial tensions.

Ideally, we need to restore the federal contribution to the city budget that existed in 1980 and to sharply increase the employment base. Regardless of changes in federal urban policy, however, the fiscal crisis in the cities would be significantly eased if the employment base could be substantially increased. Indeed, the social dislocations caused by the steady disappearance of work have led to a wide range of urban social problems, including racial tensions. Increased employment would help stabilize the new poverty neighborhoods, halt the precipitous decline in density, and ultimately enhance the quality of race relations in urban areas.

Perhaps at no other time in the nation's history has it been more important to talk about the need to promote city and suburban cooperation, not separation. The political fragmentation of many metropolitan areas in the United States has contributed to the problems of joblessness and related social dislocations of the inner-city poor. As David Rusk, the former mayor of Albuquerque, New Mexico, has pointed out, because the older cities of the East and the Midwest were unable to expand territorially through city-county consolidation or annexation, they failed to reap such benefits of suburban growth as the rise of shopping malls, offices, and industrial parks in new residential subdivisions. As areas in which poor minorities live in higher and higher concentration, these cities face an inevitable downward spiral because they are not benefiting from suburban growth. Rusk argues, therefore, that neighborhood revitalization programs, such as community development banks, nonprofit inner-city housing developments, and enterprise zones, will not be able "to reverse the downward slide of inner cities" if they are not carried out within "a framework of actions to bring down the walls between city and suburb."

Efforts to promote city and suburban cooperation will not benefit cities alone. There is mounting evidence that cities and suburbs are economically interdependent. The more central cities are plagued by joblessness, dysfunctional schools, and crime, the more the surrounding suburbs undergo a decline in their own social and economic fortunes. Suburbs that experienced increases in income during the 1980s tended to be linked to a thriving urban center. In the global economy, metropolitan regions continue to compete for jobs. Suburbs that will remain or become competitive are those with a well-trained workforce, good schools, a concentration of professional services, first-class hospitals, a major university and research center, and an efficient transportation network to link executives with other parts of the United States and with countries around the world. However, many of these elements cannot come solely from suburbs. They require a viable central city. It is important for Americans to realize that city-suburban *integration* is the key to the health of metropolitan regions and to the nation as a whole.

Reforms put forward to achieve the objective of city-suburban cooperation range from proposals to create metropolitan governments to proposals for metropolitan tax base sharing (currently in effect in Minneapolis/St. Paul), collaborative metropolitan planning, and the creation of regional authorities to develop solutions to common problems if communities fail to reach agreement. Among the problems shared by many metropolises is a weak public transit system. A commitment to address this problem through a form of city-suburban collaboration would benefit residents of both the city and the suburbs. Theoretically, everyone would benefit from mobility within the metropolitan areas, and inner-city residents would have greater means to prevent high joblessness.

The problems of joblessness and social dislocation in the inner city are, in part, related to the processes in the global economy that have contributed to greater inequality and insecurity among American workers in general, and to the failure of U.S. social policies to adjust to these processes. It is therefore myopic to view the problems of jobless ghettos as if they were separate from those that plague the larger society.

In using this cross-cultural perspective I am not suggesting that we can or even should simply import the social policies of the Japanese, Germans, or other West Europeans. As Ray Marshall has appropriately pointed out, the approaches in these other countries are embedded in their own cultures and have their "own flaws and deficiencies, as well as strengths." We should instead "learn from the approaches used in other countries and adapt the best aspects into our own homegrown solutions."

The strengths of some of the approaches in other countries are apparent. For example, in Japan and Germany most high school and college graduates leave school with skills in keeping with the demands of the highly technological marketplace in the global economy. In the United States, by contrast, only college graduates and those few with extra-specialized post–high school training acquire such skills. Those with only high school diplomas or less do not.

The flaws and deficiencies of some of the approaches in the other countries are also apparent. Except for Germany, European countries have the same gap in worker skills. Because of the generous unemployment benefits, however, the low-skilled European workers tend to be less willing to accept the lower-paying jobs that their counterparts in the United States are often forced to take. Therefore, the problems of unskilled European workers are not only restricted to low wages, they also include high levels of unemployment. As I pointed out in Chapter 6, the growing problems of unemployment among low-skilled European workers is placing a strain on the welfare state. Immigrant minorities are disproportionately represented among the jobless population, and therefore tend to be publicly identified with the problem of maintaining welfare costs. These perceptions contribute to growing intergroup tensions. Accordingly, the problems of race, unemployment, and concentration of urban poverty that have traditionally plagued the United States are now surfacing in various countries in Europe.

Just as the United States can learn from some of the approaches in the other countries, the Europeans could learn from the United States how to make their workforces more flexible instead of paying them to stay unemployed indefinitely. In particular, they could learn how to get unskilled workers into low-wage jobs that would be buttressed by maintaining certain desirable aspects of the safety net, such as universal health insurance, that prevent workers from slipping into the depths of poverty, as so often happens to their American counterparts.

It is important to discuss immediate solutions to the jobs problem in the United States. Because of their level of training and education, the inner-city poor and other disadvantaged workers mainly have access only to jobs that pay the minimum wage or less and are not covered by health insurance. However, recent policies of the federal government could make such jobs more attractive. The United States Congress enacted an expansion of the earned income tax credit (EITC) in 1993. By

1996, the expanded EITC will increase the earnings from a minimum-wage job to $7 an hour. Families with incomes from $8,400 to $11,000 will receive cash payments of up to $3,370. This expansion, and the previous expansions of the EITC in 1986 and 1990 under the Reagan and Bush administrations, reflected a recognition that wages for low-paying work have eroded and that other policies to aid the working poor—for example, the minimum wage—have become weaker.

However, even when the most recent expansion of the EITC is fully in effect in 1996 (as shown in Table 8.1), it will still fall notably short of compensating for the sharp drop in the value of the minimum wage and the marked reductions in AFDC benefits to low-income working families since the early 1970s. Nonetheless, "the 1993 law set the EITC for a family with two or more children at the level that would bring a family of four with a full-time minimum wage worker to the poverty line if the family also received food stamps and the minimum wage was modestly raised."

If this benefit is paid on a monthly basis and is combined with universal health care, the condition of workers in the low-wage sector would improve significantly and would approach that of comparable workers in Europe. The passage of universal health care is crucial in removing from the welfare rolls single mothers who are trapped in a public-assistance nightmare by the health care needs of their children. It would also make low-paying jobs more attractive for all low-skilled workers and therefore improve the rate of employment.

TABLE 8.1

AVERAGE DISPOSABLE INCOME FOR A MOTHER AND TWO CHILDREN FROM WAGES, FOOD STAMPS, EITC, AND FEDERAL TAXES (IN 1993 DOLLARS)

Year	Number of Hours Worked at Minimum Wage Throughout the Year		
	20 Hours	30 Hours	40 Hours
1972	$13,482	$14,602	$15,656
1980	11,479	12,870	13,792
1990	9,830	10,467	11,509
1993 (with EITC at fully phased-in 1996 levels)	10,612	11,956	13,653

Percentage Change in Average Disposable Income for a Mother and Two Children			
1972–1993	−21%	−18%	−13%

Source: Department of Health and Human Services. Adapted from Center on Budget and Policy Priorities (1995).

However, at the time of this writing, not only has legislation for universal health care been shelved, but the traditional bipartisan support for the EITC is beginning to erode in the Republican-controlled Congress. In May 1995, the Senate passed a budget resolution that includes an assumption that the EITC would be cut by roughly $13 billion over five years and $21 billion over seven years. As pointed out by the Center on Budget and Policy Priorities, a nonprofit public policy organization that examines federal and state fiscal policies:

> More than two-thirds of these cuts would be achieved by repealing the final phase of the 1993 EITC expansion for families with two or more children scheduled for 1996 and reducing the EITC below current levels (tax year 1995 levels) for both families with two or more children and families with one child. Ten million families with children would receive smaller EITCs than they otherwise would. . . . The 1993 EITC expansion is being phased in over several years. The final stage of the phase-in for families with more than one child is scheduled to occur in tax year 1996. *If this last stage of the expansion is repealed and the 1995 expansion is scaled back, a family of four in which a parent works full-time, year-round at the minimum wage will be pushed about $445 deeper into poverty.*

Instead of rolling back the modest expansion of the EITC, it could be argued that the earned income tax credit could be further expanded at reasonable cost to lift all poor working families who work full-time year-round out of poverty, not just those who are currently working at the minimum wage. Further expansion of the EITC and the creation of universal health care legislation ought to be issues at the top of any progressive public policy agenda today. I return to these issues in the next and final section of this chapter, but first I need to complete my discussion of proposed immediate solutions to the jobs problem.

The mismatch between residence and the location of jobs is a special problem for some workers in America because, unlike in Europe, the public transportation system is weak and expensive. This presents a special problem for inner-city blacks because they have less access to private automobiles and, unlike Mexicans, do not have a network system that supports organized car pools. Accordingly, they depend heavily on public transportation and therefore have difficulty getting to the suburbs, where jobs are more plentiful and employment growth is greater. Until public transit systems are improved in metropolitan areas, the creation of privately subsidized car-pool and van-pool networks to carry inner-city residents to the areas of employment, particularly suburban areas, would be a relatively inexpensive way to increase work opportunities.

In the inner-city ghettos, the problems of spatial mismatch have been aggravated by the breakdown in the informal job information network. In neighborhoods in which a substantial number of adults are working, people are more likely to learn about job openings or be recommended for jobs by working kin, relatives, friends, and acquaintances. Job referrals from current employees are important in the American labor market, as our discussion of employer interviews in Chapter 5 so clearly revealed. Individuals in jobless ghettos are less likely to gain employment through this process. But the creation of for-profit or not-for-profit job information and placement centers in various parts of the inner city not only could significantly improve awareness of the availability of employment in the metropolitan area but could also serve to refer workers to employers.

These centers would recruit or accept inner-city workers and try to place them in jobs. One of their main purposes would be to make persons who have been persistently unemployed or out of the labor force "job-ready" so that a prospective employer would be assured that a worker understands and appreciates employer expectations such as showing up for work on time and on a regular basis, accepting the orders of supervisors, and so on. When an information and placement center is satisfied that a worker is job-ready, then and only then would the worker be referred to an employer who has a job vacancy. Moreover, information and placement centers could coordinate efforts with the car-pool and van-pool networks to get those job applicants who lack private transportation to the employment sites.

As much of the foregoing economic analysis suggests, however, the central problem facing inner-city workers is not improving the flow of information about the availability of jobs, or getting to where the jobs are, or becoming job-ready. The central problem is that the demand for labor has shifted away from low-skilled workers because of structural changes in the economy. During certain periods, this problem can be offset to some extent by appropriate macroeconomic levers that can act to enhance economic growth and reduce unemployment, including fiscal policies that regulate government spending and taxation and monetary policies that influence interest rates and control the money supply. But given the fundamental structural decline in the demand for low-skilled workers, such policies will have their greatest impact in the higher-wage sectors of the economy. Many low-wage workers, especially those in high-jobless inner-city neighborhoods who are not in or have dropped out of the labor force and who also face the problem of negative employer attitudes, will not experience any improvement in their job prospects because of fiscal or monetary policies. Despite some claims that low-skilled workers fail to take advantage of labor-market opportunities, available evidence strongly suggests not only that the jobs for such workers carry lower real wages and fewer benefits than did comparable jobs in the early 1970s, but that it is harder for certain low-skilled workers, especially low-skilled males who are not being absorbed into the expanding service sector (see Chapter 2), to find employment today. As the economists Sheldon Danziger and Peter Gottschalk put it:

> In our view, the problem is not that more people have chosen not to work, but rather that demand by employers for less-skilled workers, even those who are willing to work at low wages, has declined. We find it paradoxical that so much attention has been focused on changing the labor-supply behavior of welfare recipients and so little has been given to changing the demand side of a labor market that has been increasingly unable to employ less-skilled and less-experienced workers.

If firms in the private sector cannot use or refuse to hire low-skilled adults who are willing to take minimum-wage or subminimum-wage jobs, then the jobs problem for inner-city workers cannot be adequately addressed without considering a policy of public-sector employment of last resort. Indeed, until current changes in the labor market are reversed or until the skills of the next generation can be upgraded before it enters the labor market, many workers, especially those who are not in the official labor force, will not be able to find jobs unless the government becomes an employer of last resort. This argument applies especially to low-skilled inner-city black workers. It is bad enough that they face the problem of shifts in labor market demand shared by all low-skilled workers; it is even worse that they confront negative employer perceptions about their work-related skills and attitudes.

If jobs are plentiful even for less skilled workers during periods of economic expansion, then labor shortages reduce the likelihood that hiring decisions will be determined by subjective negative judgments concerning a group's job-related traits. Prior to the late 1970s, there was less need for the creation of public-sector jobs. Not only was economic growth fairly rapid during periods of expansion, but "the gains from growth were widely shared." Before the late 1970s, public jobs of last resort were thought of in terms of "a counter-cyclical policy to be put in place during recessions and retired during recoveries. It is only since the late 1970s that the disadvantaged have been left behind during recoveries. The labor market changes . . . seem to have been permanently reduced private sector demand for less-skilled workers."

Given the current need for public jobs to enhance the employment opportunities of low-skilled workers, what should be the nature of these jobs and how should they be implemented? Three thoughtful recent proposals for the creation of public jobs deserve serious consideration. One calls for the creation of public-sector infrastructure maintenance jobs, the second for public service jobs for less-skilled workers, and the third, which combines aspects of the first two, for WPA-style jobs of the kind created during the Franklin D. Roosevelt administration.

Edward V. Regan has advanced a proposal for a public-investment infrastructure maintenance program. He points out that "infrastructure maintenance and upgrading can . . . benefit the economy by creating jobs, particularly for the relatively unskilled, and by raising productivity, thereby contributing to long-term economic growth." According to one estimate, $1 billion spent on road maintenance will directly generate 25,000 jobs and indirectly put 15,000 people to work. On the other hand, new construction creates fewer jobs at higher wages. Another study reports that new building projects or major construction employs 40 percent fewer workers than do maintenance projects. Just as other low-skill jobs are made more attractive by programs of health care, child care, and earned income tax credits, so would low-skill jobs in infrastructure maintenance.

Aside from creating jobs, infrastructure maintenance could lead to higher productivity. On this point, Regan states:

Intuitively, fixing roads and bridges means less axle damage to trucks, fewer road mishaps and congestion, lowered costs of goods, and increased transportation productivity. Congested and deteriorated highways, broken water mains, inadequate sewage treatment, reduced transit services—all of these infrastructure deficiencies reduce productivity, drive up costs of goods and services, and inhibit people's access to employment. Any state or local government official who has tried to attract business facilities to a particular area and has watched business decision makers turn up their noses at cracked concrete and rusting bridges knows the practical meaning of those statements.

Regan also points out that there are many other benefits stemming from an improved infrastructure that are not accounted for in standard economic measures, including shortened commuting times and reduced traffic congestion. If well selected, public investment in infrastructure maintenance could contribute to economic growth. According to the Congressional Budget Office, the national real rate of return for investments to maintain the current quality of the highway system would be 30 to 40 percent, those involving selected expansion in congested urban areas would be 10 to 20 percent.

Although the creation of infrastructure maintenance jobs will provide some employment opportunities for low-skilled workers, the condition of today's labor market makes it unlikely that many of these jobs will actually go to high school dropouts or even to high school graduates with little or no work experience. To address this problem, the economists Sheldon Danziger and Peter Gottschalk, in a recently published book, have advocated the creation of a labor-intensive, minimum-wage public service jobs program of last resort for today's low-skilled and jobless workers. They have in mind jobs such as day-care aides and playground assistants who can supervise in school gyms and public parks during after-school hours. These would be jobs for poor workers who cannot find a place in the private sector, jobs providing services that the fiscally strapped cities can no longer afford to supply through local resources.

Their plan for public service jobs differs in two important respects from recent proposals aimed at increasing work requirements and work incentives for recipients of welfare. First, their proposal is directed not just at welfare recipients but at *all poor workers* adversely affected by current economic shifts, including those who have been ineligible for, or who have chosen not to participate in, welfare. Only a small proportion of those whose labor-market prospects have diminished since the early 1970s have been welfare recipients. Second, their proposal addresses changes in the demand side of the labor market by emphasizing work opportunities and earnings supplements rather than work requirements or incentives.

It is important to distinguish clearly the view of public service jobs embodied in the proposal outlined in the Clinton administration's welfare reform plan that was pushed aside after the Republicans gained control of Congress in 1994. Under the Clinton proposal, welfare would change from an entitlement to a transitional system through which cash assistance would last only two years. For those welfare recipients who reach the time limit but fail to find jobs in the private sector, transitional public-work slots would be made available. However, as Danziger and Gottschalk appropriately point out:

> A program offering jobs of last resort *only* to welfare recipients who exhaust two years of cash assistance would have the potential for perverse incentives and serious inequities. Families who either were not eligible for welfare or chose not to participate would not have access to these jobs. Even if the incentive to go on welfare in order to gain access to the PSE jobs were small, offering jobs to welfare recipients but not to equally needy families who were trying to make it in the labor market could cause resentment.

Danziger and Gottschalk recognize the fact that if programs provided "good" public-sector jobs, local officials would be tempted to fill them with displaced but experienced workers from manufacturing and other goods-producing industries. Therefore, workers with limited experience, skills, and training from high-jobless inner-city neighborhoods would very likely be passed over. Moreover, their proposal is designed to create public service jobs that produce goods and provide services that are not available in the private sector and would not displace private-sector workers.

Their proposal offers a subminimum-wage public service job to any applicant. They would set compensation at 10 to 15 percent below the minimum wage to encourage movement into private-sector jobs as they become available. Graduated job ladders would provide rewards to workers who succeed on the job, "but wages would always be lower than [that which] an equally successful worker would receive in the private sector." These wages would be supplemented with the expanded earned income tax credit and other wage supplements (including a federal child care subsidy in the form of a refundable income tax credit for the working poor and refundable state tax credits for the working poor).

The Danziger and Gottschalk proposal obviously would not provide a comfortable standard of living for the workers forced to take public service jobs. Such jobs are minimal and are "offered as a safely net to poor persons who want to work but are left out of the private labor market." However, they maintain that their proposal is an improvement over the current system, "which offers a minimum wage if you find a job, but leaves millions of poor persons searching for work and many others poor even though they have jobs."

The final proposal under consideration here was advanced by the perceptive journalist Mickey Kaus of *The New Republic*. Kaus's proposal is modeled on the Works Progress Administration (WPA), a large public works program announced in 1935 by Franklin D. Roosevelt in his State of the Union address. The public works jobs that Roosevelt had in mind included highway construction, slum clearance, housing construction, rural electrification, and so on. As Kaus points out:

> In its eight-year existence, according to official records, the WPA built or improved 651,000 miles of roads, 953 airports, 124,000 bridges and viaducts, 1,178,000 culverts, 8,000 parks, 18,000 playgrounds and athletic fields, and 2,000 swimming pools. It constructed 40,000 buildings (including 8,000 schools) and repaired 85,000 more. Much of New York City—including LaGuardia Airport, FDR Drive, plus hundreds of parks and libraries—was built by the WPA. . . . Lester Thurow has suggested that New York's infrastructure is now decaying because no WPA has existed to replace these public works in the half-century since.

Kaus advances what he calls a neo-WPA program of employment for every American citizen over 18 who wants it. The program would provide useful public jobs at wages slightly below the minimum wage. Kaus's proposed program would not only eliminate the need to provide public assistance or "workfare" for able-bodied workers but, unlike welfare, the WPA-style jobs would be

> available to everybody, men as well as women, single or married, mothers and fathers alike. No perverse "anti-family" incentives. It wouldn't even be necessary to limit the public jobs to the poor. If Donald Trump showed up, he could work too. But he wouldn't. Most Americans wouldn't. There'd be no need to "target" the program to the needy. The low wage itself would guarantee that those who took the jobs would be those who needed them, while preserving the incentive to look for better work in the private sector.

Kaus maintains that the work relief under his proposal, like the work relief under Roosevelt's WPA, would not carry the stigma of a cash dole. People would be earning their money. Although some workers in the WPA-style jobs "could be promoted to higher-paying public service positions," most of them would advance occupationally by moving to the private sector. "If you have to work anyway," asks Kaus, "why do it for $4 an hour?"

Kaus's proposal would also place a time limit on welfare for able-bodied recipients. After a certain date they would no longer be eligible for cash payments. However, unlike the welfare program proposed in 1995 by the Republican-controlled Congress, public jobs would be available to those who move off welfare. Kaus argues that to allow poor mothers to work, government-funded day care must be provided for their children if needed. But this service has to be integrated into the larger system of child care for other families in the United States to avoid creating a "day-care ghetto" for low-income children.

In Kaus's proposal the WPA-style jobs would be supplemented with the earned income tax credit, which could be expanded at reasonable cost to lift all poor working families who work full-time throughout the year out of poverty. Because this subsidy would augment the income of all low-wage workers, those in low-level private-sector jobs would not be treated unfairly and their wages on average would be slightly higher than those in the guaranteed subminimum-wage public jobs.

Kaus maintains that there will be enough worthwhile WPA-style jobs for anyone who wants one. The crumbling infrastructure in American cities has to be repaired. Services cut back by the government for financial reasons, such as picking up trash two times a week and opening libraries every evening and on Saturdays, could be reinstated. Jobs for men and women could range from filling potholes and painting bridges to serving as nurse's aides, clerks, and cooks. "With a neo-WPA maintaining highways, schools, playgrounds, and subways, with libraries open every evening and city streets cleaned twice a day, we would have a common life more people would find worth reclaiming."

In reviewing these three proposals, the Kaus neo-WPA jobs plan is the most comprehensive because it would include not only the kind of infrastructure maintenance advocated by Regan but also the labor-intensive public service jobs proposed by Danziger and Gottschalk. And unlike the program proposed by Danziger and Gottschalk, neither Kaus's WPA-style jobs program nor Regan's infrastructure maintenance program would be targeted to poor workers. Whereas Kaus explicitly states that the pay scale for the neo-WPA jobs would be set below the minimum wage, Regan does not address the question of pay scale for his infrastructure maintenance jobs. It is reasonable to assume, however, that the pay scale for the infrastructure maintenance jobs would be lower than that for comparable levels of employment in the private sector. Nonetheless, both of these programs would very likely attract a substantial number of displaced experienced workers willing to take lower-paying public-sector jobs until they find higher-paying work in the private sector.

Given the broader scope of Kaus's neo-WPA jobs program, a higher proportion of workers with few skills and little or no work experience would be employed than would be possible under the Regan program of infrastructure maintenance. Accordingly, Kaus's program would provide many more job opportunities for workers in high-jobless inner-city ghetto neighborhoods.

The labor-intensive public service jobs program advanced by Danziger and Gottschalk is designed to generate immediate employment opportunities for workers with low skills and little or no work experience. However, since it is explicitly aimed at poor workers, it runs the risk of carrying a stigma. The WPA-style jobs advocated by Kaus avoid this problem. The program would be presented as offering jobs to any American who wants a job. Given the subminimum-wage scale, it is likely to attract only a handful of workers who could readily find higher-paying jobs in the private sector. And even if local authorities succumbed to the temptation to fill the "good" WPA jobs with displaced experienced workers, there would still be a sufficient number of labor-intensive jobs requiring little skill, training, or experience. Moreover, the experienced and higher-paid workers who accept WPA-style jobs because of layoffs in the private sector would be likely to remain in the program for only a short period of time.

Furthermore, the Kaus program of WPA-style jobs would lend itself to the kind of progressive public rhetoric that I discussed in Chapter 7—namely a public rhetoric that focuses on problems afflicting not only the poor but the working and middle classes as well. Thus, the program would promote social and economic improvements benefiting all groups in society, not just the truly disadvantaged segments of the population. This is consistent with my argument that the joblessness of the poor, including the inner-city poor, represents the more extreme form of economic marginality experienced by large segments of the population and stems in large measure from changes in the organization of the economy, including the global economy.

Because it is comprehensive, less likely to carry a stigma, and lends itself to a progressive public rhetoric of social reform, I include the Kaus neo-WPA jobs plan in my package of proposed immediate solutions to the jobs problem. However, there is the problem of administering a neo-WPA program, which is not discussed by Kaus. This program must be administered by the federal government (as was the earlier WPA program under the Roosevelt administration) in order to avoid the problem of "fiscal substitution"—that is, the shifting of spending on public employment projects from the local or state level to the federal government. This problem accompanied the implementation of the Comprehensive Employment and Training Act (CETA). The creation of public service employment through CETA in the 1970s did very little to increase the *aggregate* number of jobs in the economy because states and localities over time used the program to substitute subsidized positions for previously nonsubsidized public service jobs. This had the effect of shifting jobs from one funding source to another. Our goal here is to increase the number of jobs, and thus broad federal oversight is required.

As another way to avoid the problem of worker displacement, I would also recommend that the workers in the federal WPA-style program only produce goods and services that are not being produced in the private sector and are not presently provided by regular public-sector workers. If this problem is not addressed, considerable opposition to such a program could arise from both private- and public-sector unions and from businesses in the private sector. Accordingly, following Kaus, I have in mind useful public work that is currently not being done for financial reasons. This would include regular infrastructure maintenance; the cleaning of streets twice, not once, a day; the collection of trash twice a week instead of once a week; the opening of libraries on Saturday and in the evenings; the cleaning of municipal parks, playgrounds, and other public facilities at a level and with a frequency that would ensure their attractiveness and invite use; and the supervision of public playgrounds that would maximize safer, adult-sponsored recreation for all neighborhood children.

It is reasonable to anticipate that as WPA-style workers are used to replenish or revitalize public service staffs, certain states and localities might be tempted to scale back their regular workforce during periods of severe fiscal constraints and rely more on subsidized public service workers. To discourage this type of displacement of regular government workers, I would recommend that one WPA worker be removed for every regular worker's slot that is eliminated or not filled within a certain time period.

A WPA-style jobs program will not be cheap. In the short run, it is less expensive to give people cash welfare than it is to create public jobs. Including the costs of supervisors and materials, it is estimated that each subminimum-wage WPA-style job would cost at least $12,000. That would represent $12 billion for every 1 million jobs created. This figure does not include additional funds to augment the subminimum wage from the earned income tax credit, nor does it reflect any long-run national real rate of return for public investment in infrastructure maintenance that would contribute to economic growth.

None of the immediate solutions I am proposing involves retraining workers for higher-paying positions in the highly technological global economy. The need to retrain low-skilled workers is generally recognized by policymakers and informed observers in both Europe and the United States. However, the most serious discussions about training for the new economy have focused on young people and their transition from school to work or from school to postsecondary training. The cost of retraining adult workers is considerable, and none of the industrial democracies has advanced convincing proposals indicating how to implement such a program effectively. Moreover, a heavy emphasis on skill development and job retraining is likely to end up mainly benefiting those who already have a good many skills that only need to be upgraded.

Also, none of my immediate solutions offers a remedy for the growing wage inequality in the United States. The long-term solutions I have presented, which include those that prepare the next generation to move into the new jobs created in the global economy, are designed to combat that problem. But my specific recommendations for immediate action would address the employment problems of many low-skilled workers, including those from the inner city. They would confront the current and serious problem of the disappearance of work in the inner-city ghetto. The jobs created would not be high-wage jobs but, with universal health insurance, a child care program, and earned income tax credits attached, they would enable workers and their families to live at least decently and avoid joblessness and the problems associated with it. The United States Congress has already expanded the earned income tax credit. Universal health insurance and some kind of flexible child care program would be costly, but these programs would support *all* Americans. Furthermore, the nation has recognized the need for such social benefits and there remains considerable public support in favor of moving forward on both programs—especially in the area of health insurance—despite Congress's retreat from public policy programs to combat social inequality following the 1994 congressional elections.

Ironically, at the same time there is growing pressure in Europe to reduce the social safety net, especially the entitlement of indefinite unemployment insurance. What might evolve in the future is a movement in both directions—toward a stronger social safety net in the United States and a weaker one in Europe—that would result in similar or more comparable social welfare programs sufficient to allow workers on both sides of the Atlantic to live free of economic deprivation or severe hardship. For this to occur, however, Americans concerned about combating social inequality will have to counter the current retreat in the U.S. Congress away from public policy issues that address joblessness and poverty.

Programs proposed to increase employment opportunities, such as the creation of WPA-style jobs, should be aimed at broad segments of the U.S. population, not just inner-city workers, in order to provide the needed solid political base of support. In the new, highly integrated global economy, an increasing number of Americans across racial, ethnic, and income groups are experiencing declining real incomes, increasing job displacement, and growing economic insecurity. The unprecedented level of inner-city joblessness represents one important aspect of the broader economic dislocations that cut across racial and ethnic groups in the United States. Accordingly, when promoting economic and social reforms, it hardly seems politically wise to focus mainly on the most disadvantaged groups while ignoring other segments of the population that have also been adversely affected by global economic changes.

Yet, just when bold new comprehensive initiatives are urgently needed to address these problems, the U.S. Congress has retreated from using public policy as an instrument with which to fight social inequality. Failure to deal with this growing social inequality, including the rise of joblessness in U.S. inner cities, could seriously worsen the economic life of urban families and neighborhoods.

Groups ranging from the inner-city poor to those working- and middle-class Americans who are struggling to make ends meet will have to be effectively mobilized in order to change the current course and direction taken by policymakers. Perhaps the best way to accomplish this is through coalition politics that promote race-neutral programs such as jobs creation, further expansion of the earned income tax credit, public school reform, child care programs, and universal health insurance. A broad-based political coalition is needed to successfully push such programs through the political process.

Because an effective political coalition in part depends upon how the issues to be addressed are defined, it is imperative that the political message underscore the need for economic and social reform that benefits all groups, not just America's minority poor. The framers of this message should be cognizant of the fact that changes in the global economy are creating growing social inequality and situations which intensify antagonisms between different racial and ethnic groups, and that these groups, although often seen as adversaries, are potential allies in a reform coalition because they suffer from a common problem—economic distress caused by forces outside their own control.

In the absence of an effective political coalition, priorities will be established that do not represent the interests of disadvantaged groups. For example, in the House of Representatives, 67 percent of proposed spending cuts from the federal budget for the year 2000 would come from low-income programs, even though these programs represent only 21 percent of the current federal budget (see Figure 8.1). Without an effective political coalition it is unlikely that Congress would be willing to finance the kinds of reforms that are needed to combat the new social inequality. At the time of this writing, the momentum is away from, not toward, social programs. Instead of recognizing and dealing with the complex and changing realities that have led to economic distress for many Americans, policymakers seek to assign blame and associate the economic problems of families and

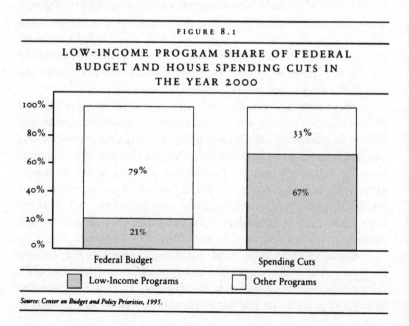

FIGURE 8.1

LOW-INCOME PROGRAM SHARE OF FEDERAL
BUDGET AND HOUSE SPENDING CUTS IN
THE YEAR 2000

Source: Center on Budget and Policy Priorities, 1995.

individuals with personal shortcomings such as lack of initiative, work ethic, or motivation. Consequently, there is very little support in favor of financing any social programs—even the creation of public service jobs for the limited number of welfare recipients who reach a time limit for receipt of welfare checks. Considering the deleterious consequences this shortsighted retreat from public policy will have for so many Americans, it is distressing that progressive groups, far from being energized to reverse the public policy direction in which the country is now moving, seem to be almost intimidated and paralyzed by the rhetoric of the Republican Contract with America.

Accordingly, the kinds of long-term and immediate-term solutions that I have proposed stand little chance of being adopted, not to mention seriously considered, in the absence of a new political coalition of groups pressing for economic and social reform. Political leaders concerned about the current shift in public policy will have to develop a unifying rhetoric, a progressive message that resonates with broad segments of the American population, a message that enables groups to recognize that it is in their interest to join a reform coalition dedicated to moving America forward.

The solutions I have outlined were developed with the idea of providing a policy framework that would be suitable for and could be easily adopted by a reform coalition. The long-term solutions, which include the development of a system of national performance standards in public schools, family policies to reinforce the learning system in the schools, a national system of school-to-work transition, and ways to promote city-suburban integration and cooperation, would be beneficial to and could draw the support of a broad range of groups in America. The short-term solutions, which range from the development of job information and placement centers and subsidized car pools in the ghetto to the creation of WPA-style jobs, are more relevant to low-income Americans, but they are the kinds of opportunity-enhancing programs that Americans of all racial and class backgrounds tend to support.

Although my policy framework is designed to appeal to broad segments of the population, I firmly believe that if adopted, it would alleviate a good deal of the economic and social distress currently plaguing the inner cities. The immediate problem of the disappearance of work in many inner-city neighborhoods would be confronted. The employment base in these neighborhoods would be increased immediately by the creation of WPA-style jobs, and income levels would rise because of the expansion of the earned income tax credit. Programs such as universal health care and day care would increase the attractiveness of low-wage jobs and "make work pay."

Increasing the employment base would have an enormous positive impact on the social organization of ghetto neighborhoods. As more people become employed, crime, including violent crime, and drug use will subside; families will be strengthened and welfare receipt will decline significantly; ghetto-related culture and behavior, no longer sustained and nourished by persistent joblessness, will gradually fade. As more people become employed and gain work experience, they will have a better chance of finding jobs in the private sector when they become available. The attitudes of employers toward inner-city workers will undergo change, in part because they would be dealing with job applicants who have steady work experience and would furnish references from their previous supervisors.

This is not to suggest that all the jobless individuals from the inner-city ghetto would take advantage of these employment opportunities. Some have responded to persistent joblessness by abusing alcohol and drugs, and these handicaps will affect their overall job performance, including showing up for work on time or on a consistent basis. But they represent only a small segment of the worker population in the inner city. Most workers in the inner city are ready, willing, able, and anxious to hold a steady job.

The long-term solutions that I have advanced would reduce the likelihood that a new generation of jobless workers would be produced from the youngsters now in school and preschool. We must break the cycle of joblessness and improve the youngsters' preparation for the new labor market in the global economy.

My framework for long-term and immediate solutions is based on the notion that the problems of jobless ghettos cannot be separated from those of the rest of the nation. Although these solutions have wide-ranging application and would alleviate the economic distress of many Americans, their impact on jobless ghettos would be profound. Their most important contribution would be their effect on the children of the ghetto, who would be able to anticipate a future of economic mobility and share the hopes and aspirations that so many of their fellow citizens experience as part of the American way of life.

APPENDIXES

NOTES

BIBLIOGRAPHY

INDEX

APPENDIXES

Appendix A

Perspectives on Poverty Concentration

Douglas Massey and Mitchell Eggers (1990) have questioned the extent of the increasing isolation of poor inner-city blacks. They state: "Although the levels of black interclass segregation increased during the 1970s, we could find no evidence that these trends account for the rising concentration of black poverty." They argue that because of persisting segregation, higher-income blacks have been "less able to separate themselves from the poor than the privileged of other groups" (Massey and Eggers [1990], p. 1186). Accordingly, an increase in the poverty rate of a highly segregated group will automatically be accompanied by an increase in the concentration of poverty. However, their research is based on census tract averages of standard metropolitan statistical averages (SMSAs), and I do not believe that this measure provides a screen fine enough to detect the changes that have occurred in the outmigration of nonpoor blacks from the more impoverished inner-city neighborhoods.

In a more recent study, Douglas Massey, Andrew Gross, and Kumiko Shibuya (1994) were able to analyze the movement of the poor and the nonpoor at the neighborhood (that is, census tract) level by utilizing data from the Panel Study of Income Dynamics, a national longitudinal study of the social and economic experiences of individuals and families, which recently appended census tract data to individual records. Because of missing address lists from 1975 to 1978, they were only able to compute the probabilities of movement between 1970 and 1973 and then 1979 to 1984. Their results show that in the early 1970s nonpoor blacks moved out of poor neighborhoods at a higher rate than did poor blacks. This supports the arguments advanced in *The Truly Disadvantaged* (Wilson [1987]), which focused on neighborhood changes in the 1970s. However, by the early 1980s this "differential had reversed" and the outmovement of the poor had become greater than that of the nonpoor (p. 431). They confirmed three factors that have contributed to the growth of concentrated poverty. Two of these factors, as noted earlier, had been suggested in *The Truly Disadvantaged:* the outmigration of non-poor whites and the rise in the number of residents in concentrated poverty areas who have become poor. The third involves the movement of poor people into poor neighborhoods.

In addition to Paul Jargowsky and Mary Jo Bane (1990; see Chapter 1), two other recent studies—by Claudia Coulton and her colleagues (1990), and Kathryn Nelson (1991)—on the significance of demographic shifts with respect to the growth of concentrated neighborhoods also relied on neighborhood measures instead of metropolitan averages. All three studies revealed that the outmigration of higher-income families from poverty areas had contributed to the rise of concentrated poverty in these areas.

Dividing neighborhoods into traditional, emerging, and new poverty areas in Cleveland, Claudia Coulton and her colleagues at Case Western Reserve University found that although more persons became poor in all of these areas during the decade of the 1970s, the most important factor in the growth of concentrated poverty in these areas was the outmigration of the nonpoor (Coulton, Chow, and Pandey [1990]).

Jargowsky and Bane (1990) focused their research on Philadelphia, Cleveland, Milwaukee, and Memphis. Using census tracts as proxies for neighborhoods, they sorted ghetto neighborhoods (that is, neighborhoods with rates of poverty of at least 40 percent) from nonghetto neighborhoods and reported a significant geographic spreading of ghetto neighborhoods from 1970 to 1980. Areas that had become ghettos by 1980 had been mixed-income tracts in 1970, although they were contiguous to areas identified as ghettos. Their results reveal that a major factor in the growth of ghetto poverty has been the exodus of the nonpoor from mixed-income areas: "The poor were leaving as well, but the nonpoor left faster, leaving behind a group of people in 1980 that was poorer than [the mix in the same area] in 1970" (p. 56).

As the nonpoor population spread outward from areas of mixed income, Jargowsky and Bane went on to state, the next ring of the city, mostly areas that were white and nonpoor, became the home of a "larger proportion of the black and poor population. The white nonpoor left these areas, which also lost population overall" (pp. 56–57). Thus, the black middle-class outmigration from mixed-income areas that then became ghettos did not result in a significant decrease in black migrants' contact with poorer blacks, for the areas to which they relocated were at the same time being abandoned by nonpoor whites, a process that increased the spread of segregation and poverty during the 1970s.

A similar point is made by Jeffrey Morenoff:

As African-American residents of all income levels flee core ghetto areas, many will relocate in neighborhoods on the geographical periphery of the ghetto, many of which are undergoing racial transition. Thus, as living conditions in core ghetto areas deteriorate, these neighborhoods should experience net population losses along with increased poverty rates, because those residents with the fewest resources are likely to be left behind. At the same time, neighborhoods along the periphery of the ghetto should be more likely than those at the core to experience gains in population (due to higher levels of in-migration), which should also contribute to poverty increases and bring about an ecological redefinition of these areas. (1994, p.14)

The most important of these studies was conducted by the economist Kathryn Nelson (1991) of the U.S. Department of Housing and Urban Development. Using new data from HUD's American Housing Survey, Nelson identified "zones of population" within large metropolitan areas and traced the residential mobility among them during the 1980s. The zones of population can be interpreted as proxies for neighborhoods. Because she was able to identify both the current and previous residence for most of the inter-metropolitan movers in these areas by zone, Nelson examined "intra-metropolitan movers at a finer level of geographic detail than the city-suburb level typically available in Census publications or microdata" (Nelson [1991], p. 1).

She found that during the 1980s all households, including those of blacks and other minorities, had high rates of outmigration from the poorest areas. Moreover, she discovered that the movement out of poor neighborhoods increased "markedly with income, among blacks and other minorities as well as for all households; and that . . . rates of black outmovement from the poorest areas were higher and more selective by income in the more segregated metropolitan areas" (Nelson [1991], p. 28). She also found that the white exodus from the poorest zones in the more segregated metropolitan areas was even higher than that of blacks and more positively associated with income. This led her to speculate that higher-income blacks in the more segregated metropolitan areas may have fewer nonghetto neighborhoods accessible to them: when they leave ghetto areas they have less space in which to disperse because of patterns of residential segregation and, as Massey and Eggers's research suggests, are more likely to have poor people as neighbors.

For a similar conclusion, see Qi Huang and Paul Attewell (1993).

Appendix B
Methodological Note on the Research at the
Center for the Study of Urban Inequality

CHICAGO URBAN POVERTY AND FAMILY LIFE STUDY

The Urban Poverty and Family Life Study (UPFLS) comprised four parts: a large survey of inner-city residents, an open-ended survey (the Social Opportunity Survey) of a smaller sample of respondents selected from the main survey, ethnographic field research, and a survey of employers in the Greater Chicago area.

The UPFLS survey. Conducted in 1987 and 1988, the UPFLS survey included a stratified probability sample of African-American, non-Hispanic white, Mexican, and Puerto Rican parents ages 18 to 44 who resided in poor neighborhoods in Chicago in 1986. It also included a supplemental sample of African-American nonparents ages 18 to 44 who lived in the same areas. Poor neighborhoods were defined as census tracts in which at least 20 percent of the residents had family incomes below the federal poverty line in 1980. Fifty-five percent of Chicago's African-American population lived in poor neighborhoods in 1980, compared with 53 percent of the Puerto Rican population, 37 percent of the Mexicans, and 3 percent of the non-Hispanic whites.

Averaging just under two hours in length, the survey was conducted by the National Opinion Research Center (NORC) staff in the homes of the respondents. Thirty-three of the interviews were conducted by telephone with respondents who either were unwilling to be interviewed in person or had moved out of Chicago. The survey covered the income and composition of the households, family background, attitudes, and social networks. It also included life-history information on employment, education, public aid, childbirth, migration, military service, detention, and relationships (parental, marital, cohabiting). English and Spanish versions of the survey were printed and administered.

From a net sample of 3,165 people, 2,490 completed the survey, yielding a response rate of 78.7 percent. Overall, 1,572 of the respondents were women and 918 were men. There were 1,183 black respondents, 489 Mexicans, 454 Puerto Ricans, and 364 whites. Of the African-American respondents, 1,020 were parents and 163 were childless. Nearly all of the non-Hispanic whites and blacks were native-born, whereas 85 percent of the Mexican respondents and 73 percent of the Puerto Ricans were not born in the mainland United States. Many of these island- and foreign-born respondents, however, migrated to the mainland U.S. during their childhood.

The Social Opportunity Survey. This survey included 167 respondents selected from the large survey who lived in the poorest census tract. These respondents were chosen by quota sampling in the proportion of 4:2:2:1 among blacks, Mexicans, Puerto Ricans, and whites. Within ethnic groups and census tracts, equal numbers of males and females from each marital and employment status (married/unmarried and employed/jobless) were selected. Open-ended questions were used to gather more detailed systematic data than that collected based on the brief responses to the main survey. Questions were organized around the following topics: opportunity and mobility, work experiences and opinions, education and expectations for their children, household composition, social classes, finances, and interviewer observations. English and Spanish versions of the survey were printed and administered.

With the permission of the respondents, the interviews were tape-recorded. They averaged an hour in length. Locating the respondents selected for the Social Opportunity Survey, especially the men, was difficult. The final group of respondents included 63 African-American women and 34 African-American men,

17 Mexican women and 14 Mexican men, 11 Puerto Rican women and 3 Puerto Rican men, and 20 white women and 5 white men.

The Ethnographic Field Research. There were two components of the ethnographic field research: intensive case studies and neighborhood participant observation, both conducted in poor city neighborhoods that had a concentration of either black, Mexican, Puerto Rican, or white residents. Two more neighborhoods were added to the study: an immigrant Assyrian neighborhood and a poor black suburban neighborhood on the Southeast Side of the city of Chicago. "Both sites were added to the study to take advantage of the research and contacts previously developed by the [research assistants], and to provide some comparisons and contrasts to the other sites. The suburban black community is similar to neighborhoods in the inner city because it is impoverished. It is different from them because it has a small population, it lacks public transportation and is physically isolated from the other communities. The [Assyrian neighborhood] is similarly particular, because many of the residents are first-generation immigrants who do not know English and live in Assyrian enclaves" (Krogh [1991a]).

The case studies were based on conversations with 99 informants, ranging from only one or two interviews to as many as thirty or forty interviews with the same informant. The average was roughly six interviews per informant. All of the conversations were tape-recorded with the permission of the informant. The total number of contacts with informants yielded almost 600 case study files. The participant observation research involved the collection of data based on the informal observations of the graduate student ethnographers. Participant observation research included walking the streets and engaging people in informal conversation; frequenting places where people congregate for recreation, social services, or the use of facilities and observing their behavior while interacting with them; and establishing relationships with individuals interviewed for the case studies in order to be introduced to other individuals and activities in the neighborhood.

Four graduate students conducted the ethnographic field research in the black neighborhoods, three in the Mexican neighborhoods, and one each in the white, Puerto Rican, and Assyrian neighborhoods. The graduate students conducted full-time field research during the summers of 1986 and 1987 and continued part-time research during the academic years 1986 and 1987. Two students extended their field research into 1988 in an effort to interview more black and Mexican men.

The Employer Survey. A sample of the firms located in Chicago and suburban Cook County and representing private employers provided the data for the employer survey. The sampling frame was based on the distribution of jobs by industry and location as listed in the 1984 edition of *Where Workers Work*. "Manufacturing firms were identified from the Illinois Manufacturers' Directory, while most other firms were identified from the Illinois Services' Directory. In addition, some retail and consumer service firms were identified from the telephone book, because the business directory listing was less complete for them than for other types of firms" (Krogh [1991a], p. 25).

The sample of firms was stratified by industry type, size, and location. Firms were stratified by industry type to reflect their distribution in the Chicago metropolitan area using the standard categories of manufacturing, construction, mining, wholesale trade, retail trade, transportation, communication, and utilities. They were stratified by size to reflect the fact that although there are more small firms than large firms, the latter provide a disproportionate number of jobs. Accordingly, firms were selected proportionate to the number of jobs they provide. Because of an expected response rate of 50 percent, 400 firms were selected in order to produce 200 completed interviews. "As it turned out, well over 50 percent of the sampled firms were willing to be interviewed, but the project did not have the resources to pursue all the potential respondents. Halfway through the field period, a 40 percent minimum response rate for every location by industry category was set. Unresolved cases in categories with response rates higher than 40 percent were not pursued further" (Krogh [1991a]). The final overall response rate was 45 percent. The response rates were similar across categories and there was no significant bias by industry, size of firm, or location.

The face-to-face employer interviews were conducted by six graduate students between July 1988 and March 1989 with representatives of the firms in the sample. The average length of time for the interviews was an hour, although many respondents were willing to speak for longer periods of time. The initial contacts and most of the interviews were with the highest-ranking official at the firm. Both closed-ended and open-ended questions were included in the survey and covered issues that ranged from hiring and recruitment practices to perceptions of the inner-city labor force.

> Most of the structured portion of the interview focused on a sample job, defined by the interview schedule as "the most typical entry-level position" in the firm's modal occupational category—sales, clerical, skilled, semiskilled, or service, but excluding managerial, professional, and technical. The distribution of our sample jobs approximates the occupational distribution in the 1980 census for Cook County, again excluding professional, managerial, and technical categories. In effect, what we have is a sample of the opportunities facing the Chicago job-seeker with minimal skills. (Kirschenman and Neckerman [1991], pp. 206–7)

As revealed in the comments presented in Chapter 5, many of the employers were not reluctant to make candid comments. In describing these responses, two of our graduate student interviewers, Joleen Kirschenman and Kathryn Neckerman, point out that "a standard rule of discourse is that some things are acceptable to say and others are better left unsaid. Silence has the capacity to speak volumes. Thus, we were overwhelmed by the degree to which Chicago employers felt comfortable talking with us—in a situation where the temptation would be to conceal rather than reveal—in a negative manner about blacks" (Kirschenman and Neckerman 1991, p. 207).

OAKLAND AND WOODLAWN NEIGHBORHOOD STUDY

This study included a survey of residents from two high-jobless neighborhoods on the South Side of Chicago. It also included six focus group discussions with the residents and the former residents of one of these two neighborhoods. The *community residents' survey* solicited responses from a representative sample of the residents of each of these neighborhoods. The survey provided information on the residents' perceptions of the quality of life in their neighborhood, the major strengths and weaknesses of their community, and existing community resources, such as the availability of social services, housing, and employment services. Data were also gathered on respondents' perceptions of how community economic development may affect them personally, as well as their concerns about the future of their community.

Through a collaborative effort, the Center for the Study of Urban Inequality, the Fund for Community Revitalization and Redevelopment, and the Metro Chicago Information Center (MCIC) research staff composed the survey questionnaire. The face-to-face interviews were conducted by staff members at MCIC, a private nonprofit research organization. A block quota sample was developed based on census tract data. The block quota technique guarantees a random dispersion of targeted respondents throughout the community.

The questionnaire consisted of approximately thirty open- and closed-ended questions, and a typical interview session lasted fifteen minutes. A total of 500 residents, 250 from both Woodlawn and Oakland, were interviewed between September 1 and November 30, 1993. The residents interviewed were adults, ages 18 and older. The vast majority of the respondents were African-American, and there was an even ratio of males and females.

In the second phase of research, six *focus groups* were convened. These groups reflected the different age and socioeconomic levels of residents in the Woodlawn and Oakland communities. Each community was represented by a group of resident adults and a group of high school students. Because of the high poverty rate in Oakland, a focus group consisting entirely of public aid recipients was formed. The sixth group consisted of former residents of Woodlawn who had relocated out of the area. The Center hired a consultant to moderate each meeting assisted by Center research staff. The meetings followed a general format for introducing the discussion topics. Each focus group meeting lasted between one and a half and two hours.

To recruit focus group subjects, the Center contacted nineteen different organizations in both Woodlawn and North Kenwood/Oakland and requested the names of residents who might be interested in participating. Focus group members were then chosen at random from these lists, and each was paid a nominal fee for participation. Consequently, these groups are not entirely representative of the general community. Certain biases may have been introduced into the discussions; for example, participants may have been more aware of certain community needs, or attuned to a particular resource, given that they are all affiliated with

one community organization or another. However, while the demographic characteristics of the focus group participants are not entirely representative of the
population in both these communities, their insights and concerns are in many
ways similar to those expressed by the general population.

In total, twenty-five Oakland residents and twenty Woodlawn residents participated in six focus groups. All participants were African-American, and 66 percent were female. Excluding the high school groups, 35 percent of respondents
were married. The educational levels of adult focus group participants were quite
high: almost two-thirds had some college experience and eight had completed
college or earned an advanced degree. The average age of the high school students was 14 years.

THE EFFECTS OF NEIGHBORHOODS ON
ADOLESCENT SOCIAL OUTCOMES

The purpose of this study was to examine the effects of neighborhoods on adolescent social outcomes in high-risk areas. The study surveyed mothers or primary
caregivers and one or two adolescent children living in poor and nonpoor (work-
ing- and middle-class) black neighborhoods in Chicago. Residents from poor
neighborhoods were oversampled. The face-to-face interviews were conducted
by the staff of the University of Northern Illinois Survey Research Center.

The sample design involved two strata: a high-poverty (50 percent or more
black, with 20 percent or more below poverty) and a low-poverty (30 percent or
more black, and median incomes of $30,000 or more) strata. Eligible households
in each tract were those with youths aged 11 to 16. Mothers and up to two eligible youths from each household were included in the sample. The high-poverty
sample involved 383 households and 614 youth. The low-poverty sample involved 163 households and 273 youth. The total sample included 58 neighborhoods with 546 households and 887 youth.

Measures of neighborhood characteristics were developed from both census
data and from interviews conducted with parent respondents. The neighborhood
unit was represented by a single census tract. Data from the 1990 census were uti-
lized to create a measure of social disadvantage for each neighborhood. This measure combines four standardized census indicators of disadvantage: poverty,
residential mobility, family structure (percentage of single-parent families), and
ethnic diversity. Three neighborhood social organization predictors were included: neighborhood control (i.e., informal and formal institutional controls),
social integration (i.e., community organizations/activities and associational ties),
and informal networks (i.e., friends and family in the neighborhood). The study
controlled for individual and family characteristics (e.g., youth, age, sex, socioeconomic status, family structure, and length of neighborhood residency) that
might affect social outcomes.

Appendix C

Tables on Urban Poverty and Family Life Study Research

TABLE I

MARRIED-COUPLE FAMILIES WITH CHILDREN UNDER 18 YEARS BY EDUCATIONAL ATTAINMENT OF HOUSEHOLDER FOR BLACK FAMILIES, 1990

Level of Attainment	Number of Families	% of All Families with Kids at Level of Attainment
Not High School Graduate	410,185	37.9
High School Graduate (or GED)	589,183	45.8
Some College/Associate Degree	580,467	49.0
Bachelor's Degree	188,126	65.1
Graduate/Professional Degree	97,610	69.3
All Levels	1,865,571	46.8

Source: *Characteristics of the Black Population, 1990 Census of Population*

TABLE 2

EMPLOYED BLACK MEN: PERCENTAGE IN MANUFACTURING AND CONSTRUCTION INDUSTRIES 1970–87 AND PERCENTAGE WHO ARE MEMBERS OF UNIONS 1969–87 BY BIRTH YEAR, MEASURED IN MARCH OF EACH YEAR

Fathers in UPFLS/living in the U.S./age 15+/without bachelor's degrees/weighted

Percentage in Manufacturing and Construction Industries

Birth Year	1970	1974	1978	1983	1987
1941–49	40	44	31	27	27
1950–55	72	57	52	31	31
1956–60	—	51	52	30	28
1961–69	—	—	35	30	21

Percentage Who Are Members of Unions

Birth Year	1969	1974	1978	1983	1987
1941–49	55	41	38	23	32
1950–55	72	60	53	36	27
1956–60	—	62	61	48	42
1961–69	—	—	36	24	35

Adapted from Krogh (1993).

TABLE 3

EMPLOYED MEN: PERCENTAGE IN MANUFACTURING
1969–87 BY BIRTH YEAR AND ETHNICITY,
EMPLOYMENT MEASURED IN MARCH OF EACH YEAR

Fathers from UPFLS/living in the U.S./age 15+/with bachelor's degrees/weighted

Birth Year/ Ethnicity	1969 %	S.E.	1974 %	S.E.	1978 %	S.E.	1983 %	S.E.	1987 %	S.E.
1941–55										
Mexican	04	9.4	37	7.0	29	5.4	33	5.8	33	3.9
Puerto Rican	24	10.5	42	8.3	27	6.6	34	6.6	34	6.1
White	49	13.4	44	10.8	43	8.4	32	7.5	24	6.5
Black	49	10.8	43	7.9	39	8.1	28	7.0	27	5.9
Older Cohort	45	7.0	41	4.8	35	4.6	30	4.0	29	3.4
1965–69										
Mexican	—	—	47	8.4	37	7.4	42	7.3	29	5.3
Puerto Rican	—	—	34	12.3	41	11.3	44	11.0	42	10.2
White	—	—	25	11.7	46	14.8	27	12.0	27	11.2
Black	—	—	39	8.0	37	6.6	25	5.4	18	3.9
Younger Cohort	54	8.7	40	6.1	38	4.8	30	4.1	23	3.1
Total	48	5.9	41	3.9	36	3.2	30	3.1	27	2.3

Adapted from Krogh (1993).

TABLE 4

ATTITUDES TOWARD WORK AND WELFARE OF CHICAGO POVERTY TRACT PARENTS BY RACE OR ETHNIC/IMMIGRANT STATUS. FIGURES REPRESENT PERCENTAGES AND NUMBER OF RESPONDENTS (IN PARENTHESES)

Attitude Variables	Black	Mexican Immigrant	Mexican American	White	Island-Born Puerto Rican	Mainland-Born Puerto Rican
If money and medical coverage were the same:						
Prefer job	80.8	89.5	83.3	87.7	78.6	79.8
	(658)	(358)	(50)	(286)	(220)	(87)
Prefer aid	16.3	5.3	13.3	10.7	19.6	16.5
	(133)	(21)	(8)	(35)	(55)	(18)
Don't know	2.8	5.3	4.9	2.5	1.8	3.7
	(23)	(21)	(2)	(5)	(5)	(4)
Plain hard work very important to get ahead[a]						
	70.5	75.9	76.4	84.5	68.5	68.2
	(721)	(315)	(55)	(306)	(222)	(88)
Plain hard work somewhat important to get ahead[a]						
	26.1	19.0	19.4	14.4	22.6	27.0
	(267)	(79)	(14)	(52)	(73)	(35)
Plain hard work not important to get ahead[a]						
	3.4	5.1	4.2	1.1	8.9	4.8
	(35)	(21)	(3)	(4)	(29)	(6)
Think people have a right to receive aid without working[a]						
	74.4	33.2	53.5	40.6	57.1	58.1
	(760)	(136)	(38)	(147)	(185)	(72)
Think people go on welfare because they don't want to work rather than for lack of decent jobs[a]						
	21.8	62.7	49.3	53.2	43.3	44.4
	(222)	(259)	(35)	(191)	(141)	(55)

[a] *Excludes "don't know" responses and those who prefer aid to work because of disability.*
Source: Urban Poverty and Family Life Survey of Chicago, 1987.

NOTES

xv   quotations from Richard Herrnstein and Charles Murray: Herrnstein and Murray (1994), p. 403.

xv   The children of the inner-city ghetto have to contend with public schools: Kenneth B. Clark was one of the first to draw attention to this problem. See Clark (1965).

xvi   It reflects the cumulative weight of poverty and racial experiences: Heckman (1995) and Patterson (1995).

xvi   Recent research reveals that additional years of schooling: Neal and Johnson (1995).

xvi   However, as the economist James Heckman points out: Heckman (1995).

xvi   the Moynihan report: For the full text of the Moynihan report and a discussion of the critical reaction, see Rainwater and Yancey (1967).

xvii   revisionist arguments by African-American scholars on the black experience: See, for example, Ladner (1973), Hill (1972), Hare (1969), Alkalimat (1969), and Staples (1970 and 1971).

xvii   Mitchell Duneier: Duneier (1992).

xvii   *The Truly Disadvantaged*: Wilson (1987).

xviii   The tendency of some liberals to deny the very existence of culturally destructive behavior: For two discussions regarding the importance of considering the influence of both culture and social structure on certain kinds of behavior, see Patterson (1995) and West (1993). For two discussions that play down structural influences and highlight cultural factors where accounting for differences in racial behavior, see Sowell (1994) and D'Souza (1995).

xx   "When O. J. gets off": Quoted in Rich (1995).

xx   In comparison with the rhetoric highlighting racial divisions: One notable exception was the extensive media coverage of the inaugural presidential

speech by Hugh Price of the National Urban League. This speech promoted interracial unity by emphasizing commonly shared problems among racial groups
and common solutions. See Price (1994).

xx   In a 1992 op-ed article in *The New York Times*: Wilson (1992).

CHAPTER I
From Institutional to Jobless Ghettos

4   the ghetto has gone "from bad to worse": Shapiro (1987).

5   many of them represented by "tiny catering places": Wacquant (1992),
p. 16.

5   quotation from Loïc Wacquant: Wacquant (1992), p. 16.

6   quotation from Bureau of the Census: In Kasarda (1993b), p. 254.

11   the growth of the central-city poverty population: Kasarda (1993a).

11   Many of the most rapid increases in concentrated poverty: The proportion of poor black Americans living in central cities rose from 38 percent in 1959
to 80 percent in 1991. In 1972, one-third of the nation's poor lived in central-city
census tracts with high concentrations of poverty, and by 1991 that figure had
skyrocketed to 60 percent (Kasarda [1993a]).

Because of the way in which poverty is defined by the U.S. Bureau of the
Census, the official figures on concentrated poverty do not reflect the depth of the
changes that have occurred. The poverty line represents arbitrary income thresholds established by the government. Anyone who lives in a family with an annual
income below one of these thresholds is designated "poor." The thresholds vary
with family size and are based on estimates of family needs. *These estimates were
calculated in 1963 using family consumption data from a survey conducted in 1955.* Although the poverty thresholds are annually adjusted for inflation by the Census
Bureau, the basic definition has never been updated to reflect changes in family
need. Accordingly, a number of experts, including a national research panel, have
recommended adjusting the official poverty measure to reflect changes in family
need and regional differences in the cost of living. See Citro and Michael (1995),
Ruggles (1990), and O'Hare, Mann, Porter, and Greenstein (1990).

The poverty threshold for a family of four was $12,092 in 1988. But, accord-
ing to recent surveys, that threshold seems to be too low. In 1989, in each month
from July through October, a Gallup poll put the following question to a representative national sample of adult Americans: "People who have income below a certain level can be considered poor. That level is called the 'poverty line.' What
amount of weekly income would you use as a poverty line for a family of four (husband, wife, and two children) in this community?" The average weekly income figure given by the respondents was converted to an annual amount and adjusted for
inflation to make it comparable to the 1988 federal government poverty threshold
for a family of four. The annual figure given by the Gallup poll respondents was
$15,017, or nearly $3,000 (24 percent) above the official poverty line. If the public's
poverty threshold were used, "the number of Americans considered poor would be

close to 45 million, instead of the nearly 32 million considered poor under the government measure" (O'Hare, Mann, Porter, and Greenstein [1990], p. vii).

In their comprehensive analysis of the official measure of poverty, O'Hare, Mann, Porter, and Greenstein (1990) state:

> The survey question used in the Gallup poll was designed to show people's perceptions of an appropriate poverty line varied according to where they lived. The question asked what level of income respondents would use as a poverty line *in their community*. The answers to the survey question varied according to which region of the country the respondents lived in. Those living in metropolitan areas would set the poverty line at a higher level than those living in non-metropolitan areas. Those in the Western portion of the United States would set the highest regional poverty line, and those in the South and the Midwest would set the lowest regional poverty lines. In every area of the country, however, the survey respondents set the poverty line for their community at a higher level than the government's poverty line.
>
> These poll results can be used to determine the number of people who would be considered poor if the public's poverty line were varied by geographic area. This is done by setting poverty lines for each area at the average levels that poll respondents from these areas said should be used to measure poverty in their communities. This approach provides a rough approximation of variations in the cost of living among different areas of the country. Using these geographically varied poverty lines, 44 million Americans would be considered poor. This is only slightly different from the 45 million said to be poor using the public's poverty line without any geographical variations. The total number of people considered poor does not change very much because, when the poverty line is varied by geographical area, decreases in some areas are offset by increases in others. Fewer people are counted as poor under the lower poverty lines used in non-metropolitan areas, in the Midwest, and in the South, but these reductions are offset by increases in the number of people considered poor under the higher poverty lines in metropolitan areas and in the West. (p. vii)

Some analysts believe that certain noncash government benefits such as housing subsidies and food stamps ought to be included as income in estimates of the number of families in poverty. O'Hare, Mann, Porter, and Greenstein pursued this point and found that

> even counting noncash benefits as income and using the public's poverty line, the number of people considered poor would still be substantially higher than under the government's poverty measure, which does not count noncash benefits. If food and housing benefits were counted as income, the number of Americans considered poor under the public's poverty line would be about 43 million, or 18 percent of the American population. If medical

benefits were also counted as income, the number of Americans considered
poor would be 39 million, or 16 percent of the population. (p. viii)

See Jencks and Edin (1990) for another comprehensive study of family income and consumption among the poor.

12   "Defining an urban neighborhood": Kasarda (1993b), p. 254.

12   defining Chicago community areas: *Local Community Fact Book—Chicago
Metropolitan Area* (1984).

12   quotation from Paul Jargowsky and Mary Jo Bane: Jargowsky and Bane
(1991), p. 239.

12   proportion of metropolitan ghetto poor in central cities: Kasarda
(1993b), and Jargowsky and Bane (1991).

14   the growth of ghetto census tracts: Kasarda (1993b). During the 1970s,
approximately three-fourths (74 percent) of the total increase in ghetto poverty was
accounted for by only ten cities. One-third of the increase was accounted for by
New York City alone, and one-half by New York and Chicago combined. When
Philadelphia, Newark, and Detroit were added, these five cities accounted for two-
thirds of the total increase in ghetto poverty in the 1970s. The other five cities
among the top ten in terms of the rise of ghetto poverty were Columbus (Ohio), Atlanta, Baltimore, Buffalo, and Paterson (New Jersey). So, when one speaks of the
rise of ghetto poverty in the United States during the 1970s, one is focusing mainly
on the industrial metropolises of the Northeast and Midwest regions of the country.

Indeed, Jargowsky and Bane (1991) found that of the 195 standard metropolitan areas that recorded ghetto poverty in 1970, 88 actually experienced a decrease
in the number of ghetto poor. Two types of cities account for the largest decreases
in ghetto poverty in their study—Texas cities such as Brownsville, McAllen, Cor-
pus Christi, and San Antonio, which experienced sharp drops in Hispanic ghetto
poverty; and southern cities such as Shreveport, Charleston, Jackson (Mississippi),
Memphis, New Orleans, and Columbus (Georgia), which recorded significant declines in ghetto poverty among blacks. These ten cities accounted for 46 percent
of the total decrease in ghetto poverty during the 1970s. Accordingly, "the decreases were not nearly as localized in a few cities as the increases" (p. 40).

However, the trends recorded during the 1970s were not repeated during the
1980s. The largest increases in the concentration of poverty occurred in mid-
western cities. The proportion of poor persons in ghettos or extreme poverty
tracts in the one hundred largest cities climbed from 12.8 percent in 1970 to 36.2
percent in 1990. In absolute numbers this represents nearly a fourfold increase
over the twenty-year period, from 222,722 in 1970 to 789,778 in 1990. Larger
cities in the Northeast (led by New York, Philadelphia, and Newark) experienced
a slight decrease in the overall poverty population and virtually no increase in the
percentage of poor people living in ghettos.

Southern cities experienced both an absolute decrease in their poverty population and a decline in the size and proportion of their poverty populations in
ghetto census tracts in the 1970s. This trend was reversed in the 1980s. The
poverty population in southern cities increased by nearly a half million between

1980 and 1990. The number of poor ghetto residents climbed from 583,945 to 886,341 during the 1980s. The proportion of the poor in ghettos rose from 23.7 to 30.3 percent. The trends in western cities were similar to those of the South—declines in the number and proportion of the poor in ghetto census tracts during the 1970s and a substantial increase during the 1980s, including an 80 percent growth in the number of ghetto poverty tracts.

14   The number of such tracts has more than doubled since 1970: Between 1970 and 1990, the prevalence of ghetto tracts increased from 6 percent of the total number of census tracts in the nation's one hundred largest cities to 13.7 percent of the total (Kasarda 1993b).

14   Paul Jargowsky's research: Jargowsky (1994). Jargowsky arrived at this figure using a slightly modified measure of ghetto poverty that does not obscure the real degree of ghettoization among blacks who live in census tracts in which a significant proportion of the residents are white. Because of the high level of racial segregation in American cities, most census tracts are nearly all black or all white. However, a growing percentage of tracts include a considerable number of both blacks and whites. Although the poverty rate for a racially mixed census tract represents all the residents of the area, it may obscure the degree of poverty concentration experienced by a particular group. For example, a mixed census tract that is 50 percent black and 50 percent white may in reality consist of two segregated areas that have little social contact and have been lumped together because of the tract boundaries. If the blacks in this census tract have a poverty rate of 50 percent and the whites a rate of 20 percent, the overall rate would be 35 percent. The area would therefore escape classification as a ghetto, even though the black area of the census tract would in fact constitute a ghetto if different boundary lines had been drawn to reflect this racial division.

This assumption was examined empirically by Jargowsky in an investigation of mixed census tracts in Dallas. Jargowsky classified these tracts as "integrated" if the proportion of blacks was between one-third and two-thirds. Using this delineation, only 31 of the 400 tracts in Dallas were integrated. "The integrated tracts contained about one thousand census blocks with an average population of just over 100 persons per block" (1994, p. 290). Using block-level data, he found that "seventy percent of the blocks and about two thirds of the residents (64.4) of the integrated tracts lived in blocks that were *not* integrated, i.e., they were not between one-third and two-thirds black" (p. 291). Jargowsky therefore felt that race-specific measures of poverty concentration in each census tract were more appropriate. Applied to the example used above, the race-specific measure for the mixed census tract (with an overall poverty rate of 50 percent) would be 50 percent for blacks and 20 percent for whites. Accordingly, the blacks in this census tract would be classified as residing in a ghetto because their poverty rate exceeds the 40 percent threshold.

14   The number of African-Americans in these ghettos: Nearly 6 million African-Americans resided in these ghettos in 1990—an increase of 35.9 percent in population since 1980. Part of this increase is due to population growth. The total African-American population also increased in metropolitan areas, but only

by 16 percent. The proportion of poor metropolitan blacks who live in ghetto areas climbed even more rapidly, from 37.2 percent in 1980 to 45.5 percent in 1990 (Jargowsky [1994]).

14   the metropolitan black poor are becoming increasingly isolated: Jargowsky (1994). The poverty rates among blacks in all neighborhoods (census tracts) in metropolitan areas decreased only slightly, from 26.9 percent in 1980 to 26.5 percent in 1990. For those in nonghetto neighborhoods, they decreased from 21.2 percent to 18.9 percent. However, for those in ghetto neighborhoods they increased from 49.5 percent to 50.8 percent.

14   The increase in the *number* of ghetto blacks: Jargowsky and Bane (1991).

14   Since 1980, ghetto census tracts have increased: Jargowsky (1994, p. 296) points out that "a direct comparison of the number of census tracts classified as ghettos in 1980 and 1990 is compromised by a change in the Census Bureau's suppression methodology, which allowed many more low-income population tracts to be reported in 1990 than in 1980. To circumvent this problem, I selected tracts . . . with at least 100 black residents. The number of such census tracts classified as ghettos grew from 3256 to 5003, a 54 percent increase. Since the number of persons in such tracts grew at a slower rate, there was an 11.9 percent decline in the population density of ghetto census tracts." The figures reported in this paragraph for the period 1980 to 1990 are based on tracts with at least 100 black residents.

14   quotation from Jargowsky: Jargowsky (1994), p. 18.

15   quotation from Massey and Denton: Massey and Denton (1993), p. 118.

15   segregation and a group's overall rate of poverty increase: It should also be pointed out that whereas the growth of concentrated poverty occurred mainly among African-Americans in the large metropolitan areas in the 1970s, in the 1980s "the growth in concentrated poverty was substantially higher among non-Hispanic whites in smaller metropolitan areas like Louisville, Kentucky, and Tulsa, Oklahoma" (Pear [1993]).

16   *The Truly Disadvantaged:* Wilson (1987).

17   the Chicago School of urban sociology: Representative studies by those identified with the Chicago School include Robert E. Park and Ernest W. Burgess, *The City* (1925); N. Anderson, *The Hobo* (1923) and *Men on the Move* (1940); F. Thrasher, *The Gang* (1927); L. Wirth, *The Ghetto* (1928); H. W. Zorbaugh, *The Gold Coast and the Slum* (1929); R. E. L. Faris and W. Dunham, *Mental Disorder in Urban America* (1931); E. Franklin Frazier, *The Negro Family in Chicago* (1932). (These were all published by the University of Chicago Press.)

17   the studies of the Chicago School: I am indebted to O'Connor (1992) for much of the discussion to follow in this section. O'Connor correctly points out:

Subsequent historical research on immigrants and the black urban experience have shown the inadequacies of the Chicago school assimilationist framework, whether as a description of the migrant experience or as a predictor of how black migrants would fare in the city. Their view of poverty, social "disorganization" and segregation as inevitable outcomes—albeit temporary ones—of the organic processes of city growth virtually ignored the role of the economy or other structural factors in shaping the trajectory of newcomers' mobility patterns. Their analysis also overlooked the role of politics and local government policies in creating and maintaining ghettos, while its inherent optimism and air of inevitability suggested that there was little room or need for intervention. (p. 5)

17 "interaction cycle" that "led from conflict to accommodation to assimilation": O'Connor (1992).

17 studies by E. Franklin Frazier: Frazier (1932 and 1939).

18 *Black Metropolis:* Drake and Cayton (1945).

18 quotation from Alice O'Connor: O'Connor (1992).

18 Using W. Lloyd Warner's anthropological techniques: Warner and Lunt (1941 and 1942).

18 *Black Metropolis* presented a much less encouraging view of black progress: O'Connor (1992).

18 quotation from Drake and Cayton: Drake and Cayton (1962), p. xv.

19 adult employment in extremely poor Chicago community areas: The figures on adult neighborhood employment presented in this section are based on calculations from data provided by the 1990 U.S. Bureau of the Census and the *Local Community Fact Book for Chicago—1950* and the *Local Community Fact Book— Chicago Area, 1960.* The adult employment rates represent the number of employed individuals (14 and over in 1950 and 16 and over in 1990) among the total number of adults in a given area. Those who are not employed include both the individuals who are members of the labor force but are not working and those who have dropped out or are not part of the labor force. Those who are not in the labor force "consist mainly of students, housewives, retired workers, seasonal workers enumerated in an 'off' season who were not looking for work, inmates of institutions, disabled persons, and persons doing only incidental unpaid family work" (*Local Community Fact Book—Chicago Metropolitan Area, Based on the 1970 and 1980 Censuses* [1984], p. xxv).

19 ratio of employed to jobless persons in the nation's one hundred largest cities: Kasarda (1993b).

20 quotation from Drake and Cayton: Drake and Cayton (1962), pp. 658–60.

20 There are three major dimensions of neighborhood social organization: Sampson and Groves (1989), Sampson (1992b), and Sampson and Wilson (1995).

20 both formal and informal networks reflect social organization: Sampson (1992b).

20 Neighborhood social organization depends on: Sampson (1992b).

21 decline in legitimate employment opportunities and drugs: Fagan (1993).

21   the sharp rise in violent crime: Figures on violent crime are from Blumstein (1994).

21   the volatile drug market in jobless neighborhoods: Fagan (1993) and Sampson (1986) and (1988).

21   the influence of the drug industry in the neighborhood: Blumstein (1994).

22   quotation from Blumstein: Blumstein (1994), p. 18.

22   quotations from Delbert Elliott: Elliott (1992), pp. 14–15. In Elliott's study, 75 percent of the black males who were employed between the ages of 18 and 20 had terminated their involvement in violent behavior by age 21, compared with only 52 percent of those who were unemployed between the ages of 18 and 20. Elliott also found that involvement in a marriage/partner relationship was associated with a sharp termination in violent behavior among black males. No significant differences in the termination of serious violent behavior by age 21 were found between black and white males who experienced one or more years in a marriage/partner relationship between ages 18 and 20. Racial differences remained for persons who were not in a marriage/partner relationship or who were unemployed.

23   what the historian Allan Spear has called: Spear (1967).

23   As Massey and Denton have carefully documented: Massey and Denton (1993).

CHAPTER 2
Societal Changes and Jobless Neighborhoods

25   In 1987–89, a low-skilled male worker was jobless: Topel (1993) and Juhn, Murphy, and Topel (1991).

25   the proportion of men who "permanently" dropped out: Juhn, Murphy, and Topel (1991). Also see Juhn, Murphy, and Pierce (1991 and 1993) and Topel (1993).

25   you see that men in the bottom fifth of this income distribution: Juhn, Murphy, and Topel (1991).

25   if jobs inside a firm have become less available: Blank (1994).

26   men who are well below retirement age are working less: Rose (1994) and Nasar (1994).

26   The proportion of male workers in the prime of their life: Rose (1994).

26   While the American economy saw a rapid expansion in high technology: Nasar (1994).

26   The growth of a nonworking class of prime-age males: Rose (1994) and Nasar (1994).

26   figures on the work experience of prime-age men with less than a high school education and prime-age black men: Rose (1994).

26   One study estimates that since 1967 the number of prime-age men: Buron, Haveman, and O'Donnell (1994).

26–7   The traditional American economy featured rapid growth in productivity and living standards: Marshall (1994). Also see Rifkin (1995).

27   Today, most of the new jobs for workers with limited education: Nasar (1994), Freeman (1994), and Holzer (1995).

27   One study found that the U.S. created: McKinsey & Co. (1994).

27   Robert Lerman and Martin Rein revealed that: Lerman and Rein (forthcoming).

27   The expanding job market in social services: Social services increased from 17 percent of total employment in 1979 to 21 percent in 1993. Lerman and Rein (forthcoming).

27   For example, "the fraction of men who have moved into so-called pink-collar jobs": Nasar (1994).

27   The large concentration of women in the expanding social service sector: Lerman and Rein (forthcoming).

27   Between 1989 and 1993, jobs held by women: Lerman and Rein (forthcoming).

27   Although the wages of low-skilled women . . . rose slightly: Blank (1994).

27   The wage gap between low-skilled men and women shrank: Blank (1994).

28   The unemployment rates among both low-skilled men and women: Blank (1994).

28   quotation from Freeman and Katz: Freeman and Katz (1994), p. 46.

28   quotation from Rebecca Blank: Blank (1994), p. 17.

28   The workplace has been revolutionized by technological changes: Marshall (1994).

29   Unlike men with lower education, college-educated men are working more, not less: In the decade of the 1980s, 79 percent worked at least eight out of ten months, up from 77 percent during the 1970s. Rose (1994) and Nasar (1994).

29   Even before the economic restructuring of the nation's economy: See Lieberson (1980).

29   "up to half of the huge employment declines for less-educated blacks": Bound and Holzer (1993), p. 395. Also see Bound and Freeman (1992); Acs and Danziger (1993); and Johnson and Oliver (1992). Studies measuring the effects of declining manufacturing on black male *income*, as opposed to employment, reach different conclusions. On the basis of these studies, declining manufacturing does not appear to have the same adverse effects on black income as it does on black employment. See Bartik (forthcoming) and Danziger and Gottschalk (1993).

29   Another study reported that since the 1960s "deindustrialization" and the "erosion in job opportunities": Bluestone, Stevenson, and Tilly (1991), p. 25.

29   The manufacturing losses in some northern cities have been staggering: Kasarda (1995).

30   Another study examined the effects of economic restructuring: Gittleman and Howell (1993).

30 "The most common occupation reported by respondents": Testa and Krogh (1989), p. 77.

30 changes in the percentage of Chicago's inner-city black fathers in manufacturing industries: For a discussion of these findings, see Krogh (1993).

31 quotation from Kasarda: Kasarda (1995), p. 239.

31 the employment and earnings of young black men across the nation: Sum and Fogg (1990).

31 Young high school dropouts and even high school graduates "have faced a dwindling supply of career jobs": Sum and Fogg (1990), p. 51.

31 John Kasarda examined employment changes: Kasarda (1995).

32 Kasarda's study also documents the growing importance of education in nine ... northern cities: Kasarda (1995). The nine northern cities were Baltimore, Boston, Chicago, Cleveland, Detroit, New York, Philadelphia, St. Louis, and Washington, D.C.

32 The jobs traditionally held by high school dropouts declined: 25 percent of the jobs held by high school graduates disappeared in these nine northern cities between 1980 and 1990, including a decrease of more than 50 percent in Detroit and St. Louis and nearly 50 percent in Cleveland and Baltimore. On the other hand, those held by college graduates rose by at least 40 percent, except in Detroit and Cleveland, which experienced more modest increases of 12 and 33 percent, respectively. Kasarda (1995).

32 "Los Angeles, which experienced a 50 percent increase": Kasarda (1995), pp. 247, 250.

32 they "were not nearly as great as the concurrent": Kasarda (1995), p. 250.

32 Robert Lerman and Martin Rein report that among all women: Lerman and Rein (forthcoming).

33 the research of Lerman and Rein: Lerman and Rein (forthcoming).

33 The proportion of less educated female workers in social services is up notably: Only 17 percent held jobs in social services in 1989. See Lerman and Rein (forthcoming).

33 Although only 4 percent of less educated employed males: Lerman and Rein (forthcoming).

33 decreases in the relative wages of disadvantaged urban workers: The decline in wages has also been notable among rural workers, although some groups suffered greater income loss than others. As William O'Hare and Anne Pauti point out: "Men, blacks, and part-time workers experienced a bigger decline in wages than did women, whites, or full-time workers. Wages of young rural workers in every sector declined, but those in extractive industries, manufacturing and trade experienced the biggest decrease in earnings. Deterioration of wages of young rural workers was found in every region of the country except New England" (1990, p. 5).

33-4 quotations from Freeman and Katz: Freeman and Katz (1994), p. 47.

34 a large number of immigrants with little formal education: Freeman and Katz (1994).

34 According to one estimate, nearly one-third of the decline in earnings: Freeman and Katz (1994); and Borjas, Freeman, and Katz (1992).

34 quotation from Danziger and Gottschalk: Danziger and Gottschalk (1995), p. 133. Also see Topel (1994).

34 The most dramatic increases in ghetto poverty occurred between 1970 and 1980: Jargowsky and Bane (1991).

35 "To make matters worse, scores of stores were forced out of business": Wacquant and Wilson (1989), pp. 91–92. The description of changes in North Lawndale is based on Chicago *Tribune* (1986).

35 Significantly fewer Hispanics and white parents felt this way: Only one-third of the employed Hispanic parents, one-quarter of white fathers, and one-fifth of white mothers felt that they might lose their jobs because of plant shutdowns.

37 "Metropolitan areas captured nearly 90 percent of the nation's employment growth": Kasarda (1995), pp. 215–16.

37 Over the last two decades, 60 percent of the new jobs created in the Chicago metropolitan area: Reardon (1991).

37 In *The Truly Disadvantaged*, I maintained that one result of these changes: This was a thesis first put forth by John Kain in his classic 1968 article. Kain (1968).

37 Although studies based on data collected before 1970: Holzer (1991). For a study based on the earlier data, see Ellwood (1986b).

37 Recent research, conducted mainly by urban and labor economists: Holzer (1991). Also see Holzer, Ihlanfeldt, and Sjoquist (1994); Ihlanfeldt, Keith, and Sjoquist (1990); Ihlanfeldt, Keith, and Sjoquist (1991); Fernandez (1991); and Zax and Kain (1992).

37 quotation from Farrell Bloch: Bloch (1994), p. 124.

38 But are the differences in employment between city and suburban blacks: See Holzer (1991), Jencks and Mayer (1989b), Frey (1985), and Grier and Grier (1988).

38 This question was addressed in a study of the Gautreaux program in Chicago: Rosenbaum and Popkin (1991).

42 quotations from Holzer, Ihlanfeldt, and Sjoquist: Holzer, Ihlanfeldt, and Sjoquist (1994), pp. 323, 343.

42 I argue that . . . inner-city neighborhoods have experienced a growing concentration of poverty for several other reasons: Research findings on the effect of the outmigration of nonpoor families from inner-city neighborhoods are mixed. See Appendix A for a discussion of this research.

43 Therefore, the economic and demographic changes: In contrast, of the nine other new poverty neighborhoods that experienced a significant drop in their white population, three (like Greater Grand Crossing) had become overwhelmingly black by 1960 after a precipitous decline in the white population during the 1950s. One had gone from being a majority black to being overwhelmingly black during the same period, one from being overwhelmingly white to being overwhelmingly black from 1960 to 1970, two from being a ma-

jority black to being overwhelmingly black from 1960 to 1970, and one from being a majority white to being overwhelmingly black from 1970 to 1980. Finally, the one neighborhood that has actually experienced a decrease in its black population since 1970 but remains predominantly black went from being 59 percent white in 1950 to being 72 percent black in 1970, then dipped to 67 percent black in 1990.

44 these demographic changes obviously can account for only a fraction: There has also been a slight but steady rise in the proportion of females in Bronzeville and a slight but steady decline in the proportion of males. The data in Table 2.1 do not specify the proportion of these females who have young children, and there have not been any notable changes in the proportion of young children in the population. It is therefore difficult to determine if these gender changes have any real or direct significance with respect to the drop in the employment rate.

45 "prudent lenders will exercise increased caution": Bach and West (1993), pp. 27–28.

46 Precipitous declines in density: Jargowsky (1994).

46 It was not until the 1960s that the FHA discontinued: Katz (1993), Bartelt (1993), Sugrue (1993), and Kelley (1993).

46 By manipulating market incentives: Katz (1993).

46 the building of freeway networks: Sampson and Wilson (1995).

47 "suburbs chose to diversify by race rather than class": Katz (1993), pp. 461–62. On the history of the suburbs in America, see Jackson (1985). For a good discussion of the effects of housing discrimination on the living conditions, education, and employment of urban minorities, see Yinger (1995).

47 "they also created barriers between the sections of the city": Katz (1993), p. 462. Also see Bartelt (1993), Sugrue (1993), and Anderson (1964).

48 quotation from Mark Condon: Condon (1991), pp. 2–3.

48 The economic mobility of these families "contributed to the sociological stability": Condon (1991), p. 3.

48 "Public housing was now meant to collect the ghetto residents left homeless": Condon (1991), p. 4.

48 "This growing population of politically weak urban poor": Condon (1991), p. 4.

48 public housing represents a federally funded: Sampson and Wilson (1995). Also see Sugrue (1993), Bartelt (1993), Kelley (1993), Hirsch (1983), and Bauman et al. (1991).

48 a fundamental shift in the federal government's support for basic urban programs: Caraley (1992); also see Orfield and Ashkinaze (1991).

49 In addition, the economic recession: Caraley (1992).

49 three unhealthy social conditions that have emerged or become prominent: Caraley (1992).

50 "allowed the minimum wage to erode to its second-lowest level": Center on Budget and Policy Priorities (1995a), p. 1.

50   "the minimum wage is 26 percent below its average level in the 1970s": Center on Budget and Policy Priorities (1995b), p. 3.

50   In the early 1970s, a working mother with two children: Center on Budget and Policy Priorities (1995b).

CHAPTER 3
Ghetto-Related Behavior and the Structure of Opportunity

51   In 1980, 21 percent of blacks but only 7.9 percent of all Mexican immigrants: Van Haitsma (1992).

52   quotation from Van Haitsma: Van Haitsma (1992).

52   Neighborhoods that offer few legitimate employment opportunities: There is a growing research literature that supports and reinforces the view that neighborhoods matter for inner-city residents. These studies present evidence that neighborhood effects do exist for joblessness, welfare receipt, school dropout rates and years of schooling, teenage childbearing, single parenthood, the level of annual earnings, political participation, juvenile delinquency, and crime. For example, in a study based on a random sample of 506 urban public school boys in Pittsburgh, Faith Peeples and Rolf Loeber found that when white and African-American youths in Pittsburgh were compared without taking their neighborhood residence into account, black youths were delinquent more frequently and were involved in more serious offenses than white youths. However, 41 percent of the African-American youths and only 2 percent of the white youths lived in "underclass" neighborhoods (measured according to an index that included six variables—family poverty, public assistance, families with a female single parent, family joblessness, births outside marriage, and male joblessness). Thus, when comparisons were made between black and white youths who *did not* live in "underclass" neighborhoods, their delinquent behavior was similar. For other recent studies on neighborhood effects, see Crane (1989); Mayer (1989); Osterman (1990); Hogan and Kitagawa (1985); Brooks-Gunn, Duncan, Klebanov, and Sealand (1993); Datcher (1982); Corcoran, Gordon, Laren, and Solon (1989); Peeples and Loeber (1994); Case and Katz (1990); Duncan and Laren (1990); and Elliott et al. (forthcoming).

53   many inner-city ghetto residents who maintain a connection with the formal labor market: See Newman (1996).

59   Not surprisingly, the rate of drug offense arrests likewise increased, "which, especially for nonwhites": Blumstein (1994), p. 15.

59   By 1990, the distribution and consumption of crack-cocaine had become widespread in the ghetto neighborhoods of Chicago: Wilkerson (1994).

59   In 1994, consumption leveled off "as heroin made a comeback": Wilkerson (1994).

60   quotations from Wilkerson: Wilkerson (1994).

60   quotation from Fagan: Quoted in Wilkerson (1994).

61 In 1984, there were slightly more than 80 homicide deaths: Blumstein (1994).

61 It is important to emphasize that the norms and actions within the drug industry: Blumstein (1994).

61 A National Institute of Justice survey: Sheley and Wright (1993), p. 1.

61 neighborhoods that integrate the adults by an extensive set of obligations: Sampson (1992b).

62 The connectedness and stability of social networks: Sampson (1992b).

62 quotation from Furstenberg: Furstenberg (1993).

62 what James S. Coleman has called "intergenerational closure": Coleman (1990).

62 As a general rule, adolescents seem to benefit: Steinberg et al. (1995). For an important theoretical discussion of networks of interpersonal communication, see Putnam (1993).

62 quotation from Steinberg and his colleagues: Steinberg et al. (1995).

63 A similar finding emerged from ethnographic research: Elliott et al. (forthcoming).

65 Nonworking poor black men and women "were consistently less likely to participate in": Fernandez and Harris (1991).

65 "It is not simply poverty that isolates women": Fernandez and Harris (1991), p. 18.

65 "social contacts were a useful means of gaining informal work": Pedder (1991), p. 37.

66 the job-search strategies that black inner-city residents most frequently reported using: Laseter (1994).

66 both black men and women more often use the public transit system: Van Haitsma (1991).

66 "Culture" may be defined as the sharing of modes of behavior and outlook: Hannerz (1969). I am indebted to Hannerz (1969) for much of what follows in this section.

67 The available research suggests that the total culture of the inner-city ghetto: Clark (1965), Hannerz (1969), Rainwater (1970), and Anderson (1991).

67 quotation from *Time* magazine article: *Time* (1977), p. 14.

67 His situation is described in the field notes prepared by a member of the UPFLS research team: Notes were prepared by Loïc J. D. Wacquant, March 1988.

70 there are also constraints on the choices they can make: I am indebted to Laura Coyne, who directed this research for a program jointly sponsored by the Pullman Foundation of Chicago and the Center for the Study of Urban Inequality, for the thoughts expressed on the problem of lack of information.

70 "not only convenient but also morally appropriate": Hannerz (1969), p. 187.

70 They may endorse mainstream norms against this behavior: Hannerz (1969).

70   In this case, ghetto-related culture "may be seen as at least to some extent adaptive": Hannerz (1969), p. 188.

70   Individuals in the inner-city ghetto can hardly avoid exposure: Hannerz (1969).

71   This, as Ulf Hannerz points out, is why some elements of culture: Hannerz (1969).

71   however, not all aspects of cultural transmission involve rational decisions: Hannerz (1969).

71   "When a mode of behavior is encountered frequently and in many different persons": Hannerz (1969), p. 185.

71   "do not go free of denunciation": Hannerz (1969), p. 187.

71-2   quotation from Ann Swidler: Swidler (1986), p. 122.

72   As Dr. Deborah Prothrow-Stith so clearly shows: Prothrow-Stith (1991).

72   Elijah Anderson points out: Anderson (1994).

72   This was the message in the pioneering works of: Clark (1965), Hannerz (1969), and Rainwater (1970).

72   "the merits of a more subtle kind of cultural analysis of life in poverty": Hannerz (1969), p. 182.

73   As Pierre Bourdieu demonstrated, work is not simply a way to make a living: Bourdieu (1965).

73   quotations from Jahoda, Lazarsfeld, and Zeisel: Jahoda, Lazarsfeld, and Zeisel (1972), pp. vii, 66.

75   Several studies reveal that the social organization of the drug industry: See, for example, Bourgois (1995) and Venkatesh (1996).

75   In social cognitive theory: Bandura (1986).

75   quotation from Bandura: Bandura (1982), p. 140.

75   "The type of outcomes people expect": Bandura (1982), p. 140.

75   A recent study on the adverse effects: Elder et al. (1995).

78   The end result, to use a term from Bandura's work: Bandura (1982).

80   quotations from Edin: Edin (1994), pp. 2-3. Edin's interviews were conducted in Chicago in 1990, and in Cambridge (Massachusetts), San Antonio (Texas), and Charleston (South Carolina) in 1992.

80   Similar findings were reported in a study by LaDonna Pavetti: Pavetti (1993).

80   Respondents in the UPFLS also pointed out the difficulty of subsisting on welfare: Comments by a woman from a poor West Side neighborhood suggest that the level of welfare benefits is also problematic for an unemployed and childless single person on welfare. "They tell you to get a job, but there ain't no jobs. They say you're on a fixed income, but they fail to realize that food and clothes are a lot with kids. Even someone without kids, they give them a fixed income—rent starts at $200. They give them, people on general assistance, they give them $158 and $70 or $80 in food stamps to last them a month. How you do that? When your rent starts at $200?"

81   Edin points out that in order to keep their families together: Edin (1994).

82   For many families, a shelter provides their last hope of staying together: Edin (1994).

82–3   quotations from Edin: Edin (1994), pp. 11, 15.

84   the typical AFDC recipient contemplates the following: Edin (1994).

85   quotation from Tienda and Stier: Tienda and Stier (1991).

CHAPTER 4
The Fading Inner-City Family

87   Changes in the family structure in the inner-city ghetto . . . are part of a process: National Center for Health Statistics (1994 and 1995) and U.S. Bureau of the Census (1993). Between 1970 and 1993, the number of unmarried adults in the United States almost doubled from 37.5 million to 72.6 million. Those who had never married made up 58 percent of this group. The number of divorced individuals more than tripled from 4.3 million in 1970 to 16.7 million in 1993. The median age at first marriage in 1993 was 26.5 years for men and 24.5 years for women—the highest figures since 1890. Blacks experience the longest delays in marriage. Note that whereas 9 percent of Hispanic women and 7 percent of white women ages 40 to 44 have never been married, 22 percent of black women in this age group have never been married.

87   Although the annual increase in the number of infants born: National Center for Health Statistics (1994 and 1995) and U.S. Bureau of the Census (1993).

88   In the African-American community, rates of marriage: Bennett, Bloom, and Craig (1989); and Franklin and Smith (1991). It should be pointed out that highly educated black women have substantially lower rates of marriage than comparable white women. In the discussion to follow, I talk about the association between the inner-city African-American marriage rate and the proportion of "marriageable"—that is, employed—males. Bennett, Bloom, and Craig point out that highly educated black women may face a problem somewhat similar to that confronting less educated black women. "For highly educated black women, there may be a shortage of 'suitable' partners, insofar as emphasis is placed on similar levels of educational attainment" (1989, p. 715).

88   education is unrelated to the question of whether divorced and separated white women remarry: Smock (1990).

88   The positive association between education and marriage: Bennett, Bloom, and Craig (1989).

89   Mark Testa, a member of the UPFLS research team, estimated: Testa (1991).

90   quotation from Testa: Testa (1991), p. 27.

91   In Chicago's inner city, single African-American men born during: Testa (1991).

91 "Ever since the growth of the one-parent family": Hechinger (1992).

91 A study relying on longitudinal data: Duncan (1984). Also see Ellwood (1986 and 1989).

91 quotation from Kathryn Edin: Edin (1994), p. 29.

92 whereas the median income of married-couple families: U.S. Bureau of the Census (1994). Also see Holmes (1994).

92 longitudinal studies also reveal: Bane and Ellwood (1983a) and O'Neill et al. (1984).

92 the available research indicates that children from mother-only households: Krein and Beller (1988), McLanahan and Garfinkel (1989), and Franklin and Smith (1991).

92 the daughters who grew up in black single-parent households are more likely to establish: McLanahan and Bumpass (1988).

92 quotation from Sanford Dornbusch and his colleagues: Dornbusch et al. (1985), p. 340.

93 black mothers in the inner city are far more likely: Based on UPFLS data analyzed by Lundgren-Gaveras (1991).

93 quotation from Van Haitsma: Van Haitsma (1991), p. 19.

93 the high percentage of black mothers who live with young children: Lundgren-Gaveras (1991).

94 Of the 12 percent of the inner-city women on AFDC: Lundgren-Gaveras (1991).

94 However, the *scientific* evidence offers little support for the claim: See, for example, Duncan (1994); Hoffman, Duncan, and Mincy (1991); Duncan and Hoffman (1991); and Bane and Ellwood (1983a).

94 the smallest increases in the number of out-of-wedlock births have not occurred: Duncan (1994).

95 Some studies reveal that a man's employment status is not related: See Testa (1991) for a review of these studies.

95 For example, one national study based on state-level data: Plotnick (1990).

95 Data from the UPFLS: Testa (1991) and Testa and Krogh (1995).

95 A study by Andrew Sum and Neal Fogg: Sum and Fogg (1990).

95 Christopher Jencks points out that: Jencks (1991). Lerman (1989) reaches similar conclusions by comparing increases in the fraction of men with and without college and noncollege education who were still single (i.e., never married).

95 Robert Mare and Christopher Winship found: Mare and Winship (1991).

96 A study by Saul Hoffman, Greg Duncan, and Ronald Mincy: Hoffman, Duncan, and Mincy (1991).

96 David Ellwood and David Rodda found no significant change: Ellwood and Rodda (1991).

96 Mark Testa and Marilyn Krogh found: Testa and Krogh (1995).

97   quotations from Testa: Testa (1991), p. 16.

97   But even when ethnic-group variations in work activity: See Testa (1991), Testa and Krogh (1995), and Van Haitsma (1991).

98   quotations from Richard Taub: Taub (1991), p. 6.

101   Thus, marriage is "not in the forefront of the men's minds": Taub (1991), p. 9.

101   "I'll get married in the future when I am no longer having fun": Laseter (1994), p. 195.

102   quotation from Furstenberg: Furstenberg (1994), p. 15.

102   the young men do "feel some obligation to contribute something to support their children": Laseter (1994), p. 40.

102   quotation from Furstenberg: Furstenberg (1994), p. 29.

105   "The labor market conditions which sustained the 'male breadwinner' family": Breslau (1991), p. 11.

105   This has gradually led to the creation of a new set of orientations: Taub (1991).

106   a youngster who grows up in a family with a steady breadwinner and in a neighborhood: Recent findings based on research conducted by Mary Corcoran and Terry Adams (1993b) reveal that black male joblessness may be related to differential exposure to work. They state that "young black men raised in neighborhoods with high levels of male unemployment work fewer hours as adults than do men raised in neighborhoods with low rates of male unemployment. Each one percent increase in male unemployment in a black man's childhood neighborhood is associated with a two percent drop in that black man's adult work hours" (p. 20). The Corcoran and Adams study is based on data from the Michigan Panel Study of Income Dynamics (PSID), a national longitudinal survey that has followed about 5,000 families annually since 1968. The sample is weighted to adjust for the oversampling of poor families. The sample used by Corcoran and Adams consists of 1,347 men (559 black and 788 nonblack) ages 25 to 35 years in 1988. In 1968, these men were children ranging in age from 5 to 15 in PSID families. "To be included in the sample, a respondent had to be observed at least three years as a child between ages 5 and 17 years and had to have headed his own household and reported earnings at least one year after age 24 years" (1993b, p. 9).

107   quotations from Elijah Anderson: Anderson (1991), p. 397.

108   quotations from Kenneth B. Clark: Clark (1965), pp. 71–72.

108   "Sex is important to her": Clark (1965), p. 72.

109   quotation from Kenneth B. Clark: Clark (1965), p. 73.

CHAPTER 5
The Meaning and Significance of Race: Employers and Inner-City Workers

111   Although empirical studies on race and employer attitudes are limited: Two of these studies—Kirschenman and Neckerman (1991) and Neckerman and Kirschenman (1991)—represent earlier analyses of our Urban Poverty and Fam-

ily Life Study's survey of employers. Also see Braddock and McPartland (1987), Braddock et al. (1986), Culp and Dunson (1986), and Holzer (1995).

111 racial stereotyping is greater among employers with lower proportions of blacks: Neckerman and Kirschenman (1991).

126 If you examine the UPFLS survey data on the employment patterns of employed inner-city black fathers: Krogh (1993).

127 only 4 percent of the 179 employers mentioned discrimination: That a lack of job opportunities was a factor in the high levels of unemployment in Chicago's inner-city neighborhoods was stated by 33 percent of the employers, and 21 percent mentioned lack of training and education. Lack of a work ethic was a reason given by 18 percent of the employers, the welfare system by 15 percent, skills mismatch by 14 percent, lack of motivation by 12 percent, and lack of transportation by 10 percent.

132 quotation from Kathryn Neckerman and Joleen Kirschenman: Neckerman and Kirschenman (1991), p. 445. Kathryn Neckerman and Joleen Kirschenman provided the first published articles on the UPFLS employer survey—also see Kirschenman and Neckerman (1991)—and brought out many of the hiring strategies of the employers in the survey that are mentioned here. I am indebted to them for many of the insights on hiring strategies discussed in this section. For related research on employer hiring strategies, see Braddock and McPartland (1987), Cross et al. (1990), and Culp and Dunson (1986).

133 city employers and selective recruitment: Neckerman and Kirschenman (1991).

135 The UPFLS employer survey revealed that only 16 percent of the employers from city firms: Neckerman and Kirschenman (1991).

135 the city employers who relied most heavily on selective recruiting: Neckerman and Kirschenman (1991).

136 A key hypothesis is that given the recent shifts in the economy: Ferguson (1993) and Holzer (1995).

136 one study conducted in Los Angeles: Johnson et al. (1996).

139 Data from the UPFLS survey show that variables measuring differences in social context: Van Haitsma (1991).

139 data from the survey reveal that jobless black men have a lower "reservation wage": Tienda and Stier (1991), p. 19.

140 quotation from Richard Taub: Taub (1991), p. 1.

140 "Immigrants, particularly Third World immigrants": Aponte (1991), p. 41.

141 Mexican immigrants are harder workers because they "come from areas of intense poverty": Taub (1991), p. 14.

141 quotations from Taub: Taub (1991), p. 14.

142 For example, one of the respondents in the UPFLS employer survey: Neckerman (1993).

142 quotation from Kathryn Neckerman: Neckerman (1991), p. 8.

142 Annual turnover rates of 50 to 100 percent are common in low-skill service jobs in Chicago: Neckerman (1991).

142   quotation from Sharon Hicks-Bartlett: Hicks-Bartlett (1991), p. 33.

143   quotation from Moss and Tilly: Moss and Tilly (1991), p. 7.

143   Because of the increasing shift away from manufacturing and toward service industries: Kirschenman (1991).

143   Neckerman argues that: Neckerman (1991).

143   What happens "when employees socialized to approach jobs and careers": Neckerman (1991), p. 27.

143   The employer interviews suggest that workers: Neckerman (1991).

143   Accordingly, "their advancement may depend on fairly subtle": Neckerman (1991), p. 27.

144   but many "did indeed espouse blue-collar ways of getting ahead": Neckerman (1991), p. 27.

144   Hispanics "continue to funnel into manufacturing": Krogh (1993), p. 12.

145   In a slack labor market . . . employers are . . . more selective in recruiting: Tobin (1965).

145   For the first time in more than two decades, the unemployment rate for African-Americans dipped below 10 percent: Holmes (1995).

145   Indeed, "the unemployment rate for black adults dropped faster": Holmes (1995).

145   the economy saw a slight decrease in manufacturing jobs during the economic recovery period: Holmes (1995).

146   whereas the unemployment rate for black youths 16 years old and older was 34.6 percent: Holmes (1995).

146   In previous years, labor-market demand stimulated: I thank the economist James S. Tobin for this insight, shared in private communication.

CHAPTER 6
The American Belief System Concerning Poverty and Welfare

149   Nor does any European city include areas that are as physically isolated . . . and prone to violence: Weir (1993a).

151   First of all, there has been a decline in mass production: In the following discussion concerning the change from the mass production system to the highly technological global economy, I am indebted to Marshall (1994).

151   "The school-to-work transition processes were informal": Marshall (1994), p. 5.

151   most of the work "was routine and could be performed by workers": Marshall (1994), p. 4.

151   "This was especially true after the New Deal policies of the 1930s": Marshall (1994), p. 4.

152   At the same time that changes in technology are producing new jobs: Friedman (1994b) and Rifkin (1995).

152   While educated workers are benefiting from the pace of technological change: Friedman (1994b) and Rifkin (1995).

152   quotation from Marshall: Marshall (1994), p. 5.

152   To encourage western European and Japanese companies to follow high-wage strategies: Marshall (1994).

153   during the worldwide recession, "the conventional wisdom": Friedman (1994a).

153   Because "capital and technology are now so mobile": Friedman (1994a).

153   In comparisons between the United States and other industrialized nations: Friedman (1994a).

153   "In most of the European Union, an unemployed worker can receive close to $1,000 a month": Friedman (1994a).

154   The U.S. economy created 35 million jobs: Friedman (1994a).

154   most of the jobs growth occurred outside central cities: Kasarda (1995).

154   "Minimum wage levels tend to be higher in Europe": Friedman (1994a).

154   Total compensation—wages, health benefits, vacations—for the typical U.S. worker: Friedman (1994a).

154   There is mounting pressure on European countries to make some adjustments: Friedman (1994).

154   A recent report based on interviews with leading government officials: Friedman (1994).

155   These leaders feel that Europe lacks both the time and the political will to change social and political habits: Friedman (1994).

155   "Direct financial housing subsidies for low-income families": Schmitter-Heisler (1991).

155   "in every year from 1984 through 1988": Greenstein (1991), p. 442.

156   Those at the bottom of the class ladder in the United States: Schmitter-Heisler (1991).

156   In 1975, 30 percent of all the poor in the United States: U.S. Bureau of the Census (1992).

156   These discouraging figures are related to such factors as "general income stagnation": Greenstein (1991), pp. 439–40.

156   Instead of helping to integrate the recipients: Schmitter-Heisler (1991).

159   T. H. Marshall's classic thesis on the development of citizenship: Marshall (1964).

159   "the whole range from the right to a modicum of economic welfare": Marshall (1964), p. 78.

159   as critics of American approaches to the study of poverty and welfare have shown repeatedly: See, for example, Castel (1978).

159   quotation from Kluegel and Smith: Kluegel and Smith (1986), p. 37.

160   The ordering of these factors remained virtually unchanged between 1969 and 1980: For a discussion of earlier research of this kind, see Patterson (1981). Also see Williamson (1974a, 1974b, 1974c) and Lauer (1981).

160   A 1990 survey using these same questions showed: Davis and Smith (1994) and Bobo and Kluegel (1994).

160   Across the 1969–90 time span: Bobo and Kluegel (1994).

160   Their findings sharply contrast with those based on a similar survey conducted in twelve European countries: Commission of the European Communities (1990).

161   quotations from Robert Castel: Castel (1978), p. 47. Also see Susser and Kreniski (1987).

161   a Harris poll taken in 1972 showed: Melville and Doble (1988).

161   The percentage of respondents in a national poll who said they agreed with the anti-welfare statement: Kluegel and Smith (1983).

161   "In the post-1980 period there was a small but real rise": Bobo and Smith (1994), p. 372. Also see Shapiro and Young (1989).

161   A more recent survey suggests that underlying such overwhelming public sentiment: Melville and Doble (1988).

162   Finally, this study emphasized "that there is today": Melville and Doble (1988).

162   Reactions to the label "welfare": Bobo and Smith (1994).

162   "The term 'welfare' has become a red flag": Bobo and Smith (1994), p. 372.

162   A recent study of attitudes toward poverty among white middle-class Americans: Iyengar (1990). Also see Bobo and Smith (1994).

162   from 1983 to 1991 the General Social Survey: Bobo and Smith (1994).

162   Throughout the 1960s and 1970s, the expanding network of poverty researchers: See Kerbo (1981) and Tompkins (1970).

163   quotations from Walter Korpi: Korpi (1980), p. 305.

163   Another irony is that despite this narrow focus, these very same American researchers: See Wilson (1987).

163   "the paradox of continuing high poverty during a period of general prosperity": Melville and Doble (1988), p. 1.

163   the General Accounting Office: General Accounting Office (1987).

164   conservative scholars such as George Gilder, Charles Murray, and Lawrence Mead: Gilder (1981), Murray (1984), and Mead (1986).

164   "*it is the moral fabric of individuals, not the social and economic structure of society*": Wacquant and Wilson, p. 99.

164   AFDC is a joint federal and state program that provides cash benefits to eligible poor families with children: See the report by the Center on Social Welfare Policy and Law (1994).

165   An average of 9.5 million children in 5 million families: Center on Social Welfare Policy and Law (1994).

165   "Between July 1972 and 1992, the combined value of AFDC and food stamps": Center on Social Welfare Policy and Law (1994), p. 10.

165 "At no other time in the past twenty-five years": Center on Social Welfare Policy and Law (1994), p. 11.

165 "what the U.S. Department of Housing and Urban Development (HUD) considers to be 'decent, safe, and sanitary' housing": Center on Social Welfare Policy and Law (1994), p. 11.

166 "In cities like Newark, Chicago, Philadelphia, Denver": Center on Social Welfare Policy and Law (1994), p. 11.

166 People tended to go on and off welfare in short spurts: Handler (1994).

166 Not only do they prefer work to welfare: See Edin (1994).

166 As unemployment in the general population rises, the probability of exiting welfare diminishes: Handler (1994).

167 "The overall picture is that one group uses welfare for relatively short periods of time": Handler (1994), p. 32.

167 Some liberals have used these figures to argue that long-term welfare dependency is a myth: See, for example, Greenberg (1993).

167 "This is because the probability of being on welfare at a given time": Handler (1994), p. 33. Also see Bane and Ellwood (1983b).

167 quotation from the House Ways and Means Committee: Quoted in Handler (1994), p. 34. See Committee on Ways and Means (1993), p. 686.

168 quotations from AFDC mother who wants "to go out there and get a job": Drawn from interviews conducted in the Oakland and Woodlawn Neighborhood Study (see Appendix B).

168 All of these subsidies and benefits designed to make low-wage work pay: Handler (1994).

169 quotation from Joel F. Handler: Handler (1994), p. 91.

169 Unlike President Clinton's proposal and other, earlier bills: Bazie and Shapiro (1994).

169 An important feature of the bill: Parrott (1995), p. 4.

170 quotation from the Center on Budget and Policy Priorities: Parrott (1995), p. 4.

170 In 1994, 4.5 million children: Parrott (1995).

170 overburdened foster care system would have to find "foster care and institutional replacements": Bazie and Shapiro (1994), p. 3. Also see Peterson (1995), Vroman (1995), Pavetti (1995), Zedlewski and Sawhill (1995), and Danziger and Danziger (1995).

170 According to one estimate: Center on Budget and Policy Priorities (1995c).

170 "the Senate welfare bill would deepen poverty for families": Center on Budget and Policy Priorities (1995c), p. 1.

170 quotation from Moynihan: Moynihan (1996), p. 33.

171 A compromise version (conference agreement) of the House and Senate bills: Center on Budget and Policy Priorities (1995d).

172 the Moynihan report: Moynihan (1965).

172 quotation from Moynihan: Moynihan (1965), p. 30.

172   some blacks were highly critical of the Moynihan report's emphasis: Rainwater and Yancey (1967).

172   a recurrent theme in the writings of black academics and intellectuals: See, for example, Ladner (1973), Hill (1972), Hare (1969), Alkalimat (1969), and Staples (1970 and 1971).

173   quotation from Robert K. Merton: Merton (1972), pp. 18–19.

174   Even though little serious research on life in the ghetto was conducted during this period: One notable exception was a study published in the late 1970s: Anderson (1978).

174–5   quotations from *Time* magazine: *Time* (1977), pp. 14–27.

175   Widely read neoconservative books: Gilder (1981), Murray (1984), and Mead (1986).

176   now cloaked in the epithet the "underclass": Following the publication of *The Truly Disadvantaged* in 1987, an unprecedented number of social scientists began to conduct research on various aspects of ghetto poverty—many of them devoted to testing the theoretical assumptions I had raised in the book. This renewed attention to the problems in the inner-city ghetto accompanied a swirling controversy over the use of the term "underclass." The controversy has been fueled by journalists and by political figures who use the term and select what is helpful to their cause—liberal or conservative—and in doing so overlook the essential facts about America's poor. For a discussion of the use, and debate on the use, of the term "underclass" among academics, see Gans (1990 and 1995), Wilson (1991a), Hochschild (1993), Ricketts and Sawhill (1986), Ricketts and Mincy (1986), and Jencks (1991).

176   quotations from Mickey Kaus: Kaus (1986), p. 22.

176   quotation from Nicholas Lemann: Lemann (1986), p. 35. Also see Lemann (1991).

176   Yet systematic research on poverty and urban migration: See Long (1974), Long and Heltman (1975), and Ritchey (1974).

176   quotations from Kaus: Kaus (1986), p. 24.

177   although Ken Auletta's study of the underclass: Auletta (1982).

177   the earlier ethnographic studies of Lee Rainwater, Kenneth Clark, Elliot Liebow, and Ulf Hannerz: Rainwater (1970), Clark (1965), Liebow (1967), and Hannerz (1969).

177   quotation from Myron Magnet: Magnet (1987), p. 130.

177–8   quotation from the Chicago *Tribune*: Chicago *Tribune* (1986), pp. 3–4.

178   quotation from Pete Hamill: Hamill (1988), p. 92.

CHAPTER 7
Racial Antagonisms and Race-Based Social Policy

183   Recent books such as Andrew Hacker's: Hacker (1992) and Bell (1992).

184   quotation from Alfred Blumstein: Blumstein (1994).

185   In 1960, the nation's population was evenly divided: Weir (1993b).

185   Across the nation in 1990: Caraley (1992).

185   In addition, the most recent economic recession: Caraley (1992).

185   Indeed, we can associate the sharp drop: Weir (1993a).

186   In each of the three presidential races: Caraley (1992).

187   to use Albert Hirschman's term: Hirschman (1970).

189   According to several demographic projections: Rohter (1993).

189   In cities as different as Houston, Los Angeles, and Philadelphia, "competition between blacks": Rohter (1993), p. 11.

189   In areas of changing populations: Rohter (1993).

189   In Dade County, there is a tendency: Rohter (1993).

189   By contrast, native-born, English-speaking: Rohter (1993).

189   They are concentrated in neighborhoods: Rohter (1993).

190   before entering the United States: Kim and Kim (1994).

190   Yet neither their educational nor their occupational: Kim and Kim (1994).

190   For example, it is estimated that 60 percent: Yoon (1994) and Min (1993).

190   "for many Koreans, small business is a bittersweet": Yoon (1994), p. 1.

190   The most destructive riot in the nation's history: Kim and Kim (1994).

190   They were joined by immigrant Hispanics: Kim and Kim (1994).

190   Korean store owners bore the brunt: Kim and Kim (1994).

191   quotation from In-Jin Yoon: Yoon (1994), p. 13.

191   In Los Angeles and New York, local-based black nationalist organizations: Yoon (1994).

191   In a scientific survey of 198 Korean store owners: Yoon (1994).

191–2   quotations from In-Jin Yoon: Yoon (1994), pp. 20–21.

192   During hard economic times: As I pointed out in a *New York Times* op-ed article, this is a theme repeatedly emphasized by Bill Clinton during his 1992 campaign for the presidency. See Wilson (1992).

194   quotation from Jennifer Hochschild: Hochschild (1995), p. 44.

194   Empirical research . . . could "uncover no evidence of class effects": Hout (1984), p. 308.

194   quotation from Hochschild: Hochschild (1995), p. 44.

194   Research by Michael Hout: Hout (1984). Also see Featherman and Hauser (1978) and Wilson (1980).

194   "Well-off black men thus could begin for the first time": Hochschild (1995), p. 44.

194   On the other hand, among the disadvantaged segments: Wilson (1987).

194   From 1977 to 1993, the percentage of blacks with incomes below 50 percent of the amount designated as the poverty line: U.S. Bureau of the Census (1994a).

194   measurement of changes in poverty: U.S. Bureau of the Census (1994b).

195   the financial gap is even greater between the two races when wealth is considered: See Oliver and Shapiro (1995) and Wolff (1995).

196   Those resources reflect a variety of advantages: Fiskin (1983).

196   quotation from Kenneth B. Clark: Clark (1967), p. 8.

196   quotation from Vivian Henderson: Henderson (1975), p. 54.

197   as specified in Title VII of the Civil Rights Act of 1964: "Title VII of the Civil Rights Act of 1964 . . . is the most comprehensive employment discrimination statute in the United States. It prohibits employment discrimination against individuals on grounds of race, color, religion, sex, or national origin by private, state, and local government employers with at least fifteen employees. Title VII also forbids employment discrimination by labor unions and employment agencies of any size, and by the executive branch of the federal government" (Bloch [1994], pp. 48–49).

197   However, if the more advantaged members of minority groups: Fiskin (1983).

197   Thus, policies of affirmative action: Fiskin (1983), Loury (1984), and Loury (1995).

197   quotation from William L. Taylor: Taylor (1986), p. 1714.

198   as long as minorities are underrepresented in higher-paying . . . positions: A recent report revealed that 95 percent of the senior management positions (vice president and above) are held by white men, who constitute only 29 percent of the workforce. Glass Ceiling Commission (1995).

198   some liberals have argued for a shift from an affirmative action based on race: See, for example, Kahlenberg (1995).

198   The major distinguishing characteristic . . . based on need: Fishkin (1983) has related this type of affirmative action to the principle of equality of life chances. Noel Salinger of the Harris School of Public Policy Studies, University of Chicago, helped to shape some of the views I express here on affirmative action.

198   the long-term intergenerational effects of having one's life choices limited by race: Heckman (1995).

200   However, "a federal policy of rapid desegregation": Jargowsky (1994), p. 310.

200   The gains, over a period of decades, could be substantial: Jargowsky (1994).

201   "But the experiment is being closely watched": *New York Times* (1994).

201   quotation from Vivian Henderson, Henderson (1975), p. 54.

201   quotation from Joseph A. Califano: Califano (1988), p. 29. For a good discussion of how programs perceived to be beneficial to blacks triggered a white backlash, see Quadagno (1994).

202   Over the past fifty years, there has been a steep decline: Bobo and Smith (1994).

202   The idea that the federal government "has a special obligation": Bobo and Kluegel (1994).

203   In 1990, almost seven in ten (69.1 percent) white Americans: By con-

trast, only 26 percent of African-Americans opposed quotas in enrolling blacks in colleges and universities and only 37.4 percent were against the idea of preferential hiring and promotion of blacks (Bobo and Smith [1994]).

203 "People whose attitudes blend antiblack feelings": Bobo and Smith (1994), pp. 382–83.

203 But these social scientists quickly pointed out that general values: Bobo and Smith (1994).

203 Bobo and Smith found that even after controlling for socioeconomic status: Bobo and Smith (1994).

203 recent studies reveal that most white Americans approve: Bobo and Smith (1994), Bobo and Kluegel (1993), Lipset and Schneider (1978), Kluegel and Smith (1986), and Kinder and Sanders (1987).

204 For example, in the 1990 General Social Survey: Bobo and Smith (1994).

204 quotation from Bobo and Kluegel: Bobo and Kluegel (1993), p. 446.

204 Furthermore, unlike "preferential" racial policies: Bobo and Smith (1994).

205 recent surveys conducted by the National Opinion Research Center: General Social Survey (1988–94).

CHAPTER 8

A Broader Vision: Social Policy Options in Cross-National Perspective

207 quotation from Robert Reich: Quoted in Friedman (1994a).

207 In previous years, only heads of state and finance ministers met "to discuss . . . high finance": Friedman (1994a).

208 "that the only way to create more jobs": Friedman (1994b).

208 It was the first time the G7 policymakers: Friedman (1994b).

208 the main hope of the ministers was that the discussions could "teach them something": Friedman (1994b).

210 quotation from Marshall: Marshall (1994), pp. 6–7.

210 Students who meet high standards: Marshall (1994).

211 quotations from Linda Darling-Hammond: Darling-Hammond (1994), p. 480.

211 funding for public education in the United States is dramatically uneven, "with wealthy schools": Darling-Hammond (1994), p. 499. Also see Educational Testing Service (1991).

211 Whereas public schools in advantaged neighborhoods: Darling-Hammond (1994).

211–12 quotation from Iris C. Rotberg and James J. Harvey: Rotberg and Harvey (1993).

212 Recent research on the nationwide distribution of science and mathematics opportunities: Oakes (1990).

212 Teacher shortages in many central-city and poor rural schools: Darling-Hammond (1990 and 1994).

212   the kind of support that would enable schools in disadvantaged neighborhoods to meet the standards that are set: Darling-Hammond (1994).

212   Since two-thirds of all new jobs will require the use of computers: Hundt (1995).

213   According to the U.S. Bureau of the Census, only 35 percent of black youths: Weaver (1995).

213   quotation from Frank C. Weaver: Weaver (1995), p. 7. Also see Krieg (forthcoming).

214   Although the empirical data on the effectiveness of existing school choice programs: Katz (1995).

214   new evidence suggests: Hoxby (1994) and Katz (1995).

214   The basic assumption underlying the act is that the role of the federal government is to "encourage experimentation": Marshall (1994), p. 21.

214   Congress appropriated $125 million for Goals 2000 in 1994: Marshall (1994).

215   The learning system in other industrial democracies: Marshall (1994).

215   quotations from Marshall: Marshall (1994), p. 7.

215   In France, children are supported by three interrelated government programs: Bergmann (1993).

216   quotation from Bergmann: Bergmann (1993), pp. 343–44.

216   quotations from Marshall: Marshall (1994), p. 3.

216   Unlike employers in Germany and Japan: Marshall (1994).

216–17   quotations from Marshall: Marshall (1994), p. 9.

217   The delay in hiring youths has a number of critical consequences: Marshall (1994).

217   According to a recent report by the U.S. Bureau of Labor Statistics: U.S. Bureau of Labor Statistics (1994).

217   the basic objective of the SWOA "is to build on the high standards encouraged by the Goals 2000 act": Marshall (1994), p. 22.

218   "The central governments continued to treat cities as a natural resource": Weir (1993a), p. 26.

219   quotations from David Rusk: Rusk (1993), p. 121.

219   Suburbs that experienced increases in income during the 1980s: Bok (1994).

220   the creation of regional authorities to develop solutions to common problems: Bok (1995), p. 13. Also see Weir (1993b).

220   quotations from Marshall: Marshall (1994), p. 26.

220–21   in Japan and Germany most high school and college graduates leave school with skills: Marshall (1994).

221   Except for Germany, European countries have the same gap in worker skills: Friedman (1994b).

222   Families with incomes from $8,400 to $11,000 will receive cash payments: *New York Times* (1994).

222   This expansion, and the previous expansions of the EITC: Center on Budget and Policy Priorities (1995a and 1995b).

222 "the 1993 law set the EITC for a family with two or more children": Center on Budget and Policy Priorities (1995b), p. 2.

223 quotation from Center on Budget and Policy Priorities: Center on Budget and Policy Priorities (1995b), p. 2.

223 they depend heavily on public transportation and therefore have difficulty getting to the suburbs: See Hughes (1993).

224 the creation of privately subsidized car-pool and van-pool networks: Based on several local transportation programs in Chicago (especially the "JobExpress" program created by the Suburban Job Link Corporation), Public/ Private Ventures, a nonprofit research organization, "has designed a research demonstration to test a transportation strategy that links inner-city residents to job opportunities outside city centers. The elements of Bridges to Work are transportation (public or private), a mechanism for connecting trained workers with available suburban jobs (a regional alliance of providers of employment services), and special support services (provided by a community agency). A four-year demonstration of the model is planned to begin in up to nine sites in Fall 1995." Public/Private Ventures (1994), p. 9.

224 the creation of for-profit or not-for-profit job information and placement centers: For this short-term policy recommendation I am indebted to James S. Tobin.

224 The central problem is that the demand for labor has shifted away from low-skilled workers: See the discussion in Chapter 2. Also see Danziger and Gottschalk (1995).

224 this problem can be offset to some extent: Bloch (1994).

225 Despite some claims that low-skilled workers: See, for example, Mead (1992).

225 available evidence strongly suggests: Danziger and Gottschalk (1995), p. 155, Holzer (1995), and Carlson and Theodore (1995).

225 quotation from Danziger and Gottschalk: Danziger and Gottschalk (1995), p. 156.

225 Indeed, until current changes in the labor market are reversed: Danziger and Gottschalk (1995).

226 Prior to the late 1970s, there was less need for the creation of public-sector jobs: Danziger and Gottschalk (1995).

226 "the gains from growth were widely shared": Danziger and Gottschalk (1995), p. 174.

226 "a counter-cyclical policy to be put in place": Danziger and Gottschalk (1995), p. 174.

226 quotation from Regan: Regan (1994), p. 43.

226 According to one estimate, $1 billion spent on road maintenance: Montgomery and Wyes (1992).

226 Another study reports that new building projects: Wieman (1993).

227 quotation from Regan: Regan (1994), p. 44.

227 According to the Congressional Budget Office: Regan (1994).

227 To address this problem, the economists Sheldon Danziger and Peter Gottschalk: Danziger and Gottschalk (1995).

228   quotation from Danziger and Gottschalk: Danziger and Gottschalk (1995), p. 173.

229   "but wages would always be lower": Danziger and Gottschalk (1995), p. 172.

229   quotations from Danziger and Gottschalk: Danziger and Gottschalk (1995), p. 173.

229–30   quotations from Mickey Kaus: Kaus (1992), pp. 259, 125.

231   "With a neo-WPA maintaining highways": Kaus (1992), p. 137.

232   to avoid the problem of "fiscal substitution": Danziger and Gottschalk (1995).

232   The creation of public service employment through CETA: Danziger and Gottschalk (1995).

233   As another way to avoid the problem of worker displacement: Danziger and Gottschalk (1995).

233   following Kaus, I have in mind useful public work: Kaus (1992).

233   A WPA-style jobs program will not be cheap: For a discussion of the cost of public-sector employment, see Danziger and Gottschalk (1995) and Kaus (1992).

234   The cost of retraining adult workers is considerable: According to one estimate, it would take an investment in education and training of "$1.66 trillion (in 1989 dollars) to restore the 1979 earnings ratios of less-skilled workers to workers with some college education, while holding workers with some college education at their 1989 levels of earnings." See Heckman, Roselius, and Smith (1994), p. 84.

235   Because an effective political coalition in part depends: Wilson (1987).

BIBLIOGRAPHY

Acs, Gregory, and Sheldon Danziger. 1993. "Educational Attainment, Industrial Structure, and Earnings: 1973–87." *Journal of Human Resources* 28: 618–48.

Alkalimat, Abdul Hakim Ibn (Gerald McWorter). 1969. "The Ideology of Black Social Science." *Black Scholar* 1 (December): 28–35.

Anderson, Elijah. 1978. *A Place on the Corner*. Chicago: University of Chicago Press.

———. 1990. *Streetwise: Race, Class, and Change in an Urban Community*. Chicago: University of Chicago Press.

———. 1991. "Neighborhood Effects on Teenage Pregnancy." In *The Urban Underclass*, edited by Christopher Jencks and Paul E. Peterson, pp. 375–98. Washington, D.C.: Brookings Institution.

———. 1994. "The Code of the Streets." *Atlantic Monthly*, May, pp. 80–94.

Anderson, Martin. 1964. *The Federal Bulldozer: A Critical Analysis of Urban Renewal, 1949–1962*. Cambridge: MIT Press.

Anderson, Nels. 1923. *The Hobo*. Chicago: University of Chicago Press.

———. 1940. *Men on the Move*. Chicago: University of Chicago Press.

Aponte, Robert. 1991. "Ethnicity and Male Employment in the Inner City: A Test of Two Theories." Paper presented at the Chicago Urban Poverty and Family Life Conference, October 10–12, 1991.

Auletta, Ken. 1982. *The Underclass*. New York: Random House.

Bach, Victor, and Sherece Y. West. 1993. *Housing on the Block: Disinvestment and Abandonment Risks in New York City Neighborhoods*. New York: Community Service Society of New York.

Bailey, Thomas. 1989. "Black Employment Opportunities." In *Setting Municipal Priorities, 1990*, edited by Charles Brecher and Raymond D. Horton, pp. 80–111. New York: New York University Press.

Bandura, Albert. 1982. "Self-Efficacy Mechanism in Human Agency." *American Psychologist* 37 (February): 122–47.

————. 1986. *Social Foundations of Thought and Action: A Social Cognitive Theory.* Englewood Cliffs, N.J.: Prentice-Hall.

Bane, Mary Jo, and David Ellwood. 1983a. *The Dynamics of Dependence and the Routes to Self-Sufficiency.* Cambridge: Urban Systems Research and Engineering.

————. 1983b. "Slipping into and out of Poverty: The Dynamics of Spells." Working paper no. 1199, National Bureau of Economic Research, Cambridge.

Banfield, Edward. 1970. *The Unheavenly City.* 2d ed. Boston: Little, Brown.

Bartelt, David W. 1993. "Housing the 'Underclass.' " In *The "Underclass" Debate: Views from History,* edited by Michael B. Katz, pp. 118–57. Princeton: Princeton University Press.

Bartik, Timothy J. (Forthcoming.) "The Distributional Effects of Local Labor Market Demand and Industrial Mix." *Journal of Urban Economics.*

Bauman, John F., Norman P. Hummon, and Edward K. Muller. 1991. "Public Housing, Isolation, and the Urban Underclass." *Journal of Urban History* 17:264–92.

Bazie, Michelle, and Isaac Shapiro. 1994. " 'Contract' Would Ultimately Deny Benefits to Five Million Poor Children." News release, Center on Budget and Policy Priorities, Washington, D.C., November 22.

Bell, Derrick. 1992. *Faces at the Bottom of the Well: The Permanence of Racism.* New York: Basic Books.

Bennett, N. G., D. E. Bloom, and P. H. Craig. 1989. "The Divergence of Black and White Marriage Patterns." *American Journal of Sociology* 95:692–722.

Bergmann, Barbara. 1993. "The French Child Welfare System: An Excellent System We Could Adapt and Afford." In *Sociology and the Public Agenda,* edited by William Julius Wilson, pp. 341–50. Newbury Park, Calif.: Sage Publications.

Blank, Rebecca. 1994. "Outlook for the U.S. Labor Market and Prospects for Low-Wage Entry Jobs." Working paper, Center for Urban Affairs, Northwestern University.

Bloch, Farrell. 1994. *Antidiscrimination Law and Minority Employment: Recruitment Practices and Regulatory Constraints.* Chicago: University of Chicago Press.

Bluestone, Barry, Mary Stevenson, and Chris Tilly. 1991. "The Deterioration in Labor Market Prospects for Young Men with Limited Schooling: Assessing the Impact of 'Demand Side' Factors." Paper presented at the annual meeting of the Eastern Economic Association, March 14–15, Pittsburgh.

Blumstein, Alfred. 1994. "Youth Violence, Guns, and the Illicit-Drug Industry." Working paper, H. John Keinz III School of Public Policy and Management.

Bobo, Lawrence. 1988. "Attitudes Toward the Black Political Movement: Trends, Meaning, and Effects on Racial Policy Preference." *Social Psychology Quarterly* 51:287–302.

————. 1991. "Social Responsibility, Individualism, and Redistributive Policies." *Sociological Forum* 6 (1):71–92.

Bobo, Lawrence, and James R. Kluegel. 1993. "Opposition to Race Targeting: Self-Interest, Stratification Ideology, or Racial Attitudes?" *American Sociological Review* 58:443–64.

Bobo, Lawrence, and Ryan A. Smith. 1994. "Antipoverty Politics, Affirmative Action, and Racial Attitudes. " In *Confronting Poverty: Prescriptions for Change*, edited by Sheldon H. Danziger, Gary D. Sandefur, and Daniel H. Weinberg, pp. 365–95. Cambridge: Harvard University Press.

Bok, Derek. 1994. "Cities and Suburbs." Paper prepared for the Aspen Institute Domestic Strategy Group. Aspen Institute, Washington, D.C.

Borjas, George, Richard Freeman, and Lawrence Katz. 1992. "On the Labor Market Effects of Immigration and Trade." In *Immigration and the Work Force*, edited by George Borjas and Richard Freeman, pp. 213–44. Chicago: University of Chicago Press (for NBER).

Bound, John, and Richard B. Freeman. 1992. "What Went Wrong? The Erosion of the Relative Earnings of Young Black Men in the 1980s." *Quarterly Journal of Economics* 107 (February): 201–33.

Bound, John, and Harry Holzer. 1993. "Industrial Shifts, Skills Levels, and the Labor Market for White and Black Men." *Review of Economics and Statistics* 75 (August): 387–96.

Bourdieu, Pierre. 1965. *Travail et travailleurs en Algérie*. Paris: Editions Mouton.

Bourgois, Philippe. 1995. *In Search of Respect: Selling Crack in El Barrio*. New York: Cambridge University Press.

Braddock, Jomills Henry, II, Robert L. Crain, James M. McPartland, and R. L. Dawkins. 1986. "Applicant Race and Job Placement Decisions: A National Survey Experiment." *Social Problems* 37: 243–57.

Braddock, Jomills Henry, II, and James M. McPartland. 1987. "How Minorities Continue to Be Excluded from Equal Employment Opportunities: Research on Labor Market and Institutional Barriers." *Journal of Social Issues* 43:5–39.

Breslau, Daniel. 1991. "Reciprocity and Gender in Low-Income Households." Paper presented at the Chicago Urban Poverty and Family Life Conference, October 10–12, Chicago.

Bronfenbrenner, Urie. 1989. "Ecological Systems Theory." In *Annals of Child Development: Six Theories of Child Development—Revised Formulations and Current Issues*, edited by Ross Vasta, pp. 1–103. Greenwich, Conn.: Jai Press.

Brooks-Gunn, Jeanne, Greg J. Duncan, K. Klebanov, and Naomi Sealand. 1993. "Do Neighborhoods Influence Child and Adolescent Development?" *American Journal of Sociology* 99:353–94.

Buron, Lawrence, Robert Haveman, and Owen O'Donnell. 1994. "Recent Trends in U.S. Male Work and Wage Patterns: An Overview." Unpublished manuscript, University of Wisconsin, December.

Califano, Joseph A, Jr. 1988. "Tough Talk for Democrats." *New York Times Magazine*, January 8.

Caplow, David. 1965. *The Poor Pay More.* New York: Free Press.

Caraley, Demetrios. 1992. "Washington Abandons the Cities." *Political Science Quarterly* 107 (Spring): 1–30.

Carlson, Virginia L., and Nikolas C. Theodore. 1995. *Are There Enough Jobs? Welfare Reform and Labor Market Reality.* Illinois Job Gap Project, Center for Urban Economic Development, University of Illinois, Chicago.

Case, Anne C., and Lawrence F. Katz. 1990. "The Company You Keep: The Effects of Family and Neighborhood on Disadvantaged Youth." Working paper no. 3705, National Bureau of Economic Research, Cambridge.

Castel, Robert. 1978. "The 'War on Poverty' and the Status of Poverty in an Affluent Society." *Actes de la recherche en sciences sociales* 19 (January): 47–60.

Center on Budget and Policy Priorities. 1995a. "Is the EITC Growing at a Rate That Is 'Out of Control'?" Washington, D.C., May 9.

———. 1995b. "The Earned Income Tax Credit Reductions in the Senate Budget Resolution." Washington, D.C., June 5.

———. 1995c. "The Administration Releases New Estimates of House and Senate Budget Bills' Effects on Poverty and Income Distribution." Washington, D.C., November 13.

———. 1995d. "The Conference Agreement on the Welfare Bill." Washington, D.C., December 8.

Center on Social Welfare Policy and Law. 1994. *Living at the Bottom: An Analysis of the 1994 AFDC Benefit Levels.* New York: Center on Social Welfare Policy and Law.

Chicago *Tribune.* 1986. *The American Millstone.* Chicago: Contemporary Books.

Citro, Constance F., and Robert T. Michael, eds. 1995. *Measuring Poverty: A New Approach.* Washington, D.C.: National Academy Press.

Clark, Kenneth B. 1964. *Youth in the Ghetto: A Study of the Consequences of Powerlessness and a Blueprint for Change.* New York: Harlem Youth Opportunity (HARYOU) Report.

———. 1965. *Dark Ghetto: Dilemmas of Social Power.* New York: Harper & Row.

———. 1967. "The Present Dilemma of the Negro." Paper presented at the annual meeting of the Southern Regional Council, November 2, Atlanta.

Cohen, Cathy J., and Michael C. Dawson. 1993. "Neighborhood Poverty and African American Politics." *American Political Science Review* 87:286–302.

Coleman, James S. 1990. *Foundations of Social Theory.* Cambridge: Harvard University Press.

Commission of the European Communities. 1990. "The Perception of Poverty in Europe." Rue de la Loi 200, B-1049 Brussels.

Committee on Ways and Means. U.S. House of Representatives. 1993. *Green Book: Background Material and Data on Programs Within the Jurisdiction of the Committee on Ways and Means.*

Condon, Mark. 1991. "Public Housing, Crime and the Urban Labor Market: A Study of Black Youths in Chicago." Working paper series, Malcolm Wiener

Center for Social Policy, John F. Kennedy School of Government, Harvard University, March, no. H-91-3.

Congressional Budget Office. 1988. *New Directions for the Nation's Public Works.* Washington, D.C., October.

Corcoran, Mary. 1995. "Rags to Rags: Poverty and Mobility in the U.S." *Annual Review of Sociology* 21:237–67.

Corcoran, Mary, and Terry Adams. 1993a. "Underclass Neighborhoods and Intergenerational Poverty and Dependency." Unpublished manuscript, University of Michigan, Ann Arbor, June.

————. 1993b. "Race, Poverty, Welfare and Neighborhood Influences on Men's Economic Outcomes." Report for Grant no. 88ASPE203A, Office of the Assistant Secretary for Planning and Evaluation, Health and Human Services, and Grant no. GAE09808, Rockefeller Foundation.

————. 1994. "Family and Neighborhood Welfare Dependency and Sons' Labor Supply." Unpublished manuscript, University of Michigan, Ann Arbor.

Corcoran, Mary, Roger Gordon, Deborah Laren, and Gary Solon. 1989. "Effects of Family and Community Background on Men's Economic Status." Working paper no. 2896, National Bureau of Economic Research, Cambridge.

Corcoran, Mary, and Sharon Parrott. 1992. "Black Women's Economic Progress." Working paper, Institute of Public Policy Studies, University of Michigan, Ann Arbor.

Coughlin, Richard M. 1979. "Social Policy and Ideology: Public Opinion in Eight Nations." *Comparative Social Research* 2:3–40.

Coulton, Claudia J., Julian Chow, and Shanta Pandey. 1990. *An Analysis of Poverty and Related Conditions in Cleveland Area Neighborhoods.* Cleveland: Center for Urban Poverty and Social Change, Case Western Reserve University.

Crane, Jonathan. 1989. "Effects of Neighborhoods on Dropping Out of School and Teenage Childbearing." In *The Urban Underclass,* edited by Christopher Jencks and Paul E. Peterson, pp. 299–320. Washington, D.C.: Brookings Institution.

Cross, Harry, G. Kewnney, J. Mell, and W. Zimmerman. 1990. "Employer Hiring Practices: The Differential Treatment of Hispanic and Anglo Job Seekers." Washington, D.C.: Urban Institute Press, Report 90-4.

Culp, Jerome, and Bruce H. Dunson. 1986. "Brothers of a Different Color: A Preliminary Look at Employer Treatment of White and Black Youth." In *The Black Youth Employment Crisis,* edited by Richard B. Freeman and Harry J. Holzer, pp. 233–59. Chicago: University of Chicago Press.

Danziger, Sandra K., and Sheldon H. Danziger. 1995. "Will Welfare Recipients Find Work When Welfare Ends?" In *Welfare Reform: An Analysis of Issues,* edited by Isabel V. Sawhill, pp. 43–47. Washington, D.C.

Danziger, Sheldon H., and Peter Gottschalk. 1995. *America Unequal.* Cambridge: Harvard University Press.

Danziger, Sheldon H., Gary D. Sandefur, and Daniel H. Weinberg, eds. 1994. *Confronting Poverty: Prescriptions for Change.* Cambridge: Harvard University Press.

Danziger, Sheldon H., and Peter Gottschalk, eds. 1993. *Uneven Tides: Rising Inequality in America*. New York: Russell Sage Foundation.

Darling-Hammond, Linda. 1994. "National Standards and Assessments: Will They Improve Education?" *American Journal of Education* 102 (August): 478–510.

———. 1990. "Teacher Quality and Equality." In *Access to Knowledge: An Agenda for Our Nation's Schools*, edited by John Goodlad and Pamela Keating, pp. 237–58. New York: College Entrance Examination Board.

Datcher, Linda. 1982. "Effects of Community and Family Background on Achievement." *Review of Economics and Statistics* 64: 32–41.

Davis, James A., and Tom W. Smith. 1994. *The General Social Surveys: Cumulative Code Book, 1972–1994*. Chicago: National Opinion Research Center.

Dornbusch, Sanford M., J. Merrill Carlsmith, Steven J. Bushwall, Philip L. Ritter, Herbert Leiderman, Albert H. Hastorf, and Ruth T. Gross. 1985. "Single Parents, Extended Households, and the Control of Adolescents." *Child Development* 56:326–41.

Drake, St. Clair, and Horace Cayton. 1945; rev. ed. 1962. *Black Metropolis: A Study of Negro Life in a Northern City*. New York: Harcourt Brace Jovanovich.

D'Souza, Dinesh. 1995. *The End of Racism: Principles of a Multiracial Society*. New York: Free Press.

Duncan, Greg J. 1984. *Years of Poverty, Years of Plenty*. Ann Arbor: Institute for Social Research, University of Michigan.

———. 1994. Testimony Before the Subcommittee on Human Resources of the Committee on Ways and Means Hearing on Early Childbearing, July 29, Washington, D.C.

Duncan, Greg J., and Saul D. Hoffman. 1990. "Welfare Benefits, Economic Opportunities, and Out-of-Wedlock Births Among Black Teenage Girls." *Demography*, November 4, pp. 519–35.

———. 1991. "Teenage Underclass Behavior and Subsequent Poverty: Have the Rules Changed?" In *The Urban Underclass*, edited by Christopher Jencks and Paul E. Peterson, pp. 155–74. Washington, D.C.: Brookings Institution.

Duncan, Greg J., and Deborah Laren. 1990. "Neighborhood Correlates of Teen Births and Dropping Out: Preliminary Results from the PSID-Geocode File." Unpublished manuscript, Survey Research Center, University of Michigan, Ann Arbor, May 8.

Duneier, Mitchell. 1992. *Slim's Table: Race, Respectability, and Masculinity*. Chicago: University of Chicago Press.

Economic Report of the President. 1964. Council of Economic Advisers. Washington, D.C.: Government Printing Office.

Edin, Kathryn. 1994. "The Myths of Dependence and Self-Sufficiency: Women, Welfare, and Low-Wage Work." Unpublished manuscript, Center for Urban Policy Research, Rutgers University.

Educational Testing Service. 1991. *The State of Inequality*. Princeton: Educational Testing Service.

Elder, Glen H., Jr., Jacquelynne S. Eccles, Monika Ardelt, and Sarah Lord.

1995. "Inner-City Parents Under Economic Pressure: Perspectives on the Strategies of Parenting." *Journal of Marriage and the Family* 57 (August): 1–13.

Elliott, Delbert S. 1992. "Longitudinal Research in Criminology: Promise and Practice." Paper presented at the NATO Conference on Cross-National Longitudinal Research on Criminal Behavior, July 19–25, Frankfurt, Germany.

Elliott, Delbert S., William Julius Wilson, David Huizinga, Robert Sampson, Amanda Elliott, and Bruce Rankin. N.d. *Beating the Odds: Overcoming Adversity in High-Risk Neighborhoods*. Chicago: University of Chicago Press. Forthcoming.

Ellwood, David T. 1986a. "Targeting 'Would-Be' Long-Term Recipients of AFDC." Princeton: Mathematical Policy Research.

———. 1986b. "The Spatial Mismatch Hypothesis: Are There Teenage Jobs Missing in the Ghetto?" In *The Black Youth Employment Crisis*, edited by Richard B. Freeman and Harry J. Holzer, pp. 147–48. Chicago: University of Chicago Press.

———. 1989. "The Origins of 'Dependency': Choices, Confidence or Culture?" *Focus* 12:6–13.

Ellwood, David T., and David T. Rodda. 1991. "The Hazards of Work and Marriage: The Influence of Male Employment on Marriage Rates." Malcolm Wiener Center for Social Policy, John F. Kennedy School of Government, Harvard University, no. H-90-5, March.

Erenburg, Sharon J. 1994. "Public Capital: The Missing Link Between Investment and Economic Growth." In *Linking Public Capital to Economic Performance*. Public Policy Brief no. 14. Jerome Levy Economics Institute, Bard College.

Fagan, Jeffrey. 1993. "Drug Selling and Licit Income in Distressed Neighborhoods: The Economic Lives of Street-Level Drug Users and Dealers." In *Drugs, Crime and Social Isolation*, edited by G. Peterson and Adele V. Harrell, pp. 519–35. Washington, D.C.: Urban Institute Press.

Faris, Robert E. L., and Warren Dunham. 1931. *Mental Disorder in Urban America*. Chicago: University of Chicago Press.

Farley, Reynolds. 1989. "Trends in the Residential Segregation of Social and Economic Groups Among American Blacks: 1970 to 1980." Paper presented at a conference on *The Truly Disadvantaged*, October 19–21, Northwestern University.

Feagin, Joe R. 1972. "America's Welfare Stereotypes." *Social Science Quarterly* 52:921–33.

———. 1975. *Subordinating the Poor: Welfare and American Beliefs*. Englewood Cliffs, N.J.: Prentice-Hall.

Featherman, David L., and Robert M. Hauser. 1978. *Opportunity and Change*. New York: Academic Press.

Feldman, S. 1984. "Economic Individualism and American Public Opinion." *American Politics Quarterly* 11:3–29.

Ferguson, Ronald. 1993. "New Evidence on the Growing Value of Skill and

Consequences for Racial Disparity and Returns to Schooling." John F. Kennedy School of Government, Harvard University, Faculty Research Working Paper Series, R93-94.

Fernandez, Roberto M. 1991. "Race, Space and Job Accessibility: Evidence from a Plant Relocation." Unpublished manuscript, Northwestern University.

Fernandez, Roberto M., and David Harris. 1991. "Social Isolation and the Underclass." Paper presented at the Chicago Urban Poverty and Family Life Conference, October 10–12, Chicago.

Fiskin, James S. 1983. *Justice, Equal Opportunity, and the Family*. New Haven: Yale University Press.

The Forgotten Half: Pathways to Success for America's Youth and Young Families. Final Report, Youth and America's Future. 1988. William T. Grant Foundation Commission on Work, Family and Citizenship.

Franklin, Donna, and Susan E. Smith. 1991. "Adolescent Mothers and Persistent Poverty: Does Delaying Parenthood Still Make a Difference?" Paper presented at the Chicago Urban Poverty and Family Life Conference, October 10–12, Chicago.

Franklin, John Hope, and Alfred A. Moss, Jr. 1967. *From Slavery to Freedom*. 3d ed. New York: Knopf.

Frazier, E. Franklin. 1932. *The Negro Family in Chicago*. Chicago: University of Chicago Press.

———. 1939. *The Negro Family in the United States*. Chicago: University of Chicago Press.

Freeman, Richard B. 1989. "The Employment and Earning of Disadvantaged Male Youths in a Labor Shortage Economy." Paper presented at a conference on *The Truly Disadvantaged*, October 19–21, Northwestern University.

———, ed. 1994. *Working Under Different Rules*. New York: Russell Sage Foundation.

Freeman, Richard B., and Lawrence F. Katz. 1994. "Rising Wage Inequality: The United States vs. Other Advanced Countries." In *Working Under Different Rules*, edited by Richard B. Freeman, pp. 29–62. New York: Russell Sage Foundation.

Frey, William. 1985. "Mover Destination Selectivity and the Changing Suburbanization of Whites and Blacks." *Demography* 22:223–43.

Friedman, Alan. 1994. "In Europe's Jobs Crisis, Growth Is No Answer." *International Herald Tribune*, March 10.

Friedman, Thomas L. 1994a. "World's Big Economies Turn to the Jobs Issue." *The New York Times*, March 14.

———. 1994b. "Accent on Education as Talks on Jobs End." *New York Times*, March 16.

Furstenberg, Frank F., Jr. 1993. "How Families Manage Risk and Opportunity in Dangerous Neighborhoods." In *Sociology and the Public Agenda*, edited by William Julius Wilson, pp. 231–58. Newbury Park, Calif.: Sage Publications.

————. 1994. "Fathering in the Inner City: Paternal Participation and Public Policy." Unpublished manuscript, University of Pennsylvania.

Gamson, William A., and Kathryn E. Lasch. 1983. "The Political Culture of Social Welfare Policy." In *Evaluating the Welfare State: Social and Political Perspectives*, edited by Shimon E. Spiro and Ephraim Yuchtman-Yaar, pp. 397–415. New York: Academic Press.

Gamson, William A., and Andre Modigliani. 1987. "The Changing Culture of Affirmative Action." In *Research in Political Sociology*, edited by R. G. Braungart and M. M. Braungart, pp. 137–77. Greenwich, Conn.: Jai Press.

Gans, Herbert. 1968. "Culture and Class in the Study of Poverty: An Approach to Antipoverty Research." In *On Understanding Poverty: Perspectives from the Social Sciences*, edited by Daniel Patrick Moynihan, pp. 201–28. New York: Basic Books.

Gans, Herbert J. 1990. "Deconstructing the Underclass: The Term's Danger as a Planning Concept." *Journal of the American Planning Association* 56 (Summer): 271–77.

————. 1995. *The War Against the Poor: The Underclass and Antipoverty Policy*. New York: Basic Books.

Garfinkel, Irving, and Sara McLanahan. 1986. *Single Mothers and Their Children: A New American Dilemma*. Washington, D.C.: Urban Institute Press.

General Accounting Office. 1987. *Unemployed Parents: Evaluation of Effects of Welfare Benefits on Family Stability*. PEMD-92-19BR. Washington, D.C.

Gilder, George. 1981. *Wealth and Poverty*. New York: Basic Books.

Gittleman, Maury B., and David R. Howell. 1993. "Job Quality and Labor Market Segmentation in the 1980s: A New Perspective on the Effects of Employment Restructuring by Race and Gender." Working paper no. 82, Jerome Levy Economics Institute, Bard College, March.

Glass Ceiling Commission. 1995. "Good for Business: Making Full Use of the Nation's Human Capital." U.S. Department of Labor, March.

Greenberg, Mark. 1993. *Beyond Stereotypes: What State AFDC Studies on Length of Stay Tell Us About Welfare as a "Way of Life."* Center for Law and Social Policy.

Greenstein, Robert. 1991. "Universal and Targeted Approaches to Relieving Poverty: An Alternative View." In *The Urban Underclass*, edited by Christopher Jencks and Paul E. Peterson, pp. 399–410. Washington D.C.: Brookings Institution.

Grier, Eunice S., and George Grier. 1988. "Minorities in Suburbia: A Mid-1980s Update." Report to the Urban Institute Project on Housing Mobility, March. Washington, D.C.: Urban Institute Press.

Hacker, Andrew. 1992. *Two Nations: Black and White, Separate, Hostile and Unequal*. New York: Scribner's.

Hamill, Pete. 1988. "Breaking the Silence." *Esquire*, March, pp. 91–102.

Hamilton, Richard F. 1972. *Class and Politics in the United States*. New York: John Wiley.

Handler, Joel F. 1972. *Reforming the Poor.* New York: Basic Books.

———. 1994. " 'Ending Welfare as We Know It'—A Wrong and Pernicious Idea." Unpublished manuscript, UCLA Law School.

Hannerz, Ulf. 1969. *Soulside: Inquiries into Ghetto Culture and Community.* New York: Columbia University Press.

Hare, Nathan. 1969. "The Challenge of a Black Scholar." *Black Scholar* 1 (December): 58–63.

Harrington, Michael. 1962. Rev. ed. 1969. *The Other America: Poverty in the United States.* New York: Macmillan.

Hechinger, Fred M. 1992. *Fateful Choices.* New York: Hill & Wang.

Heckman, James J. 1995. "Review of *The Bell Curve: Intelligence and Class Structure in American Life.*" Paper presented at the Meritocracy and Equality Seminar Series, February 2, Chicago.

Heckman, James J., Rebecca Roselius, and Jeffrey Smith. 1994. "U.S. Education and Training Policy: A Re-evaluation of the Underlying Assumptions Behind the New Consensus." In *Labor Markets, Employment Policy, and Job Creation,* edited by Lewis C. Solmon and Alec R. Levenson, pp. 83–121. Boulder Colo.: Westview Press.

Henderson, Vivian. 1975. "Race, Economics, and Public Policy," *Crisis* 83 (Fall): 50–55.

Herrnstein, Richard J., and Charles Murray. 1994. *The Bell Curve: Intelligence and Class in American Life.* New York: Free Press.

Hicks-Bartlett, Sharon. 1991. "A Suburb in Name Only: The Case of Meadow View." Paper presented at the Chicago Urban Poverty and Family Life Conference, October 10–12, Chicago.

Hill, Robert B. 1972. *The Strength of Black Families.* New York: Emerson Hall.

Hirsch, Arnold R. 1983. *Making the Second Ghetto: Race and Housing in Chicago, 1940–1960.* Cambridge: Cambridge University Press.

Hirschman, Albert O. 1970. *Exit, Voice and Loyalty: Responses to the Decline in Firms, Organizations, and States.* Cambridge: Harvard University Press.

Hochschild, Jennifer L. 1981. *What's Fair? American Beliefs About Distributive Justice.* Cambridge: Harvard University Press.

———. 1993. "Equal Opportunity and the Estranged Poor." In *The Ghetto Underclass: Social Science Perspectives,* edited by William Julius Wilson, pp. 160–72. Newbury Park, Calif.: Sage Publications.

———. 1995. *Facing Up to the American Dream: Race, Class, and the Soul of the Nation.* Princeton: Princeton University Press.

Hoffman, Saul D., Gregory J. Duncan, and Ronald B. Mincy. 1991. "Marriage and Welfare Use Among Young Women: Do Labor Market, Welfare and Neighborhood Factors Account for Declining Rates of Marriage Among Black and White Women?" Paper presented at the annual meeting of the American Economic Association, December, New Orleans.

Hogan, Dennis P., and Evelyn M. Kitagawa. 1985. "The Impact of Social Status, Family Structure, and Neighborhoods on the Fertility of Black Adolescents." *American Journal of Sociology* 90: 825–55.

Holmes, Steven A. 1994. "Birthrate for Unwed Women Up 70% Since '83, Study Says." *New York Times*, July 29.

———. 1995. "Jobless Data Show Blacks Joining Economic Recovery." *New York Times*, January 12.

Holzer, Harry J. 1991. "The Spatial Mismatch Hypothesis: What Has the Evidence Shown?" *Urban Studies* 28:105–22.

Holzer, Harry. 1995. *What Employers Want: Job Prospects for Less-Educated Workers*. New York: Russell Sage.

Holzer, Harry J., Keith R. Ihlanfeldt, and David L. Sjoquist. 1994. "Work, Search and Travel Among White and Black Youth." *Journal of Urban Economics* 35:320–45.

Hout, Michael. 1984. "Occupational Mobility of Black Men: 1962 to 1973." *American Sociological Review* 49:308–22.

Hoxby, Caroline Minter. 1994. "Does Competition Among Public Schools Benefit Students and Taxpayers?" Working paper no. 4979, National Bureau of Economic Research, Cambridge, December.

Huang, Qi, and Paul Attewell. 1993. "Testing Theories of the Underclass." Unpublished paper, City University of New York, August 11.

Hughes, Mark Alan. 1993. "Over the Horizon: Jobs in the Suburbs of Major Metropolitan Areas." A Report to Public/Private Ventures, December.

Hundt, Reed. 1995. "The Information Superhighway: Ensuring that Poor and Minority Children Do Not Fall Further Behind." Paper presented at the Children Defense Fund's Black Community Crusade for Children Working Committee Planning Retreat, July 8, Knoxville, Tenn.

Ihlanfeldt, Keith R., and David L. Sjoquist. 1990. "Job Accessibility and Racial Differences in Youth Employment Rates." *American Economic Review* 80:267–76.

———. 1991. "The Effect of Job Access on Black Youth Employment: A Cross Sectional Analysis." *Urban Studies* 28:255–65.

Iyengar, Shanto. 1987. "Television News and Citizens' Explanations of National Issues." *American Political Science Review* 81:815–32.

———. 1989. "How Citizens Think About Political Issues: A Matter of Responsibility." *American Journal of Political Science* 33:878–900.

———. 1990. "Framing Responsibility for Political Issues: The Case of Poverty." *Political Behavior* 12:19–40.

Jackson, Aurora P. 1992. "Well-Being Among Single, Black, Employed Mothers." *Social Service Review* 66 (September): 399–409.

Jackson, Kenneth T. 1985. *Crabgrass Frontier: The Suburbanization of the United States*. New York: Oxford University Press.

Jahoda, Marie, Paul F. Lazarsfeld, and Hans Zeisel. 1971. *Marienthal: The Sociography of an Unemployed Community*. Chicago: Aldine-Atherton.

Jargowsky, Paul A. 1994. "Ghetto Poverty Among Blacks in the 1980's." *Journal of Policy Analysis and Management* 13:288–310.

Jargowsky, Paul A., and Mary Jo Bane. 1991. "Ghetto Poverty in the United States, 1970–1980." In *The Urban Underclass*, edited by Christopher Jencks and Paul E. Peterson, pp. 235–73. Washington, D.C.: Brookings Institution.

Jaynes, Gerald David, and Robin Williams, Jr., eds. 1989. *A Common Destiny: Blacks and American Society*. Washington, D.C.: National Academy Press.

Jencks, Christopher. 1991. "Is the American Underclass Growing?" In *The Urban Underclass*, edited by Christopher Jencks and Paul E. Peterson, pp. 28–102. Washington D.C.: Brookings Institution.

Jencks, Christopher, and Kathryn Edin. 1990. "The Real Welfare Problem." *American Prospect* 1 (Spring): 31–50.

Jencks, Christopher, and Susan E. Mayer. 1989a. "The Social Consequences of Growing Up in a Poor Neighborhood: A Review." Working paper, Center for Urban Affairs and Policy Research, Northwestern University.

———. 1989b. *Residential Segregation, Job Proximity, and Black Job Opportunities: The Empirical Status of the Spatial Mismatch Hypothesis*. Working paper, Center for Urban Affairs, Northwestern University.

Jencks, Christopher, and Paul E. Peterson, eds. 1991. *The Urban Underclass*. Washington, D.C.: Brookings Institution.

Johnson, James, Elisa Jayne Bienenstock, and Jennifer A. Stoloff. 1996. "An Empirical Test of the Cultural Capital Hypothesis." *Review of Black Political Economy* 23 (Spring): 7–27.

Johnson, James, and Melvin Oliver. 1992. "Structural Changes in the U.S. Economy and Black Male Joblessness: A Reassessment." In *Urban Labor Markets and Job Opportunity*, edited by G. Peterson and W. Vromaneds, pp. 113–47. Washington, D.C.: Urban Institute Press.

Johnson, Waldo Emerson, Jr. 1994. "Perceptions and Patterns of Paternal Role Functioning of Adolescent and Young Adult Lower Socio-Economic Status of African-American Males: A Social Choice/Social Norms Perspective." Doctoral dissertation, University of Chicago.

Juhn, Chinhui, Kevin M. Murphy, and Brooks Pierce. 1991. "Accounting for the Slowdown in Black-White Wage Convergence." In *Workers and Their Wages: Changing Patterns in the United States*, edited by Marvin H. Kosters, pp. 107–43. Washington, D.C.: American Enterprise Press.

———. 1993. "Wage Inequality and the Rise in Returns to Skill." *Journal of Political Economy* 101:410–42.

Juhn, Chinhui, Kevin M. Murphy, and Robert H. Topel. 1991. "Why Has the Natural Rate of Unemployment Increased Over Time?" *Brookings Papers on Economic Activity* 2:75–126.

Kahlenberg, Richard. 1995. "Class, Not Race." *New Republic*, April 3, pp. 21–27.

Kain, John. 1968. "Housing Segregation, Negro Employment and Metropolitan Decentralization." *Quarterly Journal of Economics* 26:110–30.

Kasarda, John D. 1990a. "Structural Factors Affecting the Location and Timing of Urban Underclass Growth." *Urban Geography* 11:234–64.

———. 1990b. "Urban Industrial Transition and the Underclass." *Annals of the American Academy of Political and Social Science* 501:26–47.

———. 1990c. "City Jobs and Residents on a Collision Course: The Urban Underclass Dilemma." *Economic Development Quarterly* 4 (November): 313–19.

————. 1993a. "Cities as Places Where People Live and Work: Urban Change and Neighborhood Distress." In *Interwoven Destinies: Cities and the Nation*, edited by Henry G. Cisneros, pp. 81–124. New York: Norton.

————. 1993b. "Inner-City Concentrated Poverty and Neighborhood Distress: 1970–1990." *Housing Policy Debate* 4 (3): 253–302.

————. 1995. "Industrial Restructuring and the Changing Location of Jobs." In *State of the Union: America in the 1990s*, vol. 1, edited by Reynolds Farley. New York: Russell Sage Foundation.

Katz, Lawrence F. 1995. "Work-Force Preparation Policies to Promote Economic Opportunity." Paper presented at the Domestic Strategy Group Meeting on "Opportunity in the United States: Social and Individual Responsibility," Aspen Institute, August 19–23, Aspen, Colo.

Katz, Michael B. 1993. "Reframing the 'Underclass Debate.' " In *The "Underclass" Debate: Views from History*, edited by Michael B. Katz, pp. 440–78. Princeton: Princeton University Press.

Kaus, Mickey. 1986. "The Work-Ethic State." *New Republic*, July 7, pp. 22–33.

————. 1992. *The End of Equality*. New York: Basic Books.

Kelley, Robin D. G. 1993. "The Black Poor and the Politics of Opposition in a New South City, 1929–1970." In *The "Underclass" Debate: Views from History*, edited by Michael B. Katz, pp. 293–333. Princeton: Princeton University Press.

Kerbo, H. R. 1981. "Characteristics of the Poor: A Continuing Focus in Social Research." *Sociology and Social Research* 65:323–31.

Kim, Kwang Chung, and Shin Kim. 1994. "The Multi-Race/Ethnic Nature of Los Angeles Unrest in 1992." Paper presented at the annual meeting of the American Sociological Association, August 5–9, Los Angeles.

Kinder, Donald R., and Lynn M. Sanders. 1987. "Pluralistic Foundation of American Opinion and Race." Paper presented at the annual meeting of the American Political Science Association, September 3–6, Chicago.

————. 1990. "Mimicking Political Debate with Survey Questions: The Case of White Opinion on Affirmative Action for Blacks." *Social Cognition* 8:73–103.

Kinder, Donald R., and David O. Sears. 1981. "Prejudice and Politics: Symbolic Racism versus Racial Threats to the Good Life." *Journal of Personality and Social Psychology* 40:414–31.

Kirschenman, Joleen. 1991. "Gender Within Race in the Labor Market." Paper presented at the Chicago Urban Poverty and Family Life Conference, October 10–12, Chicago.

Kirschenman, Joleen, and Kathryn Neckerman. 1991. " 'We'd Love to Hire Them, But . . .': The Meaning of Race for Employers." In *The Urban Underclass*, edited by Christopher Jencks and Paul E. Peterson, pp. 203–34. Washington, D.C.: Brookings Institution.

Kluegel, James R. 1986. *Beliefs About Inequality: Americans' Views of What Is and What Ought to Be*. New York: Aldine de Gruyter.

————. 1987. "Macro-economic Problems, Beliefs About the Poor, and Attitudes Toward Welfare Spending." *Social Problems* 34 (1): 82–99.

————. 1988. "Economic Problems and Socioeconomic Beliefs and Attitudes." In *Research in Social Stratification and Mobility*, edited by Arne Kalleberg, 7:273–302. Greenwich, Conn.: Jai Press.

————. 1990. "Trends in Whites' Explanations of the Gap in Black-White Socioeconomic Status, 1977–1989." *American Sociological Review* 55:512–25.

Kluegel, James R., and Eliot R. Smith. 1983. "Affirmative Action Attitudes: Effects of Self-Interest, Racial Affect, and Stratification Beliefs on Whites' Views." *Social Forces* 61:797–824.

————. 1986. *Beliefs About Inequality: Americans' Views of What Is and What Ought to Be*. New York: Aldine de Gruyter.

Korpi, Walter. 1980. "Approaches to the Study of Poverty in the United States: Critical Notes from a European Perspective." In *Poverty and Public Policy: An Evaluation of Social Research*, edited by V. T. Covello, pp. 287–314. Boston: G. K. Hall.

Krein, Sheila Fitzgerald, and Andrea H. Beller. 1988. "Educational Attainment of Children from Single-Parent Families: Differences by Exposure, Gender, and Race." *Demography* 25 (May): 221–24.

Krieg, Richard M. Forthcoming. "Information Technology and Low Income Inner-City Communities." *Journal of Urban Technology*.

Krogh, Marilyn. 1993. "A Description of the Work Histories of Fathers Living in the Inner City of Chicago." Working paper, Center for the Study of Urban Inequality, University of Chicago.

Ladner, Joyce, ed. 1973. *The Death of White Sociology*. New York: Random House.

Laseter, Robert L. 1994. "Young Inner-City African American Men: Work and Family Life." Doctoral dissertation, University of Chicago.

Lauer, Robert H. 1981. "The Middle Class Looks at Poverty." *Urban and Social Change Review* 5 (Fall): 8–10.

Lawson, Roger, and William Julius Wilson. 1995. "Poverty, Social Rights and the Quality of Citizenship. In *Poverty, Inequality and the Future of Social Policy*, edited by Katherine McFate and Roger Lawson, pp. 693–714. New York: Russell Sage Foundation.

Lemann, Nicholas. 1986. "The Origins of the Underclass." *Atlantic*, June, pp. 31–61.

————. 1991. *The Promised Land: The Great Black Migration and How It Changed America*. New York: Knopf.

Lerman, Robert I. 1986. "Generating Poverty: Why Do Young Men Become Absent Fathers?" Paper presented at the annual meeting of the Association of Public Policy and Management, Seattle.

————. 1989. "Employment Opportunities of Young Men and Family Formation." *American Economic Review Papers and Proceedings* 79:62–66.

Lerman, Robert I., and Martin Rein. Forthcoming. *Social Service Employment: An International Perspective*. New York: Russell Sage Foundation.

Levy, Frank. 1988. *Dollars and Dreams: The Changing American Income Distribution*. New York: Russell Sage Foundation.

Lewis, Oscar. 1959. *Five Families: Mexican Case Studies in the Culture of Poverty*. New York: Basic Books.

———. 1961. *The Children of Sanchez*. New York: Random House.

———. 1966. *La Vida: A Puerto Rican Family in the Culture of Poverty—San Juan and New York*. New York: Random House.

———. 1968. "The Culture of Poverty." In *On Understanding Poverty: Perspectives from the Social Sciences*, edited by Daniel Patrick Moynihan, pp. 187–220. New York: Basic Books.

Lieberson, Stanley. 1980. *A Piece of the Pie: Black and White Immigrants Since 1880*. Berkeley: University of California Press.

Liebow, Elliott. 1967. *Tally's Corner: A Study of Negro Streetcorner Men*. Boston: Little, Brown.

Lipset, Seymour Martin. 1979. *The First New Nation: The United States in Historical and Comparative Perspectives*. New York: Norton.

Lipset, Seymour Martin, and William Schneider. 1978. "The Bakke Case: How Would It Be Decided at the Bar of Public Opinion?" *Public Opinion*, March/April, pp. 38–48.

Local Community Fact Book—Chicago, 1950. 1953. Chicago Community Inventory, University of Chicago.

Local Community Fact Book—Chicago Area, 1960. 1963. Chicago Community Inventory, University of Chicago.

Local Community Fact Book—Chicago Metropolitan Area, Based on the 1970 and 1980 Censuses. 1984. Chicago Fact Book Consortium, University of Illinois at Chicago.

Long, L. H. 1974. "Poverty Status and Receipt of Welfare Among Migrants and Nonmigrants in Large Cities." *American Sociological Review* 39:46–56.

Long, L. H., and L. R. Heltman. 1975. "Migration and Income Differences Between Black and White Men in the North." *American Journal of Sociology* 80:1391–1409.

Loury, Glenn C. 1984. "On the Need for Moral Leadership in the Black Community." Paper presented at the University of Chicago, sponsored by the Center for the Study of Industrial Societies and the John M. Olin Center, Chicago.

———. 1995. *One by One from the Inside Out: Essays and Reviews on Race and Responsibility in America*. New York: Free Press.

Lundgren-Gaveras, Lena. 1991. "Informal Network Support, Public Welfare Support and the Labor Force Activity of Urban Low-Income Single Mothers." Paper presented at the Chicago Urban Poverty and Family Life Conference, October 10–12, Chicago.

Magnet, Myron. 1987. "America's Underclass: What to Do?" *Fortune* 115 (10): 130–50.

Mare, Robert D., and Christopher Winship. 1991. "Socioeconomic Change and the Decline of Marriage for Blacks and Whites." In *The Urban Underclass*, edited by Christopher Jencks and Paul E. Peterson, pp. 175–202. Washington, D.C.: Brookings Institution.

Marshall, Ray. 1994. "School-to-Work Processes in the United States." Paper presented at the Carnegie Corporation/Johann Jacobs Foundation, November 3–5, Marbach Castle, Germany.

Marshall, T. H. 1964. *Class, Citizenship, and Social Development.* New York: Doubleday.

Massey, Douglas S., and Nancy A. Denton. 1993. *American Apartheid: Segregation and the Making of the Underclass.* Cambridge: Harvard University Press.

Massey, Douglas S., and Mitchell L. Eggers. 1990. "The Ecology of Inequality: Minorities and the Concentration of Poverty, 1970–1980." *American Journal of Sociology* 95:1153–88.

Massey, Douglas S., and Andrew B. Gross. 1993. "Black Migration, Segregation and the Spatial Concentration of Poverty." Paper presented at the annual meeting of the Population Association of America, April 1, Cincinnati.

Massey, Douglas S., Andrew B. Gross, and Kumiko Shibuya. 1994. "Migration, Segregation, and the Concentration of Poverty." *American Sociological Review* 59 (June): 1153–89.

Mayer, Susan E. 1989. "How Much Does a High School's Racial and Socioeconomic Mix Affect Graduation and Teenage Fertility Rates?" In *The Urban Underclass*, edited by Christopher Jencks and Paul E. Peterson, pp. 321–41. Washington, D.C.: Brookings Institution.

McClosky, Herbert, and John Zaller. 1984. *The American Ethos: Public Attitudes Toward Capitalism and Democracy.* Cambridge: Harvard University Press.

McKinsey & Co. 1994. *Employment Performance.* Washington, D.C.: McKinsey Global Institute, November.

McLanahan, Sara, and Larry Bumpass. 1988. "Intergenerational Consequences of Family Disruption." *American Journal of Sociology* 94:130–52.

McLanahan, Sara, and Irwin Garfinkel. 1989. "Single Mothers, The Underclass, and Social Policy." *Annals of the American Academy of Political and Social Science* 501 (January): 92–104.

Mead, Lawrence. 1986. *Beyond Entitlement: The Social Obligations of Citizenship.* New York: Free Press.

———. 1992. *The New Politics of Poverty: The Working Poor in America.* New York: Basic Books.

Melville, Keith, and John Doble. 1988. *The Public's Perspective on Social Welfare Reform.* New York: The Public Agenda Foundation, January.

Merton, Robert K. 1972. "Insiders and Outsiders: A Chapter in the Sociology of Knowledge." *American Journal of Sociology* 78:9–47.

Miller, Brent C., and Kristin A. Moore. 1990. "Adolescent Sexual Behavior, Pregnancy and Parenting: Research Through the 1980s." *Journal of Marriage and the Family* 52 (November): 1025–44.

Min, Pyong Gap. 1993. "Korean Immigrants in Los Angeles." In *Immigration and Entrepreneurship*, edited by Ivan Light and Bhachu Parmmole. New Brunswick, N.J.: Transaction Publications.

Montgomery, Michael, and David Wyes. 1992. "The Impact of Infrastructure." *DRI/McGraw-Hill U.S. Review*, October.

Moon, Henry L. 1983. *Balance of Power: The Negro Vote*. Garden City, N.Y.: Doubleday.

Moon, J. Donald. 1988. "The Moral Basis of the Democratic Welfare State." In *Democracy and the Welfare State*, edited by Amy Gutman, pp. 53–78. Princeton: Princeton University Press.

Morenoff, Jeffrey D. 1994. "Neighborhood Change and the Social Transformation of Chicago, 1960–1990." Working Paper Series, vol. 2, no. 4, Center for the Study of Urban Inequality, University of Chicago.

Moss, Philip, and Christopher Tilly. 1991. "Why Black Men are Doing Worse in the Labor Market: A Review of Supply-Side and Demand-Side Explanations." New York: Social Science Research Council.

Moynihan, Daniel Patrick. 1965. *The Negro Family: The Case for National Action*. Washington, D.C.: Office of Policy Planning and Research, U.S. Department of Labor.

Moynihan, Daniel Patrick. 1996. "Congress Builds a Coffin." *The New York Review*. January 11, pp. 33–34.

Murray, Charles. 1984. *Losing Ground: American Social Policy, 1950–1980*. New York: Basic Books.

———. 1990. "Here's the Bad News on the Underclass." *Wall Street Journal*, March 8.

Myrdal, Gunnar. 1963. *Challenge to Affluence*. New York: Pantheon Books.

Nasar, Sylvia. 1994. "The Men in Prime of Life Spend Less Time Working." *New York Times*, December 1.

National Center for Health Statistics. 1994. *Monthly Vital Statistics Report* 43, no. 5, October 25.

———. 1995. *Monthly Vital Statistics Report* 43, no. 11, May 25.

National League of Cities. 1993. "All in It Together: Cities, Suburbs and Local Economic Regions." Washington, D.C.: National League of Cities.

Neal, Derek A., and William R. Johnson. 1995. "The Role of Pre-Market Factors in Black-White Wage Differences." Paper presented at the Meritocracy and Equality Seminar Series, January 19, University of Chicago, Chicago.

Neckerman, Kathryn M. 1993. "What Getting Ahead Means to Employer and Inner-City Workers." Revised version of paper presented at the Chicago Urban Poverty and Family Life Conference, October 10–12, Chicago.

Neckerman, Kathryn M., and Joleen Kirschenman. 1991. "Hiring Strategies, Racial Bias, and Inner-City Workers." *Social Problems* 38 (November): 433–47.

Nelson, Kathryn P. 1991. "Racial Segregation, Mobility, and Poverty Concentration." Paper presented at the annual meeting of the American Population Association of America, March 19–23, Washington, D.C.

Newman, Katherine S. 1996. "Working Poor: Low Wage Employment in the Lives of Harlem Youth." In *Transitions Through Adolescence: Interpersonal Domains and Context*, edited by J. Graber, J. Brooks-Gunn, and A. Petersen, pp. 323–44. Mahwah, N.J.: Erlbaum Associates Publishers.

New York Times. 1994. "Clinton Wages a Quiet but Energetic War Against Poverty." March 30.

Oakes, Jeannie. 1990. *Multiplying Inequalities: The Effects of Race, Social Class, and Ability Grouping on Access to Science and Mathematics Education.* Santa Monica, Calif.: Rand Corporation.

O'Connor, Alice. 1992. "Race and Class in Chicago Sociology, 1920–1990." Paper presented at the annual meeting of the Social Science History Association, November 8, Chicago.

O'Hare, William, Tania Mann, Kathryn Porter, and Robert Greenstein. 1990. *Real-Life Poverty in America: Where the American Public Would Set the Poverty Line.* Center on Budget and Policy Priorities and Families USA Foundation report, Washington, D.C.

O'Hare, William, and Anne Pauti. 1990. *Declining Wages of Young Workers in Rural America.* Staff Working Papers, Population Reference Bureau, Washington, D.C.

Oliver, Melvin, and Tom Shapiro. 1995. *Black Wealth/White Wealth: A New Perspective on Racial Inequality.* New York: Routledge.

O'Neill, June, D. A. Wolf, L. J. Bassi, and M. T. Hannan. 1984. "An Analysis of Time on Welfare." Contract no. HHS-100-83-0048. Washington, D.C.: Urban Institute Press.

Orfield, Gary, and Carole Ashkinaze. 1991. *The Closing Door: Policy and Black Opportunity.* Chicago: University of Chicago Press.

Osterman, Paul. 1990. "Welfare Participation in a Full Employment Economy: The Impact of Family Structure and Neighborhood." Unpublished manuscript, Massachusetts Institute of Technology.

Park, Robert E., and Ernest W. Burgess. 1925. *The City.* Chicago: University of Chicago Press.

Parrott, Sharon. 1995. "An Analysis of the Personal Responsibility Act (H.R. 1214)." News release, Center on Budget and Policy Priorities, Washington, D.C., March 16.

Patterson, James T. 1981. *America's Struggle Against Poverty, 1900–1980.* Cambridge: Harvard University Press.

Patterson, Orlando. 1995. "For Whom the Bell Curves." Paper presented at the Meritocracy and Equality Seminar Series, February 2, Chicago.

Pavetti, LaDonna. 1993. "The Dynamics of Welfare and Work: Exploring the Process by Which Women Work Their Way off Welfare." Doctoral dissertation, John F. Kennedy School of Government, Harvard University.

———. 1995. "Who Is Affected by Time Limits?" In *Welfare Reform: An Analysis of Issues,* edited by Isabel Sawhill, pp. 31–35. Washington, D.C.: Urban Institute Press.

Pear, Robert. 1993. "Poverty 1993: Bigger, Deeper, Younger, Getting Worse." *New York Times,* October 10.

Pedder, Sophie. 1991. "Social Isolation and the Labor Market: Black Americans in Chicago." Paper presented at the Chicago Urban Poverty and Family Life Conference, October 10–12, Chicago.

Peeples, Faith, and Rolf Loeber. 1994. "Do Individual Factors and Neighborhood Context Explain Ethnic Differences in Juvenile Delinquency?" *Journal of Quantitative Criminology* 10:141–57.

Petersen, Paul E. 1995. "State Responses to Welfare Reform: A Race to the Bottom." In *Welfare Reform: An Analysis of Issues,* edited by Isabel V. Sawhill, pp. 7–11. Washington, D.C.: Urban Institute Press.

Plotnick, Robert D. 1990. "Determinants of Teenage Out-of-Wedlock Childbearing." *Journal of Marriage and the Family* 52:735–46.

Price, Hugh. 1994. Keynote address. National Urban League Annual Conference, Indianapolis, July 24.

Prothrow-Stith, Deborah. 1991. *Deadly Consequences.* New York: Harper-Collins.

Public/Private Ventures. 1994. *Annual Report.* Philadelphia.

Putnam, Robert D. 1993. *Making Democrary Work: Civic Tradition in Modern Italy.* Princeton: Princeton University Press.

Quadagno, Jill. 1994. *The Color of Welfare: How Racism Undermined the War on Poverty.* New York: Oxford University Press.

Rainwater, Lee. 1966. "Crucible of Identity: The Negro Lower-Class Family." *Daedalus* 95 (Winter): 176–216.

———. 1970. *Behind Ghetto Walls: Black Family Life in a Federal Slum.* Chicago: Aldine Publishing Co.

———. 1987. "Class, Culture, Poverty and Welfare." Unpublished manuscript, Harvard University.

Rainwater, Lee, and William L. Yancey. 1967. *The Moynihan Report and the Politics of Controversy.* Cambridge: MIT Press.

Reardon, Patrick. 1991. "Study Links City Jobless, Suburban Housing." *Chicago Tribune,* May 1.

Regan, Edward V. 1994. *Infrastructure Investment for Tomorrow.* Public Policy Brief, no. 141, Jerome Levy Economics Institute, Bard College.

Rich, Frank. 1995. "The L.A. Shock Treatment." *The New York Times,* October 4.

Ricketts, Erol, and Ronald Mincy. 1986. *Growth of the Underclass: 1970–1980.* Washington, D.C.: Urban Institute Press.

Ricketts, Erol, and Isabel Sawhill. 1986. *Defining and Measuring the Underclass.* Washington, D.C.: Urban Institute Press.

Rifkin, Jeremy. 1995. *The End of Work: The Decline of the Global Labor Force and the Dawn of the Post-Market Era.* New York: Putnam's.

Ritchey, P. N. 1974. "Urban Poverty and Rural to Urban Migration." *Rural Sociology* 39:12–27.

Rodman, Hyman. 1963. "Lower-Class Value Stretch." *Social Forces* 42 (December): 205–15.

Rohter, Larry. 1993. "As Hispanic Presence Grows, So Does Black Anger." *New York Times,* June 20.

Rose, Stephen J. 1994. "On Shaky Ground: Rising Fears About Incomes and Earnings." Research report no. 94-02, National Commission for Employment Policy, Washington, D.C., October.

Rosenbaum, James E., and Susan J. Popkin. 1991. "Employment and Earnings of Low-Income Blacks Who Move to Middle-Class Suburbs." In *The Urban Underclass*, edited by Christopher Jencks and Paul E. Peterson, pp. 342–56. Washington, D.C.: Brookings Institution.

Rotberg, Iris C., and James J. Harvey. 1993. *Federal Policy Options for Improving the Education of Low-Income Students*. Santa Monica, Calif.: Rand Corporation.

Ruggles, Patricia. 1990. "The Poverty Line—Too Low for the 1990s." *New York Times*, April 26.

Rural Sociological Society Task Force on Persistent Rural Poverty. 1993. *Persistent Poverty in Rural America*. Boulder, Colo.: Westview Press.

Rusk, David. 1993. *Cities Without Suburbs*. Washington, D.C.: Woodrow Wilson Center Press.

Sampson, Robert J. 1986. "Crime in Cities: The Effects of Formal and Informal Social Control." In *Communities and Crime*, edited by Albert J. Reiss, Jr., and Michael Tonry, pp. 271–310. Chicago: University of Chicago Press.

———. 1988. "Urban Black Violence: The Effect of Male Joblessness and Family Disruption." *American Journal of Sociology* 93:348–82.

———. 1992a. "Family Management and Child Development: Insights from Social Disorganization Theory." In *Facts, Frameworks and Forecasts*, vol. 3 of *Advances in Criminology Theory*, edited by Joan McCord, pp. 63–93. New Brunswick, N.J.: Transaction Press.

———. 1992b. "Integrating Family and Community-Level Dimensions of Social Organization: Delinquency and Crime in the Inner City of Chicago." Paper presented at the International Workshop on Integrating Individual and Ecological Aspects on Crime, August 31–September 5, Stockholm, Sweden.

Sampson, Robert J., and Walter Groves. 1989. "Community Structure and Crime: Testing Social Disorganization Theory." *American Journal of Sociology* 94:774–802.

Sampson, Robert J., and William Julius Wilson. 1995. "Toward a Theory of Race, Crime, and Urban Inequality." In *Crime and Inequality*, edited by John Hagan and Ruth Peterson, pp. 37–54. Stanford: Stanford University Press.

Schmitter-Heisler, Barbara. 1991. "A Comparative Perspective on the Underclass." *Theory and Society* 20:455–83.

Shapiro, Robert Y., and J. T. Young. 1989. "Public Opinion and the Welfare State: The United States in Comparative Perspective." *Political Science Quarterly* 104:59–87.

Shapiro, Walter. 1987. "The Ghetto: From Bad to Worse." *Time*, August 24, pp. 18–19.

Sheley, J. F., and J. D. Wright. 1993. "Gun Acquisition and Possession in Selected Juvenile Samples." *Research in Brief*. Washington D.C.: U.S. Department of Justice, National Institute of Justice.

Smock, Pamela J. 1990. "Remarriage Patterns of Black and White Women: Reassessing the Role of Educational Attainment." *Demography* 27:467–73.

Sosin, Michael. 1991. "Concentration of Poverty and Social Isolation of the

Inner-City Poor." Paper presented at the Chicago Urban Poverty and Family Life Conference, October 10–12, Chicago.

Sowell, Thomas. 1994. *Race and Culture: A World View*. New York: Basic Books.

Spear, Allan. 1967. *Black Chicago: The Making of a Negro Ghetto*. Chicago: University of Chicago Press.

Staples, Robert. 1970. "The Myth of the Black Matriarchy," *Black Scholar* 2 (February): 9–16.

————. 1971. *The Black Family: Essays and Studies*. Belmont, Calif.: Wadsworth Publishing Co.

Steinberg, Laurence, Nancy E. Darling, Anne C. Fletcher, B. Bradford Brown, and Stanford M. Dornbusch. 1995. "Authoritative Parenting and Adolescent Adjustment: An Ecological Journey." In *Examining Lives in Context: Perspectives on the Ecology of Human Development*, edited by Phyllis Muen, Glen H. Elder, Jr., and Kurt Lüscher, pp. 423–66. Washington, D.C.: American Psychological Association.

Stier, Haya, and Marta Tienda. 1994. "Spouses or Babies: Race, Poverty and Pathways to Family Life." Unpublished manuscript, University of Chicago, March.

Sugrue, Thomas J. 1993. "The Structures of Urban Poverty: The Reorganization of Space and Work in Three Periods of American History." In *The "Underclass" Debate: Views from History*, edited by Michael B. Katz, pp. 85–117. Princeton: Princeton University Press.

Sum, Andrew, and Neal Fogg. 1990. "The Changing Economic Fortunes of Young Black Men in America." *Black Scholar* 21 (January, February, and March): 47–55.

Susser, Ida, and John Kreniski. 1987. "The Welfare Trap: A Public Policy for Deprivation." In *Cities of the United States*, edited by Leith Mullings, pp. 51–68. New York: Columbia University Press.

Swidler, Ann. 1986. "Culture in Action: Symbols and Strategies." *American Sociological Review* 51 (January): 273–86.

Taub, Richard. 1991. "Differing Conceptions of Honor and Orientations Toward Work and Marriage Among Low-Income African-Americans and Mexican-Americans." Paper presented at the Chicago Urban Poverty and Family Life Conference, October 10–12, Chicago.

Taylor, Ralph B. and Jeanette Covington. 1988. "Neighborhood Changes in Ecology and Violence." *Criminology* 28 (November): 553–58.

Taylor, Robert J., Linda M. Chatters, M. Belinda Tucker, and Edith Lewis. 1990. "Developments in Research on Black Families: A Decade Review." *Journal of Marriage and the Family* 52:993–1014.

Taylor, William L. 1986. "Equal Protection, and the Isolation of the Poor." *Yale Law Journal* 95:1700–35.

Testa, Mark. 1990. "Joblessness and Absent Fatherhood in the Inner City." Paper presented at the annual meeting of the American Sociological Association, August, Washington, D.C.

————. 1991. "Male Joblessness, Nonmarital Parenthood and Marriage." Paper presented at the Chicago Urban Poverty and Family Life Conference, October 10–12, Chicago.

Testa, Mark, and Marilyn Krogh. 1995. "The Effect of Employment on Marriage Among Black Males in Inner-City Chicago." In *The Decline in Marriage Among African Americans: Causes, Consequences and Policy Implications*, edited by M. Belinda Tucker and Claudia Mitchell-Kernan, pp. 59–95. New York: Russell Sage Foundation.

Thrasher, Frederic. 1927. *The Gang*. Chicago: University of Chicago Press.

Tienda, Marta. 1989. "Poor People and Poor Places: Deciphering Neighborhood Effects on Poverty Outcomes." Paper presented at the annual meeting of the American Sociological Association, August 9–13, San Francisco.

————. 1990. "Welfare and Work in Chicago's Inner City." *American Economic Review* 80 (May): 372–76.

Tienda, Marta, and Haya Stier. 1990. "Intergenerational Continuity of Welfare Dependence: Racial and Ethnic Comparisons." Paper presented at the XII World Congress of Sociology, July, Madrid, Spain.

————. 1991. " 'Making a Livin': Color and Opportunity in the Inner City." Paper presented at the Chicago Urban Poverty and Family Life Conference, October 10–12, Chicago.

Time. 1977. "The American Underclass." August 29, pp. 14–27.

Tobin, James. 1965. "On Improving the Economic Status of the Negro." *Daedalus* 94:878–98.

Tompkins, D. C. 1970. *Poverty in the United States During the Sixties: A Bibliography*. Berkeley: Institute of Government Studies, University of California Press.

Topel, Robert. 1993. "What Have We Learned from Empirical Studies of Unemployment and Turnover?" *AEA Papers and Proceedings* 83:110–15.

————. 1994. "Regional Labor Markets and the Determinants of Wage Inequality." *American Economic Review* 84 (May): 17–22.

U.S. Bureau of the Census. 1988. "Characteristics of the Population Below the Poverty Level, 1978–84" and "Poverty in the U.S., 1985–87." Washington, D.C.: Government Printing Office.

————. 1988. "Money Income and Poverty Status in the U.S." Table 2. In *Current Population Reports*, series P-60, no. 161. Washington, D.C.: Government Printing Office.

————. 1992. "Poverty in the United States: 1992." Table 6. In *Current Population Reports*, series P-60, no. 185. Washington, D.C.: Government Printing Office.

————. 1993. "Marital Status and Living Arrangements." In *Current Population Reports*, series P-20, no. 468. Washington, D.C.: Government Printing Office.

————. 1994a. *Current Population Reports*. Published and unpublished data, March.

————. 1994b. Income and Poverty. CD-ROM.

U.S. Bureau of Labor Statistics. 1989. "Nearly Three-Fifths of High School Graduates of 1988 Enrolled in College." In *U.S. Department of Labor News Release*, no. 89-103, June.

———. 1994. "College Enrollment of 1993 High School Graduates." In *U.S. Department of Labor News Release*, no. 94-252, May.

Valentine, Charles A. 1968. *Culture and Poverty: Critique and Counter-Proposals*. Chicago: University of Chicago Press.

Van Haitsma, Martha. 1989. "A Contextual Definition of the Underclass." *Focus* (Newsletter of the Institute for Research on Poverty) 12 (Spring and Summer): 27–31.

———. 1991. "Attitudes, Social Context and Labor Force Attachment: Blacks and Immigrant Mexicans in Chicago Poverty Areas." Presented at the Chicago Urban Poverty and Family Life Conference, October 10–12, Chicago.

———. 1992. "The Social Context of Nonemployment: Blacks and Immigrant Mexicans in Chicago Poverty Areas." Paper presented at the annual meeting of the Social Science History Association, November 5–8, Chicago.

Venkatesh, Sudhir. 1996. "Private Lives, Public Housing: An Ethnography of the Robert Taylor Homes." Ph.D. dissertation, University of Chicago.

Vroman, Wayne. 1995. "Rainy Day Funds: Contingency Funding for Welfare Block Grants." In *Welfare Reform: An Analysis of Issues*, edited by Isabel V. Sawhill, pp. 11–17. Washington, D.C.: Urban Institute Press.

Wacquant, Loïc J. D. 1991. "The Specificity of Ghetto Poverty: A Comparative Analysis of Race, Class, and Urban Exclusion in Chicago's Black Belt and the Parisian Red Belt." Presented at the Chicago Urban Poverty and Family Life Conference, October 10–12, Chicago.

Wacquant, Loïc J. D., and William Julius Wilson. 1989. "Poverty, Joblessness and the Social Transformation of the Inner City." In *Reforming Welfare Policy*, edited by D. Ellwood and P. Cottingham, pp. 70–102. Cambridge: Harvard University Press.

———. 1990. "The Cost of Racial and Class Exclusion in the Inner City." *Annals of the American Academy of Political and Social Science* 501 (January): 8–25.

Waldinger, Roger. "Black/Immigrant Competition Re-assessed: New Evidence from Los Angeles." Unpublished ms., Department of Sociology, UCLA.

Warner, W. Lloyd, and Paul S. Lunt. 1941. *The Social Life of a Modern Community*. Vol. 1, Yankee City Series. New Haven: Yale University Press.

———. 1942. *The Status System of a Modern Community*. Vol. 2, Yankee City Series. New Haven: Yale University Press.

Weaver, Frank C. 1995. "Preparing Our Youth for the Information Age." *Focus*, Joint Center for Political and Economic Studies, May, p. 7.

Weir, Margaret. 1993a. "Race and Urban Poverty: Comparing Europe and America." Occasional paper no. 93-9, Center for American Political Studies, Harvard University, March.

———. 1993b. "Urban Policy and Persistent Urban Poverty." Background memorandum prepared for the Social Science Research Council Policy Conference on Persistent Urban Poverty, November 9–10, Washington, D.C.

West, Cornel. 1993. *Race Matters*. Boston: Beacon Press.

Wieman, Clark. 1993. "Road Work Ahead." *Technology Review* 96 (January): 42–48.

Wilkerson, Isabel. 1994. "Crack Means Power, and Death, to Soldiers in Street Wars." *New York Times*, December 13.

Wilkins, Roger. 1989. "The Black Poor are Different." *New York Times*, August 22.

Williamson, John B. 1974a. "The Stigma of Public Dependency: A Comparison of Alternative Forms of Public Aid." *Social Problems* 21 (June): 213–28.

———. 1974b. "Beliefs About the Motivation of the Poor and Attitudes Toward Poverty Policy." *Social Problems* 21 (June): 634–47.

———. 1974c. "Beliefs About the Welfare Poor." *Sociology and Social Research* 58 (January): 163–75.

Wilson, William Julius. 1980. *The Declining Significance of Race: Blacks and Changing American Institutions*. 2d ed. Chicago: University of Chicago Press.

———. 1987a. *The Truly Disadvantaged: The Inner City, The Underclass, and Public Policy*. Chicago: University of Chicago Press.

———. 1987b. "The Obligation to Work and the Availability of Jobs: A Dialogue Between Lawrence M. Mead and William Julius Wilson." *Focus* (newsletter of the Institute for Research on Poverty) 10 (Summer): 11–19.

———. 1988. "The American Underclass: Inner-City Ghettos and the Norms of Citizenship." Godkin Lecture, John F. Kennedy School of Government, Harvard University, April 26.

———. 1991a. "Studying Inner-City Social Dislocations: The Challenge of Public Agenda Research." *American Sociological Review* 56 (February): 1–14.

———. 1991b. "Response." *American Prospect* (Spring): 93–96.

———. 1992. "The Right Message." *New York Times*, March 17, op-ed page.

———, ed. 1993a. *The Ghetto Underclass: Social Science Perspectives*. Updated ed. Newbury Park, Calif.: Sage Publications.

———, ed. 1993b. *Sociology and the Public Agenda*. Newbury Park, Calif.: Sage Publications.

Wilson, William Julius, Robert Aponte, Joleen Kirschenman, and Loïc J. D. Wacquant. 1988. "The Ghetto Underclass and the Changing Structure of American Poverty." In *Quiet Riots: Race and Poverty in the United States*, edited by Fred R. Harris and Roger W. Wilkins, pp. 123–54. New York: Pantheon.

Wolff, Edward N. 1995. *Top Heavy: A Study of the Increasing Inequality of Wealth in America*. New York: Twentieth Century Fund Press.

Yinger, John. 1995. *Closed Doors, Opportunities Lost: The Continuing Costs of Housing Discrimination*. New York: Russsell Sage Foundation.

Yoon, In-Jin. 1994. "Who Are My Neighbors? Korean's Perceptions of Blacks and Hispanics as Employees, Customers, and Neighbors." Paper presented at the annual meeting of the American Sociological Association, August 5–9, Los Angeles.

Zax, Jeffrey, and John Kain. 1992. "Moving to the Suburbs: Do Relocating

Companies Leave Their Black Employees Behind?" Unpublished manuscript, Harvard University.

Zedlewski, Sheila, and Isabel V. Sawhill. "Assessing the Personal Responsibility Act." In *Welfare Reform: An Analysis of Issues*, edited by Isabel V. Sawhill, pp. 35–39. Washington, D.C.: Urban Institute Press.

Zelditch, Morris, Jr. 1989. "Levels in the Logic of Macro-Historical Explanation." Paper presented at the annual meeting of the American Sociological Association, August 10, San Francisco.

Zorbaugh, Harvey W. 1929. *The Gold Coast and the Slum*. Chicago: University of Chicago Press.

THE GOOD SOCIETY
by Robert N. Bellah, Richard Madsen,
William M. Sullivan, Ann Swidler, Steven M. Tipton

Bellah and his co-authors propose a new response to the country's growing social ills as America moves its domestic, economic, and social crises to the top of the political agenda. Acknowledging that we all live in and through institutions—family, school, community, corporation, religious group, the nation—they show how we can and must take responsibility for making these institutions work.

Sociology/0-679-73359-0

LABOR OF LOVE, LABOR OF SORROW
*Black Women, Work and the Family,
from Slavery to the Present*
by Jacqueline Jones

Jones offers a powerful account of the changing role of American black women, in the labor force and in the family, "free of the racism and sexism it describes, and it interprets old data in new ways" (Toni Morrison, *The New York Times Book Review*).

Winner of the Bancroft Prize
Social History/0-394-74536-1

REGULATING THE POOR
The Functions of Public Welfare
by Frances Fox Piven and Richard A. Cloward

When this ground-breaking work was first published in 1971, it dramatically revised our understanding of the welfare system and its hidden role in the larger socioeconomic framework of the United States. Substantially updated for 1990s, this analysis ranges from the early history of poor relief through the inception of welfare during the Great Depression to its massive erosion during the Reagan and Bush years. The authors provide a conceptual framework that sharply illuminates the problems current and future administrations will encounter as they attempt to rethink the welfare system.

Political Science/Sociology/Social Work/0-679-74516-5